John Bell Hood
and the Fight for Civil War Memory

John Bell Hood
and the Fight for Civil War Memory

Brian Craig Miller

The Western Theater in the Civil War
Gary D. Joiner, Series Editor

The University of Tennessee Press • Knoxville

The Western Theater in the Civil War series seeks to emphasize an emerging trend in the historiography of the nation's greatest conflict: a more general recognition that events in the West, far from being a sideshow to storied campaigns in the East, were, in many ways, even more decisive in the outcome of the war. Among the works that will be produced are scholarly monographs, biographies of leaders who need reconsideration, and edited collections that present up-to-date scholarship in this rapidly developing field.

 Copyright © 2010 by The University of Tennessee Press / Knoxville. All Rights Reserved.
Cloth: first printing, 2010.
Paper: first printing, 2014.

Cover illustration: John Bell Hood, 1863. Image courtesy of the Museum of the Confederacy, Richmond, Virginia.

Library of Congress Cataloging-in-Publication Data

Miller, Brian Craig.
John Bell Hood and the fight for Civil War memory / Brian Craig Miller.
   p. cm. — (The western theater in the Civil War)
Includes bibliographical references and index.
ISBN-13: 978-1-62190-159-4

1. Hood, John Bell, 1831–1879. 2. Hood, John Bell, 1831–1879—Public opinion. 3. Hood, John Bell, 1831–1879—Influence. 4. Generals—Southern States—Biography. 5. Confederate States of America. Army—Biography. 6. United States—History—Civil War, 1861–1865—Biography. 7. United States—History—Civil War, 1861–1865—Public opinion. 8. Collective memory—United States. I. Title.

E467.1.H58M55 2010
355.0092—dc22
[B]   2009051919

For Craig and Linda, who sparked an interest, nurtured a young mind, and loved and accepted a son unconditionally

Contents

Series Editor's Foreword — ix
  Gary D. Joiner

Acknowledgments — xi

Introduction: Rethinking John Bell Hood and the Fight for Civil War Memory — xv

Chapter 1. Sons of an Earlier Day: Hood's Journey from Boyhood to Manhood — 1

Chapter 2. A Gallant Affair on the Frontier — 27

Chapter 3. A "Soldier Indeed": Hood and the Army of Northern Virginia — 43

Chapter 4. A Crisis in Manhood? Hood and the Experience of Confederate Amputees — 87

Chapter 5. "A Forlorn Hope": The Quest to Save Atlanta — 107

Chapter 6. "Playing Hell in Tennessee" — 139

Chapter 7. Staring into the Fire of Glory and Memory: Hood, New Orleans, and the Construction of Civil War Memory — 173

Chapter 8. "A Suitable Monument": Securing the Memory of John Bell Hood — 215

Notes — 247

Bibliography — 287

Index — 307

Tables

1. Number of Demerits Awarded for Infractions at West Point ... 21
2. Rankings of Prominent Confederate Civil War Figures at West Point ... 23
3. Funds Collected for the Hood Memorial Fund through 1880 by Geographic Area ... 235

Figures

Following Page 79

General John Bell Hood in Civilian Clothes

John Bell Hood, after the Amputation of his Right Leg and Left Arm, 1864

John Bell Hood Print/Engraving, ca. 1860–1880

Hood's Headquarters during the Atlanta Campaign

Photograph Taken for the Hood Memorial Fund for Hood's Ten Orphaned Children, ca. 1879

Odlie Hood, One of Hood's Daughters, ca. 1880s–1890s

Nashville, View from the Capitol, 1864

Series Editor's Foreword

Few major figures in the Civil War cast such a contorted shadow as John Bell Hood. Controversy seemed to be his constant companion during the war, and he spent the remainder of his life defending his actions. Men who served with Hood or against him filled speeches and tracts recounting his command decisions, mostly derogatorily. As the Lost Cause movement gained momentum, Hood stood near the center. As Robert E. Lee and Stonewall Jackson were nearly deified as the epitome of Southern commanders, John Bell Hood was blamed for recklessly gambling with his men's lives, for being a drunkard and a drug addict, inept, possibly insane, and often, simply stupid. His supporters diminished as the roar of those seeking a scapegoat for Confederate defeat found an easy target. Later generations of historians have rarely been kind to Hood, often mimicking the voices of his contemporaries. Some memorials to the Confederate general do exist, of course, the most noticeable being Fort Hood in Texas. His grave in Metairie Cemetery in suburban New Orleans contains a fitting plaque. However, there are no battlefield monuments memorializing him in bronze. One reason might be that the battlefields upon which he commanded have been mostly obliterated due to urbanization. Another possibility is that generals who lose are not often lionized.

This volume by Brian Miller seeks to unravel the great mysteries surrounding John Bell Hood, attempting to separate the man from the myth. Miller does so admirably, placing Hood in the context of his time—his youth and early manhood during the changing environments of the antebellum period, military service before and through the Civil War, and the convoluted remainder of his life. What emerges is a superb examination of a very complex individual, motivated by his education and training, honed by early military successes and irrevocably altered by severe wounds that cost him the use of his left arm at Gettysburg and his right leg at Chickamauga. Upon his reentry into military service, Hood was promoted to corps commander and then army commander. The circumstances of this rapid rise led to controversy that never left him.

Although a good commander at the brigade level, Hood suffered from abysmal leadership skills as a senior officer commanding a corps, then the Army of Tennessee. Internal politics within that army assured that John Bell Hood would never be treated the same as other commanding generals, particularly Robert E. Lee or Stonewall Jackson. Following the war, Hood was forced to defend his motives and actions more than most of his contemporaries. The author deftly leads the reader through the shifting moods of Southern thought during Reconstruction and after, following Hood's path to his place in Southern memory.

Hood's place in history is tempered by the circumstances of his family. After the war, he moved to New Orleans, entered into business, married, and, despite his wounds, fathered eleven children, including three sets of twins. The great yellow fever epidemic which decimated New Orleans in 1879 all but destroyed his family and shifted public sentiment. Contemporaries and later historians began to issue theories about his behavior during the war and afterward. The author's research into Hood's actions and the general's defense of them is insightful. By tackling the myths individually, new light is shed upon the man. Brian Miller does a superb job with excellent research and a clear writing style that will satisfy historians and the general reading public alike. *John Bell Hood and the Fight for Civil War Memory* is a first-rate examination of this most controversial of generals.

Gary D. Joiner
Louisiana State University, Shreveport

Acknowledgments

One of the joys of historical writing has been the number of key people who have offered assistance to me in my work, from gathering sources to reading the manuscript and offering emotional support, encouragement, and guidance. I am grateful to the generous archivists and historians I have visited throughout the country. In particular, I thank the staff at the Southern Historical Collection at the University of North Carolina at Chapel Hill, Debbie Newman at the Arizona Historical Society, Justin Banks at Austin College, Amelia Abreu and Erin O'Brien at the Center for American History at the University of Texas at Austin, as well as Patricia Perry at Texas Tech University. Additional gratitude goes to Thomas Cartwright, Heath Matthews, and the helpful staff at the Carter House in Franklin, Tennessee, Peggy at the Curly House in Corinth, Mississippi, the staff of the Museum at Confederate Hall in New Orleans, Louisiana, and, of note, John Heiser at Gettysburg National Military Park and Lee White and Jerry Trollinger at Chickamauga and Chattanooga National Military Park.

Jennifer Ford, at the University of Mississippi Archives, embraced the topic of amputees and diligently assisted in collecting source materials and leads throughout the archives. My continued archival research was enhanced by the expertise of Wayne Everard at the New Orleans Public Library; Mary Orazio, Bill Menary, Eira Tansey, and Ken Owen at the Archives at Tulane University; and Drury Wellford at the Museum of the Confederacy. Thanks to the Filson Historical Society, who have the best card catalog in the country. Any researcher who wants to study the antebellum South should visit their facility, where they will be assisted, as I was, by Michael Veach, Noah Huffman, Becky Rice, and James Holmberg. At Duke University, a staff of patient, kind, and helpful archivists and assistants went above and beyond the call of duty, in particular Eleanor Mills, Mike Crotty, Brock Brison, Linda McCurdy, and Janie Morris. Further thanks go to the staffs at the Library of Congress and the National Archives in Washington, D.C.

After the ideas of the dissertation hit the conference circuits, I am indebted to the comments and feedback from Thomas Mackey, Robert Zalimas, Paul Bergeron, Larry Logue, Wendy Venet, Frank Towers, George Rable, and Laura Edwards. Special thanks go to each thought-provoking question from the audiences as well as those who came to speak to me after the presentation, from graduate and undergraduate students to professional and public historians. Your feedback has been taken to heart. Furthermore, I must thank Earl Hess, David Coffey, and the anonymous reader with the University of Tennessee Press, for your superb and thoughtful comments on the manuscript. It was a true honor and pleasure to have historians of your caliber comment on and enrich my work in many important and innovative ways. Thanks also to Scot Danforth and the wonderful staff at the University of Tennessee Press, especially Stan Ivester, managing editor, and Walt Evans, freelance copyeditor. Scot, you are a wonderfully kind, patient, and supportive editor and I have come to value our lunches across the country. It has been a pleasure to have you read and publish my work.

I want to thank the people of the city of New Orleans. Because of the brevity of new research done on Hood's postwar life, I spent more time in New Orleans than any other location researching this work. Sadly, as I was completing the manuscript, Hurricane Katrina devastated the gulf region and left lives and property swept away by the forces of wind and water. The hospitality and cuisine of New Orleans are exceptional. My historical knowledge of New Orleans offered me a greater appreciation for the richness of the community, and it is with a heavy heart that I complete this work at a time when they are rebuilding their lives.

Faculty mentoring has not only molded the manuscript but also my career as a historian. Gary W. Gallagher, a man who I consistently visited when I took his undergraduate Civil War class in 1998, inspired me to be a professional historian. His spoken and unspoken encouragement allowed me to blaze the trail to graduate school, and I could not have succeeded there without undergraduate mentors in the likes of William Blair, Amy S. Greenburg, and Thavolia Glymph. The faculty at the University of Mississippi, in particular Winthrop Jordan and Shelia Skemp, offered key moments of writing advice throughout my graduate education. Robert Haws, the most flexible and genuine man to work for, always made sure that the thesis, from which this dissertation came, was my top priority. He offered financial support for the dissertation when my own funds could not support traveling to research. Haws also served with eloquence as a member of my dissertation committee and asked the tough questions that forced me to come to terms with why my dissertation is important. Special thanks to my colleagues and friends at Emporia State University, particularly Ellen Hansen, Ed Emmer, Greg Schneider, Darla Mallein, and Ron McCoy, who have taken particular interest in my work. Further thanks to James Ehlers, for the hours of conversation and support. You are an exemplarily teacher, a gifted artist, and a true friend.

This dissertation would just be blank pages if it were not for the diligence and wisdom of my committee, both at the masters and doctoral level. Nancy Bercaw fostered support and guidance in developing the ideas of manhood as well as the work as a whole. Her brilliance, accompanied by her willingness to push me forward, drove this work in unexpected directions, for which I am eternally grateful on many intellectual levels. Robbie Ethridge, my friend and mentor, introduced me to the idea of the shatter zone. Her friendly demeanor and academic brilliance drove me to approach topics from all points of view, and her mentoring not only produced this dissertation, but also a published article that furthered her concept of shatter zones. Charles Wilson always made time for me in his hectic schedule to ask inquisitive questions and introduce further elements of the emergence of the Lost Cause. His true nature as a congenial scholar will always be a model in my own academic life. And of course, I thank John Neff, my advisor. His firm but gentle hand led me through the entangled world of memory. If one person can truly change your life as a historian, it would be him. My appreciations for history, my understanding of the Civil War, and my ability to convey those ideas in a classroom have all emerged because of his guidance. During a discussion on possible thesis topics in April 2001, I commented that I had always thought John Bell Hood was a fascinating character. Dr. Neff's face lit up as I told him all that I knew about Hood. He said that I might be on to something. He was always available to discuss ideas during our meetings that came to be known affectionately in the department as "Brian Time," and he gave me a sense of self-confidence and purpose, both academically and personally, as this work progressed. He encouraged me to think, to keep asking questions, and to never give up, even when there seemed no reason to continue the exploration. To him, my mentor and friend, I am forever grateful.

I have been fortunate to not only work with a supporting faculty but also some outstanding colleagues, who provided hints on sources, comments on the overall construction of the argument, or simply gave me support. My appreciation goes to Kevin McCarthy, David Hargrove, W. Scott Poole, Dennis Bradford, and Chuck Westmoreland. Special thanks to Chris Stacey, Matt Johnson, Michael Upton, Minoa Uffleman, Paul Beazley, Kimberly Burkhart,

Alice Lachaussee, Fisher Fleming, and Toby Bates for always being there when I needed them for support, a swift kick in the backside, and the opportunity just to be around them. I am also eternally grateful to Courtney Roy, who housed me in D.C. and has been the quintessential definition of a friend, and someone who both taught me how to be myself and the importance of utilizing passion in your life; Terry Bax, for the laughs, your friendship, and the writing space in K.C.; Brian Van Norman, who has been my biggest supporter in Kansas, and also the true embodiment of what a friend could and should be; Donnie Pangburn, who taught me the importance of life and living each day in order to make a difference; Ross Guthrie, who reminds me daily of how conversation enriches our lives; Rob Bennett, who taught me the importance of forgiveness, the ability to believe in myself, and the importance of believing in others; and finally Darell Parker. I stand in awe of your sacrifice, your heroism, and your ability to always make me smile. I am glad that you have been on my side throughout this project. Thanks also to Nick Messing, who has opened up a world of opportunities and has me excited to see what develops. It was difficult to put into words my gratitude to each of you listed in this paragraph!

A world of gratitude goes out to my brother Brent, who copyedited my master's thesis. You have also been my rock, whether we are visiting Hippo's in St. Louis, eating Thai food in Memphis, riding rollercoasters at Dollywood, watching baseball in Kansas City, or meeting Broadway actors at the stage door in New York. I love ya bro! My sister Brooke, who set up my first Civil War lecture at George A. Ferrell Elementary School, is someone who continues to impress me with her wisdom, maturity, and passion. I am thankful for her love and support. Finally, I am grateful to my loving parents, Craig and Linda, who took me to Civil War battlefields and museums for family vacations, instead of the beach and amusement parks. I am a historian instead of a surfer or cotton candy vendor because of their influence and guidance. Recently, I took them on a tour of Shiloh with thirty other individuals who braved rain and screaming Boy Scouts. Our Civil War journey has come full circle. Never once have they laughed at my work, told me I was in the wrong field, or uttered a negative comment about my career, and for that, I am truly blessed. They planted the seeds of historical interest in my mind. In fact, they took me to Chickamauga when I was thirteen, which emerges as the moment when I first ran into John Bell Hood.

Introduction

Rethinking John Bell Hood and the Fight for Civil War Memory

In 1897, Judge John C. West, who had served as a private in Company E of the Fourth Texas during the Civil War, delivered a Decoration Day speech in McGregor, Texas. West flexed his oratorical muscles and spoke about the important work Confederate veteran associations had promoted across the southern landscape. Intertwined within a discussion of the causes of the Civil War and the legacy of Reconstruction, West highlighted the influential role Confederate commanders had played, shaping the course of warfare through their military prowess. He stated, "Most, if not all, the leading and most conspicuous characters of the South who were noted for statesmanship and fiery eloquence before the war and for courage and military genius during that trying period have passed from the stage of action, but 'their deeds, their worthy deeds, alone have rendered them immortal.'" West called for the writing of biographies for eight prominent Confederate men. He hoped that this new body of literature would stimulate "zeal and curiosity" and prevent "gossip and tattle and nonsense," and allow southerners to engage in "profitable conversation" that would in turn guarantee a "wiser and more thoughtful generation." West assured his audience that these biographical volumes would become "Epitomes of [the] history of our country and there can be no better use of time and no higher inspiration to noble character than for the young men and women of our day to read, to study and reflect on the lives of these men and their kindred spirits who have built for themselves their posterity 'monuments more lasting than brass,' more enduring than marble." For this signal honor, West selected Robert E. Lee, Jefferson Davis, Edmund Kirby

Smith, Albert S. and Joseph E. Johnston, P. G. T. Beauregard, Thomas J. Jackson, and John Bell Hood. West fervently reiterated how the "noble character" of the eight leaders in question would fill the pages of appropriate biographies to create proper "monuments."[1]

In time, of course, historians took up the task, producing biographies that focused on the military aspects of the war. Volumes poured forth, mainly through the efforts of proponents of the Lost Cause, especially to praise the military efforts of Robert E. Lee and Stonewall Jackson. Lee and Jackson, memorialized on a higher plane than the other commanders West noted on Decoration Day, undoubtedly hold a special place in the Lost Cause ideology. Their names appear on everything from street signs to local auto repair and tire centers. Furthermore, statues arose in staggering numbers, with bronze, brass, and granite figures of Lee and Jackson in city parks, carved into mountains, and scattered across various battlefield landscapes where they commanded Confederate armies in victory and defeat. However, the same reverence given to Lee and Jackson did not trickle down to the other Confederate commanders, especially John Bell Hood.

John Bell Hood has rarely been memorialized in something "more lasting than bronze or marble." The battlefields where Hood commanded at Franklin, Nashville, and Atlanta are now covered with strip malls, pizza joints, and various forms of urban sprawl. Only recently, a plaque appeared at his grave in Metairie, Louisiana. The plaque serves not only to mark the tomb location, which is difficult to find, but also highlights the career of an individual who risked life and two limbs for the Confederate cause. Other than Fort Hood in Texas, he has no other monument, no statue, and little place in the popular memory of the Civil War.[2]

John Bell Hood, born in 1831, grew up in Mt. Sterling, Kentucky, the son of a prosperous slaveholding doctor. At the age of eighteen, Hood entered the U.S. Military Academy, graduating in 1853, ranked forty-four out of fifty-two students. Hood spent the rest of the 1850s in the U.S. Army, fighting Native Americans on the frontier, particularly in the state of Texas. When Kentucky refused to secede in 1861, Hood adopted the state of Texas as his new home, taking up arms for the Confederacy. Hood quickly rose through the ranks while commanding the Texas Brigade. Courageous and successful fighting at Gaines' Mill, Second Manassas, and Sharpsburg served notice of Hood's promise as an officer. At the same time, his personal command style instilled love and admiration from the Texas troops that fought by his side.

Severe wounds removed Hood from the field in two critical battles. At Gettysburg, Hood lost the use of his left arm. During the engagement at

Chickamauga, two months later, Hood lost his right leg, sending him to Richmond to recover from a dangerous amputation with a low survival rate. He eventually reentered military service, now as a corps commander in the Army of Tennessee, currently led by General Joseph E. Johnston. Controversy loomed between Jefferson Davis, Hood, and Johnston, ultimately leading to Johnston's removal and Hood being named commander of the Army of Tennessee. Hood faced a precarious situation as commander, as disorganization, a superior enemy force, and poor leadership skills led to failures and disaster at Atlanta, Spring Hill, Franklin, and Nashville. Hood resigned as commander in 1865 and after the war became a businessman in New Orleans. He married, fathered eleven children, including three sets of twins, and spent his postwar years defending his military career until yellow fever struck New Orleans in 1879.[3]

The biographical story of a Civil War commander like John Bell Hood is vital to our understanding of the Civil War due to his influence in shaping the outcome of the war. When American citizens, north and south, went to sleep on April 11, 1861, they woke up to a world that had completely changed with the first shots of the Civil War. Over the next four years, Americans suffered, bled, cried, and died in unprecedented numbers. The largest armies in American history marched across the landscape, looting homes and farms and leaving behind the scars of war in the form of bent rails, smoldering bales of cotton, and the charred ruins of hearth and home. When the most horrific moment in American history drew to a close, America had to change. With slavery swept away, African Americans adjusted to the meaning of freedom as their former owners adjusted to a new society that no longer could rest on the premise of slave labor.

The Civil War not only defined a generation of Americans, but also served as the turning point in American history. The citizens who endured the war left behind a vital legacy for future generations to understand how one could possibly cope with the horrors of war. The political leaders on both sides left behind a legacy of how to manage and mismanage a nation during a time of national trauma. Men left behind their homes, their families, and their careers in order to pick up arms to fight against their fellow countrymen on the other side of the Mason Dixon line. Many young men, with no prior military experience, entered the war to be commanded by a group of leaders educated in the art of war at military academies. With John Bell Hood rising through the ranks of the Confederate Army to eventually lead an army into battle, his story is vital to our understanding of the Civil War. The decisions Hood made would result in the life and death of thousands of soldiers who looked to him for leadership. By understanding John Bell Hood, we can not only come to appreciate the sacrifice Americans made during the war, but also assess the changes American society underwent as a result of war.

Historians largely agree on the main points of emphasis regarding the life of John Bell Hood. One cannot deny that Hood's tenure in the Army of Tennessee failed to secure victory for the Confederacy during the war. But, at the same time, it is the interpretation of the man and his place in Civil War history that is problematic. A perusal of the historiography of John Bell Hood reveals some misinterpretations, further compounded by a lack of documented evidence. Steven Woodworth, in a recent collection on Civil War generals who failed in battle, noted, "Some recent accounts of these two hapless generals [Braxton Bragg and John Bell Hood] lead the reader to wonder not why they held command of an army but rather why they were not in an insane asylum."[4]

In the sixty years following the contribution of Douglas Southall Freeman, who described Hood as a "young, well-trained trooper" whose "old comrades in Virginia were to remember his boldness, his bravery, his chivalry, his magnanimity," several historians have examined Hood's life beyond his early years with the Army of Northern Virginia.[5] The fact remains that Hood achieved early and brilliant success and victories. Yet, after his time with the Army of Northern Virginia is covered, three clear patterns and tendencies emerge within the historiography. First, because Hood ultimately failed at Franklin and Nashville, the Hood paradigm pivoted on finding the moment where Hood stumbled upon the narrow trail that led to his demise. One prominent historian referred to Hood's plan to invade Tennessee as one "scripted in never-never land," with the commander having "hoped," "expected," and "fantasized" to eventually meet up with Lee at Petersburg after driving his army to the Ohio River.[6]

Historians have essentially read history backward in order to discover the defining moment that produced failure. Through endeavoring in that process, they have described Hood as "fearless but brainless," "aggressive, indomitable and by standards, reckless," and following his defeats, a "battered, beaten, discredited and a hopeless cripple." By focusing solely on the details of battle, many have presumed that a military life can be explained solely through the battlefield. By diminishing Hood's interaction with his soldiers off the field, as well as in the postwar era, the image of Hood is based solely on his success rate on the battlefield, which in turn was a failure.[7]

Second, the root of Hood's failure, according to recent historians, actually may be found in events that took place several years before the Civil War began. With Hood being reared in a "world of chivalric power," his childhood emerged as the epitome of "Southern excess—too much gambling, drinking and horse racing." Scholars have stressed what they call his "academic shortcomings," pointing out the statistics of how he did in French, math, and English at West Point. However, in the midst of battle, French, math, and English seem inconsequential when dealing with the frantic pace and circumstances. Steven Woodworth implores us to forget Hood's ranking at West Point and understand that Hood "must have had some ability" for he graduated "from a fairly demanding school." Yet, historians have used these attributes of Hood's youth in hopes of foreshadowing his eventual "doom" at the military engagements in Tennessee.[8]

Third, at times, historians have argued in contradiction to available evidence, focusing on one particular set of sources that emphasized Hood's failures over his successes, both on and off the battlefield. One specific instance sprouts from how historians analyze casualty rates to determine military qualities of a commander. Some have argued that the "angry" Hood had more dead on the field at Franklin than "Grant at Cold Harbor or McClellan in all of the Seven Days." The men lost at Franklin surpassed those "lost by General George McClellan's massive Federal army in the entire Seven Days Campaign around Richmond, or by General Joseph Hooker's army stylized as the 'finest on the planet' at Chancellorsville." This statement is misleading, particularly with the vast array of different casualty totals and disputed evidence. Some sets of numbers completely discredit the assertions or draw a rather fine line between the numbers reported dead at the time of battle. Yet, historians have used the casualty rates to prove their analyses of Hood as a "reckless" individual, as he essentially "gambled" with human lives on the battlefield.[9]

The label of Hood being a "gambler" with human lives in battle provides us an opportunity to examine how historians have argued beyond available evidence, through inserting myths, rumors, and theories as facts that provide insight into why Hood ultimately failed. One work references an army tale as evidence of the "gambler," relating a story wherein Hood put one thousand dollars on one card in a faro game and emerged victorious. Using rumor over concrete, documented evidence, this framework allows for gambling to imply recklessness and incompetence, instead of understanding its place within southern culture. However, there is no evidence offered to prove that Hood ever gambled. The authors assume that Hood gambled because he grew up in the southern state known for drinking mint juleps while gambling on racehorses at backwoods race tracks.[10]

Another dominant myth swirls around Hood's life-threatening injuries and how they may have altered his psychological makeup in a significant manner. In order to deal with the physical and emotional trauma, some historians have suggested that Hood drank liquor to the point of intoxication and used drugs, specifically laudanum, to cope with his wounds from Chickamauga and Gettysburg, which relieved pain but supposedly clouded Hood's judgment.[11] Once more, rumors supplant fact, and no documentation is offered to prove Hood ever drank or abused drugs during the war. The rumor of substance abuse began with an undocumented assertion in 1940 and has continued to be reiterated time and time again in the wide range of Civil War scholarship.[12]

If Hood had been under the influence of narcotics, why did his contemporaries fail to mention it? Mary Chesnut and Jefferson Davis, who left a wealth of postwar interpretations about the war and their interactions with Hood, never mentioned any drug usage or excessive alcohol consumption that may have impaired judgment. Hood's personal surgeon's records are unavailable, leaving the idea of laudanum use as nothing more than a fabricated offering to explain defeat. Some artificial limbs arrived from Europe with a bottle of laudanum encased with the limb; yet, no sources have emerged to argue if Hood's artificial leg came with laudanum and no documents indicate Hood took the drug if he had access. These are a set of allegations that have been passed through the historiography without careful examination or foundation and need to cease until evidence surfaces.[13]

Instead of looking at the complete set of circumstances, historians relied on a problematic logic and painted Hood as too stupid, too much of a dreamer, and too hell-bent on imitating Robert E. Lee to ever be successful with his own army. Knowing Hood's tragic end, it is easy for anyone to take the ending for granted and attempt to identify, down a slippery slope toward doom, the moment where they believe failure began. Hood's ultimate failure as commander of the Army of Tennessee, in some works, trumps his success as a corps, division, brigade, and regiment commander, rendering them trivial. By undergoing the quest to discover the root of Hood's failure, the image of Hood has emerged distorted in a historiography that contradicts positive memories and contemporary accounts. By examining the historiography carefully, and uncovering how the Hood paradigm came to be constructed, we can begin to understand how some prominent historians have misrepresented John Bell Hood.

Despite the inherent problems within the historiography, many works pertaining to the military career of John Bell Hood have been well received. The military biographies, which focus on the intricacies of tactics and the implementation of battle plans, stopped short of looking at Hood extensively beyond why he failed during particular campaigns. Yet, many military studies of Hood have not yet fully explored all the available historical resources, including the *Official Records,* to assess how Hood did in other command arenas, such as gathering military intelligence and handling the day-to-day logistics of massive armies traipsing across the landscape. Instead, they have focused on social and cultural behavior as a mechanism for explaining failure, which leaves a large body of military questions unexplored. At the same time, the narrowed focus on why Hood won or lost creates historiographic problems when it attempts to understand all segments of Hood's life. Thus, it is time to reassess John Bell Hood as a man, a myth, and a memory in order to understand who he was and why we, as a historical community, have come to the conclusions presented above.

In order to reassess John Bell Hood, his life will be read forward, as a traditional biography. In other words, this book will place what we know about John Bell Hood first. Although no specific collection of John Bell Hood papers exists in the country, there is a substantial body of evidence provided through the correspondence of Hood and his fellow officers, as well as the reactions from his soldiers, in order to assist in filling in the human experience outside military decisions on and off the battlefield. When it comes to Hood's life before the war, there are a limited number of sources to help describe his childhood and his early military experience at West Point and fighting on the frontier. The same can be said with the postwar era, where our specific knowledge of John Bell Hood can be found in his limited correspondence as well as in the local newspapers reporting on his daily activities. In the end, there is enough evidence available to understand Hood's life from beginning to end, without trying to explore a specific turning point that led to failure in the Civil War.

It is difficult for the life of one individual to stand alone in not only the scope of the Civil War, but also the grand scope of American history. Thus, I will place Hood in a social and cultural context for two reasons. First, by understanding the world Hood lived within, the missing details of his early and late life can be filled in based on the communities and societies he interacted with on a daily basis. Second, by forging a cultural biography of John Bell Hood, he can be utilized as a representative of someone who grew up in both antebellum and postbellum southern society. Hood also serves as an example of what it was like for an individual coping with the failure of the Civil War in the postwar era, as communities sought to rebuild their lives, resurrect their lost honor, and remember the Civil War in a specific manner in order to assist in the reconstruction of an altered society.

A cultural context provides further insight beyond the antebellum and postwar years. After Hood departed his childhood community in Kentucky, he joined a military community at West Point. Through the proliferation of the ideals of duty, honor, and country, Hood learned how to become an active member of a select band of brothers that sought to define honor in a very specific facet, altering how Hood understood honor during his youth. As the cadets marched out of the academy, they carried with them the same ideals of honor and the same bonds of friendship and mutual admiration onto the frontier and into battle against Native Americans. When the Civil War began, military commanders, like Hood, utilized the same principles when they commanded their soldiers into battle. An officer who could successfully translate honor from the frontier to the battlefield would find early victories attainable, as John Bell Hood did on a consistent basis.

However, the Civil War erupted as a defining moment that threatened honor and manhood on a daily basis. The ideals of masculinity would be put into jeopardy when soldiers fled from the front lines and hid in the bushes away from the swirl of shot and shell. In the midst of musket fire, artillery rounds, and bayonet and cavalry charges, soldiers fell wounded in battle, losing limbs and the ability to function socially through the occurrence of posttraumatic stress disorder, and ultimately, could face death far away from their family and loved ones. For the soldiers who survived but returned an incomplete man, both physically and emotionally, the question arose if society would recognize their sacrifices and reassert their positions as men. If the armies failed to achieve victory, would a soldier who came home disfigured, shell shocked, or even perished in battle in a losing effort still be recognized as an honorable individual? Thus, the Civil War threatened the antebellum criteria of manhood and forced men and women to redefine the contours of manhood and womanhood in the midst of a society that looked very different than it did at the start of the war.

Within a cultural exploration of community and masculinity, memory emerges as a valid and important dynamic when it comes to studying history. Memory has been important both to the survivors of the Civil War and to historians in recent years. From the closing moments of the Civil War, soldiers and officers offered their opinions as to why the South failed to achieve victory. They actively constructed a series of speeches and memoirs that sought to remember the Civil War in a very specific facet. In order to collect and record the individual strands of memory, a historical society emerged in the South that sought to not only remember the Civil War as an honorable endeavor for the South but also to pinpoint the source of failure in the Confederate war effort. What many proponents of the Lost Cause concluded was that John Bell Hood's actions as a commander in 1864 hindered and in some ways obliterated the efforts toward success in the Civil War. The critical voices, though dominating the literature of the Lost Cause, did not stand alone. Defenders and critics lined up on both sides of the aisle to either support or critique Hood's efforts as a military figure. Their speeches and analysis emerged as the prominent source of evidence for recent historians to analyze John Bell Hood. However, historians, at times, have been selective in their evidence choices, allowing the critical voices to dominate both in terms of the memory of the Civil War and in the historiography of John Bell Hood.[14]

Exploring Hood's reputation and historiography reveals the relationship not only between history and memory, but also between historians and memory. In the case of Hood, as in other biographies, historians serve as the "keepers of collective memories." Within the large body of evidence available for a historian to utilize, individual memory becomes evidence, which might then ultimately influence the collective memory of an individual. Historians shaped their own collective memory based on the negative trends in social memory formation from 1865 to 1904, ultimately diminishing the available voices that sought to praise Hood. If only the critical memories pertaining to an individual like John Bell Hood are drawn into the historiography as evidence, the collective memory of Hood, both in society and the historiography, becomes slanted in a critical manner. The power of memory in the postwar era reveals how competing groups buckled under political and societal pressure in order to maintain their individual memories as part of the overall collective memory of John Bell Hood.[15]

As a historical community, we have reached a crossroads. Military historians are beginning to utilize the new military history, which pays particular attention to the social and cultural elements of a military career. One avenue to explore a new military history biography of John Bell Hood is through memory. By utilizing memory as an analytical tool, we can begin to understand how Hood's reputation was forged both during the war and well into the postwar era.

The book you are about to read is not an extensive military study that will delve into the specific details of Hood the tactician, the logistician, and the commander who failed to achieve victory. Rather, the work will utilize both a social and cultural approach, highlighting memory as a vital dynamic in understanding how Hood's reputation came to be forged within history. A memory study further allows the large body of positive and negative individual memories, which may have been discarded or diminished in previous works, to be included alongside one another to provide a more complex and nuanced portrait.[16]

With the last full-length biography on the life of Hood appearing more than two decades ago, historians now have the opportunity to appreciate new bodies of evidence and new analytical tools to reassess age-old interpretations and assessments in regard to the men who commanded in the American Civil War. It is time to rethink John Bell Hood by using memory as a mechanism to steer through a field of contradictory bodies of evidence that may not always fit the interpretation the historian wishes to convey. We now have the opportunity as a historical community to better understand not only the individual, but the society they resided within. This process can assist future historians in dealing with the tangled web of memory and the realm of contradictory evidence that does not seem to mesh with the current historiographic base. Thus, an appropriate framework, ushered in through a cultural biography, can be applied to other Civil War commanders. With that accomplished, Civil War historians can begin to recast biography in a new light, filled with new analysis and source material, which can expand Civil War studies to forge more detailed, complex, and nuanced monographs.

Chapter 1

Sons of an Earlier Day: Hood's Journey from Boyhood to Manhood

The difficulty in beginning the story of John Bell Hood stems from a lack of evidence about his childhood. Hood left no bounty of papers that chronicled the daily details of his youth. Nor did he have much to say in his memoir about his childhood before his entrance into West Point. Various census and court records have served useful in tracking the movements of the Hood family throughout the antebellum era. In the absence of direct evidence of Hood's daily childhood experience, it is possible to gain knowledge about his childhood through understanding the world around him. Given what we know of the society in which he grew to adulthood, his day-to-day experiences centered on his quest to prove himself an honorable southern man in the minds of his family and his community. Men in Kentucky, just as other men throughout the South, spent an enormous amount of time preoccupied with their masculine status among their peers. Some utilized hunting, horse racing, and controlled alcohol consumption to prove their worth. Others worked on their own personal ambition and sought the love of a woman. Hood most likely emerges somewhere in the middle, engaging in manly activities, pursuing his love interest, Sally Preston, and fostering his ambition by graduating from West Point and embarking upon a military career that would provide several future opportunities to garner notice for honorable actions on and off the field of battle.

In order to understand Hood's journey to manhood and how it may have shaped his military experience in the Civil War, we must first examine Hood's lineage to understand his family background. John Bell Hood wrote in his memoir, "Doubtless I had inherited this [military] predilection from my grandfathers, who were soldiers under Washington. They were of English origin."[1] Hood had been continually told of his male ancestors in order to solidify a bond between past generations and to establish an honorable pathway for him to follow in his own life. Thus, it should not be a surprise that a military officer had a family lineage rich in military history. In 1673, John Bell Hood's great-great-great-great Grandfather, Jasper Hood, was born. Little is known about Jasper other than he married Tryntje Luykas Andries on June 7, 1696, in New York City. The Andries family had been in the New York area since at least the 1650s. Jasper and Tryntje had five children: their first son, Jan, who died within two years of birth, another son, Jan, a daughter Aefje, and two other sons, Thomas and Lucas.[2]

Both Lucas and Thomas moved from New York to settle in western Virginia. As John Bell Hood recalled, "[My grandfathers] had settled at an early period in Virginia, and after taking an active part in the War of Independence, emigrated to Kentucky." Kentucky, with an ample supply of wild game animals and fertile soil, also held a large amount of conflict between the Cherokees and Iroquois and later, between white settlers and the native remnants. On an early expedition through Kentucky, pioneer Charles Wilkins Short wrote, "No objects meet the eye but mountains, woods and numerous rivers, which seem to roll their waters in vain." In terms of the natives, Short wrote, "The Indians have been very troublesome to us for several months past. Scarcely a week passes, but we hear of some depredations or savage outrage committed by them, on some quarter of our country."[3]

Despite the dangers, the Hood family settled in Kentucky. Lucas Hood married Johannah Van Stockholm and with her had four sons (Aaron, Andrew, Han, and Thomas) and four daughters (Cattren, Leora, Margaret, and Hannah). Andrew Hood eventually married Massa Sudduth and together they had six sons (John, Lucas, Lewis, Thomas, Andrew, Jr., and Henry) as well as six daughters (Sarchet, Martha, Rachel, Elizabeth, Peggy, and Catherine). Andrew Hood fought in the Revolution for Virginia and eventually settled along the banks of the Big Stoner in the late 1780s in Kentucky.[4]

William Sudduth, Massa Sudduth's brother, served and lived with Andrew Hood on the frontier of Kentucky. He recalled, "In the month of March 1786, Miss Hood and one of my sisters went out to a sugar camp about two hundred yards from the fort and amused themselves with swinging to a grapevine until nearly dark, the horses feeding around them." However, once darkness engulfed the landscape, local natives "caught nearly every horse belonging to the place. Several broke loose with their halters on. One they took four or five miles and stabbed in several places and turned loose and took four valuable ones with them." Andrew Hood joined Sudduth in the pursuit of the raiders, but "could not overtake them." The area where Sudduth and Hood lived came to be known as Hoods Station. Sudduth wrote, "Major Hood was allowed a guard, raised a crop and removed his family back in June and collected some other families to live at the station."[5]

Life at the station found constant interruption from native conflict in the region. Sudduth recalled one sentinel on guard duty stating "he believed there was a raccoon or something else in the branch that he had heard sneeze several times." However, the sneezing creature in the tree turned out to be a native scout, who led a party that "attempted to catch the horses three times." In response, Sudduth and Andrew and Lucas Hood launched another expedition. When the Indians had been located, the group had to use weapons to get the horses back. Sudduth wrote, "Lucas Hood and Harry Martin were one on each side of me with their guns cocked and up to their faces to shoot, but the [Indian horseman] fell so quick as to save their fire."[6]

In the midst of the horse-stealing conflict with local natives, one of the settlers, Frederick William Wills, who served in both the War of 1812 and various Indian engagements on the frontier, emerged as "one of the leading citizens of the settlement," having been "industrious" and a "thorough-going man possessed of far more than ordinary mental capacity." Wills's father also served in the Revolution, further solidifying a family lineage steeped in military heritage. Wills eventually presided over the marriage of Andrew Hood's son Lucas and his own daughter, Frances Wills.[7]

Lucas Hood gained a reputation as an Indian fighter. He joined "the Kentucky Militia with General Harmer on his ill-fated expedition against the Indians of Little Turtle [Miami] in 1790." John Bell Hood's grandfather also served as a scout with General "Mad" Anthony Wayne and eventually fought at the Battle of Fallen Timbers on August 21, 1794. Lucas Hood, "an Ensign in the 36th Regiment of Kentucky Militia," met an early death when he had been scalped and left for dead at Fallen Timbers.[8]

Before his unfortunate death, Lucas Hood and Frances Wills had four children: Andrew, William, John W., and a daughter, Frances. Andrew and his son Thomas Jefferson Hood eventually served as representatives to the Kentucky Constitutional Convention in 1849. John W., born on June 1, 1798, followed his two brothers and became a doctor by studying medicine at the University of Pennsylvania in 1829 and 1830. He married Theodosia French. Unfortunately, the records are incomplete and the exact date of the marriage is unknown. The couple lived in Owingsville, Kentucky, a community known to have one of the first iron foundries in the West, which operated from the start of the nineteenth century for ten years. In Owingsville, Theodosia gave birth to her first child, John Bell Hood, on June 29, 1831. Two more sons, William and James, as well as a daughter, Olivia Keziah, arrived after the family moved to Mount Sterling, Kentucky.[9]

The Hoods' Mount Sterling homestead stood upon a hill, surrounded by a fence made of limestone. The home, one and a half stories, consisted of a "kitchen, pantry and dining room" on the first floor. The grounds contained a large orchard that Doctor Hood utilized to provide medical instruction for other potential frontier doctors, away from his own homestead. Despite the expansive grounds, the Hood children did discover the tools their father used in his medical instruction. On one occasion, Lizzie Hood and her friend, Mary Davis Reid, awaited the return of her father and the medical students, who had journeyed out onto the property to engage in medical instruction. When the dinner bell clang across the hills and the men returned to the house, the two girls went to examine the makeshift medical school for themselves. Discovering a series of boxes, the girls curiously lifted the lids to peer at the contents. Suddenly, a leg toppled from the box, which sent the girls darting back to the house, screaming each frantic step along the way.[10]

To keep his medical instruction current, John Hood needed a constant supply of bodies to use for scientific study. Hood made several deals with the local jails in the region to retrieve the bodies of executed criminals. For John Thompson, a black man scheduled to be executed for murder, Hood struck a deal to provide him with all the whiskey he could drink in exchange for his body after the execution. Thompson agreed and Hood used the body to continue his instruction in the orchard.[11]

Despite the prominence of medical instruction in the community of Mount Sterling, nothing could stop the waves of disease that plagued the Kentucky frontier. Cholera and smallpox swept through the region, resulting in a growing orphan population. In the summer of 1833, a cholera epidemic struck Lexington and spread eastward, leaving a path of misery and destruction. J. P. Harrison wrote, "I am fearful that it will be an epidemic in Kentucky." Robert Davidson stated, "Early in June, 1833, the epidemic made its appearance, and filled every house with mourning. In the short space of nine days, fifteen hundred persons were prostrated, and dying at the rate of fifty a day." The epidemic claimed the lives of about five hundred settlers, resulting in an environment in which, according to Davidson, "The streets were deserted. The marketplace was desolate. . . . The graveyards were choked. Coffins were laid down at the gates by the score, in confused heaps."[12]

Within Mt. Sterling by July, according to local resident Jilson Harrison, "There are twenty-five or thirty cases of cholera in town, five fatal—Harry Richardson, Henry Landers (a wagon maker), the eldest daughter of Dr. Slavens (Martha Ann Slavens) and two Negroes." Approximately four hundred citizens fled the community. Harrison, who remained behind, kept "calomel and Opium or Laudanum near by." Dr. John Slavens, who had lost a daughter to the cholera outbreak, recommended a course of action. He wrote, "If you value your life, eat no vegetables of any kind, no matter how prepared. Keep out of the night air, rain and hot sun as much as possible. Nearly all the cases can be traced to some impropriety of eating or exposure. I am satisfied that the disease is not contagious, no, no more than worms or croup in children."[13]

The primitive medical knowledge of the time failed to recognize that cholera had been spread through water contamination, instead of vegetables or weather exposure. The rampant spread of disease further solidified the fears some townspeople had with their local physicians. Ellen Green wrote, "You will recollect Dr. Tomkins. He has turned out to be a perfect sort. . . . He is now strolling about the streets absolutely barefoot—all from the . . . habit of at first moderate drinking—which can be more horrible." A local physician stumbling through the town, intoxicated, a few months after the major outbreak of cholera did little to calm the nerves of the concerned citizens. In other cases, skill alone could raise alarm. William Blackburn wrote to a family member, "I know you prefer Dr. Caldwell and I am entirely willing you to employ him. At the same time, I have many apprehensions of his skill. I wrote regretting you to go to my fathers to avoid Scarlet fever. If you have done so it will be unnecessary to discuss the Mt. Sterling physicians."[14]

Despite some concerns with local physicians, John W. Hood rose as a prosperous doctor and used his medical practice to eventually teach medicine as well as gain landed capital, both in acres and in slaves. The Hood family had been lucky in terms of maintaining the health of their family at Mount Sterling, surviving the cholera outbreak intact. In 1825, the Hood family owned two lots in Owingsville, as well as four slaves. On one of the lots, John Hood constructed "a two-story house of logs, walled it with hand-dressed planks and covered it with a roof of clapboards." Joel Hart, an up-and-coming stonemason who emerged as Kentucky's "most noted sculptor," built the fireplace and also a chimney for the Hood residence, which survived as one of the oldest homes in Owingsville. The census records reveal that in 1830, there were five persons counted at the Hood residence, two white males and three white females. Furthermore, the census also counted three male slaves under ten, three female slaves under ten, one female slave between twenty-five and thirty-six, and one free black male between twenty-four and thirty-six, a total of seven slaves and one free black.[15]

The 1840 census reveals nine persons counted in the Hood residence, which would include Hood, his wife, and three of the children, leaving four members living in the household not immediate members of the family. In

1840, the Hood family also held eleven slaves: three black males between ages ten and twenty-four, two black males between ages twenty-four and thirty-six, two black females under the age of ten, three black females between the ages of ten and twenty-four, and one black female between the age of twenty-four and thirty-six. Again, the family also had one free black male living with them between the age of thirty-six and fifty-five. The 1850 census recorded seven members of the Hood household. However, the slave schedule of 1850 cannot be located. By the end of his life, John W. Hood held well more than six hundred acres of land and an estate valued at $9,760, which ranked above all in the county, with the exception of "about two dozen inhabitants." Although the hard data on enslaved members of the Hood household remains incomplete, the census records do prove that the Hood family had slaves counted in both the 1830 and 1840 census.[16]

Some of the property acquired by the Hood family had been given by relatives. Hood's mother, Theodosia French, was the daughter of James French and Keziah Calloway. James French had served in the Revolution and has been appointed a justice of the peace and a county surveyor in the 1790s in Kentucky. John Adams appointed him "federal commissioner for the first division of Kentucky and charged him with the responsibility of serving under the act which provided 'for the valuation of lands and dwelling-houses and the enumeration of slaves within the United States'" in 1798. The French family's political influence also lent itself to landed wealth, which James French left to his daughter upon his death in 1835. Thus, the home that Theodosia French and John W. Hood built in Mount Sterling had been courtesy of the land from James French as well as "an additional bequest of $700."[17]

Theodosia's only brother, Richard French, quickly emerged as a prominent political figure in Kentucky. French had attended private schools before studying law and worked as a lawyer in Winchester, Kentucky. Shortly after being admitted to the bar, French went to the Kentucky state House of Representatives from 1820 to 1826 and served as a judge on the circuit court in 1829. Representing the Jacksonian Democrats, French decided to try his hand on the national political scene and successfully received election to the House of Representatives in the fall of 1834. However, French failed to garner reelection in 1836. He had an unsuccessful run for governor of Kentucky in 1840 and decided to return to the House of Representatives in Washington, elected to two terms in 1842 and 1846. After leaving the House of Representatives on March 3, 1849, French returned to Covington, Kentucky, to practice law until his death on May 1, 1854.[18]

Much of French's political career had been devoted to protecting the institution of slavery in Kentucky. The growing belief that slavery represented a necessary evil facilitated an antislavery crusade within the state of Kentucky. In 1840, Cassius Marcellus Clay, a member of the Kentucky state legislature, fervently argued that the institution of slavery had been a detriment to Kentucky's economy. Yet many of the citizens, despite their dislike for the institution, were not willing to accept Clay's argument and shelve a system that had become so intertwined within the social and economic fiber of the state. In the meantime, abolitionist organizations, sentiments, and speeches appeared throughout the state, in forty seven of the one hundred counties. Bath and Clark County, where the Hood family had resided, had either held "a public antislavery meeting," participated in the "nomination of an antislavery candidate to the state Constitutional Convention," or held some sort of abolitionist talk or rally.[19] Thus, while John Hood held slaves, his homestead had been immersed in abolitionist sentiment and activity, following a pattern that covered almost half of the state.

Despite the presence of an abolitionist movement in Kentucky, southern men utilized slavery to define their own manhood. In the antebellum era, southerners defined masculinity through twin pillars: honor and mastery. Honor, the first pillar in defining an individual as a man, could only be achieved through participating in honorable acts. Before any honorable acts could take place, the southern man had to first internalize his own self-worth. Honor had to be internalized in order for an individual to have an "understanding of who he is and where he belongs in the ordered ranks of society."[20]

Once the internal definition had been secured, southern men affirmed their honor in society by following "a set of expectations determined and perpetuated by the community." The community usually defined the set of expectations through public rituals. Honorable acts included seeking "revenge against familial and community enemies," showing the proper physical appearance to display "inner merit," chivalrous acts to defend "male integrity," and "reliance upon oath-taking as a bond in lieu of family obligations and allegiances." Once a sense of self-identity emerged, both internalized and confirmed from the public, southern men could then take part in the second pillar of manhood: mastery. Mastery, exhibited through control of women, slaves, land, and their own household, helped secure the internalized definition and secured their internalized honorable manhood in the eyes of the community.[21]

The South underwent a transition from defining manhood in the eighteenth century through a republican model, meaning men, "as head of a household," who "place the good of the community above individual desires" and emerge as someone who has "subordinate self-interest to the commonwealth." Yet, with the turn of the nineteenth century, everything changed with the emergence of the self-made man. Men now received encouragement to pursue "wealth, power, and self-advancement," without a "sense of responsibility to neighbor or nation." The transition had been driven also by "the institutions southern students attended, the parental directives they received, and the peer culture they created."[22]

At the outbreak of the Civil War, historians have argued that "men internalized a sense of manliness through relationships to wives, children and slaves," while also seeking to maintain and head an "autonomous, self-sufficient household." Thus, southern manhood required "an independent household and landownership, a submissive wife and children, and ideally, slaves." In order for men to define themselves as men, they were dependent on having sought out a loving woman, bearing children, and holding slaves in order to exert mastery for the public to see. The relationships between men and women in the South were much more than women being dependent on men. Men were equally dependent on their families to exert their internalized definition of honor. Furthermore, dependency varied in different circumstances at different times, depending on the nature of the household.[23]

However, even though a majority of southern men lived without owning land or slaves, they still resided in a society dominated by the elite manly conceptions of honor and mastery. If a community had no direct connection to slavery, southerners had to seek additional ways to define manhood and assert mastery outside human or landed capital. Historian Stephen Berry argues that many men did not see honor as the only thing to "constitute a reason for living." Berry sees many men as seeking éclat, "a term comprising power and honor but bigger than both of them." Instead of solely relying on honor, men followed what southern planter James Henry Hammond argued as the keys to living. Hammond wrote, "There are two things worth living for, love in life, immortality after death." Love included relationships with both men and women, and immortality could be achieved with an ambitious career that created an impact that could last for years into the future. Berry's insightful analysis offers another level of understanding how men sought to define themselves as men. Honor, mastery, ambition, and love all emerge as possible avenues for men to internalize and then display their manhood for all to see.[24]

Yet, the existence of both slavery and an active antislavery movement poses a serious problem for Kentucky males in displaying their own honor.

If the Deep South utilized slavery to display honor and mastery, how would the young men of Kentucky, who grew up in counties filled with abolitionist sentiment, be recognized as honorable men throughout the rest of the South? Kentucky, as a border state, not only underwent a transition on how they defined slavery after 1830, but also a transition in what elements of society could be utilized to define a southern man.

Newspapers published around the time of John Bell Hood's birth, as well as in subsequent years, continually discussed what being a man entailed in the state of Kentucky. Some of the assessments of men were far from flattering. One newspaper writer, who published near where John Bell Hood grew up, questioned the very nature of man. He wrote, "What is man? Originally dust; engendered in sin; brought forth with sorrow; helpless in his infancy; extravagantly wild in his youth; mad in his manhood; decried in his age; his first voice moves pity; his last commands grief." Described as "a dunghill blanched with snow," men displayed the following qualities: "if poor, despised; if rich, flattered; if prudent, mistrusted; if simple derided; his beauty, a flower; his strength, grass; his wit, a flash; his wisdom, folly; his judgment, weakness; his art, imperfection; his glory, a blaze."[25]

Part of that transition rests in the role religion played throughout Kentucky. To forge any sense of community on the frontier, many settlers turned to the church, which, according to historian John B. Boles, "bound people together in close-knit spiritual families and as such performed a much-needed service for the mobile population." Samuel R. Brown, who wrote a travel guide during the antebellum era, stated, "It is a solemn truth, that religion is no where more respected, than in Kentucky." With religion dominating the Kentucky frontier, some citizens called into question whether the community rituals utilized to display honor were appropriate. Ritualized violence, in the form of dueling, existed throughout the state, prompting several citizens to call for its end. Kentucky outlawed the practice in 1799, punishable by fines of up to $5,000. However, over the next thirty years, the state legislature added revisions, allowing for gentlemen to get around the law.[26]

On February 3, 1813, Kentucky became the first state in the Union to pass a law outlawing the carrying of a concealed deadly weapon. The law read that no one could carry "a pocket pistol, dirk, large knife, or sword in a cane, concealed as a weapon, unless when traveling on a journey." Violators of the law would be forced to pay a fine of $100, of which $50 would go to the informant who turned in the violator. The law worked, according to British visitor Elias Pim Fordham, who traveled throughout Kentucky in 1817–18. Fordham noted, "Nothing is more common than for men in Kentucky to quarrel about politics, and the pistol used to be the universal resort. But as almost every duel was fatal, the legislature took effectual means to prevent dueling. The dirk is now generally worn, and not unfrequently used in the lower parts near the Tennessee line." Despite the effectiveness of the early law, the Kentucky Supreme Court struck it down in 1822, arguing that "it is the right to bear arms in defense of the citizens and the state that is secured by the constitution." Through the ruling of the Supreme Court, Kentucky returned to carrying concealed weapons without the threat of fines.[27]

Another way to display the criteria of manhood was the mastery of alcohol consumption. Yet, Kentucky also saw the rise of prohibition in the midst of the reform culture of the 1830s and 1840s. Hensh Gorn, a resident of Kentucky, wrote to his mother of a trip that included his stop at a home where "dance and cards, music, crackers and mint juleps made the time pass merrily away." Whiskey also served on the frontier as a form of currency. A perusal of advertisements in antebellum Kentucky newspapers reveals the importance whiskey played in ensuring the survival of the frontier economy. Elijah H. Elliott, a grocer in Paris, Kentucky, placed a notice of a new bounty received in his store. Elliott had a variety of food items, spices, medicines, shoes, housewares, several flavors of brandy, wine, personal care items, ammunition, and tobacco products. He noted, "All the above articles will be sold low for Cash, or exchanged for Whiskey, Tallow, Bees-wax, and all articles in the produce line." Thus, whiskey emerged so entrenched in Kentucky society that its monetary value could purchase goods to ensure survival.[28]

The availability of alcohol did not guarantee that everyone drank freely, especially in the emerging prohibition atmosphere. How then could young men display their manhood? Young men, like John Bell Hood, had to internalize their own definition of manhood at a time when the world around them underwent reconstruction of manhood's contours. They could pay particular attention to hunting, gambling, and horse racing in order to display honor to a region that began to turn away from slavery, violence, and alcohol as contours of manhood. With young John Bell Hood reluctant to acquire slaves at any point in his life, honorable manhood displayed through a mastery over slaves or land remained untenable. Furthermore, following in his father's footsteps to medical school did not guarantee any recognition of elite manly status, especially with the fluctuating world of masculine definitions in antebellum Kentucky. The pursuit of honorable status does not stand alone as a reason why someone like Hood would have engaged in horse racing, drinking, and gambling. With the members of Kentucky society separated on the frontier, men gathered to hunt, fish, and gamble or eat. Through these avenues, words and gestures were exchanged in the presence of those who would recognize them as gentlemen.[29]

We cannot deny, however, that the actions of a young man constantly conveyed his status and worth in society. John Bell Hood had to discover a way to assert his reputation among his peers. Thus, by age fourteen, young men across the South regularly engaged in fighting, wrestling, gambling, drinking, and swearing, especially because they utilized the imitation of "the mannerisms of older brothers and fathers" to secure their status as men. With Hood's father busy with the medical training of future doctors, young Hood received a similar state of parenting from his father as other youths across the South.[30]

Young men, like John Bell Hood, could actually turn to recreational activities that many enjoyed throughout the South, such as hunting, riding horses, or drinking, to develop their own sense of honorable manhood. When the young Hood played, he actually was laying a foundation to define himself as a man in future years. Boys in the South had to learn at an early age that they must pay careful attention to a complex symbolic code of social manners and behaviors to attain the same level of manliness as their fathers.[31]

As a youth, when John Bell Hood participated in hunting, he took part in an approved community ritual that allowed for the display of honor. Though southern youth could exhibit a masculine ethos through a number of avenues, hunting allowed for an elaborate display of manhood one could perform before a wide variety of audiences, justifying the manly act. Boys would begin displaying mastery by setting traps and using dogs to retrieve their kill. Young men also learned how to ride horses, which would be necessary for hunts as they matured in age and stature. If a young boy could prove he was capable of mastering dogs and traps, he could move beyond trapping and attain the ultimate symbol of masculinity: a gun. Guns, usually presented to a southern boy as a gift from his father or another male relative, allowed the youth to understand how mastery worked. When a southern man held a gun, the firearm represented "the dominion of white men over slaves, animals, and the natural world, as well as their responsibilities toward white women and children as protectors and providers." As a young bachelor, a southern male may not have the opportunity to prove his honor through mastery over a household or slaves, especially if he did not own slaves, like John Bell Hood. Hunting allowed a young man to prove he could exhibit mastery, through control over "dogs, horses, equipment, slaves and liquor." Thus, the event of the hunt allowed the emergence of a white male fraternity, with initiation undergone through the spilling of blood within the fields and forests around their homes.[32]

Hunting instilled additional values beyond guaranteeing a public recognition of manhood. Hunting allowed a youthful man to display self-control. By possessing self-control, a hunter could increase his chances for a successful kill, for "calmness improved marksmanship, coolness prevented hasty decision making, and silence concealed the hunter from his prey." A newspaper writer in Charleston, South Carolina, in 1851, wrote, "You feel an exultation beside the fallen deer which many have failed to experience in the moment of much more important triumphs. But of course you will take care to conceal this when your comrades come up—of course it is nothing to you to kill a deer." With southern white males believing only they were capable of exerting self-control, hunting allowed them to "prove themselves worthy of this mantle of power." The youthful southerners who embarked upon hunting expeditions also gained valuable training for a future in the military. By taking part in hunting expeditions as a youth, John Bell Hood may not only have found an opportunity to display his mastery as part of his masculine development, but also learned critical skills that would be necessary for a career as a military officer.[33]

Mastery could take place in other forms than hunting. Young men could display honor by mastering horse riding. The handling of horses not only had masculine connections to Kentucky, but larger societal ones at the same time. The budding bluegrass region emerged as a haven for horse breeding and horse racing. Numerous local newspaper advertisements proclaimed their horses available for stud. One advertisement proclaimed the availability of "The valuable and fine breeding horse, Grand Turk," who stood "in fine health" and could be viewed at his home stable. The owner declared, "Turk's color, and breeding as to size and figure is not surpassed by any horse in Kentucky." Right below the notice on Turk stood another for "The elegant and well bred horse, Sir William." William remained at the same stable as two other worthy horses, "the very large and noble Jack, The Duke of Bourbon," as well as Tom Foot, a "very fast and elegant" pony. The breeding prowess and promise of several Kentucky horses displayed a sense of nobility and aristocracy, with the animals receiving titles of nobility and descriptions fit for the most refined gentlemen throughout the state.[34]

Proper breeding of horses could produce a colt that would eventually participate and win the regular bout of horse races run throughout the state's northern regions. Horse racing provided an avenue for men to gamble, with betting sports serving the function "of reducing other kinds of 'dangerous, but often inevitable social tensions.'" Just like the act of a duel, gambling offered a way for men to use a prescribed code of honor to affect both their "personal and group status, which depended so largely upon public perceptions." Men placed bets whenever the opportunity arose, ranging from local barbeques to taverns. Yet, in northern Kentucky, the horse race emerged as the premier location for men to be seen by the public as well as be seen betting on the racing fortunes of a horse.[35]

Hunting, horses, and youthful drinking all provided avenues for young John Bell Hood to transition from a young boy to a young man. However, recreational activities were not enough to assert his own personal ambitions. Because Hood decided not to become a physician like his father, he could find some guarantee of manly status in one location that would display his ambition: the military. A masculine culture had always been present in the military, as serving in the armed forces authenticated manhood.[36]

Men used military experience to secure their masculinity in three ways. First, the military created a unified white male community and allowed for the formation of manly bonds between men, leaving women and minorities on the fringes. By spending time with other men in the military, men would learn how to identify with one another and also how to prove their mastery over women and minorities. Second, soldiers regarded their weapons and uniforms as symbols of masculinity. Military weaponry and uniforms, exclusive for soldiers, allowed the man to display his honor through his sword and his uniform. Third, southern men, by engaging in battle, proved themselves legitimate heirs to the revolutionary military tradition forged in America. By joining the military, a young man could prove to his family that he possessed the same level of manly courage as the previous generations. Hence, military service for John Bell Hood possessed all the possibilities for a young boy to prove himself a man within a society dealing with fluctuating definitions of honor and masculinity.[37]

When John Bell Hood chose another career path than his father or brothers, he exhibited a key component of honor: independence. By becoming a cadet, Hood would enter a world where his father and mother could no longer remain completely in charge of his life and well-being. West Point could afford Hood a chance to prove his manly worth by completing his education and attaining an officer position within the U.S. Army. When Hood would don his gray uniform, he proved himself worthy of following orders and upholding responsibilities. Hood recalled in his memoir, "Doubtless I had inherited this predilection from my grandfathers, who were soldiers under Washington." Hood needed to join the military not only to prove his manly worth to himself and his family, but also to sustain a proud family lineage rooted in military service.[38]

West Point offered young men who demonstrated themselves to be "mathematically inclined" at the local level a chance for honorable advancement in society. Yet, West Point offered no guarantees in the antebellum period. With the nation entering a lull in major military endeavors following the War of 1812, military advancement tended to lean toward the politically connected. A friend of Jubal Early wrote, "I presume I shall remain in the army, and perhaps be a captain by the time I am sixty. It seems like a joke, but damn me if I don't think there is a good deal of truth in it." Yet, in the wake of the Mexican War, Hood stood a reasonable chance of finding promotion, with new tracts of territory needing to be explored and policed against Indian violence. With the lack of educational opportunities in the South, West Point seemed the logical choice for someone of Hood's background and ambition.[39]

Hood's familial political connections proved vital for the young man with a keen military interest. Prior to the outbreak of the Civil War, cadets at West Point needed a political appointment, either from a congressman or "the President 'at large.'" Furthermore, a cadet had to pass an entrance examination. One young man described the examination process, stating, "There were about twenty of us marched in at once. The mathematical examination consisted of questions in vulgar and decimal fractions. . . . We were then called upon to read, I read an extract from Blair which was satisfactorily done. I was then called upon to write [a sentence]. This I done and was sent to my seat. This closed the examination." No one wanted to increase the toughness of the entrance exams, fearing the embarrassment of political appointees failing. Yet, more than half the appointees in a given year still failed the examination.[40]

For Hood, his great uncle on his mother's side, Judge Richard French, represented the 9th District of Kentucky in the United States Congress. Thus, an appointment at West Point came through on January 27, 1849, with Hood summoned to report to duty on July 1, making him a member of the class of 1853. Future presidents, such as Martin Van Buren and William Henry Harrison, wrote to the superintendent to make sure their children or family friends received extra attention while at West Point. Hood did not have that luxury. He would have to work harder to become an army officer who, according to Lieutenant Colonel William Baumer, was "an honorable, courageous, self-reliant, clear-thinking man . . . [with] a broad grasp of the essentials of his profession."[41]

Hood, like many cadets before and after him, possessed "a strong liking for military life, a desire to be a West Pointer with all the implications of conforming to a certain pattern." Before he departed for school, his father remarked, "If you can't behave, don't come home. Go to the nearest gatepost and butt your brains out." In his departing words of advice, Hood's father reminded the new cadet of the importance self-control played in exhibiting the signs of manhood. In order for Hood to maintain his transition from boy to man, he had to display mastery over himself.[42]

As a doctor, Hood's father certainly knew the benefits of higher education. The system of higher education created in the United States rested on four principles. First, it produced scholar-gentlemen, an idea taken from the Renaissance. Second, from the Reformation, many believed education fostered "moral, ethical and religious development." Third, education, used to produce civic leaders, received sponsorship from the state and had been introduced through the American Enlightenment. Finally, the scientific revolution brought the idea of "using education to master the physical world for man's progress therein."[43] John Bell Hood would graduate as a scholar-gentleman, and become a civic leader who held high moral and ethical standards and utilized his education to advance the world around him, in a military manner. The knowledge attained from a higher education would not only teach Hood how to serve as a model officer but also as a model man in society.

When Hood arrived at the gates of West Point, he attempted to understand the military culture of the 1850s. The West Point curriculum, rooted in the ideals of duty, honor, and country, closely corresponded with southern ideals of honor and manhood. A young southern man, who had spent his youth working to preserve his family honor, would now arrive at West Point with the chance to expand that notion of honor to include his fellow cadets and his country. In order for honor to be maintained, the cadet had to prove his self-worth through his duty to the academy's curriculum and to duty to protect their country. To chart their progress, cadets could view their grades every Saturday, which adhered to a 3.0 scale adapted by Sylvanus Thayer in 1817. A 3.0 conveyed a perfect recitation. Passing, a grade of 2.0, marked the borderline, with unacceptable performance falling below a 2.0. Furthermore, when students arrived at the academy, they were divided into groups and attended classes based on their skills and abilities, as judged by their instructors. The ranking system allowed the superintendent to remove any emotional attachment to a cadet when it came to a critical decision about their future outside the academy. Upon graduation, cadets who ranked high in their class received engineer appointments, while lower-ranked cadets went to assigned positions in the infantry.[44]

Thayer based the West Point curriculum on the French language, owing to many texts being available only in this language, as well as mathematics, the fundamental basis for engineering. Cadets studied algebra, trigonometry, geometry, and French in their first year. As sophomores (third-class cadets), the same courses would be studied, adding drawing and analytical geometry.

In the third year (second-class cadets), students undertook courses in physics, chemistry, and topographical drawing, with physics now rising to prominence, just as mathematics had in the first two years. In the final year, cadets engaged in engineering, mineralogy, and ethics, the latter defined as a course in "rhetoric and moral and political science." Although the courses shuffled around over time, essentially each West Point cadet could expect a curriculum rich in mathematics, science, foreign language, and courses geared toward producing engineers.[45]

Yet, the cadet could not only rest on his performance inside the classroom. Each January and June, the cadets participated in a rigorous exam session. Prior to the examination, the instructor would place all the covered topics of the semester on slips of paper and throw them into a hat. Once the slips had been mixed up, the instructor would draw a slip of paper and write down an exam topic for each name on the class roster. However, the students were not privy to their selected topic unless they broke the honor codes and either bribed the instructor or broke into his office or home to take a peek at the list. The arbitrary choice of topic could make or break a student, as the exams had to be passed to remain in good standing. James Whistler, the prominent American artist, entered West Point in 1851. Completely stumped during his chemistry examination, he stated to his instructor, "I am required to discuss the subject of Silicon. Silicon is a gas." His instructor replied, "That will do, Mr. Whistler," and promptly failed the budding artist, resulting in his dismissal from the academy. Whistler later reflected, "Had silicon been a gas, I would have been a major general."[46]

Outside the classroom and the examination process, cadets embarked in a summer encampment in order for officers to train cadets on the art and science of soldiering. Cadets rose thirty minutes earlier, waking at 5 a.m., but went to sleep at the same time, 9:30 p.m. The first-class cadets usually did the instructing, which could range from using artillery pieces to constructing bridges. Yet, a majority of the time for beginning cadets was spent learning infantry tactics and marching. Still, standards of behavior and dress were rigorously maintained. One cadet remarked during a day of drill, "I have changed my pants four times in one day and had my boots blackened as many times. If you step out of your tent with your coat not buttoned with *every* button and hooked in the neck, and with *clean* white gloves you are reported." With the cadets routinely firing artillery pieces, the process of keeping clean white gloves to avoid demerits proved challenging, at the very least.[47]

Hood witnessed a few structural changes to the academy between 1849 and 1853. He observed the construction of the Central Barracks in 1850 and

1851. A new mess hall appeared in 1852 and the academy tore down the South Barracks to make room for the new campus construction. A telegraph office appeared at West Point, with a line running from the academy back to New York City. On September 1, 1852, Robert E. Lee received an appointment as superintendent of the military academy. Lee replaced Captain Henry Brewerton, who had served since 1845. As superintendent, Lee continued to maintain a high level of discipline. Lee refused to allow cadet Henry DuBois to leave for home to attend a wedding, explaining that if he granted a leave to DuBois, he would have to do so for everyone, and that would cause a set of "serious interruptions that would take place to their studies and duties. The whole time of the Cadets is necessary to master their Course at the Academy, and any withdrawal of their attention affects them injuriously." As superintendent, Lee also served to witness an expanded curriculum, more books in the library, and new facilities, as well as telescopes available for research. Furthermore, a new course was added to the curriculum in 1853: dancing.[48]

Despite new barrack construction, many parts of the daily routine did not change. When John Bell Hood wanted to bathe, he had to either use the primitive facility near the cemetery (not in the barracks) or, in warmer weather, walk to the river. Latrines, to the south of the barracks, provided toilet facilities before indoor plumbing arrived in the barracks in 1904. When Hood arrived, he received a furnished room complete with "iron bedstead with mattress and blanket, a table, straight-backed chair, lamp, broom with dust pan and scrub brush, tin pail, pitcher, mirror and washstand."[49] Yet, the room had to be placed in a precise pattern to avoid the accumulation of demerits. The order for proper room upkeep read as follows:

> Bedstead—against door; Trunks—under iron bedsteads; Lamps—clean on mantel; Dress Caps—Neatly arranged behind door; Looking Glass—between washstand and door; Books—neatly arranged on shelf farthest from door; Broom—Hanging behind door; Drawing books—under shelf farthest from door; Muskets—in gun rack and locks sprung; Bayonets in scabbards; Accoutrements—Hanging over musket; Sabers, Cutlasses and swords—hanging over muskets; Candle Box (for scrubbing utensils) —Against wall under shelf nearest door and fire place; clothes—neatly hung on pegs over bedsteads; Mattress and Blankets neatly folded; Orderly Board—over mantel; chairs—when not in use under tables.

The order from the commandant concluded, "Orderlies of rooms are held responsible for the observance of the above mentioned arrangement."[50] Thus, with the strict orders for the maintenance of a room, it is no wonder that several cadets, including Hood, earned numerous demerits for problems in their room upkeep.

The food Hood ate at West Point received a review from a congressional delegation, which commented, the food "was neither nutritious, nor wholesome, neither sufficient nor nicely dressed." Breakfast usually included " 'the remains of the meat of the former day's dinner, cut up with potato with considerable gravy,' bread, butter and coffee." For the midday meal, Hood usually dined on "roast beef, veal or mutton, boiled potatoes, and bread." The final meal of the day, known as tea, consisted of "bread, butter, and tea or coffee, supplemented occasionally by cornbread and molasses." Though the menu tended to change daily, Hood never saw any desserts, except a pudding made with stale bread to save money, or vegetables other than potatoes. One cadet found a nest of three mice in his pudding, which got the menu changed to turkey and goose for a month. Another discovered a comb in his pudding. Cadets usually remarked on finding insects in the sugar or cockroaches in the soup, as well as "sour molasses" and "rancid butter." They routinely complained of the boring food. Furthermore, cadets had little time to eat and when they did, the food sometimes had an odd taste. Cadet Tully McCrea wrote, "They have caused an improvement in our mess hall fare until it now presents a respectable appearance. If the cleanliness only equaled the quality, I would be satisfied. But I see no change in that respect. Last night my coffee tasted so plainly of soapsuds, that had not been wrenched from my cup, that I could not drink it."[51]

As a new cadet, known as a plebe, Hood found himself subjected to the hazing of older comrades. West Point cadets adhered to a system where younger cadets always bowed to the upperclassmen. When one cadet entered his final year, he said, "We acquire that air of importance, that show of dignity and condescension to our inferiors which forms the great characteristic of First Class Men." Yet, the first-class status allowed upperclassmen to play pranks on their lower-class brethren. Such acts of trickery included "cutting the plebe's tent ropes, stealing his clothes and grabbing a sleeping plebe by the ankles and pulling him off his bed." In fact, John Schofield, a member of Hood's class, particularly enjoyed stealing clothes, which forced a cadet to miss roll call and receive demerits or show up wrapped in a blanket. One historian has described the pranks, which Hood surely engaged in as an upperclassman, as "feats of manhood."[52]

At first glance, pranks may seem to undermine the very foundation of manhood at West Point that was rooted in both duty and honor. However, although not the most honorable route, the shared experience of both being the victim and benefactor of a prank furthered the bonds of brotherhood between cadets. Particularly, the moments for bonding came outside pranks in the moments of free time that fostered a shared experience. Cadets, like Hood, routinely played sports, hiked, read, or participated in the Dialectic Society, an organized debate society that met on Saturdays to argue a topic of the day. Furthermore, professors and instructors belonged to the Napoleon Club, which met and invited cadets to hear grand lectures on military campaigns, complete with maps in the heralded Napoleon Room.[53]

For his time spent at the academy, Hood received $28 a month. Yet, he never saw much of the money, as it could only be used to purchase items such as razors, mirrors, clothing, and other necessities. The money usually did not meet the bill needed for monthly upkeep with Spartan standards. He also had to protect his gray uniforms. With heavy shoes and a hat that weighed five pounds, Hood had to maintain proper appearance, despite discomfort. One verse at the academy read, "Your coat is made, you button it, give one spasmodic cough, and do not draw another breath until you take it off!"[54]

What money Hood did save could very well have been spent at the local tavern, Benny Haven's, or even farther to Garrison's Landing on the other side of the river, or even to travel all the way to New York City. Benny Haven's remained in business throughout the antebellum years, especially when many cadets, including Jefferson Davis, Edgar Allen Poe, George Pickett, and John Bell Hood snuck away to taste the spirits as well as the buckwheat flapjacks that made the food served back at the academy fade briefly from memory. No doubt, when Hood attended for a beverage, he sang along to Benny's anthem, set to the tune of the song "Wearin' o' the Green." The lyrics read as follows:

> Come, fill your glasses fellows, and stand up in a row
> To singing sentimentally, we're going for to go;
> In the Army there's sobriety, promotion's very slow,
> So we'll sing our reminiscences of Benny Havens, oh!
> Oh, Benny Havens, oh! Oh, Benny Havens, oh!
> So we'll sing our reminiscences of Benny Havens, oh![55]

Haven had originally worked for a sutler but ended up fired when he was discovered selling rum to a cadet. Haven and his wife set up a tavern in 1824 in Highland Falls. Mrs. Haven cooked, usually buckwheat cakes and roast turkey, while her husband took care of serving the liquor at the tavern, a post he filled for many years and well after the Civil War. In fact, Haven even agreed to hold kegs of rum for some cadets when they went on leave.[56]

However, a trip to Benny Haven's could expose a cadet to the other dreaded horror of the academy: the accumulation of demerits, awarded on a point system for rule infractions. Thayer introduced the demerit system, which ultimately lowered a student's class standing, no matter what grades they had attained in class. Historians have focused on Hood's demerit accumulation to foreshadow his eventual military failures. Such infractions could include "the smell of tobacco smoke in the quarters, swearing, failure to attend church, whistling during study hours and lack of neatness" (see Table 1).[57] Hood's behavior his first year earned him eighteen demerits, ranking him forty-seventh out of 221, in terms of having the least number of demerits. In his second year, Hood accumulated sixty-six demerits, ranking him 109/209. In his third year, Hood accumulated an additional ninety-four demerits, placing him 116/224 among all cadets, with 196 demerits. This total fell just four shy of the number for expulsion in his final year at the military academy, placing him 204/225. Thus, his four years produced 374 demerits, which was average for a West Point graduate in the years before the Civil War.[58]

Yet, what did Hood earn demerits for? According to the academy records, Hood "received numerous demerits for having his room out of order, his bed not properly folded, clothes not folded properly, for being absent or late, or for loitering or visiting." His demerits also emerged from "visiting the Commandants Tent with a cigar in his cap" or from using chewing tobacco. But, within this "average" number of demerits, very few were earned for infractions of military principle. In his four years, Hood did receive a demerit "for being out of uniform, having worn the wrong collar to church," and he received two demerits during "formation drills." In one instance, he got a demerit because the squad he led swung their arms while marching. However, Hood never received any demerits for being late to military instruction, nor "for the cleanliness of his weapons, [or] for his performance at military drill or training," or "the condition of his military equipage."[59] Hood loved military training and always arrived prepared for the daily exercises. Thus, Hood excelled at the classroom that would teach the most tangible lessons in readiness for the Civil War: the lessons in preparing for battle.

Hood's behavior did not equal Robert E. Lee, who graduated from the academy without any demerits. There is no record indicating whether Lee was scrupulous in his behavior or in his effort, which was available through hard work, to erase demerits from his record. Neither did it equal James B. McPherson, who received only a few demerits at the top of Hood's class. Though Hood's behavior and academic records are not as pristine as Lee's, his records are superior to many others, especially those expelled from the academy for poor academic and behavioral performance. At the same time, his records are equal to many others, particularly in the area of military professionalism. Joshua Sill received twenty-three in one day and John Schofield,

TABLE 1
Number of Demerits Awarded for Infractions at West Point

Number of Demerits Issued	Possible Offenses to Acquire Demerits
One Demerit	Rifle or equipment dusty Clothing not properly adjusted Blotted paper or misspelled word Dating paper incorrectly Yawning in ranks Spots on mirror
Two Demerits	Late for a formation Buttoning clothes in ranks Bed in disorder Returning book late to the library Carrying rifle improperly Dusty room Not wearing gloves in ranks when required Asking irrelevant or unnecessary questions
Three Demerits	Absence card not properly posted Borrowing arms or equipment without authority Losing articles Unintentionally going off limits on the reservation Dozing at a lecture or instruction Borrowing or lending clothing for inspection Sentinel failing to make a challenge
Four Demerits	Asking an improper question Rifle or equipment rusty Unmilitary bearing Dropping rifle at ceremony Hands in pockets Unintentional absence from drill
Five Demerits	Failure to keep a dental appointment Concealing articles from the tactical officer Gum chewing on post or in ranks Putting articles other than laundry in a laundry bag Dozing or laughing at divine service Carrying food from the mess hall without authority Not wearing the required insignia Being late at a formation Intentionally going off limits on the reservation Returning from hop five minutes or less late Marcher failing to keep section properly closed up
Seven Demerits	Absence from any duty or ceremony, unintentional Attempting to send a telegram without authority Changing room in barracks without authority Contracting a debt without authority Using profane or improper language

like Hood, also earned 196 in his senior year, including thirty related to military infractions. Philip Sheridan received 189 his final year, with several for "failing to perform adequately in military drill, and not paying attention at military instruction."[60]

Demerit accumulation worked hand in hand with classroom grades in determining a cadet's ranking. Many historians have interpreted Hood's performance at West Point to assert that he did not possess the qualities to command an army. However, Hood actually had a similar ranking to other southern cadets, who, like himself, entered the academy without the benefits of private education in the North. Most northeastern cadets had advanced mathematics training prior to entering West Point, which usually ensured a northerner at the head of every class. For Hood, in his fourth-class year, he finished with a ranking of 52/74 total cadets. He ranked forty-fifth in mathematics, sixty-first in French, and fifty-sixth in English. In his third-class year, Hood placed thirty-fourth in mathematics, fifty-third in French, and fifty-fourth in drawing, leading to a class ranking of 39/63. Hood remained in a similar position in his second-class year, with a ranking of 41/57. He finished forty-first in philosophy, forty-third in chemistry, and thirty-fifth in drawing. In his final year, Hood placed forty-fifth in engineering, fifty-second in ethics, forty-sixth in minerals and geology, forty-second in infantry tactics, and forty-fifth in artillery tactics, in a class that had fifty-five members.[61]

However, despite earning lukewarm marks in his last two years, Robert E. Lee, who served as superintendent during Hood's final year, never wrote home to Hood's parents to inform them of poor academic performance, a customary ritual for the superintendent. Military education, according to one historian, may even hinder performance on the battlefield, with commanders spending time anticipating their adversary and crediting them with "equal skill and knowledge" instead of acting decisively. Many students who excelled at West Point failed to garner distinguished military careers or a prominent role in civilian life following their education. Yet, there are exceptions, with Robert E. Lee and George McClellan graduating at the top of their class, respectively. At the same time, U. S. Grant ranked twenty-one out of thirty-nine, and Philip Sheridan stood thirty-fourth out of fifty-two; average performances that did not hinder successful service during the Civil War. Even James Longstreet, who performed admirably as a corps commander under Lee and had the foresight to see the failure of the Pickett-Pettigrew-Trimble Assault at Gettysburg, ranked near the bottom of his class overall, a dismal fifty-four out of fifty-six (see Table 2).[62] Thus, academic performance at West Point cannot always guarantee how well a graduate would perform on the field of battle, making Hood's educational performance as a precursor to failure a problematic historical notion.[63]

The class of 1853, with fifty-two total cadets, graduated in June. Members of the class included James B. McPherson, ranked first, John Schofield, ranked seventh, John Bowen, ranked twelfth, and R. O. Tyler, ranked twenty-second.

TABLE 2
RANKINGS OF PROMINENT CONFEDERATE CIVIL WAR FIGURES AT WEST POINT

Year of Graduation	Future Civil War Figure (Cadet)	Ranking	Class Size
1826	Albert S. Johnston	8	41
1827	Leonidas Polk	8	38
1828	Jefferson Davis	23	33
1829	Robert E. Lee	2	46
	Joseph E. Johnston	13	46
1830	John Magruder	15	42
1837	Braxton Bragg	5	50
	Jubal Early	18	50
	John Pemberton	27	50
1838	P. G. T. Beauregard	2	45
	William J. Hardee	26	45
1840	Richard Ewell	13	42
1842	Gustavus W. Smith	8	56
	D. H. Hill	28	56
	R. H. Anderson	40	56
	Lafayette McLaws	48	56
	Earl Van Dorn	52	56
	James Longstreet	54	56
1843	Samuel French	14	39
1844	Simon Buckner	11	25
1845	Edmund Kirby Smith	25	41
1846	Thomas J. Jackson	17	59
	George Pickett	59	59
1847	A. P. Hill	15	38
	Henry Heth	38	38
1853	John Bell Hood	44	52
1854	J. E. B. Stuart	13	46
	Stephen D. Lee	17	46
	William Pender	19	46
1856	Fitzhugh Lee	45	46
1859	Joseph Wheeler	19	22

Philip Sheridan, who was suspended one full year for striking an officer during an altercation, ranked thirty-fourth. Hood graduated with the ranking of forty-fourth in his class.[64]

Though Hood did not leave West Point at the top of his class, he departed with a wealth of knowledge on the war experience. His training in drilling, artillery, and cavalry taught him all the necessary information to be a professional soldier in the United States Army. Hood graduated West Point with an understanding of practicing the principles of duty, honor, integrity, and protecting your country in order to exhibit manly characteristics. His fellow cadets also provided several opportunities for Hood to take part in a shared honorable experience through the formation of strong bonds of brotherhood. The bonds, rooted in a shared experience, underwent construction immediately as Hood stepped onto the grounds of the military academy. Each cadet had to undertake the same admissions experience. All suffered through the same inclement weather, the same unappetizing meals, the same strict rigors of discipline, and the same fears of classroom participation and examination. Each cadet bore hazing at the hands of their upper-class comrades as well as the military rigors experienced in the summer encampment. A West Point education, though free, did not come without costs. Thus, to survive, Hood had to turn to his fellow cadets and bond over a shared experience. The bonds of brotherhood, fashioned in the halls of West Point, shifted when Hood graduated and traveled to the frontier. Furthermore, the bonds would remain when cadets took up arms against one another when the nation plunged into a bloody and horrific Civil War.

The antebellum culture of Kentucky provided an environment of extreme contradictions and fluctuating definitions. Slavery remained a vital institution for economic wealth as well as an outlet for proving elite status and maintaining honor and mastery. At the same time, the abolitionist spirit tore at the state and threatened to completely undermine how men thought of themselves as men. Citizens began to abhor the violence taking place in their communities and questioned the appropriateness of dueling. Though southern men received encouragement to partake of alcohol, a temperance movement swelled within the state to cease alcohol consumption. Hood's upbringing did not signify a world of recklessness and carelessness that would eventually lead to military defeat. He simply followed a preset protocol of behavior to prove himself a man among his peers in southern society and to fulfill his own ambitious agenda to become a successful officer in the United States Army. By selecting a military career over one rooted in medicine, Hood could assert his masculinity and pay homage to a military lineage rooted in the Revolution. The experience would also prepare Hood to deal with the tests that the Civil War would bring, both in the military arena and in his own personal perceptions of manhood. Yet, for John Bell Hood, West Point would constitute only the beginning of a long journey of proving himself honorable and masterful in the eyes of both his father and southern society.

Chapter 2

A Gallant Affair on the Frontier

Those early days in California brought out character.
—Ulysses S. Grant

Thus, while most of the Confederacy's ranking generals received their initiation to battle in the Mexican War, Hood had won his spurs against the Apaches and Comanches on the Texas Frontier.
—Historian Harold B. Simpson

As John Bell Hood prepared to graduate from West Point, his relative Richard French again exerted his political influence in a letter to United States Army Adjutant General Samuel Cooper. French said, "A nephew of mine, John Hood, is about to graduate at West Point, and writes me he wishes to be attached to the Dragoon . . . and if that cannot be done, to the [Mounted] Riflemen.—If consistently with the law, it can be done, I shall esteem it a particular favor." Despite the letter from French, Hood graduated without receiving an appointment to either of the requested locations. Instead, Hood found himself appointed as a brevet second lieutenant with the Fourth Infantry Regiment. Hood accepted the appointment, writing, "I received your letter enclosing me a certificate of appointment to the position of Bv't [Brevet] 2nd Lieut. U.S. Army, my age is twenty-two years, residence Mount Sterling Kentucky, appointed a cadet July 1st 1849 and born in the State of Kentucky and hereby accept the appointment of the President, and have the oath prescribed by law and enclose you the Certificate."[1]

The completion of his education at West Point afforded John Bell Hood the opportunity to begin his career as a professional member of the military. Once a soldier finished at West Point, they usually ended up serving somewhere on the American frontier. The American government utilized the military to fortify the Pacific Coast as well as supervise the miles and miles of frontier that had been acquired from the Louisiana Purchase, the Mexican War, and the Gadsden Purchase. With only 16,000 soldiers in the standing army, the task of securing the frontier emerged as extremely difficult. Furthermore, the frontier afforded soldiers the chance to assert their manhood through participating in the characteristics of a military culture, which included "self-sacrifice, duty and honor, toughness and stoicism, courage and a love of adventure." Thus, Hood, who had strengthened his understanding of duty and honor at West Point, would now have to look within himself to find the strength and courage to deal with the daily trials of an unknown world.[2]

With his education and training complete, Hood prepared to test the merits of military professionalism while serving on the fringes of the American frontier. Yet, to make his military appointment official, Hood needed to take an official oath before Judge George Gist on July 18, 1853. By repeating the oath, Hood declared, "I will bear true allegiance to the United States of America, and . . . I will serve them honestly and faithfully against all their enemies or opposers whatsoever; and observe and obey the orders of the President of the United States, and the orders of the Officers appointed over me." Hood traveled onboard a ship from New York City, where he had been stationed for a few weeks on the coastal defenses at Fort Columbus, to Panama. Hood then embarked upon a ship headed for San Francisco. When he arrived in California, Hood wanted to take a carriage to Benica Barracks. However, the carriage ride would cost an outrageous $20 in gold. As Hood later remembered, "This aspect of affairs—our pay being only about $60 a month—compelled us to hold consultation with our brother officers and to adopt the only alternative: to proceed on foot." Hood reported for duty at Fort Jones in northern California, where he reported to Colonel Buchannan, his commander.[3]

The fort, encompassing more than 640 acres, contained two officers' quarters, an officers' as well as a company kitchen, and a guardhouse. Furthermore, the fort also had a hospital, granary, and stable as well as a commissary, quartermaster store, and supply office. In the few years Hood spent at Fort Jones, several buildings would be added, including an orderly room, more officer quarters, a mess room, permanent housing for the soldiers, and a home for the assistant surgeon. The space in California was large enough to hold thirty-four soldiers. Joseph K. F. Mansfield, a visitor to the fort, described it by saying, "Of course, [the buildings are] quite indifferent, but such as other people enjoy and sufficient for the present." Another described the fort as holding buildings like "rough log pens, cover over, with places for a door and window but left without these luxuries as well as without floors."[4]

Despite its location on the frontier of California, Fort Jones remained well stocked. J. C. Bonnycastle, a first lieutenant at the garrison, reported, "The supply of clothing on hand is ample, and the arms on hand are sufficient in number for the present strength of the Company." George Crook, a second lieutenant with whom Hood formed a strong friendship, noted that the fort contained three horses and fourteen mules. He said, "The horses are employed in pursuit of deserters and riding on Quarter Master duties, and the mules are employed in hauling wood, and water for the Post and for the transportation of provision, ammunition and for troops when on Indian expeditions." The commissary, where Hood dined as an officer, contained a wealth of the plain solid fare of the military, including pork, ham, bacon, flour, meal, bread, beans, rice, coffee, sugar, vinegar, pickles, and apples. Yet, despite the cornucopia of edible delights, the food had to be cooked over open fires, owing to the post kitchens not containing a single stove. With the chimneys deteriorating, the cooking process brought forth a series of complaints from the officers stationed at the fort. Thus, Captain D. A. Rupell ordered two stoves, one for the officers and one for the company kitchen. According to post records, the stoves never arrived during Hood's stay.[5]

Yet, the lack of stoves only proved an annoyance, and griping became simply a source of distraction from the twin threats present at Fort Jones: Indian attacks and disease. Surrounding Fort Jones, the Modoc, Pitt River, and Cloud River Indians lived, who one officer described as "murderous and warlike." Yet, the Shasta tribe, also in the region, had remained peaceful mostly because the civilians had extended "kind treatment, trifling and well timed presents." However, Lieutenant J. C. Bonnycastle recommended moving all of the tribes to a reservation because of the influx of white settlers and their effects on the region's animal populations. He reported, "During the past winter I have known them to suffer from hunger. . . . the game has been so hunted by Whites as to render it wild, so that the Indians are unable to kill much with their arrows and it is difficult for them to procure powder and ball." Bonnycastle even provided some food for the natives who traveled to Fort Jones in peace. Yet, the lieutenant could not guarantee protection, because of those who had "separately advocated an extermination of the Indian race." Thus, Bonnycastle predicted a war in northern California within a year, as the Native Americans would try to purge the landscape of white settlement one final time.[6]

However, despite his predictions, Bonnycastle did not want warfare to break out. He reported a month later that he had close to two hundred members of the Shasta tribe camped at Fort Jones. The officer promised care for the tribe in exchange for a "voluntary promise from all of the bands, to refrain from stealing or in anyway molesting the whites." Bonnycastle believed the tribe would remain at peace as long as "some white man [does not] make a wanton attack upon them." In fact, the officer even proposed the idea of removing the Shasta tribe from northern to southern California. However, he discovered that they were "not generally willing to leave this part of the country."[7] Hood's few years at Fort Jones thus remained a peaceful endeavor, with some white officers extending their hand of protection and support to the peaceful natives, whose way of life had been shattered by the increasing encroachment of white settlers.

Even though the physical threat of Indian violence had been minimized, the same could not be said of the biological threats of disease. One officer remarked, "The general health of the command is, at present, good, but many of the soldiers are very liable to returns of chill and fever contracted during last summer." Several of the soldiers felt under the weather, with many having chills and fever in 1853 and the spring of 1854, many cases of which were not recorded on the sick reports.[8]

To stay distracted from Indian conflict and the threat of disease, Hood spent the hot summer days hunting animals, cultivating wheat, and selling the surplus goods for profit, eventually earning $1,000 in gold. Hood needed the money, because the California gold rush that continued to spill over from 1848 and 1849 had inflated prices throughout California. Ulysses S. Grant, who had been serving as quartermaster in California and in Oregon Territory, noted the problems that the Pacific Coast posed for soldiers serving in the military prior to Hood's arrival. He wrote, "Prices of all kinds of supplies were so high on the Pacific Coast from 1849 until at least 1853—that it would have been impossible for officers of the army to exist upon their pay." Grant noted that at Benicia, "flour was twenty five cents per pound; potatoes were sixteen cents; beets, turnips and cabbage, six cents; onions, thirty seven and a half cents." Grant, who moved to Fort Vancouver in Oregon Territory, raised a crop of potatoes to help offset the costs of food that arose because of the gold rush in the San Francisco area.[9]

Hood's days in California ended because of actions undertaken in Washington, D.C. After a brief respite away from the army, Albert Sydney Johnston accepted command of the newly formed Second Cavalry, authorized by Congress on March 4, 1855. Until the appearance of the First Dragoons in 1833, cavalry had only been raised to meet immediate threats and then quickly disbanded. However, with the resistance of the Seminole Indians to removal in Florida, the Second Dragoons emerged from an act of Congress on May 23, 1836. The Second Dragoons fought the Seminoles, patrolled the fringes of Georgia, and eventually served with distinction in the Mexican War by traveling with General Winfield Scott to Mexico City. Following the engagement in Mexico, the dragoons again served on the frontier, engaging Native Americans throughout present-day Texas, New Mexico, and California. President Franklin Pierce believed in expanding the military for protection of the frontier. He stated, "I find in existing circumstances a necessity for an increase in our military force, and it is believed that four new regiments—two of infantry and two of mounted men—will be sufficient to meet the present exigency. If it were necessary to weigh the cost in a case of such urgency it would be shown that the additional expense would be comparatively light."[10]

Pierce had simply echoed the recommendation of others before him. Winfield Scott, serving as general in chief, called for the army to be "increased by the addition of at least two regiments of dragoons and two regiments of infantry." Volney Howard, a congressman from Texas, told his fellow representatives that he feared the increasing Native American presence on the Texas frontier. He called the Indians "well mounted and the most expert riders in the world." He declared, "You can neither fight nor pursue them with infantry or artillery. Out of reach of the guns of the fort and these corps might as well be a thousand miles distant. They never can come up with the enemy." With the wave of settlers expanding beyond the first line of forts established in the 1840s, the 2,886 soldiers who protected the Department of Texas, almost two thousand miles long, simply could not protect the continuing encroachment. Under this pressure, the army built more forts in 1851–52. Logically enough, it now needed more men to arm those strategic positions.[11]

Jefferson Davis, the secretary of war in 1855, encouraged the development of the First and Second Cavalry by a congressional order on March 3, 1855. Davis, who had served in the First Dragoons, created the cavalry to meet the increasing threat from Native Americans following the Mexican War. The soldiers would be hand selected to serve among "Jeff Davis' Own." Albert Sydney Johnston and Davis had developed a deep friendship since West Point, and when it was offered, Johnston took command of the Second to "defend the far-flung Texas frontier from the depredations of the Comanches." Many high-ranking officers transferred from the Second Dragoons to help fill the regiments. With a limited number of soldiers, Johnston thought it prudent to track down and pursue groups of Kiowas and Comanches instead of placing his soldiers where he thought the Native Americans might strike. Each company obtained horses from a procurement team operating throughout Ohio,

Indiana, and Kentucky, providing enough of the "best-blooded stock" so that each company could ride matched horses of a particular color. Company A rode grays, while Company K had roans. Companies G and H rode on browns, Companies B and E received sorrels, and Companies C, D, F, and I all mounted bays.[12]

The Second Cavalry emerged as a who's who for future officers of the armies that would later grapple in the Civil War. The officers who served grew to know one another and develop firm and lasting friendships that would strengthen during the oncoming Civil War. Among the officers serving under Johnston were Lieutenant Colonel Robert E. Lee and Captain Edmund Kirby Smith. Each of these officers eventually became full generals for the Confederacy. Major William Hardee attained a lieutenant general position while Earl Van Dorn, Fitzhugh Lee, and Charles Field rose to the rank of major general. Others among the cavalry won a brigadier's star, and Major George Thomas and George Stoneman eventually served in commanding positions for the Union army.[13]

However, to get into the Second Cavalry, a member of the military, like Hood, would have to undergo the rigors of a highly political position. To get appointed, Hood used his faint political channels through the influence of his friend from Kentucky, John Breckinridge. When Hood wrote to Breckinridge on May 12, 1855, he stated, "I presume you remember my having asked of you the Session of Congress before this last to use your influence towards my getting transferred to one of the Cavalry Regiments, in case an increase of the army should be brought about." Hood let Breckinridge know that he had submitted an application but had also heard of someone declining an appointment. Hood wanted Breckinridge to use his "influence so [as] soon as you get this" to make the transfer happen. Yet, Hood needed the actions to take place quickly, for he feared that by July 1, a new class from West Point would come into the army and take away any available position. He concluded, "I will beg of you to aid me so soon as you can with convenience. I will forward this by express hoping it will reach you very soon."[14]

Hood even took it upon himself to write directly to Jefferson Davis, and also asked that the president of the United States, Franklin Pierce, receive his application, apparently after failing to get his friend John Breckinridge to act on his behalf. Hood did pause to apologize for violating "the usual rule laid down in the Regulations of such applications," but he personally feared that "delay in other departments" would deter the application from ever arriving. The letter to Davis of April 1855 apparently paid off, with Hood receiving appointment in August. When Hood departed for Jefferson Barracks, Missouri, the selected rendezvous point of the Second Cavalry, Lieutenant Philip Sheridan replaced him at Fort Jones in California. While in San Francisco, Hood met a young, red-haired banker at Lucas, Turner and Company by the name of William T. Sherman. Hood described Sherman at the meeting as having a "piercing eye and nervous impulsive temperament."[15]

Recruiting officers for the Second Cavalry traveled throughout the nation and received orders to reconvene in September south of St. Louis. The cavalry spent a brief time in Missouri, where the soldiers trained and received appointment to their respective companies. Hood, appointed to Company G, received his brown thoroughbred horse. The Second Cavalry was ordered to Texas on September 27. Then, on October 27, 1855, owing to the lack of direct railroad tracks to Texas, the cavalry, with 750 men and eight hundred horses, as well as five ambulances and twenty-nine wagons, headed overland toward Fort Belknap in Texas.[16]

The members of the Second Cavalry received a specific uniform for their new duties. It consisted of "gray trousers, a short blue tunic with yellow trim, brass shoulder scales and a black slouch hat with the brim pinned up on the right side with an eagle (Austrian style), and with black ostrich plumes on the left side slanted back from the crown." Edmund Kirby Smith further described the uniform, stating that "cavalry boots worn over the pants, knife and revolver belted to the side and a double barrel gun across the pommel, complete the costume as truly serviceable as it is unmilitary." The soldiers of the Second Cavalry carried either a Springfield rifle carbine, a removable stock carbine, or a breech-loading Perry carbine. Every soldier got a Colt navy revolver and a dragoon saber. All of the items would be carried on the soldier or attached to their Crimsley or Campbell saddles.[17]

The journey to Texas had its share of eventful circumstances. One soldier had been caught stealing a watch from a civilian, which resulted in his traveling in chains. Another soldier reached such a point of intoxication that he fell from his horse, consequently died, and was buried along the side of the road where he fell. On December 12, the Second Cavalry briefly stopped at Fort Washita, in the Indian territory, where they received greetings from Captain Braxton Bragg. As the cavalry crossed into Texas, the winter weather stormed across the frontier, "freezing several horses to death." Yet, the cavalry troops endured the freezing temperatures and eventually arrived at Fort Belknap. Albert Sydney Johnston ordered Companies B, C, D, G, H, and I to Fort Mason, northwest of present-day Austin. Johnston traveled with the six companies on January 2, 1856, across the frozen rivers, and arrived at Fort Mason on January 14. Companies A, E, and K remained behind at Fort Belknap.[18]

The Second Cavalry's creation took place as a reaction to the increased Native American presence on the Texas frontier. With an exponential increase in settlers, from Stephen F. Austin's arrival in 1821 to the declaration of Texas independence on March 2, 1836, white settlement produced a shattering wave of individuals who brought alcohol, disease, slavery, and the fur trade. As tribes underwent displacement, removal, and repositioning across the western landscape, the Comanche, the chief group to declare the Texas frontier their new home, mainly followed the migratory patterns of the buffalo, an essential element for their subsistence. However, the migratory patterns of the buffalo sometimes intersected the new encroachment patterns of white settlers. The Comanche attacked and raided those settlements for several reasons. First, white settlement disrupted the Comanche hunting patterns and forced some to take lengthy detours to either hunt buffalo or travel into Mexico for trade. Second, more and more settlers competed with the Comanche for limited resources, especially with governmental measures that encouraged land speculation and the pursuit of precious metals, particularly gold. Once the Comanche utilized force against a group of settlers, the United States Army increased its presence on the Texas frontier and therefore spurred the rise of military outposts.[19]

The main outpost for the Texas frontier rested in Fort Mason. On May 15, 1851, as part of an elaborate defense system following the Mexican War, the fort underwent construction because of settlers continuing to move westward. Fort Mason helped extend an original line established in the late 1840s that had been manned by Texas Rangers. With the arrival of Federal cavalry, the need for the rangers dissipated. The new "middle line forts" would provide the necessary protection against a large territory that held Comanche, Kiowa, and Lipan-Apache Indians. Yet, Fort Mason had been inactive for almost all of 1854 and part of 1855, allowing many local civilians to strip it of any useful resources, which meant that the first task of the Second Cavalry would be to rebuild the dilapidated fort. The arrival of the six companies allowed the fort to again act as an important defensive location along the Texas frontier. Moreover, Fort Mason served as a central location for command, with Albert Sydney Johnston, George Thomas, Earl Van Dorn, Robert E. Lee, and Richard Johnson all using the fort as a command position.[20]

The Second Cavalry saw Fort Mason as a suitable headquarters because of its prominent location. The wife of Albert Sydney Johnston, Eliza, expressed

"... the view from the fort is one of the grandest and most extensive that I have ever seen." The fort, constructed on Post Hill, offered a fine view of the two main water sources in the area: the Llano River, nine miles to the south, and the San Sabo, twenty-three miles to the north. Furthermore, several streams, including Comanche Creek and Mason Creek, provided ample drinking water for the soldiers stationed in the region. One inspector to the fort reported it as "elevated and salubrious and located within 400 yards of an unfailing supply of pure spring water." Plus, Post Hill sat in a region rich in natural resources, including "limestone, sandstone, cedar and oak," all utilized to construct the necessary buildings for the fort.[21]

Colonel J. F. K. Mansfield, the inspector general of the army, visited Fort Mason in July 1856 to inspect the facility. Mansfield seemed pleased with the available medical care attainable at the fort, writing, "Dr. Swain appeared to be well qualified for the occasion and the sick cared for. The post is healthy." With a spring bubbling forth an adequate water supply, Mansfield approved the natural resources, including "abundant wood and grazing for the animals and the transportation of supply not heavy." The soldiers had to rely on local wild animals, like deer and turkey, in addition to beef provided by the local farmers. Yet, for the most part, the soldiers in Texas ate "bacon, ham, spiced meats" as well as "beans, potatoes, rice, dried fruits, vegetables from the post garden" and "wild grapes or plums, coffee, bread and sweets made at the post bakery."[22] Hence, the fort had adequate supplies to continue operation on the Texas frontier.

During its early existence, Fort Mason had been relatively quiet in terms of Native American conflict. As time progressed, however, conflict spiraled in the mid-1850s until the arrival of the Second Cavalry. As Robert S. Neighbors remarked, "Our frontier has, for the last three months, enjoyed a quiet never heretofore known. This state of things is mainly attributable to the energetic action of the Second Cavalry, under the commander of Colonel A. S. Johnston."[23]

Because Johnston's command was so important in protecting the Texas frontier, he appointed Robert E. Lee commander at nearby Camp Cooper on March 27, 1856. Johnston needed Lee to help the camp recover from a horrific ordeal the proceeding winter. Supplies had been delayed by the "winter weather of unprecedented severity, accompanied by heavy snow and ice in the streams." The weather caused the animals to succumb to the elements "in numbers," and the men were "frequently prevented from moving at all for days together, by drifts of snow, and frozen rivers." A few days before Lee arrived, one soldier noted, "The Cavalry here are in a poor condition to do anything." Lee realized that the location of Camp Cooper needed to be changed and decided to ride around the frontier searching for a new location.[24]

When Lee would go for a ride on the frontier to look for new defense locales, he would usually take someone with him, which afforded Hood the opportunity on several occasions to reconnect with his old superintendent from West Point. While stationed in Texas, Lee taught Hood how to conduct himself as a "model gentlemen." As the two officers rode across the Texas frontier, Lee decided to offer Hood a bit of advice on women, after undergoing the impression that Hood might "form an attachment for some of the country lasses." Lee said, "Never marry unless you can do so into a family which will enable your children to feel proud of both sides of the house." Hood valued the moment where Lee could offer "fatherly advice." Although Lee had not been officially stationed in Texas from 1857 to 1860, he stopped on several occasions in the region to visit and attend court-martial hearings. Furthermore, Lee also had been stationed at Fort Mason in December 1860, following the official secession declaration of South Carolina.[25]

For the most part, Hood remained in Texas for the years leading up to the Civil War, with the exception of an extended furlough to visit his ill father in Mount Sterling, Kentucky. He departed Fort Mason on March 17, 1856, and later asked for the furlough to be extended an additional sixty days. He wrote to Jefferson Davis, stating, "My father's health is still very distressing and in the same state of mind I represented him to be in my first application. His business is in the greatest confusion and I am the only child he will allow to attend to it for him." Jefferson Davis approved the extension on July 17, 1856. Any tension between Hood and his father over discarding a career in medicine for the military had eroded, with Hood utilizing his furlough to spend quality time with his father. The extension allowed Hood to sell his ailing father's property. At the same time, Hood assisted with determining a proper course of action for the Hood family following the death of Dr. Hood. Hood returned to Fort Mason in December 1856. Unfortunately, he would never see his father again. He died on November 30, 1857.[26]

With Hood back at Fort Mason throughout 1857, his company, along with Company B, remained at the fort, while Johnston scattered the rest of the companies across the Texas frontier. Yet, the fort constantly had to deal with a lack of cavalry horses. Each company had been short on horses and continually requested more animals from the military or tried to obtain them on personal expeditions. Several of the horses succumbed to eating "too many oak acorns and dry oak leaves." With increasing levels of Native American conflict throughout the region, Hood, who had recently received a fresh supply of horses, decided on July 5, 1857, to lead a scouting expedition of twenty-five men in search of Comanche Indians. Hood and his men received thirty days of rations and loaded their saddlebags with their mess kits and a pile of bacon, coffee, and hardtack. To find their way, John McLoughlin, a prominent Delaware scout and guide, accompanied the expedition. Hood remembered, "I was young and buoyant in spirit; my men were well mounted and all eager for a chases as well as a fray."[27]

Following the North Llano to the west from the fort, the scouting party traveled between the Concho River and Mexico. Yet the journey proved taxing "upon the dry plains without water or the sight of game." On July 19, the soldiers did spot a deer, which "the sight went forth a shout of joy from the men, who then felt confident that fresh water was not very far distant." When the soldiers stumbled upon a few watering holes, the water appeared "scum-covered" and the soldiers dealt with the pungent odor emanating from their only source by holding their "breath while he partook of the distasteful but refreshing draught." Hood observed many horses showing "great fatigue and leg-weariness." Yet the soldiers were prepared for any possible military action. When the cavalry expedition stumbled upon an abandoned Indian camp, Hood noted, "They had eaten one of their mules or horses, and this sign, together with others about their bivouac, bore clear evidence that the party had become quite formidable." Fortunately, for the cavalry expedition, "Every man was armed with an army rifle and a six-shooter; a few of us had sabers and two revolvers, whilst I was armed with a double-barrel shotgun loaded with buck shot and two Navy six-shooters," recalled Hood.[28]

With fatigue increasing on the ride, as well as the lack of water, Hood abandoned the original trail and headed toward the Devil River. Before departing, Hood received word that the Tonkaway Indians would raise a white flag at their reservation. When Hood and his party arrived, the flag clearly flapped in the breeze. A group of Comanche approached Hood, displaying a white sheet. Then, they dropped the sheet and charged forward. A group of approximately one hundred Lipan-Apache and Comanche Indians attacked the expedition party along Devil's Run. The natives ignited tall fires in hopes of scaring the cavalry horses. Instead, a great cloud of smoke engulfed the prairie, making it difficult to see the native warriors, who were armed with "tough buffalo hide shields" as well as "iron tipped lances" and "rifles or bows and arrows." The fighting became a brawl, with hand-to-hand combat. During the fight, Hood fired a double-barreled shotgun to stop two warriors trying "to pull him from the saddle" by cutting his bridle reigns. Sergeant Shannon disposed of a warrior chief "by parrying his lance thrust and then cleaving his skull open with a saber stroke." Herman G. Rost, who had survived the Mexican War, barely survived an attack by three Indians, who tried to grab his legs to throw him from his horse. Rost eventually used his revolver to kill one warrior, while another soldier arrived in time to save Rost from being pulled down.[29]

The warriors continued to discharge rifles, with the Native American women crouched behind the lines, loading the rifles and then passing them forward to the men, who would fire toward the cavalry command. Hood charged forward, firing his revolver. Clearly outnumbered, Hood attempted to overwhelm a numerically superior force by taking a stronger defensive position. He later remembered the engagement as "a most desperate struggle" with adversaries "all painted, stripped to the waist, with either horns or wreaths of feathers upon their heads." During the fighting, Hood had "his hand pinned to his bridle with an arrow." In order to remain in command, Hood broke off the arrowhead and "withdrew the shaft from the wound. A handkerchief, wound tightly around his hand, staunched the bleeding." As Hood dealt with his first war injury, a cry rang out among the Native Americans to signal an end to the attack after Hood had pulled his men back fifty yards to dismount and regroup.[30]

Hood lost two members of his party and had five wounded, including three sustaining major injuries. In terms of the horses, one had been killed, with three injured and the rest beaten around the "face, head and neck with the tough buffalo hide shields." The Native Americans, losing nineteen, including two minor chiefs, retreated toward the Rio Grande. A relief expedition of infantry arrived from Camp Hudson the following day to assist the soldiers, as well as bury the dead. The survivors departed for Fort Clark, where they remained a few days to rest and where Hood wrote his official report of the engagement. After being away from Fort Mason for five weeks and riding nearly five hundred miles, Hood and his men returned on August 8, 1858.[31]

Upon return, General Twiggs, the commanding officer at Fort Mason, said, "Lieutenant Hood's affair was a gallant one, and much credit is due to both officer and men." In a letter to Albert Sydney Johnston, Captain Richard Johnston wrote, "It was a gallant affair and reflects credit not only upon him, but also upon the Regiment of which he is a member." Furthermore, Winfield Scott, the commanding general of all United States troops, also remarked on Hood's gallant performance.[32]

The military engagement with the Native Americans presents a moment when Hood utilized his training acquired at West Point. By effectively leading his troops, Hood rallied his men, even after a surprise ambush threatened the welfare of the entire company. Hood utilized Mahan's tactical training when he pulled back to a better defensive position to protect his men from a larger enemy force. Furthermore, despite the ferociousness of the battle, Hood sustained few casualties and inflicted more on his adversaries. Hood's experience in battle not only reinforced his scholastic lessons at West Point, but also created an opportunity to bond with the soldiers he commanded. With victory secured, the soldiers of the Second Cavalry realized that they could trust both Hood and his leadership instincts.

After recuperating from his injuries sustained in battle, Hood took over Company E on December 16, 1857, from Captain George Stoneman. A change in companies meant a change in duty assignment, with Hood first going to Camp Cooper for several months. When Robert E. Lee relinquished command of Camp Cooper in October 1857, the camp consisted of a bake house, a forage, a few stables and storehouses, several kitchens, and quarters, as well as a guardhouse and hospital. Yet, improvements could not be made because of a continual rejection of pleas for more War Department funding. Desertions increased and relations with local Indians declined, while officers tried to find a new location for Camp Cooper. Lee had tried to find a new location, but the main source of contention rested in the scarce water supply. Lee reported that although he had located "many pretty sites and more desirable than [Camp Cooper]," he could not find an adequate spring, owing to the high level of salinity in the river water. With violence increasing on the frontier, the present location of Camp Cooper was simply not desirable. In the few weeks since the departure of Lee, "approximately 600 horses had been taken by the Indians, and 7 people had been killed," as well as $60,000 worth of property taken or destroyed in the region. On August 3, 1858, Hood moved to Camp Colorado, located directly north of Fort Mason, and seized the opportunity to work on completing the necessary structures of a new camp. Yet, Hood and his soldiers had to deal with inclement weather in October, forcing "Hood to use the stable as sleeping quarters for his men." However, the troops completed living quarters by the start of 1859.[33]

The move to Camp Colorado coincided with a renewal of Native American attacks along the Texas frontier. On October 21, 1858, a scouting party discovered, as one soldier noted, "the bodies of Joshua Jackson, Mrs. Jackson, their daughter about sixteen years, and a little boy aged about seven years." The scouting party buried the family and looked for two members still missing. When word came back to Hood at Camp Colorado, the officer immediately sent Sergeant Alby with fifteen soldiers to assist in recovering the missing children. Post records do not indicate that the children were ever recovered.[34]

With the loss of the Jackson family, local officials contacted the secretary of war to argue that the inhabitants of Texas needed immediate protection. Hood played host to a squad of rangers who visited Camp Colorado four times in the two months following the Jackson family's murder. With extra military protection, Hood commenced with his rebuilding project. On February 1, 1859, he earned a promotion from second lieutenant to first lieutenant, and he departed Camp Colorado for Fort Belknap on February 7. However, Hood returned to Camp Colorado twice. First, in June 1859, Hood returned to properly inspect the buildings and issue an official report to the quartermaster general. He returned a second time to take over for Captain Whitting for two months in the fall of 1859.[35]

In November and December 1860, while on leave, Hood received an appointment to serve as chief of cavalry at West Point, a coveted assignment. While Hood had excelled in military exercises at the academy, his efficient handling of the cavalry throughout Texas proved to U.S. Army commanders that Hood would be a great choice to instruct at West Point. Hood initially wanted to decline the order because of rising sectional tension evident throughout the country. Colonel Cooper, serving as adjutant general, said, "Mr. Hood, you surprise me. This is a post and position sought by every soldier." Hood decided to accept the position, which would take him away from Camp Wood, along the Nueces River, where he had been since 1859. However, before leaving for the point, the oncoming war forced Hood to remain loyal to the South. He resigned his commission with the Second Cavalry of the United States. Secretary of War Simon Cameron received the notification and approved it on April 25, sending orders for Hood's resignation to be announced on April 27, 1861. Hood stopped in Indianola, Texas, to offer a farewell to his soldiers, then departed for Kentucky.[36]

When Hood and his fellow officers resigned from the United States Army, many government officials reacted in disgust. Secretary of War Simon Cameron, in the summer of 1861, wrote, "At the national Military Academy they were received and treated as the adopted children of the republic. By the peculiar relations thus established they virtually became bound by more than ordinary obligations of honor to remain faithful to their flag." Cameron expressed that only one in 70,000 received a West Point education, at the expense of the federal government.[37]

In the early spring in 1861, Hood returned to his home state of Kentucky, one that can truly be identified as a border state, in order to meet with Breckinridge, then serving as governor. Many settlers there had come from other regions of the slaveholding South. Some Kentuckians owned slaves, while others detested the rise of abolitionists in the region. At the same time, the state had admired Henry Clay for his devotion to the nation and watched railroad construction link Kentucky to the North. Thus, it comes as no surprise that the state overwhelmingly voted for John Bell, the Constitutional Union candidate in 1860, who advocated keeping the country together. Kentucky remained neutral, ignoring Lincoln's initial call for troops in 1861 after the firing on Fort Sumter. It failed to join with other Confederate states, who sought its alliance. On May 16, the Kentucky House adopted a resolution that stated the people "shall take no part in the civil war now being waged, except as mediators and friends to the belligerent parties; and that Kentucky should, during the contest, occupy the position of strict neutrality." As the state continued to deal with neutrality issues throughout the early war years, Kentucky would eventually send approximately 75,000 soldiers to the Union ranks and about 35,000 to fight for the Confederacy.[38]

But, for the time being, if Hood wanted to join the Confederacy, he would have to leave the Union and, more important, the national army. When it became clear to Hood that Kentucky would not travel the road to secession anytime soon, he departed his home state and traveled to Montgomery, Alabama, the current capital of the Confederacy, and signed up for the Confederate army. He wrote in his memoir about Texas, "So deeply impressed had I become with its vast and undeveloped resources that I had, just prior to the war, determined to resign and make it my home for life. Therefore when Kentucky failed to act, I entered the Confederate service from the State of Texas, which thence forth became my adopted land."[39]

With his West Point education, Hood had earned the knowledge to serve as an efficient officer. His experience on the frontier, exhibited through battle, put the education to the test, and Hood passed with accolades. He had been appointed to watch over the construction of Camp Colorado and Camp Wood and even received an appointment to instruct the cavalry at West Point. Yet, in order to attain the level of military professionalism Hood desired, he departed his home state and adopted Texas as his new home. As he left the United States, Hood had been adequately prepared for the Civil War. However, no training could prepare Hood, as well as his fellow officers, for the horrors of a bloody and destructive war that loomed on the horizon.

Chapter 3

A "Soldier Indeed": Hood and the
Army of Northern Virginia

R. M. Gray, a soldier who fought for the Confederacy during the Civil War, offered an early impression of both the physical and personality features of John Bell Hood. He stated, "Lieut. Gen. John B. Hood was one of the noblest looking men I ever met. In response his features were more massive and quiet than was precisely the thing for admiration. But when lit up by the emergency of battle they became wonderfully impressive." Gray described Hood as "a large and firmly formed man," who had a "fresh complexion" and appeared to have German ancestry, from his "light hair and blue eyes." When John Bell Hood spoke, the "tone of his voice was kindness." He also acted "void of show or parade." Furthermore, Gray witnessed how Hood interacted with his fellow soldiers. He stated, "He possessed that faculty of binding men to him by ties stronger than mere sense of duty, which is so necessary for a great leader to have."[1]

Early in his career, John Bell Hood realized one of the most important criteria for success in military command: the bonds between soldier and commander. Time and time again, Hood asked his soldiers to participate in difficult military tasks, ranging from brutal offensive charges to holding a critical defensive position during the climax of battle. In turn, the bond between soldier and commander was reciprocal, as the soldier had to both trust and respect his leader. His men had heard tales of Hood's gallantry on the frontier, displayed through the capacity to achieve victory against a formidable opponent. However, Hood could not stand alone on his reputation in the days preceding war. He needed to make sure his men trusted him to the point where they would follow him anywhere in battle. A strong bond with his men would not only bring about more military victories, it would also increase Hood's reputation in the army and foster his ambition to move up the ranks. By having a strong reputation, Hood also could secure his own sense of manhood by achieving an honorable military career, grounded in victories and secured in a noble reputation. His service with the Texas brigade would begin his journey through the Civil War at attempting to achieve a noble reputation among the ranks of both the Confederate army and the Confederate populace. While the Texas Brigade needed a strong commander like Hood, Hood, in turn, needed the Texas Brigade to secure his manhood through military service. As Val Giles, a member of the Fourth Texas stated, "The Texas Brigade made Hood."[2]

Hood's journey with the Texas Brigade began shortly after Kentucky failed to secede in early 1861. After signing up for the Confederate army, Hood traveled next from Montgomery, Alabama, to Richmond, Virginia, where he reported to Robert E. Lee on May 5. Lee remarked, "I am glad to see you. I want you to help me." Instead of leaving him in Richmond at the Ballard House, a local hotel, Lee stated, "I wish you to go to Yorktown and report to Colonel Magruder." Hood departed immediately and arrived at Yorktown, Virginia, in time to spend the evening "gazing intently every few minutes in the direction of Fortress Monroe." On May 31, Hood received orders to be placed "in charge of all the cavalry on the York River for the purpose of establishing a camp of instruction and of making judicious disposition of the pickets and videttes." Hood had to not only drill the cavalry but also teach them discipline. Yet, with Hood ranking only as first lieutenant, Magruder ordered his promotion to captain, then major, in order to continue commanding the cavalry. Hood led the cavalry in the swamps of Virginia and harassed Union forces at Fortress Monroe.[3]

On July 12, 1861, Hood ordered his cavalrymen to dismount, and they attacked a group of Union soldiers near Newport News. Hood remembered the assault causing "great consternation and the enemy ran in all directions through the woods." As the dismounted Confederate cavalry charged, the Union forces ran, incurring several casualties, including two officers. Hood's group only lost one horse. The skill in routing the Union troops earned Hood early accolades. Captain Thomas Goode said, "For our victory all knowledge a great indebtedness to the gallant bearing and skillful conduct of Maj. Hood, who is every inch an officer and deserved well of his country." Newspapers paused to pay Hood "a high compliment" for his "gallant conduct and cool bearing." Another simply remarked that Major Hood had acted "very manfully."[4] The southern press had begun to solidify Hood's manly reputation in the eyes of Confederate society.

While newspapers remarked on Hood's gallant actions, his fellow military commanders also paused to glance at Hood's military capabilities. John Magruder sent a message to Lee. He called Hood "the efficient commander of the cavalry of my department" and offered that the victory had emerged as "a brilliant little affair." Lee sent his congratulations to Hood on July 15 and also forwarded the details to Jefferson Davis. Hood continued to drill the soldiers and educated them "in the duties of soldiers" until September. Hood's actions had garnered another promotion to lieutenant colonel. He returned to Richmond, where he received orders to organize the Fourth Texas Infantry.[5]

The men who gathered in Austin, Texas, in July 1861 to form the companies that would eventually coalesce into the Fourth Texas regiment underwent a leadership change early in their existence. Hood replaced Colonel R. T. P. Allen of the Fourth Texas in the fall of 1861, mostly because the Texas troops refused to serve under Allen. The soldiers from the Fourth Texas, according to Chaplain Davis, encompassed "representative men from all portions of the State—young, impetuous, and fresh, full of energy, enterprise, and fire—men of action." Prior to the war, the group had been "attorneys, doctors, merchants, farmers, mechanics, editors [and] scholastics." The regiment also included cowboys and at least one Native American. Individuals who spotted the Texas regiment offered a series of praiseworthy observations. One said, "The men are a stalwart set of soldiers and will do fine service when they reach the field of action." A newspaper reporter remarked, "Such men as these will make quick work of the Yankee racers when they get the chance."[6]

Immediately, Hood had to establish himself as a suitable commander who could win over his eclectic group of soldiers, especially after the Texans had stubbornly refused to fight. His physical presence impressed the men. One writer described Hood as a man who stood "six feet two inches in height, broad full chest, without any surplus flesh, light brown hair and beard, blue eyes, with the softest, tendered expression, except when excited, then flashing with lighting." Beyond his physicality, Hood also brought an aura of military professionalism that demanded respect. One man remembered Hood as someone who stood "commanding in appearance, dignified in manner, courteous to officers and men, and yet strict in his ideas of discipline. He was a man of great personal magnetism, capable of holding the love and commanding the respect of all who came within his influence."[7]

However, Hood could not just stand around and expect his men to be impressed. He needed to find ways in which to both heighten the pride of the regiment and to teach military discipline to soldiers that could quit on him. Hood drilled his inexperienced soldiers on the fields in the Richmond area, where the Fourth Texas was stationed in the fall of 1861. Hood recalled "drilling this splendid body of young men and educating them in the duties of soldiers." He told his soldiers, "No regiment . . . should ever be allowed to go forth upon the battle-field and return with more trophies of war than the Fourth Texas—that the number of colors and guns captured, and prisoners taken, constituted the true test if the work done by any command in any regiment."[8]

Hood had the luxury of time to drill his soldiers, with few major military battles occurring in the fall of 1861. The Union army, fresh off a humiliating defeat at the Manassas railroad junction on July 21, underwent a command change, with General George McClellan replacing Irvin McDowell to command the disheveled Union army stationed in Washington, D.C. McClellan would take the rest of the year to drill the Union army into a formidable opponent and prepare for a military campaign that would not begin until the following spring. Because both the North and the South initially expected the war to be over after one major battle, the reality of a long war engulfed both sides of the Mason-Dixon Line. In other words, both the Union and the Confederacy had to form large armies that would be trained and properly disciplined to orchestrate the many military battles in the year ahead.[9]

Fresh off a few months of drilling, members of the Fourth Texas departed the Richmond area in November 1861 to spend their winter encampment along the Potomac River. Before their departure, the Fourth Texas was combined with members of the First and Fifth Texas to form the Texas Brigade. Under the leadership of recently appointed Brigadier General Louis T. Wigfall, the Texans marched to Dumfries, Virginia, located twenty miles from Centreville, the center of Confederate command where General Joseph Johnston had remained since the victory at Manassas. With McClellan gathering a large army around Washington, D.C., the Confederate military had to be prepared for any major thrust of Union soldiers into northern Virginia.[10]

In order to pass the time waiting to see if anything would happen militarily, the Texans created a theater company, eventually calling themselves "Hood's Minstrels," complete with "a brass band and a choir of singers." Soldiers from other regiments eagerly wanted to attend the performances, which cost twenty-five cents. Yet, the winter winds in an open-air performance made for light crowds. The soldiers decided to build their own theater, complete with a curtain. Val Giles described the curtain as getting "his inspiration from Dante's Inferno. It was painted on a fly tent representing devils, jinn, sea monsters, with green eyes and red tongues, all engaged in mortal combat." Giles thought the curtain was "a pretty good show in itself." Comfort from the elements drew sold-out audiences and special guest stars. Harry McCarty, the author of

"Bonnie Blue Flag," made several appearances to sing patriotic songs throughout the existence of Hood's Minstrels.[11]

Hood also took the winter months to further instill the values of military action within his soldiers. As a commander, he expected each soldier to obey orders, including "putting out the lights at night, as men if restless themselves must not disturb others, for to sleep when the chance offered was an important duty." Hood taught his soldiers individual lessons in manhood, through understanding "personal responsibility—each member must feel that in their conduct in camp, when around cities and towns, no comrade must be allowed to bring disgrace upon the regiment." If such disgrace took place, Hood forced the soldiers to discipline one another. The experience bound "officers and men together with ties that have never been forgotten, and which death itself has not been able to sever."[12]

By instilling a sense of personal responsibility among his soldiers, Hood taught his men a lesson learned in his youth: mastery of oneself. By forcing his soldiers to practice self-control, Hood formed a regiment that would always maintain a high level of honor. The Fourth Texas had come to reflect the personality of their commander, who spent each day of the war working hard to secure an honorable reputation among the army ranks. By commanding an honorable group of men, Hood continued making great strides in securing his own internal sense of self-worth.

When the winter snows began to melt, the Texas Brigade underwent a leadership change. Brigadier General Wigfall, fresh off a victory in the Texas senate election, left his military position, allowing for Lieutenant Colonel James Archer, the commander of the Fifth Texas, to assume command of the brigade. With the Eighteenth Georgia joining the Texas Brigade in the winter months, the men departed the winter quarters at Dumfries, Virginia, and moved quickly to camp a few miles west of Fredericksburg. Many of the soldiers left behind their quarters as a means of deceiving the Union troops into thinking that the Confederate army still was in the vicinity of the Manassas railroad junction.[13]

As the soldiers prepared to depart camp, Hood made a rousing speech to motivate the men for the coming campaign. He said, "You are now leaving your comfortable winter quarters to enter upon a stirring campaign—a campaign which will be filled with blood, and fraught with the destinies of our young Confederacy. Its success or failure rests upon the soldiers of the South." Hood showed a strong sense of belief in his men, pointing out that he felt "no hesitation in predicting that you, at least, will discharge your duties, and when the struggle does come, that proud banner you bear, placed by the beauty in the keeping of the brave, will ever be found in the thickest of the fray." Hood called on his fellow soldiers to "stand or fall together." With the concluding remarks, and the tossing of a "handsome bouquet," the soldiers offered "three cheers for Colonel Hood."[14]

The men moved slowly out of camp. One soldier described the dampening chill with many men "all wet to the skin" and that they had to walk with "mud over shoe tops everywhere." Hood decided to set an example for his men. He dismounted his horse when approaching a cold stream. He declared, "Come on, men, right through. It's not deep." Hood charged forward through the stream, which was "more than half-leg deep to him." As Hood emerged from the chilly water on the other side, Val Giles recalled, "Of course, he was well prepared to set such an example, for he wore waterproof boots that came well up on his thighs, so he passed over dry-shod." The example proved effective, as the Texans, "with a shivering whoop," plunged into the stream, which Giles remembered "came up to the middle of some of the shorties."[15] Hood remounted his horse and dealt with the chill infused by the cold water, as he waited on the other side for his devoted men to rejoin him.

By the time the Texas Brigade reached Fredericksburg, Hood's actions thus far in the war had earned him a promotion, from colonel of the Fourth Texas to brigadier general over the Texas Brigade on March 3, 1862. Hood's brigade consisted of the First Texas, commanded by Alexis T. Rainey, the Fourth Texas, in control of John Marshall, as well as the Fifth Texas, commanded by James J. Archer, and the Eighteenth Georgia, affectionately called the "Third Texas," with William T. Wofford at the helm. Because Hood's promotion would increase his duties beyond just commanding the Fourth Texas, the members of the regiment began collecting funds in hopes of presenting their old colonel with a gift to express their gratitude.[16]

Privates from the Fourth Texas presented a horse to Hood a few weeks following his promotion as a token of both appreciation and congratulations on the promotion. First Sergeant J. M. Bookman offered the horse with these words: "In you, sir, we recognize the soldier and the gentleman. In you we have found a leader who we are proud to follow—a commander whom it is a pleasure to obey; and a horse we tender as a slight testimonial of our admiration." The men appreciated Hood's openness and his constant encouragement for the soldiers to visit him in headquarters whenever possible. In the midst of battle, Bookman said the soldiers would "look for your [Hood] commanding form and this proud steed as our guide, and gathering there we will conquer and die. In a word, General, 'you stand by us and we will stand by you.'" Hood expressed his "gratitude at this mark of confidence" and promised that his men "should not look in vain for a rallying point when the struggle came."[17] One steed represented the devotion and friendship exhibited between the men of the Fourth Texas and their beloved commander, feelings that would not die even in the glory and defeat to come.

The promotion did not mean that Hood would end his moments of bonding with his fellow soldiers. However, it did mean that Hood would now forge more intimate bonds with his fellow officers, rather than the rank and file soldiers. Through his promotion to brigadier general, Hood now had to alter how he interacted with other men in order to relate to other officers, rather than just his fellow soldiers. For example, one Sunday evening in March 1862, Hood gathered with his fellow officers and Chaplain Nicholas A. Davis around a campfire. The chaplain later remembered that Hood, despite his status as lacking baptizing, showed "religious interests." Hood "picked up the Bible and opened it as we sat quietly by our fire," recalled Davis. He read aloud from Psalm 118, verse 17, which states, "I shall not die but live." Hood then asked that all those seated at the fire "open and read in like manner." The religious experience allowed for a moment of bonding between the officers, as they truly believed that "the Lord is our refuge and strength."[18] In a private moment, Hood's early reputation as a man having a caring and deep personal side shines through, especially because he showed mutual admiration for his fellow officers. Thus, for Hood, forging a bond remained a paramount part of his leadership style.

The moments of bonding took place during the major military operations emerging across the Virginia landscape in 1862. On March 17, Union commander George McClellan began moving his Army of the Potomac on ships bound for the Yorktown Peninsula, Virginia. The Union plan called for McClellan's army to capture the capital city of Richmond. Yet, this time, the attack would come from the southeast, because General Irvin McDowell's efforts to capture the city from the north had failed in July 1861. McClellan arrived at Fortress Monroe on April 2, 1862. Meanwhile, the Texas Brigade, still in Fredericksburg, received immediate orders to march on April 6. With April showers soaking both the soldiers and the roads, the Texas brigade moved slowly toward Yorktown and established a position along the old Revolutionary War trenches on April 19.[19]

By the time the Texas Brigade had arrived outside Yorktown, McClellan had laid siege to the city and spent several days getting his men into position. The Confederate army, under the command of General Joseph E. Johnston, held the Union soldiers at bay until May 3, 1862, when Johnston decided it would be prudent to pull the Confederate forces back toward Richmond. The Confederates fell back to Williamsburg, where they engaged McClellan in battle on Monday, May 5. Johnston, suffering 1,682 casualties, inflicted 2,283 and gained a clear path to continue his movement back toward Richmond, where a stronger defensive position could be formed.[20]

However, the Texas Brigade did not take part in the battle at Williamsburg. Johnston, fearing the Union advance up the York River to the east of Williamsburg, sent several Confederate units, including the Texas Brigade, to form a defensive position near Eltham's Landing, where the Pamunkey River flows into the Mattapony River to form the York River. On the afternoon of May 7, 1862, General Joseph E. Johnston ordered Hood's Brigade to "feel the enemy gently and fall back," but to avoid any general engagement along the York River at Eltham's Landing. Johnston wanted to ascertain the speed at which Union gunboats were moving up the York River to join McClellan's advancing force from Williamsburg. With no general engagement expected, the Texas Brigade was ordered not to load their rifles before leaving camp that day. Hood remembered, "I leaped from my horse, ran to the head of my column, then about fifteen paces in rear, gave the command, forward into line, and ordered the men to load." Hood's Texans, fully displaying their bravery, charged forward and engaged the Federal army in a brief skirmish. Minié balls flew rapidly, hitting Corporal Sapp of Company H in the head. According to some wartime reminiscences, a Union corporal prepared to fire directly at Hood's head. Fortunately for Hood, Private John Deal quickly "dropped on his knee," took aim, and fired at the Union soldier, saving Hood's life. Ironically, Deal had disobeyed orders, having loaded his rifle prior to leaving camp. Bravery almost ended the military career of Hood, if it were not for the quick thinking of a disobedient private. Afterward, according to eyewitness Val Giles, Hood "complimented John on the fine shot he made, but chided him very gently for loading his gun without orders." Appropriately, Deal never received further punishment for his timely disobedience.[21]

Despite his brush with death and orders from Johnston to avoid a general engagement, Hood's soldiers smashed forward, driving the Union troops backward toward the woods. Hood then called to his men to advance and "feel the enemy." Hood's men drove "the enemy a distance of one and a half miles through a most difficult forest," according to Hood's report. He stated, "I captured some forty prisoners and secured eighty-four stands of arms, the density of the forest and large area over which the engagement extended prevented my securing more of the latter without permitting my men to straggle." Hood suspected that the enemy he engaged had been "considerably reinforced" and that "the loss of the enemy in killed and wounded was heavy." Hood estimated, mostly owing to the thick forest that made visibility difficult, inflicting at least three hundred casualties, while sustaining eight killed and twenty-eight wounded. He reiterated his pleasure as to how his soldiers performed, writing, "The conduct of officers and men, one and all was beyond all praise."[22]

Johnston, despite the bravery and audacity of the Texas troops, became annoyed with Hood's own apparent lack of obedience. Johnston rode up to Hood and said, "General, I sent you up to West Point to check the enemy, but not to bring on a general engagement." Hood replied, "Well, General, those people were so saucy that the boys wanted to give them a little thrashing and I let them do it." Johnston asked Hood, "What would your Texans have done if I had ordered them to charge and drive the enemy back?" "I suppose, General," Hood replied, "they would have driven them into the river, and tried to swim out and capture the gunboats." Johnston capitulated and responded, with a smile, "Teach your Texans that the first duty of a soldier is literally to obey orders."[23]

Despite the disobedience, Hood's personal enthusiasm and the fighting capacity of his soldiers caught Johnston's eye, as well as those of other Confederate commanders. Major General Daniel Harvey Hill reported, "Hood, with a single brigade attacked their advance on the 7th and drove them back to their gunboats. [U.S. commander William] Franklin troubled us no more. His experience gained with the Texans had been ample and satisfactory." Gustavus Smith, the Confederate commander overseeing the effort to stop the Union advance up the York River, remarked, "The Texans won immortal honor for themselves, their State and their commander, General Hood, at Eltham's Landing." He further remarked, "All the troops engaged showed the finest spirit, were under perfect control, and behaved admirably. The brunt of the contest was borne by the Texans, and to them is due the largest share of the honors of the day at Eltham." Robert E. Lee remarked, "They have fought grandly, nobly and we must have more of them." Lee even requested that some Texans be sent to him immediately, especially because they served "as an example of daring and bravery."[24]

After a successful battle, local civilians embraced their soldiers and showed their appreciation through gifts of applejack and peach brandy. Yet, Hood feared that his men may not be able to exercise self-control over the flowing liquor from the grateful populace. In order to prevent his troops from breaking rank to partake in the celebration, Hood issued a report that smallpox had broken out in the area. This fabrication made a lasting impression on his troops. Later, as the army marched westward from the York River toward Richmond, Hood found one of his soldiers lying drunk in the middle of the road. Hood asked, "What is the matter with you, sir?" The inebriated soldier stammered, "Nossin' much, I reckon, General. I just feel sorta weak and no account." Hood ordered the man to stand and rejoin his company, but the soldier was too drunk to stand on his own accord. To assist the drunken private to his feet, Hood asked other soldiers along the road to help the man rejoin his company. As the soldiers offered their assistance, the intoxicated private cried out, "Don't you men that ain't been vaccinated come near me. I've got the smallpox." Hood, realizing his false report of smallpox had been linked to the liquor itself, laughed and decided to leave the man in the road, acknowledging, "Some teamster will pick him up."[25]

By maintaining discipline with a personal touch, Hood showed his ability to command without breaking the bonds of trust and admiration formed between him and his men. Even when he had to instill discipline, Hood never lost sight of his care for the personal well-being of each member of the Texas Brigade. One morning, Hood discovered William H. Lessing, a member of the Fourth Texas, leaning up against a tree. The fourteen-year-old had failed to have his gun loaded while on guard duty. When Hood questioned the young lad, the soldier replied, crying, how he was "so tired and hungry." Immediately, Hood called for relief to be sent immediately for the guard post and commanded Lessing to go directly to his headquarters tent for breakfast.[26]

Following Eltham's Landing, the Texas Brigade fell back with the rest of the Confederate army to the outer limits of Richmond. McClellan, following the victory at Williamsburg, continued his pursuit throughout the month of May, and by early June formed a strong military position, stretching southeast from Mechanicsville to Fair Oaks, Virginia. On June 7, some members of the Texas Brigade scouted in a wooded area and discovered soldiers from the Seventy-first Pennsylvania. Instead of being ordered to dig trenches, the soldiers heard, "Forward boys! Give them hell!" The skirmish resulted in fifty Union casualties before the Texans regrouped and fell back, prompting Hood to issue an order of congratulations. The next morning, the Texans attacked a Federal work detail, prompting one Union soldier, captured in the incident, to remark, "The firing of the Texans was so accurate and their movements so cunning and Indian-like, that . . . [we] never wish to make their acquaintance again." The actions of the Texas brigade throughout the Peninsula campaign prompted one newspaper to report, "I send you . . . a single prediction that when 'the fight' takes place the Texas Brigade will kill more Yankees, storm more batteries, and capture fewer prisoners than any brigade in the service."[27] Only time would tell if the prediction would prove accurate.

With the wounding of Joseph E. Johnston and the mental collapse of Gustavus Smith during the Battle at Seven Pines in early June, Robert E. Lee took command of the Confederate forces around Richmond. On June 25,

1862, Union forces attacked the Confederates at Oak Grove. With the Confederates able to hold their own at Oak Grove, the next day, Lee ordered soldiers under the command of A. P. Hill and D. H. Hill to attack Union soldiers stationed east of Mechanicsville, the right anchor of McClellan's line. The Confederates dislodged the Union soldiers, who fell back to the southeast near Gaines' Mill, where John Bell Hood would be asked to take his Texans into battle once more.[28]

As the Union fell away from Richmond, Lee wanted to continue his momentum and decided to attack again at Gaines' Mill, on June 27, 1862. Lee had asked if Hood's force could break the strong Union position on Turkey Hill, to which Hood replied, "I shall try, sir." Lee asserted, "This must be done." And try he did; Hood personally led the charge into the Union force, "down the slope, through a peach orchard, across the branch, up the hill over the log breastworks." The field, littered with the remnants of the previous battle, did not deter the Texans, as they "pressed forward, driving the enemy from his well-selected and fortified position." The charge resulted with the Texas Brigade breaking the center of the line, despite the Texans being cut down "like wheat in a harvest" with a barrage of Union artillery once the Confederates reached the open fields. Hood had commanded the men to "fix bayonets and charge . . . up the steep hill, through the abates, and over the breastworks, upon the very heads of the enemy." Hood's force held up against a feverish counterattack, signaled by the ground trembling "like an earthquake" and the sound of "a noise like the rumbling of distant thunder." In his memoir, Hood recalled how his Texas soldiers always stood ready to heed the request of Lee, stating, "If a ditch was to be leaped, or fortified position to be carried, General Lee knew no better troops upon which to rely."[29]

During the battle, Lieutenant Colonel John Cheves Haskell saw Hood reforming his brigade. Haskell stated that Hood "spoke to me, offering to help me as I was very bloody. When I told him that I was not seriously hurt, he told me he was about to charge the battery which was sweeping the level beyond the field." As Haskell prepared his men to join Hood on the right, a shot struck Haskell in the right arm, "crushing and tearing it off at the shoulder." Haskell recalled, "When it struck me it seemed to knock me up in the air and spin me around two or three times, though I suppose that was imaginary, then dashed me down with a force that knocked all the breath out of me. When I came to, I found my arm wrapped around my sword blade in a most remarkable manner."[30]

As Haskell lay wounded, the Texans and Georgians moved forward, with Hood holding "a sword whose bright blade reflected the level beam of a sun still above the horizon," according to one eyewitness. As another Texas soldier remarked, "The secret of our success is found in the discretion exercised by Hood at the top of the hill, where so many had fallen before us, when, instead of halting and making a fight, as others had done, he gave the word, and our brave men rushed headlong from the hill, and, at short range and with cold steel, drove the enemy from their hiding places." Another soldier feared to make the attack, but when he caught sight of "old Hood resting on one foot, his arm raised above his head, his hand grasping the limb of a tree, looking as unconcerned as if we were on dress parade," the soldier decided, "I just determined that if he could stand it, I would."[31]

Although Hood had commanded his men in small skirmishes and demonstrations earlier in the war, Gaines' Mill marked the first major battle for John Bell Hood. Hood followed his orders by attacking with a relentless determination to drive the Union army away from Gaines' Mill. When the charge began, Hood displayed his personal courage by leading at the front. Hood regrouped his men, even after the Union had unleashed a ferocious counterattack, when other men may have fled from the field. In fact, Hood used the Union offensive as a moment when he could not only rally his men, but also serve as a personal example, as he stood among the roar of artillery and the crackling of rifle fire. When other soldiers saw Hood, they rose to their feet and charged forward again, despite the field in front of them being littered with casualties. Hood utilized the moment not only to prove his strength as a military officer in front of other untrained officers and green troops on the field of battle, but also to display his own honor by fighting as gallantly as possible.

However, the moment that would garner both Hood and the Texas Brigade accolades for their gallantry came at a heavy price. During the Battle of Gaines' Mill, the Texas Brigade lost 572 men, with more than half (253 casualties) coming from the Fourth Texas, which Hood personally led in the charge. One soldier noted of the battlefield that evening, "The smell of blood is sickening." As a result, the Union soldiers retreated back across the Chickahominy River. The battlefield, littered with human casualties, was a sickening site. "I tell you of a truth, a battlefield is awful when you see thousands of angry warriors rushing upon each other, yelling like so many hell hounds from the infernal regions," said N. J. Brooks, a cavalryman from Georgia. He described the image of seeing "hundreds of bombs bursting and men falling," as well as "horses running away, killing themselves and riders, cannons firing, clouds of dust rising." The disturbing portrait of war prompted Brooks to think that if everyone could witness the same sight, "There would be a ten-fold greater clamor for peace among them than there ever was for war."[32]

The horrifying scene of dead and dying men sickened Hood and visibly moved him. One officer remembered Hood crying upon a cracker box. Hood sobbed, "Just look here, Major, at these dead and suffering men, and every one of them as good as I am, and yet I am untouched." Chaplain Davis noted, "After the battle was over Gen. Hood manifested that kind feeling for his men that a long and severe campaign together is sure to beget. All night he rode and walked to have them [the wounded] gathered and sent to places of comfort—the hospitals where they could have their wounds cleansed and dressed." Following the battle, Hood called to the Fourth Texas during a morning roll call, "Is this the Fourth Texas?" One soldier replied, "This is all that remains." Hood turned his horse away to hide his tears once more.[33] As Hood took in the nearly 50 percent casualty rate of his old regiment, he understood the deep sacrifice his men made to save the Confederate position, and mourned for the men he had bonded with and then lost to the violence of war.

In the midst of his grief, the bloody engagement also saw the reemergence of Hood's old friendships formed on the frontier. The Union's Second Cavalry, of which Hood had been a proud member for six years prior to the war, attacked the Fourth Texas during the battle in order to regain some stolen artillery. Hood remembered, "Major Whitting, who was captain of my company on the frontier of Texas, commanded the former in this bold attack to recapture these guns; his horse was killed under him, and he fell stunned, though unharmed, at the feet of my men, and was taken prisoner." In addition, Hood, while surveying the wounded, heard a cry from Captain Chambliss, another old friend from the Second Cavalry. When Chambliss's identity had been confirmed by one of Hood's soldiers, Hood immediately sent word to Chambliss that he would arrive shortly. Hood rode to see his wounded friend at daybreak and recalled meeting "with the same warmth of feeling which had characterized our intercourse previous to the war." Hood had Chambliss transported to a hospital and made sure he had the same level of attention that a Confederate officer would receive. The attention assisted in Chambliss making a full recovery.[34]

Later, Hood went to Libby Prison, where Chambliss and another Union officer with whom he had served on the frontier had been transferred. The guards at the prison probably wondered why a Confederate officer would visit captured Union soldiers. Hood had served with the two officers in Texas during his frontier days and wanted to show his concern "about their welfare."[35] Thus, while Hood's uniform proved his allegiance to the Confederacy, his experience in the United States Army not only shaped how he thought about being a soldier but also how he thought about his fellow officers. Hence, the bonds formed between officers in the 1850s on the American frontier could not be crushed by the hand of war.

Despite the horrific casualties, the charge that allowed Lee to achieve victory at Gaines' Mill drew notice from fellow soldiers and officers. Isaac Gordon Bradwell, who had served with the Army of Northern Virginia, remembered much later, "Too much cannot be said for the brave fellows who assaulted McClellan's center at Gaines's Mill, a position equally as strong as that held by him at Malvern Hill and Meade's at Gettysburg."[36] General Samuel W. Melton noted, "They are, incomparably, the best fighters in the [C]onfederacy; men upon whom one could depend under all circumstances—who seem to fight for the very love of it." General Thomas "Stonewall" Jackson had the opportunity to witness Hood's soldiers in action at Gaines' Mill. Jackson, in his official report, wrote that, "The fourth Texas, under the lead of General Hood, was the first to pierce these strongholds and seize the guns." Jackson called the fighting displayed here an "almost matchless display of daring and desperate valor." Following the battle, Jackson surveyed the ground and gave his famous and often-cited quotation, "The men who carried this position were soldiers indeed!"[37]

Arthur H. Edey felt so inspired by the actions of the Texas Brigade that he wrote a song dedicated to the brigade on October 1, 1862. The song worked to honor the bold actions in battle, as well as to mourn the loss of those who fell. The lyrics read:

> Down by the valley mid thunder and lightning
> Down by the valley mid jottings of might
> Down by the deep crimsoned valley of Richmond
> The twenty five hundred moved on to the fight
> Onward, still onward to the portals of glory
> To the sepulchral chambers yet never dismayed
> Down by the deep crimsoned valley of Richmond
> Marched the bold warriors of Hoods Texas Brigade
>
> See ye the fires and flashings still leaping
> See ye the tempest and jettings of storm
> See ye the banner of proud Texas
> In front of her columns move steadily on
> Hear ye the music that gladdens each comrade
> Riding on wings through torrents of sounds
> Hear ye the booming a down the red valley
> Rainey imbuckles his swarthy old hounds

Fifth Texas I saw your brave column
Rush through the channels of living and dead
Fourth Texas why weep your old war horse
He died as he wished in the gear of your head
West Point ye will tell on the pages of glory
How the blood of the South ebbed away neath your shade
And how the sons of Texas fought in the red valley
And fell in the columns of Hood's Texas Brigade.

Fathers and mothers ye weep for your jewels
Sisters ye weep for your brothers in vain
Maidens ye weep for your sunny-eyed lovers
Weep for ye shall never behold them again
But know yet that victory the shrine of the noble
Encircles the house of death, newly made
And know that freedom the shrine of the mighty
Shines forth on the banners of Hood's Texas brigade.

Daughters of southland come bring ye bright flowers
Weave ye a chaplet for the brow of the brave
Bring the emblems of freedom and victory
Bring ye the emblems of death and the grave
Bring ye some motto befitting a hero
Bring ye exotics that never will fade
Come to the deep crimsoned valley of Richmond
And crown our young chieftain Hood of the Texas Brigade.[38]

    The engagement at Gaines' Mill, particularly the charge of the Texas Brigade, saved the city of Richmond and ushered in McClellan's withdrawal from the Peninsula. The victory at Gaines' Mill, produced through the heroic actions of the Texas and Georgia soldiers, as well as the commanding ability of John Bell Hood, emerged as the only battle victory for the Confederacy on the Peninsula. Yet, the apparent momentum produced from the victory carried Lee to victory, at the expense of Hood's soldiers at Turkey Hill. With McClellan backing his way toward Harrison's Landing on the James River, the Confederates again engaged the Union army at Glendale and Malvern Hill on June 30 and July 1, respectively. Lee correctly surmised that McClellan's attempt to take Richmond had come to an end. But, a Union force in Washington, under the command of John Pope, could link up with McClellan or apply pressure to Richmond from the north if McClellan decided to again move up the Peninsula. Thus, Lee decided to rush his army northward to meet Pope's force on very familiar terrain for some soldiers from the Army of Northern Virginia: the fields and forests around Manassas railroad junction. On August 8, 1862, Lee sent word to Hood to "proceed to Hanover Junction as soon as practicable" and pushed Hood in that his soldiers "must march." In terms of supplies, Lee wanted Hood to take his "wagon trains and batteries" but send ill soldiers to Richmond to recover. Five days later, he ordered Hood to join Longstreet at Gordonsville, because Union commander Ambrose Burnside had departed the city of Fredericksburg.[39]

The march to return to Manassas proved an exhausting endeavor. On one evening, Hood stopped his soldiers at two in the morning, and many of them fell down to sleep where the lines had stopped. As the soldiers rested, a group of officers examined a barrel left behind for foraging. When the examination concluded, the barrel was kicked and it rolled down a hill toward the sleeping Texans. Suddenly, "the old grey mare," a favorite animal in the regiment, had been scared by the barrel and went dashing up a hill. However, the animal had been "loaded with kettles, tin cups and frying pans," and the sound startled many of the exhausted soldiers into a half awake daze. With a cry of "Look Out," the soldiers bolted "down the slope over a well-constructed fence, which was soon leveled to the ground, and had continued their flight several hundred yards before they awoke sufficiently to recover their wits." When the soldiers realized what had happened, they "boldly march[ed] back, convulsed with laughter." Thus, the popular tune sung among the Texas Brigade, "The Old Grey Mare Came Tearing out O' the Wilderness" was born.[40]

On the march northward toward Manassas, Lee noted that Hood's men had been "attacked by a considerable force which had crossed at Freeman's Ford. After a short but spirited engagement the enemy was driven precipitately over the river with heavy loss." The engagement, on August 22, 1862, resulted in at least two hundred Union casualties, according to Hood's report. Undaunted, the Texas Brigade moved forward, arriving at Manassas and taking a position to attack on the evening of August 29 along the Warrenton Turnpike. However, the evening attack had, for the most part, been mild in terms of cost, with Hood losing fewer than one hundred soldiers. Lee noted, "The enemy was repulsed by Hood after a severe contest and fell back, closely followed by our troops." With the soldiers facing some resistance along the turnpike, Lee and Longstreet agreed that the fight would continue the following morning. Shortly after dawn, Hood quickly surveyed the situation and warned Richard Anderson, who had been maneuvering during the night, that his men needed to shift in order to move away from the direct range of Union artillery.[41]

That afternoon, Hood's men stepped forward once again. A member of the Tenth New York said, "Companies had barely time to discharge their pieces once before the Rebels were almost upon them." "The Texans didn't give them time to reload but with fixed bayonets moved upon them and getting within eight or ten paces emptied their guns at them—they couldn't stand but fled, we killing them at every step," recalled a private from the Fifth Texas. Hood called the rush of soldiers "the most beautiful battle scene I have ever beheld." The force of the Texas soldiers caused one New York private to remark, "The right and left flanks of the enemy almost surrounded us. Where the regiment stood that day was the very vortex of Hell!"[42]

Hood, as he had at Gaines' Mill, personally led the troops forward, shouting, "Men, I shall have you to charge that artillery. Don't waste your fire on the infantry. If you only go close enough, they will run. Kill the horses, so that they cannot carry off the guns." The soldiers obeyed, moved swiftly, and captured a battery. They "were not found where he [Hood] had ordered them to halt." In fact, the troops went up the hill, ran "over the battery," and routed the Union troops in the valley beyond, "pouring their deadly fire" upon the enemy. One Confederate soldier noted, "The fight I was wounded in was a severe fight—our entire force engaged the entire Yankee force. We whipped them." Although the task before the Texans had been bloody, Chaplain Davis wrote, "We could afford to hazard the destiny of one of our best officers in the dreadful attempt. It was *made* and *done*. The shout of victory was first heard in the Fourth Texas, under Hood's command." In this case, Davis again intermixed praise for the soldiers and Hood, acknowledging that Hood "performed the duty assigned with great satisfaction, and filled the most sanguine expectations of all upon the field." Though writing in retrospect, Davis attributed the Texas Brigade's success to the actions of their commander. Hood served as the key reason why the Texans had fought so courageously. As Hood himself remarked, "As to their gallantry and unflinching courage, they stand unsurpassed in the history of the world."[43]

The month of August, climaxing with the battle at Manassas, resulted in more than one thousand casualties, half of the Texas Brigade. Colonel William Wofford, commanding the Eighteenth Georgia, reported that his "regiment lost in killed 19 and wounded 133." He remarked, "I cannot find words to express the gallantry of my regiment, both officers and men." One soldier witnessed the destruction and commented, "My God! My God! So many dead all around!" After the battle, an eyewitness recalled his own impressions of Hood and his military ability. The witness said of Second Manassas that, "It was here that both [Hood's courage and genius] found a field of exercise, and gallantly as the brigade has ever borne itself, it was on the 30th of August that it was by itself eclipsed, and brightly as the Lone Star has ever shone, it was a memorable day that it rose high and gave forth a more resplendent light than ever before." The soldier proclaimed that Hood and his soldiers gained "immortal honor" through the attack that resulted in the destruction of two Union regiments. Proof of the gallantry was through Hood's men "capturing twelve guns and nine strand[s] of colors." Hood simply had been "unfailing as has ever been."[44]

Despite gallantry shown on the field of battle, not everyone liked Hood. His favored position in the Army of Northern Virginia occasionally caused conflict. At the conclusion of Second Manassas, Hood's men captured some Federal ambulances and Hood allowed the men to keep them for the brigade's personal use. General N. G. Evans, who outranked Hood, ordered that the Texans turn over the ambulances. Hood refused because "he did not consider it just" to yield the ambulances "to another brigade of the division, which was in no manner entitled to them." Evans had Hood arrested for disobeying orders. Hood's arrest sent an angry shockwave over the Texas Brigade. Rev. Nicholas Davis noted, "The men were not willing to go into an engagement without him, and many had positively declared that they would stack arms." Cries came from among the soldiers of "Give us Hood" as well as "If there is any fighting to be done by the Texas Brigade, Hood must lead it."[45]

Hood remained under arrest as the Army of Northern Virginia began a new campaign into Maryland. In fact, his men refused to go into action along the Boonesboro Gap at South Mountain unless Hood returned. To appease the Texas Brigade, Lee first called out to the soldiers, "You shall have him, gentlemen." Next, Lee asked Hood to apologize to end the controversy. Lee stated, "General, here I am just upon the eve of entering into battle, and with one of my best officers under arrest. If you will merely say that you regret this occurrence, I will release you and restore you to the command of your division." Hood refused and said, "I am unable to do so, since I cannot admit or see the justice of General Evans' demand for ambulances my men have captured. Had I been ordered to turn them over for the general use of the army, I would cheerfully have acquiesced." Lee pondered, and after asking Hood to apologize, again with the same refusal, he said, "Well I will suspend your arrest till the impending battle is decided." Lee made the decision despite the fact that Hood refused to apologize to Evans. The news brought great pleasure to the troops. As Hood rode to the front of the army after his release, "he was cheered long and loud by each regiment of the division." The soldiers immediately joined the battle at Boonesboro, and with bayonets drove the Union troops out of position and halted any Union attempt to return to Harpers Ferry, Virginia.[46]

The ambulance situation presents a window into the relationship between Hood and Lee. Hood's relationship with his commander had grown since his days at West Point. The time on the frontier allowed for Hood and Lee to establish a more meaningful bond between fellow officers. Early on, Lee realized Hood's potential as a commander, as he placed the Texas Brigade in key positions, both at Gaines' Mill and at Second Manassas, ensuring victory. Now, Hood defied his superior officer by refusing to apologize for holding the ambulances. Despite Hood's blatant disobedience, Lee turned the other way to allow Hood upfront for another critical military endeavor. For Lee, the prospect of having Hood on the front lines clearly trumped the parameters of military discipline.

Hood's return to command invigorated the Texas Brigade as they engaged the Union army outside the quiet town of Sharpsburg, Maryland, along Antietam Creek. Despite their high spirits, some soldiers had grown tired, owing to the engagement at South Mountain and a long, arduous march since the Peninsula campaign. One soldier noted that many of his fellow troops were "barefooted and ragged" and "foot-sore, weary and hungry, but full of patriotic ardor and inspired faith in the justice of our cause." The soldiers also had been forced to survive on green apples and green corn and complained of hunger. This forced Hood to ask Lee if his soldiers could prepare breakfast in the middle of the night on September 16, 1862, under a constant drizzle that confounding campfire efforts. Furthermore, the soldiers faced the danger of fire from Union sharpshooters.[47]

As dawn approached, Hood's soldiers, now numbering close to two thousand, had their breakfast interrupted as the Union army attacked. A staff officer, looking for Hood, arrived during breakfast to state, "General Lawton sends his compliments with the request that you come at once to his support." A Georgia soldier wrote, "Just as we began to cook our rations near daylight, we were shelled and ordered into formation. I have never seen a more disgusted bunch of boys and mad as hornets." The Texas Brigade, in the vicinity of the West Woods, stopped the Union offensive, directed by Joseph Hooker, and drove the army back across the bloody Miller Cornfield. The Texans, offering a rebel yell, fired a volley into the Union line, described by one Union soldier as "a scythe running through our line." Yet, Union artillery battered the advancing rebels, forcing Hood to pull back along the treacherous ground littered with the scars of war. With Union artillerists double-loading their Napoleon guns, the artillery fire shattered Hood's soldiers. One officer saw "an arm go thirty feet into the air and fall back again." He called it "awful." Another soldier recalled, "Whole ranks went down and after we got possession of the field, dead men were found piled on top of each other." With the fierce artillery fire, Hood called out to an aide of Jackson, declaring, "Tell General Jackson unless I get reinforcements I must be forced back, but I am going on while I can!"[48]

Clearly, Hood's aggressive style was seldom emulated. Alphonso Avery, a soldier from North Carolina, said, "Here it was that, for the first time in the war, I saw our men fix their bayonets in action, which they did at the command of Gen. Hood, who was riding up and down the line." Robert E. Lee recalled, "The battle now raged with great violence, the small commands under Hood and Early holding their ground against many times their own numbers of the enemy, and under tremendous fire of artillery." Bold fighting allowed the Confederate army to hold onto their position at the battlefield's northern end. Hood's men had again fought gallantly, suffering one thousand casualties within the Texas Brigade. The First Texas lost 82 percent, with the Eighteenth Georgia suffering 57 percent and the Fourth Texas losing 54 percent of their regiment. The scene of destruction upset Hood to the point where he responded harshly to his commander when Lee inquired where the Texas Brigade was located. "They are lying on the field where you sent them. My division has been almost wiped out," Hood replied.[49]

Despite staving off the early Union attack, the rest of the day, fought along a sunken wagon road and over a small bridge, ended in a military draw, with A. P. Hill arriving in time to stop Union corps commander Ambrose Burnside's attempt to cut off Lee's retreat. The Confederate army, halted in their attempt to take the war north, eventually withdrew from Maryland. Lee, even with Hood's outburst, thought highly of Hood and his actions in battle, and for good reason. Hood himself wrote, "It was here I witnessed the most terrible clash of arms by far, that has occurred during the war. The two little giant brigades of this division wrestled with this mighty force, losing hundreds of their gallant officers and men but driving the enemy from his position and forcing him to abandon his guns on our left." When Henry Kyd Douglas rode an errand for Jackson to the West Woods, to the area where Hood had fought, he observed a horrific scene. He wrote, "The dead and dying lay as thick over it as harvest sheaves. The pitiable cries for water and appeals for help were much more horrible to listen to than the deadliest sounds of battle. Silent were the dead, and motionless. But here and there were raised stiffened arms; heads made a last effort to lift themselves from the ground." Another soldier witnessed a horse "dragging his own entrails from the gaping wound of a cannonball." The animal eventually let out a piercing scream and fell dead. The bloodiest day in American history again heightened the fighting reputation of the Texas Brigade. The gallant efforts of the Texas troops, in a defensive position this time, as well as their great loss, prompted Lee to reconsider the arrest for misconduct that had fallen on Hood before the battle. Ultimately, Lee decided to clear Hood's arrest from the record during the retreat back into Virginia.[50]

Beyond the field of battle, political figures worked to raise the status of John Bell Hood. Colonel J. B. Robertson wrote a letter to Senator W. S. Oldham in Texas. The colonel urged the senator to use political influence "in making General Hood a major general." Robertson observed, "He is one of the best officers we have." Robertson fervently believed that several others held the same "universal sentiment" regarding Hood. Additionally, Major Thomas J. Goree, Longstreet's aide, wrote to his mother after the battle of Sharpsburg, saying, "It is very probable that Genl. Hood will be promoted to Major Genl. for his gallantry in these various contests. No man deserves it more. He is one of the finest young officers I ever saw . . . and had we had many more of the like sort at Sharpsburg, we would have whipped the Yankees worse than they were ever whipped before." Hood's dynamic and brave presence among the Texas Brigade could not be denied. His reputation, both as a commander and a fighter, was scarcely equaled.[51]

Goree's intuition proved true, for after Sharpsburg, "Stonewall" Jackson wrote a letter to General Lee, requesting Hood's promotion to major general. In his letter, Jackson emphasized that Hood had rendered "distinguished service." In the fighting at Antietam's West Woods and Cornfield, Hood's "duties were discharged with such ability and zeal, as to command my admiration." Jackson concluded by stating, "I regard him as one of the most promising officers in the army."[52]

While Hood's status rose among his peers and superiors, resulting in a rank promotion on October 10 to major general, a publication appeared that threatened Hood's status and reputation. In the aftermath of Sharpsburg, Hood's chaplain, Nicholas Davis, wrote *The Campaign from Texas to Maryland with the Battle of Fredericksburg,* which detailed the actions of the Texas Brigade. It should come as no surprise that Davis spoke highly of Hood and the Texans at Sharpsburg. Yet, Davis cast a critical eye upon Major General Lafayette McLaws, who Davis blamed for the Confederate failure to secure victory in Maryland. McLaws had "thwarted the plans of a great army, and made its victory only half complete." Davis wrote, "We want more of our own men. Men who, when the fight begins, will not stand and 'listen to the battle shout from afar,' but will rush forward at the word and carry the field by storm."[53] According to Davis, because of McLaws's tardiness, the Confederacy suffered defeat and the Texans acquired more casualties than required.

McLaws immediately took exception to the publication and wrote Hood, who he pinpointed as the source of Davis's part in tarnishing McLaws's reputation. Hood responded, "The book you refer to was not written under my auspices, and today is the first time my attention has been called to the paragraph you refer to." Hood stated that he had not read the book and that Davis had used the adjutant general's office to secure source material. Hood defended himself vigorously, pointing out how he had not even mentioned McLaws in his report. Hood stated, "But I certainly have no right or desire to blame you or Genl. [D. H.] Hill, I had been fighting since sunrise that morning, and my ammunition was exhausted an hour and a half before your arrival."[54]

McLaws received Hood's letter and responded, "The whole tenor of the publication is so unfounded [and] so maliciously false that one naturally seeks for a motive which would prompt a writer to turn out of his path to utter a baseless slander." McLaws argued that Lee commanded him to wait until receiving further notice, when Lee would instruct him and his men to move into action. After marching several hours through the twilight, McLaws argued that his men needed rest and food, so some "made fires and cooked their breakfast." Yet, Davis had asserted that McLaws stopped his men "to strip and roll up their clothes, to prevent getting them wet, and then halting for some time, for them to make their toilette." After resting nearly two hours, according to McLaws, Lee called him forth and, as McLaws noted, "I immediately mounted my horse and rode to the head of my command then under way."[55] For McLaws, the issue of protecting his honor and his reputation presented the paramount problem.

McLaws appreciated Hood's letter, particularly because he had spoken to other commanding officers about the pamphlet. He wrote to Hood, "I am very glad that you denied that the pamphlet of Mr. Davis was published under your auspices for I tell you frankly that it has been the opinion of many who have read it, that you must have been a party to its publication or must have known its contents before publication." Hood wrote back four days later, requesting to meet with McLaws in person. Hood believed McLaws correct to defend himself and wanted Chaplain Davis to correct the error. Yet, Davis had left for Texas. Hood assured McLaws that upon his return, Davis would be "glad to correct his statements." Even if Davis was in no particular hurry to return to the Texas troops, Hood offered to have someone or even himself write to Davis immediately to "save you from the disagreeable necessity of doing so yourself."

To close, Hood asked McLaws to "correct the idea prevailing in the minds of any of your friends, that I had anything to do with the book of Mr. Davis."[56]

As early as 1863, Hood found himself embroiled in an interpretation of the war, one involving both memory and an honorable reputation. Whether Hood knew about the pamphlet or even helped write it remains unclear. However, Davis recalled in his memoir that Hood stated he was "thoroughly of the opinion, that the victory of that day, would have been as thorough, quick and complete, as on the Plains of Manassas, on the 30th of August, if General McLaws had reached the field with his men, even as late as nine o'clock." Hood needed to alleviate any finger pointing, particularly since he had found favor with Lee and Jackson. Evidently, Hood immediately contacted Nicholas Davis, who wrote to McLaws nearly two months later and declared, that "from information since received I feel that I have done you injustice, in the severe remarks." Davis declared himself willing to "make an honorable amend for that injury" and planned on correcting the item through the issuance of a second edition. Of note, Davis wrote the response July 30, 1863, at a moment when the Confederacy was again contemplating on a failed northern invasion. Davis did not want to stir up any controversy, particularly, "in an hour like this."[57]

Even with the McLaws controversy, Lee continued to think highly of Hood as a military commander. Part of Lee's admiration for Hood rested with his view of how the Texas soldiers fought on the Peninsula and at Sharpsburg. Lee, in a letter to General Lewis T. Wigfall, dated September 21, 1862, implored the general to raise more troops from Texas. Lee pleaded, "I need them much. I rely upon those we have in all tight places, and fear I have to call upon them too often. They have fought grandly and nobly, and *we must have more of them*." Throughout 1862, Lee had called upon Hood and his men to lead daring and risky attacks, which resulted in each instance with heavy casualties. Lee's reasoning stood based upon how he could always turn to Texas to achieve his military goals. He concluded his letter, "With a few more such regiments as Hood now has, as an example of daring and bravery, I could feel much more confident of the campaign."[58]

Following the Confederate withdrawal from Sharpsburg, the Texas Brigade moved to Winchester, Virginia, and came to rest on the grounds of an aristocrat. One soldier noted, "We had little to do but eat, drink, sleep and talk." The owner of the estate came to see Hood about his men "prowling around his premises" and "trying to steal something." Hood reassured the gentleman that his men did not steal and agreed to send some Texas soldiers to guard his estate. As Val Giles remembered, "Shoats, chickens, geese, ducks and bee-gums disappeared every night." The gentleman grew "mad as a hornet" and went to see Hood. He stated, "Send me an honest set of Christian soldiers, if you have such in your division. I don't want any more of your damned Texans. Give me a guard from some other State that will protect my property."[59] Hood agreed to find some Christian men and sent for soldiers from the Eighteenth Georgia.

Lee eventually moved the troops from Winchester toward Fredericksburg, where Hood and his troops arrived November 23, 1862, after a march through "shoe-top deep mud" and rain. Following his October promotion to major general, Hood would now command a division as his soldiers faced off against Union commander Ambrose Burnside in mid-December. The division included the Texas Brigade, the Third Arkansas, who fought gallantry at Sharpsburg and replaced the Eighteenth Georgia, as well as units from Alabama and North Carolina. Hood's division, under the command of General James Longstreet, had been initially positioned at Hamilton's Crossing, located south of the heights beyond the town, where Longstreet had anchored his line. With the Union army gathered on the other side of the Rappahannock River, the Confederates realized the battle would be imminent. Longstreet moved Hood closer to the heights outside town. Burnside, after being delayed awaiting pontoon bridges to cross the Rappahannock River, finally began bridge construction on the morning of December 11.[60]

Once the bridges had been completed, Burnside moved his army and finally attacked on the morning of December 13. During the battle, Hood sat and watched the action that mainly took place on his left and right, with no major action to his front. Soldiers from the Fifty-fourth and Fifty-seventh North Carolina, recently added to Hood's division, saw some significant action at Fredericksburg. Many of the green North Carolinians surged forward in pursuit of the fleeing Union soldiers from New Jersey. But suddenly, a round of Union artillery fire brought the Southern pursuit to a halt. One Union artillerist, after seeing one shot knock down eighteen Confederates, remarked, "It was an awful sight to see their poor fellows going up in the air." Hood called to halt their progress. One North Carolina soldier walked by a group of Texas soldiers, "wiped the powder grime from his weather-beaten face with his sleeve of his coat and wrathfully exclaimed, 'Durn ole Hood, anyhow! He jes didn't have bus'ness ter stop us when we'uns was ah-whippin' the durn blue-bellies h—ll an'back, an eff we'uns hadder bin you Texicans he'd never o'dis it.'" Hood did lose 343 at Fredericksburg from his division, of which 224 came from the Fifty-seventh North Carolina and forty-six from the Fifty-fourth North Carolina.[61]

What the irate North Carolinians did not realize is that Hood had pulled the soldiers back once they reached the open ground. This time, at Fredericksburg, with the victory in hand, Hood did not stand willing to bleed his division any further than necessary to secure victory. He had "expected orders every moment to move either to the right or to the left." Longstreet even told Hood that "when an opportunity offered he should move forward and attack the enemy's flank." During the battle, Val Giles remembered, "Under all circumstances, no matter how sudden or unexpected an attack might be, he [Hood] was such a thoroughly trained soldier that he never showed the least bit of nervous excitement under fire." Yet, at Fredericksburg, Hood detected an "uneasiness and suspense" among his soldiers and appeared to try hard to "suppress his own anxiety." Most of Hood's division did not move, but stood fast, and "Hood seemed made of steel." However, Longstreet wanted Hood to attack the flank, and after the war, regretted "not bringing the delinquent to trial." Longstreet wrote that although he offered Hood's reluctance to follow orders to the official records, the incident went no further, mostly owing to Hood being in "high favor with the authorities." But an overwhelming Confederate victory prevented Longstreet from pushing the matter any further.[62]

Longstreet's dissatisfaction with Hood's performance seems out of place considering the actions of the Texas Brigade so far in the war. Time and time again, Hood had personally led his men forward, with waves of attacks resulting in piles of Confederate casualties. Hood stood prepared to attack to the left or right. Yet, with the Union army clearly obliterated on the streets of Fredericksburg and at the face of the Stone Wall in front of Marye's Heights, a grand charge from John Bell Hood was simply unnecessary to achieve victory. Hood's previous offensive maneuvers had been vital in either securing victory or preventing the collapse of the Confederate position. At Fredericksburg, the Confederate line under Longstreet's command never stood at the precipice of failure. Most of Hood's division was not needed to win a clear-cut victory, and his men welcomed the opportunity to rest.

As the Confederate army spent time in winter quarters in 1863 following the victory at Fredericksburg, Lee and Hood frequently visited and conversed. The friendship, evolving from a relationship between a superintendent and a plebe at West Point to colleagues on the frontier, did not prevent Lee from disciplining his officer. During one particular conversation, Lee voiced his criticism of Hood's men "burning fence rails, killing pigs and committing sundry delinquencies of this character." Hood "warmly" defended his troops and even recommended Lee send his chief of staff to inspect the area around Hood's camp. Lee responded, "Ah, General Hood, when you Texans come about, the chickens have to roost mighty high."[63]

With the winter snows making the gathering of supplies necessary, Hood's division remained in winter quarters south of the Fredericksburg area. James Crowder described his winter dwelling, remarking, "Some of the boys has got little loge cabin dabed with [mud] and some got holes dug in the ground and covered over with dirt and some of them has got tents with chimleys to them and others has got [tent] flys to stay in[.] [T]he house that my mes built is ten feate wide and twelve feate long[.] [W]e have got hit covered over with board." By the beginning of 1863, the Texas Brigade gathered a collection and donated $5,945 for "the relief of the sufferers of Fredericksburg." Furthermore, the winter months also saw a theater constructed and a resurrection of the famed theatrical group, Hood's Minstrels. Hood attended several of the dramatic and comedic performances, with Lee and Longstreet also occasionally in attendance.[64]

As the winter winds gave way to the emerging spring weather, Hood's division participated in a day of fasting and prayer on March 27. One soldier reported, "I heard a good sermon preach and prar made by severl good men tho the boys is all gone a fishing since we donte have to drile to day." Following the day of fasting and prayer, Longstreet ordered Hood's division to move on Suffolk, Virginia, and support Fort Huger, a Confederate fortification and a target of Union warships moving into the region. Hood's division supported the Confederate artillery inside the fort that disabled several ships on April 17. However, the Union gunboats remained on the offensive. On April 19, Union soldiers stormed the fort and captured "five pieces of artillery and about 140 Confederates." Hood considered a counterattack but decided against a possible high cost for little again.[65]

The heavy loss of men throughout much of 1862 had changed Hood's perception of warfare. Instead of charging forward at all costs, Hood exercised prudence at Fredericksburg and Fort Huger in order to first assess the position. Realizing that the gains resulting from the battle would not be worth the cost, Hood held his Texans back from making another charge that could inflict heavy casualties for minimal gain. Hood also understood the reciprocal nature of the bond he had formed with his men. By garnering a mutual trust, Hood knew his soldiers would be ready to fight when called upon. At the same time, his men expected Hood to act as a wise commander and make sure their battle sacrifice was worth the effort. By understanding this reciprocal relationship, Hood proved to his men that their fighting tenacity could sometimes best be used in a subdued fashion.

Because of the action at Suffolk, the soldiers of Hood's division missed the crucial and costly battle at Chancellorsville, Virginia. Hood wrote to Lee on April 29, 1863, from Suffolk, stating, "I presume we will leave here so soon as we gather all the bacon in the country. When we leave here, it is my desire to return to you. If any troops come to the Rapidan please don't forget me. I have not lost many men." Hood did pause to lament one particular loss to Lee: Captain Turner, the leader of the sharpshooters, from the Fifth Texas, who died in a gunboat fight. Hood declared, "A more noble and brave soldier has not fallen during this war." Hood concluded, "I hope however we will accomplish all we came here for."[66]

With Union commander Joseph Hooker now in charge of the Army of the Potomac, preparing to cross the Rapidan River and attack Lee near Chancellorsville, Lee called for Hood's division to move closer to Fredericksburg. Hood gathered his men and said, "My men I haven't called you around me to listen to a speech. I only wish to say, that we are going to meet the enemy. Our friends are probably fighting them now." As one soldier noted, he departed without "one mouthful of rations cooked up and marched all day before eating anything." Hood moved the army quickly and relentlessly. One soldier wrote, "We had little flour along that we cooked at night—also a little bacon. We marched 27 miles that day and stuck up camps for the night—and orders was to be ready to leave the next morning by light." Despite the speed of the march, Hood's division did not make it to the Chancellorsville area in time for the battle in early May, 1863.[67]

Even without Hood's division, the Army of Northern Virginia successfully stopped another Union campaign to capture the capital city, Richmond. However, Lee lost more than ten thousand troops and his prominent corps commander, "Stonewall" Jackson. With a void in leadership created by the death of General Jackson at Chancellorsville, Lee called upon Hood to step up and take a more prominent role. With the Confederate army growing in both size and confidence, Lee decided to reorganize the Army of Northern Virginia through the creation of a new corps, the largest body of any army organization during the Civil War. Lee even considered Hood, as well as Richard Anderson, for command of the newly constructed Third Corps that ultimately went to Ambrose Powell Hill, the elder officer who Lee called "the best soldier of his grade." Lee did call Hood a "capital officer" and realized Hood's potential as a corps commander if duty so dictated. Thus, Lee decided to write a letter to Hood. He said, "I wished for you very much in the last battle, and believe, had I had the whole army with me, General Hooker would have been demolished; but God ordered otherwise." Lee grieved over the death of Jackson, but hoped that the army could "endeavor to follow the unselfish devotion and intrepid course he pursued." Lee concluded, "I rely much upon you. You must so inspire and lead your brave division as that it may accomplish the work of a corps." Lee appreciated Hood's observations about how the large numbers of soldiers placed within the three corps would be difficult to maintain at their present size. He said, "I am much obliged to you always for your opinion. I know you give it from pure motives. If I am not always convinced, you must bear with me." At Lee's invitation, Hood now would have to prove himself further as a commander who could step in and fight to the same level that had given Jackson success under Lee. Lee signed the letter as "now and always your friend." His trust in Hood remained clear. Now, it was up to Hood to respond to Lee's call.[68]

Despite the loss of Jackson and the need to reorganize the Confederate army, the South had again achieved a clear victory over the Army of the Potomac. Hooker withdrew back across the Rapidan River. Lee stood at a critical crossroads. His soldiers, despite the setback the previous year at Sharpsburg, had won two decisive victories against a stronger opponent on separate occasions outside Fredericksburg. However, things seemed more perilous for the Confederacy throughout the rest of the country. With Union commander William Rosecrans threatening Braxton Bragg's army in Tennessee and Ulysses S. Grant moving against Confederate forces near Vicksburg, Mississippi, Lee had to make a decision about his next move. Secretary of War James Seddon envisioned sending George Pickett and possibly Hood to join Joseph Johnston near Jackson, Mississippi. Lieutenant General Longstreet formulated a plan where his corps, including the divisions of Pickett and Hood, would travel to assist Bragg in Tennessee, and it was hoped their movements would alleviate pressure on Vicksburg. Yet, Robert E. Lee had a different vision. In order to succeed at Vicksburg, Lee reasoned, the Army of Northern Virginia should move North, invading Maryland and Pennsylvania. Despite hesitation from certain cabinet members and from Jefferson Davis, Lee's plan received an endorsement.[69]

As Lee made plans for the upcoming campaign, Hood's division, stationed at Culpeper, Virginia, remained busy, as they participated in a grand review on May 27, 1863. Despite the unusually warm temperatures, Hood's men obliged, mostly owing to the invitations Hood had sent to local women. A soldier wrote that the review "was a beautiful sight to look at . . . but not in the least beautiful or pleasant to the ones who were in the review." Furthermore, the men withstood the heat "to suffer a little to have the curiosity of the nice ladies satisfied." Hood ordered the whole division "in line of battle across a field (I should have said fields)." The review, "quite a show," offered the "beautiful" young ladies on horseback a moment of entertainment. Following the review, one soldier noted, "We had a sham fight. The artillery showed off very well firing several rounds and the infantry made a charge with a yell. . . . It reminded me of the winding up of a circus."[70]

Hood would have the opportunity to further prove his worth to Lee with his division remaining with the Army of Northern Virginia. The soldiers moved north toward Harrisburg, the capital of Pennsylvania and a vital rail center that connected Philadelphia to the central part of the state. William Youngblood, from Alabama, offered a reminiscence of Hood during the Gettysburg campaign. When the Confederate force reached the Shenandoah River, Youngblood inquired of General Hood if he could remove his clothing to wade the river. Hood replied, "No time could be allowed for dressing and undressing." Despite it being a "hot June day," Youngblood remembered the water as "biting cold, so cold that I crawled upon a projecting rock in the middle of the stream until I was forced to leave it."[71]

John C. West, a private in Company E, Fourth Texas, further described the long road into Pennsylvania. West stated, "We left the camp from which I now write on the fifteenth day of June, under a burning sun and a brazen sky. The march was conducted by that unmerciful driver, our beloved General Hood, who simply strikes a trot and is satisfied that the Texas Brigade at least will camp with him at nightfall." On the march into Pennsylvania in June 1863, Hood met Lieutenant Colonel Arthur Fremantle, an officer in the British army, who was traveling with General Lee. Fremantle noticed how other Confederate soldiers were "pointing and laughing at Hood's ragged Jacks." He described the troops from Texas, Alabama, and Arkansas as men who "carry less than any other troops; many of them have only got an old piece of carpet or rug as baggage; many have discarded their shoes in the mud; all are ragged and dirty, but full of good-humor and confidence in themselves and in their general, Hood." Rumor also had it that Hood's men were "accused of being a wild set, and difficult to manage." Yet, the impression Hood's soldiers made upon Fremantle and the citizens of Pennsylvania did not deter the Texans in the least. Fremantle noted, "They answered the numerous taunts of the Chambersburg ladies with cheers and laughter."[72]

Fremantle also noted that "by his Texan and Alabamian troops he [Hood] is adored." The Briton described Hood as "a tall, thin, wiry-looking man, with a grave face and a light-colored beard, thirty-three years old, and . . . accounted one of the best and most promising officers in the army." Fremantle observed Hood firsthand as the Confederate forces attacked at Gettysburg,

Pennsylvania. On the morning of July 2, 1863, Hood talked with Longstreet about the plans for the day's attack. In a battle planning session, Lee fervently declared, "The enemy is here, and if we do not whip him he will whip us." Yet, Longstreet remained hesitant and said, "The General [Lee] is a little nervous this morning; he wishes me to attack; I do not wish to do so without Pickett. I never like to go into battle with one boot off."[73]

Under orders from Lee, Longstreet slowly moved south, delayed by a late start as well as the possibility of being seen by Union signalmen on Little Round Top. Thus, Hood did not send troops forward into battle along the Emmitsburg Road at Seminary Ridge until approximately 4 p.m. Yet, prior to the attack, the solders had undergone a rigorous march. Hood stated, "So imperative had been our orders to hasten forward with all possible speed that on the march my troops were allowed to halt and rest only about two hours during the night from the 1st to the 2d of July." The veteran troops, hot, tired, and thirsty after the long morning march, prepared to attack at places later known as Devil's Den and the Round Tops. Hood had fervently protested the position to Longstreet three different times, asking for permission to "move to the right and fall on the enemy's left flank on Little Round Top." Longstreet refused and the men marched forward. The Union bursts of artillery increased in ferocity. Captain Barziza, from Texas, wrote, "The enemy's shells screamed and bursted around us, inflicting considerable damage. It is very trying upon men to remain still and in ranks under a severe cannonading. . . . The men are all flat on the ground, keeping their places in ranks, and as a shell is heard, generally try to sink themselves into the earth."[74] Hood regretted that his men had to move forward into the artillery salvo. In the months following the battle, Hood readily offered criticism to Richmond's socialites and dignitaries over Longstreet's decision to obey Lee's orders instead of following his own advice.

Hood ordered the men forward, crying, "Fix bayonets, my brave Texans; forward and take those heights!" Hood further shouted, "Forward, my Texans, and win this battle or die in the effort." Another Texan responded, "Follow the Lone Star Flag to the top of the mountain!" Shortly after the troops moved forward, splashing across the waters of Plum Run, John Reed witnessed an artillery shell that "seemed to burst immediately over the group" of officers and aides, which included Hood, gathered in a peach orchard. Reed witnessed Hood sag in the saddle, and "the staff officers crowded around and helped him to dismount." Fragments from the shell ripped through his left hand, forearm, elbow, and bicep.[75]

John Cheves Haskell also witnessed the wounding. He remembered, "I was ordered to take two batteries to Hood and he turned, apparently to give me orders, but on the instant was struck on the arm by a shrapnel shot and reeled and fell from his horse utterly prostrated and almost fainting." Though Haskell noted the wound did not seem "very severe," it shocked Hood "much more than a much more severe one would ordinarily have done." As Hood received medical attention from Dr. John T. Darby, his chief surgeon, he ascertained the situation and called on Evander Law, his second in command, to take over. Hood's left arm would be spared amputation, but remained paralyzed.[76]

When Fremantle last saw Hood, he stated that, "He looked rather bad, and has been suffering a good deal; the doctors seem to doubt whether they will be able to save his arm." Fremantle later wrote that "the most serious loss was that of General Hood.... I heard that his Texans are in despair." Yet, his soldiers surged forward and continued a heavy day of fighting that failed to dislodge the Union troops holding Little Round Top. This forced the Texans to eventually return to where the attack had commenced. Private John C. West wrote, "I believe the wounding of General Hood early in the action was the greatest misfortune of the day." Without him in command, his division would suffer 597 casualties.[77]

After receiving medical attention, Hood traveled from Gettysburg almost two hundred miles in an ambulance to Staunton, Virginia, in the heart of the Shenandoah Valley. On his journey, Hood did not ride alone in the ambulance. Wade Hampton, also wounded at Gettysburg, shared the ride. Hampton could not sit up on the journey, while Hood could not lie down. Hood healed quickly from his wounds and traveled with his physician, Dr. Darby, to Richmond. He would remain there for a little more than a month, with one eye on his recovering injuries and the other on the field of battle that continued to call him.

While in Richmond, the wounded officer garnered immediate notice of the female populace, particularly Sally Preston and Louise Wigfall, the daughter of Hood's former commander. Wigfall, after spending time with Hood, said, "A braver man, a purer patriot, a more gallant soldier never breathed than General Hood.... He was a man of singular simplicity of character and charm of manner—boyish in his enthusiasm—superbly handsome, with beautiful blue eyes, golden hair and flowing beard—broad shouldered, tall and erect—a noble man of undaunted courage and blameless life."[78]

However, the call to the battlefield trumped any romantic notions for Hood at this juncture in his career. He missed his men and the thrill of battle. The soldiers of his division, especially the Texas Brigade, also longed for Hood to regain command. As Major Thomas Goree wrote, "The Texas Brigade is not in the condition I would desire to have it. The morale of it is bad." Longstreet had replaced Evander Law, who led Hood's division at Gettysburg, with Brigadier General Micah Jenkins. However, Jenkins proved unpopular with Hood's men and fellow officers, thus providing a window of opportunity for Hood to return to command.[79]

Hood's recovery, precipitated by the fighting juices that flowed through his veins, allowed him to continue his service in the Army of Northern Virginia, with visible signs of his wound on display. Major Joseph B. Cumming remembered, "We were sitting on a log, General Hood taking his breakfast, one arm, as I remember, in a sling."[80] However, with crisis brewing in Tennessee, Hood disregarded his injuries, and he served a detached duty with the Army of Tennessee. Lee had sent Longstreet's corps to reinforce Bragg, who faced a tough Union force, commanded by General William Rosecrans, in the vicinity of Chattanooga. With this detachment of Longstreet's corps, Hood would never again rejoin the Army of Northern Virginia. On September 8, 1863, Longstreet's soldiers passed through Richmond and Hood joined his soldiers once more, leading the march into the Carolinas and Georgia. With the retaking of Chattanooga by Union forces, Longstreet's march was plagued by "poor rail lines, inadequate rolling stock" as well as "a wide variety of rail gauges." The difficult travel conditions meant that Hood's division did not arrive until September 18.[81]

The opening day of the Battle of Chickamauga commenced on September 19, 1863. Brigadier General St. John Richardson Liddell saw Hood for the first time and found him "affable," but the "conversation was too short to enable me to form an estimate of his ability and military views." During the opening action of the battle, R. M. Gray, a Confederate soldier, remained pressed flat against the earth in order "to avoid the hurricane of death which was hurtling above our heads." Suddenly, one soldier cried out, "There is Genl Hood." Gray remembered turning his head and seeing Hood "quietly upon his horse." Hood "sat as calmly and as unmoved, amid the missiles of the enemy, as I could have done in my tent watching the contest just before him, he saw that decisive moment had come." Another soldier witnessed Hood riding with "his hat off in a token salute, his left arm still in a sling, and his noble countenance still pale from the wound received at Gettysburg." The soldiers cheered. Hood quieted the soldiers and said, "Boys, I am glad to see you. You must whip this battle here." Hood decided the moment had arrived and ordered the soldiers forward "like a whirlwind upon the enemy." The Union troops "broke and fled in dismay." Gray said, "I still heard that firm determined voice as we pursued giving orders to those around him. How he escaped is alone to be accounted for by special interposition of providence."

Braxton Bragg noted, "Hood, later engaged, advanced from the first fire, and continued to drive the force in his front until night."[82] The battle would stretch into another day of fighting, and Hood's luck in escaping enemy missiles began to fade.

The battle that continued on September 20 resulted in Rosecrans ordering the center of his line to move left to fill a gap that had supposedly been created in a Confederate attack. However, when the Union soldiers moved to brace for the attack, they accidentally opened a real gap in the Union position. Thus, when the Union soldiers moved, Longstreet's corps attacked right into the gap, with Hood's division leading the way. Hood called out, "Move up men: those fellows are shooting at the tops of the trees." The attack proved successful, splitting the Union army in half, overrunning Rosecrans's headquarters, and sending the commander fleeing for his life back to Chattanooga, while Union corps commander George Thomas fought to the bitter end at Snodgrass Hill. Thomas earned the nickname the "Rock of Chickamauga" and the Confederacy earned a stunning and convincing victory. Joseph Cumming remembered, "Chickamauga was one (if not the one) of the bloodiest battles of the war." As Alphonso Avery, a member of the Sixth North Carolina, stated, "And when the war has closed, [this] victory achieved on the stream of death, will be pronounced the most complete of any that has been won from the beginning of the Revolution."[83]

During the battle at Chickamauga, Hood, while riding to lead his soldiers into action, grasped for a regimental flag after cheering on some South Carolina soldiers. At that moment, a Minié ball smashed through his right femur, shattering the bone and again removing him from the battlefield. With Dr. John T. Darby still in Richmond, Dr. T. G. Richardson, chief medical officer of the Army of Tennessee, performed the amputation, four inches from the hip, right behind the Confederate lines. Hood told his physician, "I am in your hands, gentlemen; do as you think best." One soldier recalled hearing that even after his leg had been shattered, Hood "never lost his composure for a moment, and gave orders clearly and coolly before allowing himself to be taken from the field." Upon hearing of the operation, the Texas Brigade resolved to raise funds, accumulating nearly $5,000, to purchase an artificial leg from France for their hero.[84]

Ironically, Hood, in his postwar years, recalled a wounding superstition held within the ranks of the Texas Brigade. Hood, since the beginning of command with the Texas soldiers, normally rode a horse into battle by the name of Jeff Davis, the horse he received from his soldiers in 1862. As Hood himself recalled, "he [Davis] generally received the bullets and bore me unscathed."

However, at Gettysburg, Hood's horse had been lame, and thus, Hood had to command from a different mare and had been shot from the horse. At Chickamauga, his horse had been wounded on the first day of action, prompting Hood to again mount another steed, and again, had been shot from his horse. Thus, he and his soldiers believed that "when mounted on old Jeff, the bullets could not find me." Hood recalled that the horse survived the war and went to a family in Seguin, Texas, where it passed away and had been "buried with appropriate honors."[85]

Hood's wounding and amputation at Chickamauga sent a shockwave throughout the army. Rumors of his death spread like wildfire on a scorched prairie. When Hood fell, General Benning rode to speak with General Longstreet. He said, "General Hood killed, my horse killed, my brigade torn to pieces, and I haven't a man left." When word traveled to Virginia to meet the ears of Robert E. Lee, he wrote, "I am grieved to learn of the death of Gen. Hood." Lee further stated, "I am gradually losing my best men." Two days later, Lee still had not been notified that Hood was alive. He wrote in a letter to James Longstreet, "I grieve for the gallant dead and mourn for our brave Hood."[86]

Further sentiments regarding the rumored death of Hood came from other Confederate soldiers, officials, and southern newspapers. William Bailey, in the First Louisiana, noted in his diary on September 23, "Gen. Hood of Texas reported killed," but three days later noted that he had only "lost a leg." John B. Jones, the Confederate War Department clerk, noted, "Hood is said to be dead." Hood's obituary even appeared in newspapers on September 20, 1863. The obituary stated, "Hood, Major-Gen. John B., an officer in the Confederate service, reported killed at Chickamauga." The obituary glorified the military career of Hood by making careful note of all Hood's woundings, from his days fighting "Comanches and Lipans near the head of the San Pedro River" to his command of "the largest division in Gen. Longsteet's corps."[87]

However, the swirl of rumors resulted in clear confusion as to the outcome of Hood's injury. Four days after his initial comment on Hood's death, John Jones wrote, "Hood is not dead, and will recover." Newspapers, such as the *Daily Picayune,* later reported, "We have to mourn the loss of many gallant men and officers." Yet, the *Picayune* reported Hood losing a leg, changing the tone in the newspapers from death to amputation. Robert Kean, head of the Confederate Bureau of War, more than a week after the battle, wrote, "General Hood, reported killed, has lost a leg above the middle of the thigh, and is reported doing as well. Our best men fall in every battle." When Lee received word of Hood's survival, he wrote in a letter to Jefferson Davis that the news gave him "great relief." General Braxton Bragg wrote, "Major-General Hood, the model soldier and inspiring leader, fell after contributing largely to our success, and has suffered the irreparable loss of a leg. That his valuable life should be spared to us is, however, a source for thankfulness and gratitude."[88]

The widespread notice of his wounding and apparent demise, as well as Kean's significant description of Hood as one of the "best men," reflects Hood's status to those who did not march with the army daily. One resident of Richmond noted how the Confederate task emerged "dampened by the loss of General Hood, who died under the operation of amputating his leg. He left here two weeks ago scarcely able to manage his wounded arm. His loss is a severe one, second only to that of Jackson."[89] The diarist made a powerful observation, ranking Hood's death directly behind Jackson on the scale of crucial losses during the Civil War. Albert Sydney Johnston, absent from the top two, had been considered one of the greatest losses in the Confederacy early in the war.

Yet, the correct news eventually arrived to the Confederate populace. Henri Garidel expressed relief, writing, "General Hood, so it says, is not dead but is very ill from having his right leg amputated. He is a handsome man. He is 6 feet 2 inches tall. He used to stand up very straight." Garidel noted Hood's earlier visit to Richmond in 1863, remarking that "he had his arm in a sling." Additionally, Garidel wrote, "He is a famous general and commands the Texans. I pray to you, God, to keep him from dying. We need him."[90]

Hood's ability to regain command of a force received tremendous praise from his superior officers and ranking Confederate government officials. His survival and bravery led to more recommendations for promotion to the rank of lieutenant general in the Confederate army. Longstreet wrote how Hood "handled his troops with the coolness and ability that I have rarely known by any officer, on any field." Bragg agreed with Longstreet, simply stating, "I cordially unite in this just tribute." James A. Seddon, the Confederate secretary of war, responded, "I cannot too warmly express my appreciation of the character and services of this distinguished officer." Jefferson Davis, in responding to the secretary of war, wrote, "The services of Major General Hood, and his character as a soldier and patriot, are equal to any reward, and justify the highest trust." Davis, though, thought a promotion was a hasty decision and wanted more details as to why Hood should receive advancement. In an additional letter to Senator Wigfall, Seddon wrote, "I have felt the deepest interest for your friend, and I trust I may say mine, the gallant Hood. He is a true hero, and was the Paladin of the fight."[91]

After Hood's wounding and the Confederate victory at Chickamauga, the newspapers echoed positive sentiments about Hood and his abilities. The *Atlanta Daily Appeal* wrote, "He is peculiarly a soldier—a soldier as much by nature as education—who, it seems, to my imperfect judgment, is fitted to any military position to which he may be called." Even at this early stage, a southern newspaper endorsed Hood for more responsibility. The *Daily Confederate,* out of Huntsville, Alabama, made note of Hood's "noble countenance."[92] Hood, viewed as the tragic hero, suffered two debilitating wounds in the course of two months. The wounds transformed his image into a minor celebrity in the Confederate press. Now, the approval of Hood's ability and character rang out not only through the Confederate ranks but through the home front as well.

As the accolades and promotion emerged around him, Hood had to deal with the painful reality of his now phantom limb. The day following his field operation, Hood traveled to a private residence in Armuchee Valley, fifteen miles from the Chickamauga battlefield, where the officer remained until the end of October. Yet, by October 8, Hood had asked when he could return to duty. His physician noted his progress, remarking, "He sat up yesterday for twenty minutes and I hope soon to see him moving on his crutches." Hood's progress allowed for him to next travel to Atlanta at the end of October. After a few days' rest at the home of Colonel J. S. Thrasher, Hood traveled next to Wilmington, North Carolina, for a few days, with an eventual destination in Richmond to recover from his injuries. One newspaper reporter remarked, "Somewhat bleached by illness rendering his delicate features more delicate, with soft hair of light brown and silky beard nearly golden, he looks like a mild, sensitive and amiable man, as no doubt he is in private life, as he is a courteous and gallant soldier in the field." Another writer remarked, "The General is looking hale and hearty, despite the suffering and exhaustion occasioned by the loss of a limb, and expresses himself in the best of health and spirits."[93]

On November 16, the *Daily Picayune* reprinted a report from the *Charleston Courier* that tracked Hood's travels from Chickamauga to Richmond. Hood passed through Branchville, South Carolina, in a private car, "attended by Surgeon Darby of the Confederate service and accompanied by Gen. Gustavus W. Smith and wife." The party rode in an "elegant and comfortable car belonging to and lent by a liberal citizen of Augusta." For the most part, Hood rode upon a litter "seeming not suffering from his wounds and in fine spirits, although only convalescent from an attack of typhoid fever, which supervened the amputation of his leg." The *Courier* longed for Hood's return to the field, where he would "again make the enemy quall before his prowess." Upon arrival at their destination, Smith and Hood were to be the guests of General Whiting.[94]

As 1863 drew to a close, Hood's soldiers had a productive year of fighting, heavily contributing to military actions at Gettysburg and securing victory at Chickamauga. Unfortunately, the year also brought the young commander two critical wounds, rendering him a useless arm and a phantom leg. Hood's two heroic red badges of courage sent him into and created a stir in Confederate high society, to the point where Hood emerged as a celebrity. Upon meeting or seeing the wounded soldier, influential members of society echoed the tributes of valor and noble courage printed in the papers and spoken from within the Confederate military ranks. His "noble" reputation, solidified by military performance and unfortunate wounding, would set the stage for new tasks dealing with the reality and ramifications of being a Confederate amputee.

General John Bell Hood in civilian clothes. Courtesy of the National Archives.

John Bell Hood, after the amputation of his right leg and damaged left arm, 1864. Courtesy of the Historic New Orleans Collection, New Orleans, Louisiana.

John Bell Hood print/engraving, ca. 1860–1880. Courtesy of the Library of Congress.

Hood's headquarters during the Atlanta campaign. Courtesy of the Library of Congress.

Photograph taken for the Hood Memorial Fund for Hood's ten orphaned children, ca. 1879. From the Campbell Family Papers #155, Southern Historical Collection, Wilson Library, University of North Carolina at Chapel Hill.

Nashville, view from the capitol, 1864. Courtesy of the National Archives.

Odlie Hood, one of Hood's daughters, ca. late 1880s–1890s. *Courtesy of Louisiana Historical Association Collection, Manuscripts Department, Tulane University Libraries.*

Chapter 4

A Crisis in Manhood? Hood and the Experience of Confederate Amputees

After losing his leg at the Battle of Chickamauga in September 1863, recently promoted Confederate General John Bell Hood traveled to Richmond to recover from his wounds. Hood convalesced at the home of socialite and famed diarist Mary Chesnut. Mary Preston, a visitor to the Chesnut home, shouted, "Come here, Mrs. Chesnut. They are lifting Hood out of his carriage, here at your door." As Hood received assistance onto a sofa in the drawing room, Mary Chesnut gazed at the wounded Hood for the first time since he had left for Chickamauga. While Chesnut and Preston acted as if Hood sat in their midst completely unharmed, others gathered for a luncheon "looked as if it would be a luxury to pull out their handkerchiefs and have a good cry." As the ladies of the home attended to Hood, he received a plate of cut-up oranges. Hood remarked, "How kind people are! Not once since I was wounded have I ever been left without fruit, hard as it is to get now." Someone in the crowd remarked, "The money value of friendship is easily counted now. Oranges are five dollars apiece."[1]

There are relatively few historical monographs that directly describe the prominent role limb amputation played in the lives of either Confederate or Union soldiers. Yet, at times, amputation has occasionally been recognized for its role in shaping the amputees' quality of life and attitudes in a postwar society. In Hood's example, amputation had multifarious effects on his life, career, and on the historical memory of him as an officer. Hood, who would later be strapped to the saddle to command the Army of Tennessee, has been accused of depending on drugs and alcohol to deal with the pain from his injuries. One historian argues that Hood fathered eleven children in the postwar period in order to "refute any inference that he might be a 'lame' lover due to his crippled body." In this particular instance with Hood, amputation has been interpreted to hold the key to a wide range of personal manifestations, ranging from irrationality to chemical dependency to a fear of emasculation.[2]

However, it is clear that amputation had a far more nuanced and pervasive effect on southern society following the Civil War than has so far been acknowledged. Prewar notions of masculinity and manhood, as we have seen already evolving within a slave society, underwent still further transformations because of the war's trauma. In fact, the Civil War stripped away the masterful facade of honorable manhood through the return of physically altered southern men. Chiefly, although the war became a venue wherein Confederate men could find new definitions of individual and societal worth, it also produced new challenges to the older definitions. When a Confederate soldier faced permanent disfigurement from combat, the scalpel and saw, they had no idea how southern society would view their injuries. Would an amputee be able to find love in a physically shattered state? How would the hampering of their military career ambitions affect their status in society?

Amputation in the Confederate army initially presented a crisis in the definition of honor and manhood.[3] The Civil War challenged every definition of honor, manhood, and mastery in multiple ways. As the war came to ravage and scar the southern landscape, elite southern men lost the ability to define their manhood through mastery as land became barren and African Americans fled toward Union lines and the prospect of freedom. Although manhood was defined through multiple avenues, the critical disruption that the outbreak of the Civil War placed on southern society allowed the importance of other criteria, such as a solid marriage and the complete male physique to become relatively more important. Ultimately, southerners would view the actions of their soldiers as honorable. Confederate soldiers returned home without limbs to a world that had reassessed and reconfigured their definitions of manhood in order to allow amputees, who had risked their manhood by losing a limb, an honorable place in southern society. Southern men and women incorporated the imperfect southern male body within their traditional notions of manhood, and did so by blending traditional gender models within their celebration of their veterans and the construction of a Lost Cause mythology.[4]

With Hood leaving behind little written reaction to his amputation, we can turn to the experience of other amputated Confederate officers in order to understand the profound impact the injury played on the quality of their lives, both during and after the war. Though death was expected in defending a country, being maimed and rendered incomplete was more feared than death.

Confederate Lieutenant Colonel Henry Watkins Allen said, "A man ought always to expect to be killed in battle, and should be willing and prepared for death always before he goes into it." Courage, climaxed through death on the battlefield, remained a vital characteristic necessary for success in war. Allen's attitude offers insight as to why Confederate soldiers would reject an amputation. Though death was always a possibility in war, amputation could hinder the manly and noble effort through a soldier losing any part of his wholeness, instead of dying on the battlefield as a complete man. Interestingly, Allen was shot in the leg at the Battle of Baton Rouge on August 2, 1862, and refused amputation, saying that he "would rather die." For four months, Allen recuperated, but felt pain continually. In a letter, Allen wrote, "My right leg is giving me much trouble. I fear it will never get well!" Once Allen could use crutches, he visited his old regiment, the Fourth Louisiana, who "seized his hands and kissed them," while others "picked him up in their arms, embraced him, and bore him aloft through their camp, cheering and weeping as they went." Allen simply "wept like a child." Allen continued to believe in the Confederate cause, living in exile in Mexico in June 1865 as a physically whole man. He died the following year, owing to illness directly resulting from his injury, and that may have been avoided with amputation.[5]

The experience of Henry Watkins Allen allows us to see that the battlefield and the threat of amputation shaped the ways in which southern men, like Hood, regarded their own personal honor and the uncertain future that awaited them. So powerful were these concerns that the only option available to men desiring to control their fate was the desperate recourse of rejecting medical treatment. Though some men could view their scars as "badges of honor," a soldier could continue to find honor on the battlefield with a scar, but an amputation rendered that possibility an extremely difficult one, at best. Officers and soldiers chose to utilize the battlefield to exhibit valor and bravery as an avenue to define or redefine their manhood. However, while a soldier spent weeks or months in a hospital bed, the battle raged onward without them. Thus, to continue using the battlefield as a testing ground for honor and manhood, soldiers needed to return as soon as possible to continue the fight. Soldiers returned to battle in order to not lose a chance for self-definition by rejecting the option of amputation.[6]

J. S. Woods, a physician during the war, stated, "Amputation is almost never warrantable; but the prospect of success warrants the effort to save the life [at the expense of] the limb." The vast numbers of Confederate amputations were enough to disturb any doctor or soldier, for that matter. Within the Union ranks, 29,980 recorded amputation operations took place during the war. The Confederate medical records in no way match the accuracy of those of the North. Though the numbers may not be precise, estimates suggest nearly twenty-five thousand Confederates underwent amputation during the four years of warfare. The number of amputations seems low, compared to the number of gunshot wounds inflicted. From 1861 until the end of 1862, 77,293 gunshot wounds inflicted on Confederate soldiers were treated on the battlefield and in hospitals, with 4,241 soldiers not surviving, resulting in a mortality rate of 5 percent. In a study of the major amputations that targeted only 18,718 out of the estimated 25,000 total Confederates, a staggering 6,282 perished, with a fatality rate of 33 percent. The survival rate depended heavily on which limb was severed. More concrete data pertaining to Confederate amputations emerges from specific battle details. During the battles around Richmond in 1862, the following Confederate amputations took place: 45 of the forearm, with a 13 percent mortality rate; 192 of the arm, with a 28 percent mortality rate; 132 of the lower leg, with a 43 percent mortality rate; and 172 of the thigh, with a 59 percent rate of death.[7]

The reason behind the large piles of amputated limbs rests in the advanced weaponry of the war coinciding with Napoleonic tactics lagging behind technological improvements. With an importation of more than 500,000 Enfield rifles early in the war from England, the large size of the projectile, combined with a powerful discharge from the rifle, utterly destroyed human flesh and shattered bone to a point where it could not be stabilized and expected to heal. With a relatively low-velocity soft lead projectile, the bullet struck and shattered bone, splintering the flesh around it. Furthermore, "the wound would also be contaminated by bits of clothing the bullet carried with it." Thus, owing to the extreme structural damage and infection, the wound stood a minute chance of healing properly without amputation. If the injured limb remained, the body could become infected by "gangrene, blood poisoning or any number of other highly efficient killers." Amputation became a common tactic to ensure survival of the wounded soldier.[8]

G. M. B. Maughs, a physician serving during the war, offered his advice on when to amputate, considering amputation "the most serious and abused of field operations." He argued that amputation should only take place when the limb had been shot off, leaving an irregular stump, or when the limb sustained "injury to the large blood-vessels and nerves." Believing that surgeons rushed to amputation, Maughs hypothesized that amputation at or above the knee would result in a 50 percent mortality rate. Furthermore, as the cut moved closer to the pelvis, any amputation in the upper thigh resulted in a mortality rate of 80 to 90 percent.[9] Hood survived such an amputation, but with a high mortality rate, it was necessary for surgeons to exercise caution in every possible situation.

Yet, that was not always the case, and some surgeons fervently disagreed with Maughs. Francis Sorrel, in his medical report, noted the success of some Confederate operations near the hip, including Private James Kelly, General Richard Ewell, and General John Bell Hood. The success of these, and others, according to Sorrel, attested to "the skill and ability of Confederate Surgeons in the performance of an operation, regarded heretofore as almost uniformly fatal." When amputation did not take place for injuries above the knee, out of 221 cases, only 116 soldiers recovered, a survival rate of 52 percent. In terms of the seventy-seven who received amputation, forty recovered and thirty-seven died, a survival rate of 48 percent. Whether the injury above the knee underwent amputation or was left alone, the survival rates in both cases are quite similar. Sorrel called these figures "favorable" and "far surpassing . . . any heretofore reported or known to the profession."[10]

But, of course, no numbers can reflect the misery and pain associated with the amputation of a limb. For Confederate soldiers, chloroform, the anesthetic of choice in the South, could be administered if available, as well as a shot of whiskey. Yet, chloroform and whiskey did not always mean that the patient would have a painless ordeal. Postoperative pain had little remedy. Charles Hutson, recuperating from a wound attained at First Manassas, the first major land engagement of the war, wrote, "As the hospital was crowded with groaning men, some undergoing the agonies of amputation, I very gladly accepted the kind attention of a gentleman named Lamotte, who soon proved that he understood well the art of dressing wounds." Hutson understood the ramifications of amputation and was relieved that he did not have to undergo any further surgery. Sam Watkins, a private in the Army of Tennessee, witnessed the mortal wounding of General Lucius Polk and stated that, "General Polk's leg had been shot almost entirely off. I remember the foot being twisted clear around, and lying by his side, while the blood was running through the litter in a perfect stream." With the horrors of the hospital and battlefield fresh in mind, the memories of many soldiers contained several heart-rending recollections of pain and agony.[11]

As soldiers and officers alike entered the hospital tent, their thoughts tended to drift toward their family, their survival, their fellow comrades in arms, and also to their religion. Conversely, they often had to decide immediately whether they would allow their manly appearance to be altered in order to preserve their lives. The soldier could succumb to death, knowing that they had died an honorable death in battle. Yet, because they also defined their own personal manhood through the preservation of the physical wholeness of their physique, many soldiers rejected amputation, sometimes violently. Additionally, officers defined their manhood through the ability to lead their men into battle. Thus, the loss of a limb could render not only a loss of a command position but also the possibility of advancement in command. As the war progressed, soldiers received constant word from the home front on the destruction of property and routinely heard word on the flight of African Americans to freedom. The loss of capital, both in property and in slaves, threatened both the basis of mastery and the whole social fabric that developed masculine ideals. Ultimately, when a southern man rejected amputation, they rolled the dice and hoped that southern society would embrace their wound as honorable and continue to recognize their prewar status following the war. Therefore, rejecting amputation in order to maintain the complete male physique emerged time and time again in the latter stages of the war. Although many soldiers eventually succumbed to complications resulting from resisting amputation, for many this death was preferable to a loss of honor.[12]

For Confederate officers who accepted amputation, they faced a unique set of circumstances. Despite their own personal notions of honor, some officers turned to their personal physicians to make the decision. A Minié ball struck General Thomas "Stonewall" Jackson on the middle left finger at the Battle of Manassas on July 21, 1861. Jackson, who received injury while waving his soldiers forward into battle, received medical attention after the guns had ceased to thunder across the landscape. The regimental doctor examined his finger and declared that amputation needed to take place at once. Jackson refused and galloped off upon his horse to find Hunter Holmes McGuire, his medical director, who splinted the finger with two sticks. Jackson and his finger made a full recovery because Jackson preferred the advice of his own doctor. Jackson, knowing his own body and trusting McGuire's advice, chose to avoid amputation in order to remain available for combat at a moment's notice.[13] Jackson's example clearly demonstrates the interplay of different motives in determining whether or not amputation would take place. Furthermore, he presents a case of following the advice of a trusted surgeon over a desire to maintain a complete body.

The idea of returning to battle seems more plausible in Jackson's case, because he again faced amputation on the evening of May 2, 1863, during the battle of Chancellorsville. A Confederate volley raked Jackson and his officers during a reconnaissance mission. McGuire argued that the left arm required amputation and Jackson replied, "Yes, certainly; Dr. McGuire, do for me whatever you think is best." The amputation, two inches below the shoulder, commenced because Jackson agreed with the opinion of his friend and surgeon. With the risk associated with so many amputations, Jackson also knew that his surgeon realized the danger presented if the amputation did not take place. After the amputation, Jackson noted his new noble badge of courage, stating, "Many would regard them [wounds] as a great misfortune. I regard them as one of the blessings of my life." A captain responded, "All things work together for good to those who love God." Lee reflected on Jackson's amputation by stating, "He has lost his left arm, but I my right arm." As the myth of Jackson grew throughout the South, the Southern commander always, in the mind of the "Lost Cause," encapsulated the highest ideals of honor and manhood. In fact, Jackson viewed his wounds as a blessing from God. Unfortunately, for Jackson, the blessing transformed into pneumonia, which killed him on May 10.[14]

By Jackson declaring his missing limb a blessing, southerners could begin to see the honorable results of losing a limb for the sake of defending the Confederacy. Although several soldiers faced death because of complications after an amputation, many Confederate officers and soldiers lived with a missing limb as a constant reminder of their own personal sacrifice. Some men refused to allow amputation to ruin their internal definitions of manhood and followed a particular rule for discharged soldiers, "What you have lost in body, try and make up in energy, decision and mental vigor."[15]

Jackson was not the only high-ranking Confederate officer to undergo amputation and live, even for a brief period of time. On August 28, 1862, Major General Richard Ewell suffered an injury at the hands of a Minié ball that struck his kneecap at the battle of Groveton, Virginia. Ewell's attendants came to his aid at once, but he exhorted, "Put me down and give them hell. I'm no better than any other wounded soldier." Initially, Ewell insisted on amputation, hoping that an operation would expedite a return to command in the field, even though Doctor Hunter McGuire refused and hoped to save the leg. Jubal Early also tried to convince Ewell to save the leg, and eventually, Ewell conceded. However, the doctor found the leg in horrible condition. As Campbell Brown, who examined the leg after amputation, wrote, "When the leg was opened we found the knee-cap split half in tow [sic], the head of the tibia knocked into several pieces and that the ball had followed the marrow of the bone for six inches breaking the bone itself into small splinters and finally had split into two pieces on a sharp edge of the bone." As the surgeon prepared for surgery, Ewell stated, "Tell the doctor that I will be if it shall be cut off, and that these are the last words of Ewell." As the saw began to cut the bone, Ewell horrifically remarked, "Oh My God."[16]

Ewell barely survived the operation and ended up six miles away at a home called Dunblane. Ewell emerged as a minor celebrity among the women. During his recovery, as one lady remarked, "He impressed us all as not only heroic and strong but as having the nicest consideration for others." Class trumped the notion that a missing limb could render a wound anything but a noble scar. After he recovered, Ewell departed the care of the women at Dunblane and headed to Richmond. A woman remarked as he left, "We missed all the pleasant things, but worst of all we missed the man whose fortitude and patient endurance had drawn our hearts to him."[17]

Ewell's experience at Dunblane reveals a dependency on the women who ushered in the healing process. Men even joked that veterans missing a limb would invoke greater sympathy from southern women and had a better chance with the ladies than those who had survived the war intact. Women noted, "The cause glorifies such wounds" and "A hand is a bad thing to lose, but it won't hurt you among the ladies of Savannah." As the *Southern Field and Fireside* magazine asked, "What but a woman 'makes the Confederate soldier gentlemen of honor, courage, virtue and truth, instead of cut-throat and vagabond?'"[18]

Thus, when the defeated amputated men returned home, they had to be dependent on women not only for recovery but also for assistance in reconstructing their shattered manhood from their wartime failure. Historian LeeAnn Whites argues that the trials of devoted women allowed the fulfillment of gender ideals as written by an Augusta editorial in the postwar period. Prior to war, southern men, the "towering oaks," shared the landscape with women, who represented a "clinging vine." Once the war shattered the southern landscape, the "oak was riven by a thunderbolt, its spine cracked." The vine now had to "hold the splintered oak erect, it if would only cling around with its caressing tendrils and bind up its shattered brow." In other words, the love of a devoted woman could begin the process of reattaching the broken limbs to the shattered tree of southern manhood.[19]

The reliance on women may increase further if the amputated soldier returned to find his property destroyed or his slaves freed. Thus, the Reconstruction era allowed the crisis in defining manhood to move from the battlefield to the household. When men returned home, what remained of the household provided an arena for defeated soldiers to reassert their manhood. For Confederate amputees to be perceived as an honorable and masterful man in their own households, they needed to function as regularly as possible. Serving as an integral part and head of the household could continue the public ritual of asserting and maintaining some sense of mastery. Yet, some men were wounded to the point that they needed the assistance of a loving woman in the transition back to society. At the same time, women used this opportunity to assert female mastery over their wounded husband. While women gained a unique type of authority through caring for their wounded mate, they did not attain complete mastery, as societal ideals of mastery trumped individual circumstances within households. Thus, amputated men embraced the household as an appropriate arena to reassert mastery.[20] No matter what the case, women were crucial in shaping the constructions and reconstructions of manhood in the postwar period.

The haunting image of broken limbs scattered across the southern landscape haunted women in life and in sleep. The time necessary to prove worth in battle remained a source of contention for some women. One southern woman wrote her husband after Shiloh, stating, "If you could come home now, I think you ought to be satisfied; you have been in a hard fought battle; and won glory enough, certainly for me." In a letter to her husband, Will, on January 22, 1863, Emma Crutcher recalled a dream she had about him. She wrote, "But when I fell asleep again, I dreamed that you did come home, not exactly as I had imagined, however. I thought a middle aged gentlemen called on me one day, told me he was an army surgeon—that Captain Crutcher had been wounded in the leg—not however to endanger his life, for he was rapidly recovering and would be home in a few days." The dream did not reveal the death of her husband, but an injury that would render him to a condition of being "lame for life." When Emma learned of his amputation, she wrote, "And my only sensation was maximized joy! Now, thought I, he will never leave me again, for he will be of no use, in the army, and—if I die, he will never marry again, for no one but me would love a lame man—he is mine now."[21]

The absence of her husband during the war altered how Emma Crutcher defined herself as a woman. Victoria Bynum argues, "The ideals of feminine duty so carefully inculcated in white women from birth—ironically, as a means of ensuring social stability—strengthened the convictions that underlay women's disorderly behavior." Thus, any women who encouraged their husbands to desert undertook unruly behaviors. In order for a woman to define herself as a woman, she needed the company of a man. As Elizabeth Fox-Genovese argued in her discussion of slaveholding women invoking "honor," women "were invoking an ideal of excellence that could not be divorced from their identification with their men."[22] In other words, women needed men to understand the gender boundaries that defined womanhood. In theory, a man would never walk out of a relationship if he needed his wife to care for his lifelong injury. At the same time, women made demands on their husbands to return home and return the household back to the way it had always been, with a woman defining herself through her husband. In her mind, as well as the minds of women across the South, a maimed man could only remain dependent on his wife, who would understand and embrace the noble scar. Emma Crutcher herself wrote, "I read, somewhere once, and was much struck with the novelty of the idea, that the study of your dreams was one of the best methods of arriving at self-knowledge—that there, and only there, could we see our motives divested of all the self-deceptions." In a way, the dream of the injured husband brought to the surface all the concerns and feelings that Crutcher held in the midst of war. Yet, she defended herself as not being selfish in the dream. She stated, "If I am selfish, you have fostered that feeling in me. But you came home and the meeting was all my imagination pictured, and I awoke, sighing that it was not reality, lameness and all. If I only regarded my own feeling without thinking of duty, I had rather take you now, lamed for life, than wait for months and maybe years longer, with the chance of [not] having you back with me." As Crutcher exemplifies, the horrific experience of war left Confederate women searching for their husbands to return to them, in any form that would reinforce and reestablish a pattern of men once again placing the family before duties to the country.[23]

In fact, the Confederate government issued a call to women for reaction to Confederate amputees. After the loss of Atlanta to Union General William Sherman in September 1864, beleaguered Confederate President Jefferson Davis embarked on a goodwill tour of Georgia. Sensing a growing disillusionment among the Confederate populace, Davis stopped in Macon on September 23 to speak to a crowd containing a large female contingency. Davis called on the southern women to build a new aristocracy. He said, "When the war is over, and our independence won, (and we will establish our independence,) who will be our aristocracy? I hope the limping soldier." Davis predicted an honorable place for the wounded Confederate veteran. Yet, the returning soldiers could not embark on the journey alone. Davis remarked, "To the young ladies I would say when choosing between an empty sleeve and the man who had remained at home and grown rich, always take the empty sleeve. Let the old men remain at home and make bread."[24] The future of an honorable aristocracy did not rest in the men with complete male physiques who had avoided military service. It rested in the new honorable man: the amputated war veteran. In order for a new aristocracy to replace the old order, Confederate women would be pivotal in their preference for amputees over whole men.

Yet, what would happen to the women who did not heed the call of Jefferson Davis? In particular, women could undergo social ostracizing from the southern populace and even in the southern newspapers. In one instance, two women were traveling by streetcar in New Orleans, when a gentleman, described as a "Knight of the Crutch," who, despite his amputated limb, took the women's tickets to the box at the front of the car, a traditional act of chivalry on New Orleans streetcars. As the amputee hobbled toward the front, the women sat silently, ignoring the act of chivalry. Unfortunately, for the women, one eyewitness vented his frustration in the local newspapers. He cried, "Did you thank him? Not a bit of it! Isn't it a gentlemen's duty, whether he has one leg or two, to wait on and be polite to a lady? Certainly it is! But were you two ladies? Perhaps so!" The man went on to remark that women needed two attributes to possess the ideals of " 'true-lady-hood': courtesy, and a delicate thoughtfulness and consideration for the comfort and convenience of others, especially the unfortunate." It appeared a social crime that the women refused to act in a cordial manner to the gentlemen, but his war injuries made the situation even more embarrassing for the stature of New Orleans women on streetcars throughout the city. The witness concluded with a sarcastic prediction, stating, "I wonder if you two are 'Women's Rights' women? If so, how will you manage to get your 'tickets' into the ballot box independent of the assistance of a gentleman with or without a crutch?" After some thought, the writer concluded, "I suspect that you are 'Women's Rights' women, and, before dismissing you, I would advise you to think seriously of this matter, for gentlemen are sometimes just a little tricky on Election Day."[25] The experience on the streetcar draws attention to a host of local and national political issues during the Reconstruction era. Furthermore, the definitions of womanhood on New Orleans streetcars remained dependent on women acting courteous and thoughtful to their gentlemen assistants, especially if the gentlemen sacrificed a limb during the war.

Yet, for the most part, southern women did not need a call from the president to realize their necessary role in assisting amputated men. While in Richmond, Lizinka Campbell Brown, Richard Ewell's fiancée, emerged as his primary caregiver. Brown, daughter of a former senator and minister to Russia, had been described as "an able, strong-minded woman." According to eyewitnesses, she materialized as the guardian of her fiancé's health and spirits. Visitors noted how she was "watching over him with sleepless vigilance and cheering him by hopeful and recreative converse." In a letter to Ewell, Brown wrote, "While I sympathize in your terrible suffering and loss, it is only womanly to remember that one of its consequences will be to oblige you to remain at home and make me more necessary to you."[26]

For Lizinka Brown, the definition of womanhood underwent reconstruction, as she now faced the reality of her future husband's injuries. In order to feel vital to the war effort, the injured man had to place his livelihood in the hands of the willing and devoted woman. Yet, the injury also secured any fears that Brown had about the status of her own relationship with Richard Ewell. In a way, amputation provided more security to a relationship that could be tested with flirtation from the female throngs for the heroic generals. At the same time, she also implies that not many women would care for an unwhole man, making her sacrifice in caring for an amputated man the adhesive securing the two individuals in a relationship. She wrote, "That whereas I thought before you ought to marry and could very well marry a younger woman, now I will suit you better than any one else, if only because I will love you better." In her mind, Brown's love and devotion expanded with amputation and Ewell would have no choice but to remain dependent on her love and care. In fact, once the two married and Ewell returned to battle, she went with him and not only took care of Ewell, but also his military affairs. Colonel James Conner said, "She manages everything from the General's affairs down to the courier's who carries his dispatches. All say they are under petticoat government."[27]

The case of Richard Ewell remains a fascinating place to examine the importance of appearance and character in shaping men's notions of manhood in the postwar era. One afternoon, Ewell, walking down the street with his wooden leg, encountered a major who, upon seeing the leg, asked, "Does it hurt?" Ewell thought the major to be jesting but then noticed that the major also had a wooden leg. Thus, he replied, "Yes. Does yours hurt you?" The major paused and said, "No. I have gotten accustomed to mine." In this brief conversation, the major reinforced how Confederates dealt with the daily reminder of sacrifice.[28]

The sacrifice did not go unnoticed. On another occasion, Ewell spoke with Duff Green, another man who had lost a leg in the Civil War. As their conversation commenced on a street corner in Richmond, a factory owner from Georgia saw the two injured men looking "homely" on the street and offered them jobs at his factory. The gentlemen instantly recognized the sacrifice of the men, more visible than a wound covered by clothing, and offered his services. Yet, the factory owner assumed that the missing legs signaled Ewell and Green being lower class. Owing to their physical injuries, it would have been difficult for either amputee to assert an honorable and masterful appearance on a street corner. Nevertheless, Ewell and Green turned down the man, who did not realize they had been officers in the Confederate army. He said, "Well gentlemen I beg your pardon but you looked like common folks mightily." The factory owner, like others throughout the Confederacy, sought to provide maximum care for those who visibly gave life and limb for their glorious cause. Also, Ewell and Green did not take the remarks of the factory owner as an insult to their honor. In the antebellum era, the factory owner's remarks may have precipitated a duel for failure to recognize an honorable gentleman. Instead, the former officers both understood the fluctuating nature of manhood and accepted the owner's remarks as nothing more than charity easily deflected. Amputation had changed the notion of honor because appearance no longer guaranteed recognition of class and elite status in post-Confederate society.[29]

The interplay between Ewell, Green, and the factory owner conveys the crisis in manhood in the postwar South. With the system of slavery destroyed and the landscape of the South in shambles, elite southern gentlemen could not longer guarantee that others on the street would recognize their status, formerly rooted in public rituals designed to display honor and mastery. Southerners could have utilized the complete male physique to define manhood. Yet, with calls from Jefferson Davis for amputees to emerge as the new aristocracy, the line between the elite and the common wounded soldiers in the postwar period blurred beyond recognition. Amputated men did not perceive manhood in the same manner as society, forming a fraternal bond between amputated Confederates. At the same time, as Elliot Gorn has argued, scars reflected the marks of lower-class men who had to resort to fistfights, duels, and outright brawls to protect their manhood.[30] Thus, the factory owner recognized Ewell and Green as "common folks" because of the scars they had received throughout the course of the Civil War, which, prior to the war, had been recognized as signs of lower-class status. Furthermore, neither Ewell nor Green at the time exhibited any part of the public rituals necessary in the antebellum era to prove honor and mastery. Thus, post-Confederate society had to adjust their antebellum notions of manhood to accommodate the elite men who had not only lost their slaves and maybe their property but also had been scarred by the horrors of war.

Edward Pollard, a newspaper writer, wrote an impassioned description of Ewell. He stated, "The spectacle of a worn and mutilated man looking prematurely old, mounted on a white horse that had often snuffed the battle with defiance, but was now scarcely more than a crippled skeleton." Despite the "sorrowful picture" created by Ewell wandering the streets in a "dilapidated sulky," Pollard recognized the devotion exhibited by Ewell. He said, "It was a sorrowful picture but a nearer view disclosed a man remarkable even in the ruin of health and constitution, whose gray eye was as sharp and fierce as ever, and whose precise conversation showed that the vigor of his mind was as yet untouched."[31] In the experience of war, all men suffered and sacrificed. Yet, for the amputee, the picture of sacrifice, despite the condition of the soldier, always remained in focus.

Using the experience of other Confederate amputees, we can garner a better understanding of the experience General John Bell Hood may have faced with his amputation. Even with the lack of medical records for Hood, it seems plausible that his personal journey through amputation would resemble that of other Confederate officers. Following his first wounding at Gettysburg, Hood refused to stand by and watch the rest of the war progress. He needed to exhibit his manhood through his ambitious agenda to reach the top of the military command ladder, and thus he needed to return to the battlefield as quickly as possible. Yet, the proving of manhood was costly as Hood lost his leg at Chickamauga. From the battlefield at Chickamauga, Hood traveled to Augusta and then to Wilmington, North Carolina, before moving on toward Richmond. On his journey, according to the *Richmond Enquirer,* Hood found his escorts in surgeon Darby, General Gustavus Smith, and his wife. Hood and his party traveled by "an elegant and comfortable car belonging to and lent by a liberal citizen of Augusta." On his journey, Hood remained in "fine spirits" and was "not suffering from his wounds," despite an earlier attack of typhoid fever. The paper called Hood a "brave and distinguished officer" and hoped he would "resume his post in the field, and again make the enemy quail before his prowess."[32]

With the rumors of his death behind him, as well as adequate progress on the healing of his wounds, John Bell Hood's approval from the Confederate citizens rose to new heights as he quickly recovered. Hood wrote to General John Robertson on January 2, 1864, stating, "I am improving daily, and hope soon to be able to ride and walk again." His speedy recovery allowed him to attend many societal events. In particular, one evening, Miss Mary Preston, dressed as a member of a Greek chorus, delivered a charade entitled "Knighthood":

> *Knight,* is my first, my second is a name
> That's doubly linked unto enduring fame;
> The gentle poet of the Bridge of Sighs,
> The hero, cynosure of the tenderest eyes.
> HOOD, whose keen sword has never known a stain,
> Whose valor brightened Chickamauga's plain;
> Well might he stand in glory's blazing roll
> To represent to future times my whole;
> For goodlier Knighthood surely never shone
> Round fair Queen Bess upon her stately throne
> Than his, whose lofty deeds we proudly call our own.[33]

Hood's presence in the city during the winter of 1863–64 made him an instant celebrity, as scores of women flocked to see the amputated general. Just like Richard Ewell before him, Hood had seen action in the war and had lived to tell the stories of heroism and failure. The constant attention forced Hood to experience a "hectic flush of fever on his face." Hood said, when visiting with Mary Chesnut, "This is the first house I have had myself dragged to. I mean to be as happy a fool as a one-legged man can be. But send me off now. So many strangers scare me. I can't run as I did before."[34]

When Hood made his first public appearance on horseback in January 1864, the Richmond press made immediate note of the event. Hood "appeared on Main street, groomed by a single servant; his lost limb supplied by an artificial one." As Hood tested out riding a horse for the first time since Chickamauga, a "crowd of spectators congregated on the sidewalks, and hats were instinctively lifted from scores of heads, while cheers broke forth from several points." Even though Hood needed the support to heal from his injuries, it is no wonder he returned to the field of battle in March 1864. The thrall of the crowds, as well as his desire to once again find honor in battle, led Hood to finish the war on the battlefield. The press noted that "The General rode erect, and well, 'like Harry with his beaver up,' and his appearance gave promise of an excellent report of himself when he again appears on the field." Hood later remembered that his restoration exceeded expectations and permitted that he never required an ambulance upon return to battle.[35]

Throughout his recovery period, John Bell Hood consistently called on Mary Chesnut for friendship and carriage rides, of which Chesnut happily obliged. Hood asked Chesnut to throw him a casino party, go to taffy pulling with him, and called on her for a carriage ride where the two discussed Mr. Chesnut in a flattering manner. On one ride, Hood asked a friend of Chesnut, Mr. Brewster, what the symptoms were of a man being in love. Brewster stated, "When you see her, you breath is apt to come up short. If it amounts to mild strangulation, you have it bad. You are stupidly jealous, glowering with jealousy, and with a gloomy, fixed conviction that she likes every fool you meet better than she does you." Hood replied, "Well, I have felt none of these things so far, and yet they say I am engaged to four young ladies. That's a liberal allowance, you will admit, for a man who cannot walk without help."[36]

Hood's gallant deeds and the loss of his limb drew suitors, from the likes of Sally Preston and Louly Wigfall. Mary Chesnut paid a visit to the Wigfall residence and found Hood "stretched full length on a sofa with a rug thrown over him." With Hood nearby at the gathering, Wigfall's father joked that as Chesnut departed for the ride, her husband had asked "if he should have a doctor for the party when you get back, since it was freezing out of doors." Then, Wigfall remarked that Chesnut replied she would not risk freezing "even for any two-legged animal in the world." Chesnut did not appreciate the attempt at humor and scolded her guest. "You have been too long in Texas. Your jokes are too rough," stated Chesnut. "Where is your American prudery, to talk before ladies of legs, off and on?" Furthermore, Chesnut proclaimed, "And never did I dream that people would say such things about a man's horrible mutilation before his face." Wigfall could only declare himself "ill-bred."[37] Thus, Mary Chesnut understood the important role women had to play in order to facilitate the recovery process of wounded Confederate officers and soldiers. Chesnut may have made the remark earlier, but found it completely inappropriate to jest at the expense of a wounded individual who had sacrificed in the war. She thought it hypocritical for socialites to ostracize anyone, especially when they themselves had avoided military service altogether.

Throughout his recovery, Hood had forged a friendship with Jefferson Davis and his family. Hood even accepted an invitation to sit in the Davis pew at St. Paul's Episcopal Church. Davis helped Hood down the steps after the service. As Hood remembered, "Often President Davis was kind enough to invite me to accompany him in his rides around Richmond, and it was thus I was for the first time afforded an opportunity to become well acquainted with this extraordinary man, and illustrious patriot and statesman of the South." Hood flattered Davis on numerous occasions, including when Davis had offered vocal criticism of the Confederate officers in the field. Hood responded, "Mr. President, why don't you come and lead us yourself? I would follow you to the death." Hood's future career in the Confederate military would escalate further from the friendship forged with Davis. Davis learned to trust in Hood and would call on him to report details from the battlefront.[38]

On the evening of February 5, 1864, Hood attended a reception at the request of Jefferson Davis and received a "perfect ovation." At the reception, Mr. Preston helped navigate Hood through a crowd of well-wishers, "handling him as tenderly on his crutches as if he were the Princess of Wales's new-born baby." Hood departed the reception for an evening at Ives's Theater aboard a carriage with a host of ladies, including Sally Preston. When the party arrived at the theater, Preston sat behind Hood, instead of next to him. Mary Preston turned to Preston and stated, in French, "Don't you see this man is making you more conspicuous, twisting his neck off, looking back, than if you would come sensibly alongside." Sally Preston responded, "Stop it! Do you suppose nobody speaks French but you?" Major Von Borcke, a Prussian officer who was in attendance, remarked, "And if she scolds you in German, I will understand." Preston caved into pressure and reluctantly sat next to Hood. Despite the initial cold treatment from Preston, Hood enjoyed the evening. Breckenridge remarked, "Watch Hood! He has not seen the play before and Bob Acres [the actor] amazes him."[39]

The relationship between John Bell Hood and Sally Preston dominated his period of recovery. In the spring of 1863, Hood traveled to Richmond routinely and spent time with the Chesnut family. At the time, Sally Preston resided with the Chesnuts, and when Hood requested to meet her, Preston declined. Mary Chesnut described Preston as "the very sweetest woman I ever knew" but also that she "had a knack of being 'fallen in love' with at sight and never of being 'fallen out of love' with." Yet, Preston, according to Chesnut, had the uncanny ability to cast "a spell upon her lovers," to the point where many ended up "killed or died of the effects of her wounds." In one instance, when Chestnut asked her nephew, Johnny Chesnut, if he had any romantic interest in Sally Preston, Johnny cried, "No, never." He continued, "I dare not. I would prefer to face a Yankee battery. They say So-and-So is awfully in love with Miss S.P. Then I say, look out! You will see his name next in the list of killed and wounded."[40]

Hood told his friend John Darby his thoughts on Preston. When anyone asked Darby what the general had said, he replied, "Only a horse compliment—he is a Kentuckian, you know. He says, 'You stand on your feet like a thoroughbred.'" Hood later admitted that he "surrendered at first sight" upon seeing Preston and admitted to her that every time he went into battle, he fought for "god, my country and you!" Despite his feelings, Hood still had to deal with the stigma of Preston being quite the coquette of suitable gentleman. With his injuries, Hood became quite the ladies' man as well, rumored among the gossipers of Richmond as being attached or engaged to several women. On one occasion, Hood admitted to Preston that Richmond society had him betrothed to four different women, of which one included Preston herself. She responded, "Richmond people are liberal, as you say. I never heed their reports. They say I am in engaged to Shirley Carter and to Phil Robb." Hood replied, "I think I will set a mantrap near your door and break some of those young fellows' legs, too."[41]

With Preston's track record, Hood remained diligent in his romantic pursuit, even after the wounding curse cast true. Chesnut told Preston, "It was odd . . . that Hood was always lucky till he fell in love with you." Yet, Preston continually avoided showing true romantic interest. Despite displaying a cold shoulder toward Hood, the general did not give up his pursuit of Miss Preston. One evening in February 1864, Hood brought Preston along with him to an evening with the Chesnuts. Hood and Preston arrived with a man by the name of Cy. Preston stormed out of the carriage and declared, "He [Hood] spoke so harshly to Cy as we got out of the carriage. I saw how he hurt Cy's feelings, and I tried to soothe Cy's mortification." Hood responded, "You see, Cy nearly

Hood and the Experience of Confederate Amputees

caused me to fall by his awkwardness and I stormed at him. But she salved it over. She told Cy how good he was, and I could not do without him." Preston responded, "I hate a man who speaks angrily to those who dare not resent it!"[42] While Hood laughed off the matter as a "good joke," it was clear that Sally Preston sent Hood a clear signal that his feelings of admiration and romance were anything but mutual.

Surely, Hood knew how Preston felt about him. Yet, she continually sent mixed signals. During another night at the theater, Chesnut reported, "The crowd surged that way, and she [Preston] held out her arm to protect him from the rush. After they had all passed she handed him his crutches, and they too moved slowly away." Preston, in some ways, felt obligated to protect her "wounded knight." Thus, Hood remained continually optimistic. On a ride one evening with General Breckenridge to visit Mary Chesnut, she asked Hood, "How did you enjoy the ride? I saw you from the window." Hood's reaction consisted of no smile, but "a lazy queer twinkle of inward delight in his eye." Hood remarked, "Oh, a delicious day. I am dying to tell somebody, and I know for her sake you will be cautious. You see, I asked her [Preston] if she liked me as well as anybody else." Preston responded with a yes. Hood pressed again, asking "Better than anyone else?" Preston repeated her previous answer. So Hood pushed further, inquiring, "Then will you let me try to make you love me?" Preston responded, "That's just as you please." Hood noted her response echoed with "cool indifference."[43] Though Hood remained romantically optimistic, Chesnut certainly realized that the exchange of feelings failed to produce a blossoming romance.

With such a public relationship, many in Richmond naturally assumed that Hood and Preston were engaged to one another. One evening, Hood and Varina Davis, the wife of the Confederate president, attended a dinner party. As the two sat in conversation, both Davis and Hood overheard Preston in another room of the house, proclaiming, "Engaged to that man! Never! For what do you take me?" The sadness that encapsulated Hood's brow forced Varina Davis to change the subject. She told Hood of an officer who, after hearing of Hood's injuries, said "he would wince and dodge at every ball." Hood melancholy responded, "Why wince when you would thank God for a ball to go through your heart and be done with it all?" Davis later told a friend that the event displayed a "high tragedy" and Hood had "the bitterness of death in his tone."[44]

Despite any hurtful remarks, Hood refused to discount Preston, and the two announced an engagement in February 1864, after Hood pressed the issue on several occasions. During one carriage ride, Hood held out his hand and

Preston stated, "Ah! Don't do that. Let it all rest as it is. You know I like you. You want to spoil all." Hood replied, "Say yes or say no. I will not be satisfied with less. Yes—or no, is it?" His ultimatum caught Preston off guard, and as he continually held out his hand to her, she panicked and put her hand into his. Hood's demeanor immediately changed and Preston later told Chesnut, "I pulled my hand away by main strength." Hood declared at once that he would speak to her father and seek his permission for the engagement. Yet, when she told Mary Chesnut the engagement story, Chesnut doubted her sincerity and simply remained unconvinced that Preston truly liked Hood.[45]

Even though Hood needed physical and emotional support to heal from his injuries, remaining in Richmond did not afford him the opportunity to prove his worth as the Civil War continued to rage. The chaotic courtship of Sally Preston did little for Hood in terms of securing his manhood in the face of amputation. Thus, it is no wonder Hood decided to return to the battlefield in March 1864, taking a commanding role with the Army of Tennessee. The recovery period allowed Hood to visit with General John Breckenridge in Richmond. Breckenridge spoke eloquently to Hood, stating, "My dear Hood, here you are beloved by your fellow-soldiers, and, although badly shattered, with the comfort of having done noble service, and without trouble or difficulty with any man." In the opinion of Breckenridge, Hood's stature for service to the Confederate army did not decline with the unfortunate wound that resulted in his right leg being amputated four inches below the hip.[46]

In fact, Hood's devotion to the cause, and his willingness to return to the field of battle in 1864, continued his personal quest for military recognition and, at the same time, would solidify his relationship with Preston. The battlefield allowed Hood to return to a place he knew how to operate away from the excess of societal social circles. Hood had the opportunity to remain behind in a civil appointment but refused, and stated, "No bomb-proof place for me; I propose to see this fight out in the field." Hood thought his return to war would strength his romantic relationship, but that backfired. Preston spoke candidly about Hood's injuries, stating, "I never cared particularly about him, but now that he has chosen to go with those people, I would not marry him if he had a thousand legs, instead of having just lost one." Preston indicated that Hood's injuries would not force her to love him, despite Hood's hopes that Preston could be there for him. Yet, as the talk among Hood's friends and associates, as well as the town became "leg, leg, leg," referring to Hood's amputation, Preston refused to change her feelings about her suitor. She ultimately became romantically involved with another man and refuted the gossip of Hood's supporters, who had become critical of Preston for rejecting the injured officer. She confronted the gossipers and deflected criticism by referencing someone else in their social circle. "Don't waste your delicacy! Sally is going to marry a man who has lost an arm, so he is also a maimed soldier, you see; and she is proud of it. The cause glorifies such wounds."[47]

Preston made it a point to halt any further criticism by pointing out that she would still love and care for an amputated man, even if his name was not John Bell Hood. Preston eliminated any guilt she may have acquired by leaving Hood by courting another amputee. Although the cause rendered the Confederate sacrifices to a glorious position, the cause could not push Preston to love Hood. By the end of the war, the romance had died permanently, despite Hood's repeated and persistent attempts to ignite a romance between the two.[48]

When the Civil War drew to a dramatic close, southern men could no longer define manhood through antebellum notions of honor and mastery or the complete male physique, as some officers returned physically shattered. When Confederate amputees, like John Bell Hood, returned home to a world devoid of slavery, southern society reconfigured their notions of the complete male physique to make room for the incomplete war hero. Because the Confederate soldier and officer fought for an honorable and manly cause, society recognized the sacrifice displayed in a visible red badge of courage by not allowing an absent limb to become a symbol of feminization. As amputees adjusted to a new form of manhood in the postwar period, so did women. Confederate women, who had sacrificed throughout the war, continued their sacrifice and ensured the love of a man by offering unconditional support in reconstructing personal notions of manhood.

Manhood underwent redefinition, as independence, exhibited through wealth and through physical mastery, no longer stood at the center of manhood. Manhood now could include recognition of some dependency in a loving relationship. The love of a wife and the support of a community could provide the necessary crutches for the Confederate amputee to survive and readjust to the fluctuating world void of slavery and honorable public rituals. In other words, women and a supportive society could fill the "empty sleeve" by fulfilling masculine notions of bravery and honor. Without them, Confederate amputees, including John Bell Hood, may have given in to the feminized ideal of the South, presented by a victorious North. Thus, some officers, like Hood, returned to the battlefield to reassert their manhood and continue their ambitious goals. Yet, a return did not necessarily equal success, which Hood would discover in due time.

Chapter 5

"A Forlorn Hope": The Quest to Save Atlanta

It was natural enough, after the failure of General Johnston to check our advance, other tactics should have been employed, and no man could have been found who could have executed this policy with greater skill, ability and vigor than General Hood.
—*General Frank Blair*

When John Bell Hood departed Richmond to return to battle, he believed that he could assist the Confederacy in achieving victory. However, Hood did not return to the Army of Northern Virginia, where he had gained military renown over the previous two years. Hood, now permanently detached from the Army of Northern Virginia, joined the Army of Tennessee at Dalton, Georgia, as a corps commander on February 24, 1864, under the command of General Joseph E. Johnston. In fact, Confederate officials had wanted him to return to battle within a few weeks of his injury. As early as October 1863, Braxton Bragg kept President Davis up to date on Hood's condition, writing, "He is reported much improved." Bragg wanted Hood to be promoted to command a corps with the Army of Tennessee. By the end of the year, Hood's name even emerged as a recommendation to Jefferson Davis to fix the command problems in the Trans-Mississippi West. Ultimately, Hood would end up with the Army of Tennessee. Yet, in a letter to Davis on February 6, Herschel Johnson questioned the selection. He said, "I have thought much about your sending Genl. Hood to Genl. J[ohnston]. I know his gallantry and merit. But is it not well to consider seriously whether he is physically equal to the arduous duties of the position?"[1] Davis disagreed and decided to let time judge whether or not Hood had reached a physical point suitable for a return to command.

Despite Hood's injuries, President Davis sent him not only because he trusted him as a commander, but also as a friend and confidant. Their friendship had been solidified through carriage rides, dinner parties, and church services during Hood's recovery in Richmond. Davis knew that Hood would provide details on the state of Johnston, a man the president simply distrusted and in some ways, despised. When Hood returned to command with the Army of Tennessee, his allegiance would always lie with his commander in chief, with whom he had formed a personal friendship in the midst of resurrecting his honor following amputation.

On the field, however, Hood would have to pledge his allegiance to his commanding officer, Joseph E. Johnston. Johnston had commanded Hood in early 1862, when Hood's Texans charged against a Union force at Eltham's Landing. Johnston, who had been wounded in May 1862 at the Battle of Seven Pines, had not come into contact with Hood in several months. Yet, Hood's growing reputation preceded him, as Johnston called for Hood on February 18, stating, "Lieutenant General Hood is much wanted here." When Hood stopped to visit Sally Preston in Columbia, South Carolina, Johnston had telegrammed to Hood, "We want you much," and stood excited about what Hood would bring to the army as a corps commander. Once Hood arrived at the end of February 1864, Joseph Johnston breathed a sigh of relief. He wrote to Senator Wigfall, stating, "Hood's arrival gave me much comfort," and a month later, he wrote, "My greatest comfort since getting here—indeed the only one in a military way—was Hood's arrival."[2]

Even before Hood arrived in Georgia, he had been placed in a difficult position. Davis had sent him to keep an eye on Johnston, from whom Hood would receive orders during the upcoming campaign. As a corps commander, Hood had the responsibility of leading several thousand troops into battle under the direction of Johnston's orders, something he had never done. In fact, in the last two major battles, Hood had to leave the field because of injuries from shot and shell. If Hood did not agree with the orders, or if Johnston acted in any way that Hood thought hurt the chances of Confederate success, he was supposed to write to Davis. With Hood wanting his return to battle to be a successful endeavor, he needed to achieve success, both in the eyes of the public and in they eyes of his commander in chief, who could promote him to command an entire army. Hood would have to walk a delicate tightrope, balancing his responsibilities as a subordinate commander to Johnston and an informant to Jefferson Davis. Furthermore, he would now again have to adjust to leading a new group of men with whom he had not spent months forming bonds that aided the leadership process.

Johnston, despite his disfavor with Jefferson Davis, received command of the Army of Tennessee in December 1863. The appointment came out of sheer desperation, from Davis's point of view. Though Braxton Bragg had achieved a resounding Confederate victory at Chickamauga in September 1863, he failed to hold the city of Chattanooga, particularly when Grant arrived to take command of all Union forces in the Chattanooga area. By the end of November, Bragg and his army had been driven into northern Georgia, in a state of utter disarray. The Confederacy continued to face a loss of soldiers, both through desertion and death. Now, with the state of Tennessee in Union hands, Chattanooga could be used as a launching point to invade other areas in the Deep South. Jefferson Davis had no choice but to turn to Johnston, to reshape the Army of Tennessee into a fighting force that could keep the Union out of the heart of the Confederacy.

As commander of the Army of Tennessee, Joseph Johnston possessed, according to one soldier, the confidence of everyone "except the stragglers—who have not manhood enough to fight." Johnston possessed "skill as a strategist" and had the ability to place an army into the field that was "tolerably well disciplined and tolerably well officered." With Johnston instilling confidence back into the Army of Tennessee, he now had a corps commander in Hood who could assist in protecting Georgia from the Union armies. However, many of the soldiers in the field wondered if Hood's injuries would alter his ability to effectively command, especially because he had returned to the field of battle so quickly after surviving an amputation with an 80 percent mortality rate. Yet, Hood proved himself healthy in the months following his new appointment, saying, "I have been riding all over this country with Gen. Johnston and have been in the saddle every day enough to have fought two or three battles, without feeling any inconvenience." Witnesses concurred with Hood. General Wheeler told Bragg that Hood "rides fourteen or fifteen miles a day without much fatigue." When Hood arrived with the army, he brought a carriage, according to Halsey Wigfall. Yet, Hood sent the carriage back "and rides everywhere on horseback. He is out nearly every day and rides from twelve to fifteen and twenty miles without dismounting." Hood even expected to soon "walk with a cane."[3]

Joseph Cumming recalled seeing Hood throughout 1864. He wrote, "He wore a wooded leg, but except when in the saddle, moved only on crutches. In this campaign, leaving in the morning his quarters of the night before, he would go on crutches to the side of his horse, pass the crutches over to an orderly, and while another orderly would support him from behind, he would raise his left food into the stirrup." The orderly would then have to pass "the right wooden leg over the horse's back, and place the right wooden foot in the stirrup. Thus mounted the General could ride long distances at a slow pace." The soldiers called Hood "Old Pegleg." Even with his injuries, Hood persevered. Thomas Clayton, serving as an engineer with the Army of Tennessee, wrote a letter to his wife Emma. Clayton said, "Gen. Hood is one of the best men I ever saw in my life. I feel sorry for him every time I see him. He is so badly crippled but it is astonishing how he can use himself, can mount his horse alone, with only one leg and one arm—one having been so much disabled by a wound as not to be able to use it."[4]

For his first task back in the saddle, Hood faced a precarious situation, as General Ulysses S. Grant, now commander of all the Union forces, set into motion a grand overland campaign in the spring of 1864. Grant, riding with the Army of the Potomac, would attack Lee in Virginia. Grant instructed Major General William T. Sherman, in command of Union forces around Chattanooga, to move into Georgia, with his sights set on the Army of Tennessee and Atlanta, a major industrial city and rail center in the heart of the Confederacy. If Sherman captured Atlanta, he would sever the Confederacy's ability to transport military provisions across the South. Johnston and the reconstructed Army of Tennessee had to hold Georgia at all costs, if the Confederacy wanted to achieve victory in the Civil War.

In the midst of preparing for the Union invasion, Johnston remained unaware of the clear motive behind Hood's correspondence to Jefferson Davis on the army's status. Johnston did approve the first letter to Davis, in which Hood merely offered that the army could use "an addition of ten or fifteen thousand men" in order to advance. Hood offered his eagerness "for us to take the initiative." He further requested more horses for the artillery to prepare for the oncoming offensive. Because Davis perceived his corps as being made up of mostly "untried troops," Hood also "hope[d] to do good work." With Davis perceiving Hood's command position as challenging, if Hood could find success, his favor could only continue to grow. In his letters to Davis, Hood assured the president that he wrote with the best interests of the Confederacy in place. Hood remarked, "You find, Mr. President that I speak with my whole heart, as I do upon all things in which I am so deeply interested." "God knows I have the interest of my country at heart," Hood wrote, "and I feel speaking to you that I am so doing to one who thoroughly appreciates and understands my feelings."[5]

Hood wrote not only to Jefferson Davis but also to Braxton Bragg, who now assisted Davis with orchestrating the war behind a desk in Richmond. Hood needed time to assess the state of the army. He wrote, "I am an earnest friend to the President and am ever willing to express my ideas in regard to the coming campaign." In another letter, Hood told Bragg, "How unfortunate for our Country, it is for the Generals in the field to fail to cooperate thoroughly with the Authorities of the Government and not act together. I can't express to you how much it worries me." Hood conveyed to Bragg that in the coming campaign, Johnston may not act aggressively enough to save Atlanta. Hood understood the importance of an offensive maneuver. If Johnston moved north, he could recapture Chattanooga and gain momentum to retake Tennessee and Kentucky. Hood noted that "to retain Tennessee would be of more value to us [Confederacy] than a half dozen victories in Virginia." Johnston, however, decided to keep his defensive position at Dalton, Georgia. Hood wrote, "I . . . am sorry to inform you that I have done all in my power to induce General Johnston to accept the proposition you made to move forward. He will not consent." [6]

Yet, for Johnston, moving his force to retake Chattanooga was not a simple task. As Joseph Cumming remembered, "Sherman had a powerful veteran army of quite double the size of Johnston's." Cumming also saw the terrain as being advantageous to Sherman's move toward Dalton from Chattanooga, which Sherman did with increasing pressure. Johnston expected Sherman to attack his right at Dalton along Rocky Face Ridge and used Hood's corps to protect the ridge. Hood's corps did participate in some light skirmishing along the ridge on May 8. However, Sherman sent the brunt of his attack against the Confederate left along Dug Gap. Johnston was about to be flanked, which meant the Union army could cut off his main line of supply, the Western and Atlantic Railroad, about fifteen miles from Dug Gap.[7]

Thus, Johnston decided to pull the Army of Tennessee out of Dalton and move South to Resaca, a town on the Western and Atlantic Railroad that would protect his supply line. Joseph Johnston later said, "At Dalton the great numerical superiority of the enemy made the chances of battle much against us." Even if Johnston had been able to strike a decisive blow against Sherman, the Union forces "had a safe refuge behind the fortified pass of Ringgold." Hood wrote to Davis and Bragg and told them how an offensive movement would be necessary, but Hood concluded, "It is for the President and yourself [Bragg] to decide."[8]

On May 12, 1864, the day when Johnston would order all of his army to protect Resaca, John Bell Hood paused to partake in a religious ceremony.

Shortly after midnight, Hood received baptism from Leonidas Polk, an Episcopal bishop from Louisiana, through some rainwater that had been collected in a "tin cup of ordinary army variety." Colonel Walter Rogers, an eyewitness to the baptism, remarked that Hood "looked happy and as though a burden had been lifted." Another eyewitness, who stood in the shadows, reported, "There stood the battered old hero (barely thirty years old). There the Warrior Bishop Polk. And there stood your humble servant with a flaring tallow candle in one hand and a horse bucket of water in the other."[9]

The details of Hood's religiosity prior to his baptism are sketchy. We do know that Hood attended church services during his recovery in Richmond. Yet, no records indicate he was religiously active as a child. As a wave of religious fervor swept through both Union and Confederate forces throughout the war, Hood joined his fellow soldiers in finding a deeper purpose in life. Of note, Hood asked Polk to baptize him at a critical juncture in his life. Although he had participated in some light skirmishing already, Hood's corps would surely see major combat action in the coming days, particularly with the speed that Sherman's army had advanced. It seems reasonable that Hood paused to cleanse his soul in preparation for the upcoming military engagements. Hood also could utilize the baptism to bond with his fellow soldiers, who also may have been caught up in the religious fervor.

Hood had found success in battle earlier through his close relationship with his Texas Brigade. However, in Georgia, Hood now commanded a group of men he had never met. No bond of trust existed prior to Sherman's advance. Hood's reputation from his days fighting in Virginia did give him some leverage. Captain George C. Binford, part of the Eighteenth Tennessee in Hood's corps, said, "I expect we will like him very much." Thomas Clayton wanted to serve "with Hood for he will give me a better opportunity to learn and improve myself than anyone else." With Johnston placing Hood's corps at positions he perceived as critical, Hood would have to use success in battle to bond with his soldiers.[10]

Hood tried to replicate his command style, which had worked effectively in Virginia, with his new corps in Georgia. He issued a brief note "to say to the officers and men of this corps that though he comes among them a stranger he trusts they will not be strangers long." In his new role, Hood wanted "to share their hardships and their dangers, their pleasures and their triumphs." Hood knew that his men had to have the right amount of discipline and willingness to comply with orders if the corps were to achieve "the highest point of military efficiency." He concluded, "A short period will perhaps elapse before the opening of the campaign. Let us employ each day with singleness of purpose in perfecting our drill, our organization, and our discipline, and we may confidently await the trial of arms."[11]

At Resaca, Hood had again been placed on the right portion of the Confederate line. The Union army moved forward on May 14, lightly skirmishing along the right portion of the line. Hood wrote to Johnston, stating "The enemy is advancing—they are now in the vicinity of my infantry skirmishers. They are extending also to my right—I am rapidly getting ready to meet them." Though Hood's corps had been successful in the skirmish, Confederate scouts discovered the Union line was vulnerable on the left. Johnston repositioned some of the Confederate forces and at 4 p.m., Hood attacked the Union left. One Illinois soldier saw Hood's line "formed in admirable order, their flags floating gaily, many of their officers mounted, and a light line of cavalry riding in the rear and upon either flank." As Hood's corps charged forward, a shrill rebel yell echoed across the landscape. Union troops fell back. Chaplain Deavenport observed, "The enemy were driven hastily from their entrenched position, leaving knapsacks, haversacks, guns." Yet, Union soldiers had been repositioned to stop the onslaught of Hood's advance. Hood wrote to Johnston, "The enemy are now extending to my right." Darkness fell, forcing Hood to wait until the next morning to continue his attack.[12]

Hood wanted to attack the next morning. However, Johnston received word of Sherman bringing up reinforcements. If Hood attacked, his corps, which had been successful the day before, could face obliteration. Hood staved off an assault by Union troops on the afternoon of the fifteenth, but he did not attack, as Johnston discovered Sherman was again about to outflank him. Johnston, in order to save his army, pulled out of Resaca and headed south along the Western and Atlantic Railroad toward Adairsville. With a large amount of open terrain, Johnston had to come up with a better strategy to stop Sherman's advance. He decided to create the illusion that his army had gone to Kingston, to the east. Anticipating that Sherman would divide his force at Adairsville, Johnston placed the bulk of his army at Cassville, to the southeast, where Hood would await the arrival of the divided Union army and attack. Johnston, who was baptized by Polk on May 17, believed he finally had Sherman where he wanted him in order to achieve victory.[13]

Johnston ordered Hood to attack the Union forces on May 19. As Hood marched forward during the midmorning hours, he noticed a large force of Union soldiers to his right, which had the ability to flank his army. Hood halted the attack and pulled back. Johnston changed strategy and decided to pull the entire Confederate force back a few miles and wait for Sherman to attack. Johnston declared to the army, "You will now turn and march to meet his advancing columns . . . Soldiers, I lead you to battle." Morale soared in the ranks with the opportunity of battle. Hood would be able to deliver a striking blow from the new position, yet he never attacked because of the appearance of Yankee cavalry. Joseph Cumming recalled, "Unfortunately this promising movement was thwarted by General Hood's failure to attack owing to wrong information communicated to him by one of his staff officers." Johnston concluded that he had "to cancel the attack and order Hood to withdraw," and his army needed to fall back toward Allatoona Pass. Thus, the morale changed as one staff officer said, "I could not restrain my tears when I found we could not strike." Johnston's plans for destroying the Union army at Cassville fizzled under the weight of numerical superiority. After Johnston's military decision, Burton Butler remarked, "It is said around here that Genl Johnston is flanked on the right and left, which forces him back but he says his army is in good spirits and eager for a personal engagement."[14]

After the war, Johnston reacted to the failed attack at Cassville and accused Hood of fabricating the report of Yankee cavalry in the vicinity that halted the attack. Johnston wrote, "[Hood's] erratic movement [was based] upon a wild report." Hood had displayed, according to Johnston, "extraordinary disobedience." Hood responded that Thomas C. Hindman, who had suffered casualties at the hands of the fabricated Yankee cavalry, served as proof enough of the situation and concluded, "It was not a mistake."[15] In a strange twist of fate, Joseph Johnston, the chronic retreater, had wanted to fight, but John Bell Hood, the chronic fighter, opted instead for retreat. Johnston, as commander of the army, made the decision to call off the attack and again gave Sherman the advantage by retreating farther into Georgia.

Hood, angered at two thwarted attempts to attack at Cassville, vented his frustrations back to Richmond. On May 21, 1864, Hood sent Colonel Brewster, a personal friend, to see Jefferson Davis and personally deliver a letter. He wrote, "Colonel Brewster has been with us since we left Dalton and can give you an account of the operations of this army since the enemy made their appearance in our immediate front. He leaves for Richmond today and I think it would be well for you to have a conversation with him in relation to our affairs." Hood slightly changed his tactic of reporting to Davis by sending an eyewitness, who happened to be a personal friend, to report on Johnston's lack of aggressiveness. Though Hood's actions again defy military maxims of how to treat a fellow officer, especially a superior officer, Hood had to obey his president. The reports not only won Hood continued favor with Davis, but also plunged Johnston's reputation to new lows, despite all he had done to rebuild the Army of Tennessee. Davis, when speaking to Mary Chesnut, noted how Johnston had routinely rejected the imploring of Hood to attack and that "so much retreating would demoralize General Lee's army."[16]

With Johnston pulling the Army of Tennessee south to Allatoona Pass, the two armies did not attack one another for about a week. Sherman continued to advance, forcing Johnston to again move his army to avoid being flanked. Hood's corps, moved to the southwest, took up a position at New Hope Church, where on May 25, 1864, Hood, outnumbered four to one, attacked a Union force. The fighting location, later known as the "hell hole," witnessed repeated assaults. Hood boldly inflicted 1,600 casualties, while only suffering three hundred. One soldier from Mississippi called the early action in north Georgia "our debut or introduction to the famous Georgia campaign, which was followed by a series of hardships, battles and skirmishing for several months afterwards, picket fire never ceasing day and night."[17]

Hood requested to attack again at New Hope Church on the twenty-eighth, but the repositioning of the Confederate forces had been sluggish, with frequent pauses. The terrain proved a more formidable deterrent in the middle of the night than the weakened Union force, which should have been ahead along Little Pumpkinvine Creek. As Hood arrived, Wheeler's cavalry discovered Union forces had moved up on the other side of the creek and had dug in, forming a strong series of breastworks. When word arrived at Johnston's headquarters of the strong Union position, Johnston again cancelled his plan for Hood to attack. In his memoir, Johnston again blamed Hood for repeating the mistakes of Cassville at New Hope Church. In reality, the Union troops had not completed moving to the other side of the creek. But, "Hood's weary, sleep-starved troops were forming in the jungle-like woods for an assault."[18] With a larger Union force dug in at a strong position, Hood, if he attacked, could have committed a costly error.

Despite the recent failures of the Army of Tennessee to defeat Sherman's army, Sidney Champion, in a letter to his wife, wrote, "Johnston will whip Sherman at this point—our force is inferior to the enemy—but we are [a] determined army—hopeful and cheerful—and our leader is a great man." Champion, a soldier among the ranks, assessed that Johnston's strategy "is so far above our comprehension—that we can't understand it until we see its effect." Thus, Champion and his fellow soldiers, who noted that "Johnston has inspired the army with renewed confidence and great enthusiasm," felt certain that Johnston would "rank in history next to Genl R E Lee." Joseph Cumming, another soldier in the Army of Tennessee, realized that the army had retreated ninety miles, but said, "Every time it was attacked it had repulsed the attacks; every time it fought it had been victorious." Johnston had always withdrawn the army "in perfect order, and had not left behind a single piece of artillery, or even an ambulance or any of its wounded" and ensured the soldiers "had been regularly and abundantly fed."[19]

While Sherman waited for the rest of his army to reposition at Allatoona, Johnston again repositioned his army along the mountains north of Marietta, Georgia. As the Confederates awaited the arrival of the Union forces, an artillery shell struck General Leonidas Polk on June 14 and killed him. Hood wrote to Johnston, lamenting, "I am too sad to come over this evening. 'Tis hard that one so noble generous and brave as our friend . . . should be taken from us." Yet, the absence of Hood's spiritual counselor did not deter him from aggressive military action. Hood's corps continued to be repositioned as Sherman extended his lines, resulting in his corps being moved southwest to Kolb Farm on June 21. The next day, Hood attacked on his own accord, without orders from Johnston, forcing the Union to fall back. General Jacob Cox, a Union commander, noted the "good generalship of the effort." Despite the effort, however, the Union force could not be dislodged. Hood incurred more than 1,500 casualties, compared with only two hundred Union.[20]

With Sherman again closing in, Johnston remained concerned about his ability to hold his position just west of Marietta at Kennesaw Mountain. Yet, the position did afford Johnston the opportunity to dig in. He awaited the attack from Sherman, which came on June 27, 1864. The attack, which commenced at 8 a.m. with artillery, bled both armies. As Dr. T. P. Lockwood, a surgeon from the Sixth Mississippi, stated, "Wounded Confederates, wounded Yankees, wounded Negroes, and wounded foreigners from the slums and scums of Europe. . . . Many of them sick with pneumonia. The first night my ward alone was crowded with 160 of these wounded." A long night awaited the doctor. The following morning he remarked, "There were eighty of the wounded and sick dead in the ward, and the remainder in a critical and pitiful case." The victory for Johnston came at the expense of about seven hundred soldiers, compared to Sherman losing nearly three thousand in the frontal assaults.[21]

In the course of a week, the Army of Tennessee engaged in two major offensive maneuvers. Though Hood failed to achieve victory at Kolb's Farm, Johnston gained a triumphant victory at Kennesaw Mountain, in a campaign that had so far been marred by flanking maneuvers and the appearance that Johnston had only retreated. In the course of two months, Johnston had given up ground, but the city of Atlanta remained, for the time being, safely in Confederate hands. Johnston had lost only a few thousand casualties in two months, compared to several thousand that Lee lost during a similar series of maneuvers and battles in Virginia during the same weeks. By Johnston attacking at Kennesaw, he proved that when the time was right, he would attack. Despite his victory, Johnston could not hold his position, as Sherman, with the numerical upper hand, again attempted to outflank Johnston. With Johnston having to abandon Kennesaw Mountain, the reality set in that sometimes you have to fight, even if the time and location are not of your choosing.

By early July, even with a victory at Kennesaw Mountain, Johnston had retreated all the way to Atlanta, exposing north Alabama to Federal forces. With the Confederacy's crucial supply of saltpeter for gunpowder coming from the caves of northern Alabama, as well as Sherman now approaching the gates of Atlanta, Jefferson Davis grew more anxious in Richmond. Davis wrote to Johnston to warn him of the situation. Johnston replied, "We have been forced back by the operations of a siege, which the enemy's extreme caution and greatly superior numbers have made me unable to prevent. I have found no opportunity for battle except by attacking entrenchments."[22] Johnston's reply sent a message to the Confederate president that the attack at Kennesaw may have been a fluke, in terms of the grand scheme of the campaign. With the already bad blood between the two men now reaching a boiling point, Davis wanted a clear plan from Johnston on how he would attack Sherman. Without it, Johnston would set into motion a series of events forcing Davis to make a decision he felt would be the best hope of saving the Confederacy.

As Sherman pressed to capture Atlanta, grumbling emerged over Johnston's lack of an aggressive strategy to stop the Union advance. One Confederate citizen sarcastically remarked, "I think old Johnston will clean out Sherman in a few days. I know we will . . . when we fight." Johnston had written Bragg after Kennesaw Mountain, stating that he had been unable to stop Sherman, mostly owing to the larger force as well as the flanking maneuvers the Union army utilized. On July 9, the Confederate army pulled back behind Peachtree Creek, north of Atlanta. President Davis, frustrated with Johnston, sent General Braxton Bragg to "proceed to Georgia" and "confer with Johnston." Bragg would now serve as another eyewitness, beyond military reports and the letters from Hood, on the state of the Army of Tennessee. When Bragg arrived, he reported, "Our army is sadly depleted" and he found "little encouraging."[23]

Jefferson Davis stood at a crossroads. He had to make sure Atlanta held for the sake of saving the Confederacy, particularly with Lee now under siege at Petersburg. Davis still hoped that the northern populace would become disillusioned with the war, to the point where they would elect someone in November's presidential election who would negotiate an end. Davis's grudge against Johnston could have resulted in his removal from command earlier in the campaign, especially before the attack at Kennesaw Mountain. Yet, Davis wanted to see what Bragg would report. Bragg's arrival did little to promote enthusiasm among the troops. Robert Patrick, a Confederate soldier, wrote, "The army hates him, and cannot endure him." He remained upset that Bragg received more pay that Lee, yet "he remains in Richmond doing nothing." Patrick, exploring his own pessimism, thought that if Bragg was in town, "we may expect to hear of something gone wrong in a few days." The Confederate soldiers knew that if Bragg had arrived to personally survey the army, a change in command could come within a few days.[24]

Hood informed Bragg of the several failed opportunities to take the offensive in the preceding months. In a letter delivered to Bragg in person, dated July 14, 1864, Hood reiterated that over the course of the last two months, "we had several chances to strike the enemy a decisive blow. We have failed to take advantage of such opportunities." While at West Point, Hood had been schooled in the importance of the defensive position as clearly superior on the battlefield. Yet, he had also learned the importance of aggressiveness. Hood knew that Bragg and Davis wanted someone in command who could aggressively attack Sherman in order to win a military, social, and political victory. Hood described the current position of the army as a "very difficult one" and urged "we should not under any circumstances allow the enemy to gain possession of Atlanta." Hood claimed to have offered offensive suggestions, declaring, "I have, general, so often urged that we should force the enemy to give us battle as to almost be regarded as reckless by the officers high in rank in this army, because their views have been so directly opposite. I regard it as a great misfortune to our country that we failed to give battle to the enemy many miles north of our present position." Hood concluded that he wanted Bragg to tell Davis that he "shall continue to do my duty cheerfully and faithfully and strive to do what is best for our country, as my constant prayer is for our success."[25]

Bragg sent a brief declaratory note to Davis on July 15, initially stating, "The best interests of the country demand a change but policy dictates some delay. Hood is the man. I write fully by messenger today." After having time to complete a full report, Bragg jotted down, "I have made General Johnston two visits, and been received courteously and kindly. He has not sought my advice and it was not volunteered. I cannot learn that he has any more plans for the future than he has had in the past." Bragg did report a high level of morale among the army and believed that Johnston now stood "more inclined to fight." Yet, among the corps commanders, Hood had always insisted on attacking, while Hardee had concurred with Johnston in favoring "the retiring policy." Bragg decided to endorse Hood, with some reservations. He wrote, "If any change is made Lt. Gen. Hood would give unlimited satisfaction, and my estimate of him, always high, has been raised by his conduct in this campaign." Bragg stood impressed with Hood's reputation and actions on the current campaign and believed that he would achieve what Davis wanted in an effort to save Atlanta. However, he called Hood not "a man of genius, or a great general." In the current situation, dubbed by Bragg as an emergency, Hood was "far better . . . than anyone we have available."[26]

While Bragg advocated for a change in commander, Davis had to make the ultimate decision. He could accept Bragg's recommendation and select Hood or he could turn elsewhere. He could choose William Hardee, a corps commander in the Army of Tennessee. However, Davis had offered Hardee command of the army after Bragg and he turned it down, forcing Davis to select Johnston. The other corps and division commanders had not distinguished themselves enough to draw notice from Davis. He could also have looked outside the Army of Tennessee. Robert E. Lee could not and would not abandon the Army of Northern Virginia in the trenches protecting Petersburg.

Davis could have turned to P. G. T. Beauregard, but he had failed to distinguish himself since the early victory at Manassas. Beauregard had declared victory on the first day at Shiloh, but had been handily defeated the following day. Beauregard had also given up Corinth, a bad sign for a president who needed someone to fight to protect a city. Davis could have asked Bragg, but with Bragg's performance with the Army of Tennessee at Chattanooga, he would have not been able to survive the ramifications from both his government and the soldiers if Bragg returned to command. In the end, John Bell Hood was the only logical answer, considering the need to save Atlanta and the desire to appoint a commander who would not easily give up the city.

Jefferson Davis turned to Robert E. Lee to help figure out who should command the Army of Tennessee. Davis asked Lee, "General Johnston has failed, and there are strong indications that he will abandon Atlanta. He urges that prisoners should be removed immediately from Andersonville. It seems necessary to relieve him at once. Who should succeed him? What think you of Hood for the position?" Lee did not advise a change in command at the time he issued a telegram, stating, "I regret the fact stated. It is a bad time to release the commander of an army as that of Tennessee. We may lose Atlanta and the army too." Yet, when Lee sat down to write a letter, he realized that Davis planned on changing commanders. He said, "I had hoped that Johnston was strong enough to deliver battle. If Johnston abandons Atlanta, I suppose he will fall back on Augusta. This loses us Mississippi and the trans-Mississippi communications." Lee wrote that "Hood is a good fighter, very industrious on the battle field, careless off, and I have had no opportunity of judging his action, when the whole responsibility rested upon him."[27]

As an army commander, Lee had opportunities to witness Hood lead a brigade and a division when Hood led attacks at Gaines' Mill and Sharpsburg. Yet, Lee, in his correspondence to Davis, now failed to give his full endorsement for promoting Hood to command. He hinted that Hood might not be fit for full command duties, despite his earlier hopes that Hood's ability would fill the void left by the death of General Jackson. Also, it is not clear what Lee meant when referring to Hood as "careless off" the field of battle. Lee had spoken to Hood about his soldiers' behavior but never disciplined him. It is possible Lee was referring to Hood's men chasing chickens or the ambulance episode that led to Hood's arrest. Whatever the reason, Lee hesitated to endorse Hood.

More important, Lee also removed himself from the feud between Davis and Johnston. By not fully endorsing Hood, Lee spared himself from becoming involved in the internal strife within the Confederate government. At the end of the letter, Lee again presented a contradiction, "I have a high opinion of his gallantry, earnestness and zeal."[28] Lee ultimately believed that Hardee had more experience with managing an army, but Davis would never be able to ask Hardee again, especially after an earlier refusal at another critical juncture. Lee understood the dangerous situation the Army of Tennessee faced. By remaining ambivalent about Hood, Lee spared himself any burden of blame for Davis's decision. Lee never made clear which is more important: combativeness or managerial skills. Davis needed a fighter and ignored Lee's hesitation to endorse Hood. In the end, combativeness won over managerial skills, as Hood ascended to the commanding rank.

Even with a change in commander necessary in Davis's mind, he had to give Johnston credit for rebuilding the shattered Army of Tennessee throughout 1864. Johnston wrote about his army to Davis, stating, "These troops, who had been for seventy-four days in the immediate presence of the enemy, laboring and fighting daily, enduring toil, exposure and danger with equal cheerfulness, more confident and high spirited than when the federal army presented itself near Dalton." Here, Johnston reiterated how he had rebuilt a shattered army from scratch.[29] Yet, despite his high standing among the soldiers and his ability to rebuild and supply an army, Johnston commanded a force that had allowed Sherman near the gates of Atlanta.

On July 16, Davis requested that Johnston reveal his plans for the current military crisis. Johnston responded, "My plan of operations must . . . depend on that of the enemy." Johnston further painted a portrait of ambivalence in his response, stating, "We are trying to put Atlanta in condition to be held for a day or two by the Georgia militia that army movements may be freer and wider." Davis had heard enough. The following morning, a courier handed Brigadier General Samuel Wragg Ferguson, a member of the South Carolina cavalry, an order received in the midst of bullets flying "fast and thick." Ferguson remembered, "It was the order relieving Genl. Johnston and placing Genl Hood in command. For the first time in the war, my heart failed me and I doubted of our ultimate success." Johnston's telegram from the War Department stated, "I am directed by the Secretary of War to inform you that, as you have failed to arrest the advance of the enemy to the vicinity of Atlanta, far in the interior of Georgia, and express no confidence that you can defeat or repel him, you are hereby relieved from the command of the Army of Tennessee." The telegram orders that Johnston "immediately turn over to General Hood" control of the army.[30]

The same day, Hood received a note from Secretary Seddon, stating, "You are charged with a great trust. You will, I know, test to the utmost your capacities to discharge it. Be no less wary than bold." When Hood received word, Thomas Clayton said, "I [never saw a] man astonished in all my life. . . . This army will now have some fighting to do I expect. Hood has been oppressed all the time to falling back." In his memoir, Hood called the promotion an event that was "totally unexpected." James W. Ratchford, Hood's adjutant general, claimed after the war that Hood appeared shaken and requested that he had Ratchford "say nothing about it to anyone." When Lieutenant Halsey Wigfall went to congratulate Hood on the promotion, he noted, "He [Hood] spoke very sadly and said he hardly knew if it were a subject of congratulations." Wigfall believed that Hood "seemed to feel very fully the weight of responsibility thrown upon him."[31]

Johnston responded to the orders in a telegram written to the secretary of war. He said, "Your dispatch of yesterday received and obeyed—command of the Army and Department of Tennessee has been transferred to General Hood. As to the alleged cause of my removal, I assert that Sherman's army is much stronger, compared with that of Tennessee, than Grant's compared with that of Northern Virginia." Despite the superior force, Johnston proclaimed, "Yet the enemy has been compelled to advance much more slowly to the vicinity of Atlanta than to that of Richmond and Petersburg, and penetrated much deeper into Virginia than Georgia." In a reference to Hood, and possibly Hood's reports to Davis, Johnston concluded in a sharp tone, "Confident language by a military commander is not usually regarded as evidence of competence."[32]

Johnston sent Hood a note of congratulations in the early morning and Hood responded, "I accept your congratulations. . . . I desire to have a conversation with you, and for that purpose will be over early in the morning." Johnston agreed and met with Hood, offering advice on the necessity of attacking before he departed. After being removed from command, Johnston now understood that Davis wanted an attack at all costs. However, Hood, as well as fellow corps commanders Hardee and Alexander Stewart, met with Johnston and decided to issue a telegram pleading to postpone Johnston's removal, at least until the situation at Atlanta ended. Unfortunately for Johnston, the president and many citizens of the South wanted Atlanta not given up without a clear fight. Davis, after weeks of riding the fence, firmly stood his ground, rebuffed the telegram, and said, "A change of commanders, under existing circumstances, was regarded as so objectionable that I only accepted it as the alternative of continuing a policy which has proven disastrous." The change of command took place to "promote the general good." Davis declared that the order "had been executed and I cannot suspend it without making the case worse than it was before the order was issued." Thus, Hood would take Johnston's place immediately, which he acknowledged by informing Davis, "I have assumed command of the army and department of Tennessee."[33]

As he departed, Johnston issued an address to his soldiers. He stated, "I cannot leave this noble army without expressing my admiration of the high military qualities it has displayed." The army, throughout the campaign, exhibited "endurance of toil" and "brilliant courage." Johnston promised to watch their future victories. He concluded, "To one and all I offer the assurance of my friendship, and bid you an affectionate farewell." General C. H. Stevens responded, "We know you were doing the best possible, and we would hail with joy your return to command us. Our most sincere well wishes for the future. You have the love, respect, esteem and confidence of the officers and men in this brigade." One soldier recalled, "We passed his headquarters. He stood with head uncovered. We lifted our hats. There was no cheering! We simply passed silently, with heads uncovered. Some of the officers broke ranks and grasped his hand, as the tears poured down their cheeks."[34]

As Hood ascended to command of the army, Confederate newspapers took up the issue of changing commanders at a critical juncture. The situation appeared to some as if a "national calamity" had taken place. The soldiers were "disheartened and disgusted" over the removal of Johnston at "the climax of his campaign," according to the *Charleston Mercury*. "A Southern army is a huge ganglionic nerve," remarked the paper, which has a continual flow of "intelligence and individuality as can be found in any mass of the community." With the damage done, the newspaper tried to inject optimism, because Hood remained "popular as he is with the army" and he would receive all the necessary support from "the people and the general government . . . which Johnston . . . has but partially received."[35]

Other newspapers appeared dumbfounded, and the appointment excited "much surprise." Though no one could deny Hood's early military success, he had failed to garner accolades since his separation from the Texas Brigade. One newspaper writer noted, "Other division commanders have been as successful as Hood." The reporter wanted Hardee to be appointed because of his "seniority and by greater experience to the promotion." "When and where," the writer questioned, "has Hood displayed the capacity to command one of the largest armies of the Confederacy and to conduct a campaign on which the salvation of the cause in a great measure depends?" Despite Hardee's earlier refusal of command, the writer was not ready to accept Hood as the best choice.[36]

Newspapers, hesitant to fully endorse Hood, offered other suggestions beyond Hardee. The situation in Atlanta "calls for an officer of proved ability of the first order." The commander deemed most appropriate for the position was Beauregard, and he should have been sent "if a malignant jealousy, unparalleled outside the bottomless pit, could be quenched for love of the country." Beauregard's service in holding Petersburg before Lee arrived made him a natural choice for newspaper editorial staffs. But, as one writer noted, "a cold snaky hate must be gratified at whatever cost to the country. To appease this hate, people in Georgia must be sacrificed as cheerfully as were the people in Mississippi and Tennessee in the days of Pemberton and Bragg." Though Hood had been admired by the newspaper writer, Beauregard ultimately got the endorsement to command the army.[37]

Despite the mixed reviews from the newspapers, Hood had to concentrate his energy on the reaction of the men who now served as his corps commanders in the Army of Tennessee. When Major General Patrick Cleburne received word of the change, he remarked, "Oh, Hell, Oh, Hell. Issue the order to the troops." William Hardee, irked at being passed over for command despite his early refusal, would have resigned if Atlanta had not been swinging in the balance. Samuel French declared his sorrow for Johnston's removal, and Benjamin Cheatham also expressed "regret." Hood would have preferred someone else to command his old corps, but he listened to Hardee, who argued that "Cheatham was the best man at my disposal." Cleburne, who by no means rooted for Johnston, believed that William Hardee deserved the commanding position. Thus, for John Bell Hood, the men he counted on to orchestrate the upcoming campaign remained cautious, suspicious, and even openly hostile about Hood's promotion.[38]

The reaction of the corps commanders, in many ways, mirrored the soldiers' reactions within the ranks of the Army of Tennessee. Word of Johnston's removal traveled quickly. James Palmer, a soldier from Mississippi, noted in his diary that the removal of Johnston caused "great dissatisfaction among the soldiers for they all loved Johnston as a protector and guide." First Lieutenant John Henry Marsh wrote that the removal of Johnston "caused the greatest gloom that has ever been known to pervade this army. But we have reconciled ourselves to the change; and earnestly hope it is for the best." William Harvey Berryhill wrote, "Hood is a great General but cannot manage to keep up the spirit of the army as Johnston did." With Johnston gone, Berryhill noted "some signs of demoralization" and he heard "of desertions occasionally."[39]

The man who had rebuilt the Army of Tennessee from the shattered fragments created by Braxton Bragg departed after spending several months leading the men, and earning their respect and admiration. J. P. Cannon observed strong men weeping, "while others cursed, and not one approved the change." Johnston held "the confidence and love of the army of Tennessee" and "no man in the Confederacy, not even the great Lee himself" could have replaced Johnston at a time when Sherman held "three men to our one." A Texas soldier wrote, "Every soldier's head hung low when we heard that our gallant commander had to give up the command of the Army." Captain Kay, an artillery commander, said, "Every man looked sad and disheartened and felt that evil would result."[40]

Robert Patrick, the Confederate soldier who had earlier expressed his displeasure with Braxton Bragg, blamed Bragg for the removal, stating, "I have no doubt old Bragg has something to do with this." Patrick noted that, "Hood is a fighting man. When we first fell back below the Chattahoochee Hood insisted upon Johnston fighting the enemy there." Yet, even with the fighting spirit induced by John Bell Hood, Patrick hesitated to give his endorsement in a full-scale attack against Sherman. He wrote, "This is all very fine talk, but we are not strong enough to go into a pitched battle. If we had been, Johnston would have tried it long before this." In the end, the respect and admiration for Johnston could not be denied. Patrick ascertained, "From what I can learn the army is dissatisfied with the change."[41]

Hood did have the benefit of the soldiers knowing his reputation. Sidney Champion wrote, "Hood will make a few commands but the army had every confidence in the old Genl [Hood] and are willing to trust him." Alex Spence, a member of the First Arkansas, wrote, "They know he will fight—the Federals will never be able to get Atlanta. We will hold it at all hazards." A few days later, Spence noted, "The troops have the utmost confidence in Genl Hood's ability as a commander, and all are satisfied to go where he says go."[42] The Spence family correspondence reveals that Hood had earned the trust of some of his soldiers.

Hood needed victories to solidify any respect or admiration from his men. His army suspected why he had been given command. Joseph Cumming said, "General Hood was obviously appointed to the command of the army, under implied or expressed orders to abandon Johnston's wise policy and to attack Sherman at any hazard." The victories Hood sought would have to come against a superior Union force that had held Johnston at bay for several weeks. Hood simply had to prove himself on the battlefield, not only to his soldiers but to the southern populace. He possessed a reputation in the southern papers as "not only to be a fighting man, but a man who knows how to fight." As John Snow wrote, "He has never commanded an army before, but he has shown himself a fine officer as a division and corps commander. He has the characteristic of being a fighting character." Snow, who knew Hood would fight, thought the replacement of Johnston would "very soon bring matters to an issue."[43]

Sherman, commanding the Union force, learned of Johnston's replacement through the Georgia newspapers. Grant wrote to Sherman, stating, "General Johnston has been relieved of command and General Hood takes his place, much to surprise of the army and public; also that this change indicates that there will be no more retreating, but that Atlanta will be defended at all hazards and to the last extremity." Sherman asked General John Schofield about Hood, because Hood and Schofield had attended West Point together. Schofield stated. "He was bold even to rashness, and courageous in the extreme." Oliver Otis Howard, in a letter to his wife, wrote, "Hood was a classmate of McPherson. He is a stupid fellow, but a hard fighter." Nevertheless, Sherman now knew that Hood would attack instead of the usual flank-and-retreat maneuvers exhibited under the command of Johnston.[44]

Jefferson Davis, William T. Sherman, and citizens in the Confederacy expected Hood to attack. And attack he did. Annie Carmouche, a citizen of New Orleans, remembered that Hood "knew what the people wanted, and right or wrong, he led our army up so close to the Federal breastworks that the men had to lie down." Carmouche blamed the citizenry who "clamored for action," as Johnston had done all he could to "have his men mowed down to no purpose, for well he knew by now the South had no reserve force to fill their places." President Davis tried to assist Hood by sending him Major General William L. Smith to serve as chief engineer, a man who had won the "highest reputation" when serving Lee in Virginia. As one Atlanta newspaper predicted, any battles around the city would be "the greatest battle of the war."[45] Thus, the battles to protect Atlanta, some of the most critical for the Confederate war effort to either deliver independence or blaze the trail toward defeat, placed enormous pressure on John Bell Hood. Would the newly minted commander, who had sought a commanding role all his military life, be ready for the task?

On July 18, Hood issued a circular to the Army of Tennessee, explaining his acceptance of command. He wrote, "I feel the weight of the responsibility so suddenly and unexpectedly devolved upon me by this position, and shall lend all my energies and employ all my skill to meet its requirements." Hood turned to the soldiers, as he always did, in hopes of gaining their confidence. He requested, "I look with confidence to your patriotism to stand by me, and rely upon your prowess to wrest your country from the grasp of the invader, entitling yourselves to the proud distinction of being called the deliverers of an oppressed people."[46]

The army would have to accept Hood immediately, as he intended to engage Sherman in battle at once. James Robinson, in a letter to his wife, stated, "Hood issued an address to the army which means fight in every word." Hood promised his men that they would embark upon a journey that would force Sherman to "fight us on even ground and no longer attack entrenchments." Hood further promised to "defend Atlanta to the last." He assigned Cheatham to command his old corps and then offered an attack at Peachtree Creek on July 20, only a few days after taking over as commander. Hardee, who would drive the Union troops backward toward Peachtree Creek and the Chattahoochee River, had been ordered to destroy the Union force. When Hood asked his corps commanders if they understood the plan, they all answered yes. Hood did warn that Hardee might encounter some Union troops already in breastworks, but the rest would be throwing them up as the battle commenced. Thus, "a bold and persistent attack," with the "point of the bayonet" would be needed to obtain Confederate victory.[47]

Yet, the best laid plans do not always manifest themselves as desired. The attack did not commence until 4 p.m., instead of at 1 p.m., from Hardee, owing to the slow movement of Benjamin Cheatham. Hardee moved too far forward, making it difficult to maneuver in such a way to coordinate with Cheatham. Thus, without telling Hood, Hardee decided to simply follow Cheatham. The troop movement did avoid some potential overlaps and allowed the Confederates to attack along the Union line at a weaker position. But ultimately, the attack failed. George Thomas, commanding the Army of the Cumberland, noted, "The enemy attacked me in full force at about 4 p.m., and has persisted until now, attacking very fiercely, but was repulsed handsomely by the troops all along my line. Our loss has been heavy, but the loss inflicted on the enemy has been very severe." Union Brigadier General John Geary noted, "General Hood had massed the greater part of his entire army in this furious assault upon a single corps (and that one the smallest in our army) and was whipped back to the ground he had left in the morning."[48]

Hood lost approximately 2,500, compared to Sherman losing 1,900. Hood essentially, as Major General Gustavus Smith remembered, orchestrated a similar plan to what Johnston had envisioned before his removal. Smith remembered, "If Hood's orders had been promptly obeyed, this attack would probably have resulted in a staggering blow to Sherman." Hood's corps commanders had failed to achieve victory, especially because Hardee, according to one historian, "employed only a third of his available force, and in the case of the Tennesseans was delivered in a half-hearted fashion." Though Alexander Stewart's soldiers did find some success, the Union soldiers regrouped and drove the Confederates back, despite their ability to inflict a heavy number of casualties on the Union forces. Wherever the Confederates held a numerical advantage, they failed to fight with the gusto needed to achieve victory. Furthermore, they only fought hard where they were outnumbered, resulting in failure.[49]

Union troops continued to press along the lines the following day. That afternoon, Hood declared, "with a strange, indescribable light" in his eyes, "At once I attack the enemy. He has pressed our lines until he is within a short distance of Atlanta and I must fight or evacuate. I am going to fight." R. M. Gray wrote, "We held the position however and gave them such a warm reception that they gladly retired. This was a brilliant affair for us and we began to believe that Hood would be able to keep his promise." The battle did afford Hood the opportunity to set a clear tone that trying to save Atlanta would mean a fight, instead of a strategic retreat. Yet, during five brutal hours along Peachtree Creek, several Union divisions pushed back the advancing Confederates. Private James Palmer from Mississippi noted, "We made a charge on the enemies' breastworks. We repulsed the enemy to their third line of for tifications. We were then forced to fall back to our fortifications with a heavy loss of men. We lost one man over half our brigade." Following the engagement, Gray stated, "Silently we turned our faces towards the city and sadly bade adieu to our unfortunate comrades who slept the sleep that knows no wakening upon that bloody field. We arrived in the city about midnight and found all excitement and bustle. We supposed that Atlanta was then to be surrendered."⁵⁰ In other words, while some may have thought the campaign over, Hood, despite the casualties, had other plans.

Hood did not cease and again attacked the Union army east of Atlanta on July 22 at Bald Hill, near Decatur. Joseph Cumming recalled, "General Hood continued his aggressive tactics, attacking with inferior forces against Sherman's strong lines, manned by superior numbers, and generally getting the worst of it." As John W. Fuller later wrote, "Hood hoped this simultaneous attack upon front and rear would crush such portion of Sherman's army as might stand between." Hood ordered Hardee's corps to attack the left portion of the Union line, commanded by General James McPherson, and Cheatham would join in the attack to push the Federals back. However, as the Confederates got into position to attack, McPherson moved two divisions, placing them in a position perpendicular to the main line. The maneuvering allowed the Federals to easily meet Hardee's attack.⁵¹

When news of the attack hit Richmond, the papers reported, "Everybody is applauding General Hood and his noble army for the skill and gallantry displayed by them in this engagement." In her diary, Ellen Renshaw House noted, "Gen. Hood whipping the Yankees. Has killed four Gens., captured 23 pieces [of] Artillery and the fight still going on." House had heard that Hood had "been whipped and fallen back before Atlanta" but later corrected her self, noting, "It proved false. Hood whipped the Yanks in one of their grand flank movements." Henri Garidel confirmed the news that spread quickly, writing, "He [Major Smith] had big news. Hood had in fact beaten Sherman in Georgia and had taken 2,000 prisoners and 22 cannon." The impression produced in Confederate society came from telegrams that Hood sent to Richmond, where he chronicled the attacks made by Hardee and Cheatham, as well as Wheeler's cavalry routing the Union near Decatur. Hood did not know the extent of casualty numbers, but concluded, "Our troops fought with great gallantry."⁵²

The attack by Hardee and Cheatham garnered some success, with the Confederates holding part of McPherson's line at the end of the day. However, the attacks were again uncoordinated and the Confederates failed to win a complete victory. When the smoke cleared from the gallant effort, Richard Wharton said, "Heavy loss. I got wounded in right leg and left the field." In reality, Hood lost nearly 5,500 casualties. Hood's number of casualties, with an army of about 35,000, remained low compared to previous Confederate engagements at Shiloh, Sharpsburg, and Murfreesboro, where the Confederates had an army roughly the same size. The South lost more than ten thousand at Shiloh, almost fourteen thousand at Sharpsburg, and nearly twelve thousand at Murfreesboro. Though the attack afforded some success, the condition of the Confederate army in 1864 could not withstand a large number of casualties, especially if the effort failed to achieve complete success.[53]

In the aftermath of the attack near Decatur, Hood learned that one of the four thousand Union casualties was General James McPherson, the second Union commander, following Nathaniel Lyon at Wilson's Creek in 1861, in charge of an army to fall during the Civil War. In his war memoir, Hood recalled his emotional reaction to the death of McPherson. Reminiscing about the bonds of friendship forged at West Point, Hood wrote that "the announcement caused me sincere sorrow. Although in the same class, I was several years his junior, and, unlike him, was more wedded to boyish sports than to books." McPherson assisted Hood on several occasions during their stay at West Point, especially after Hood had participated in "some merry-making." The following day, after a night at Benny Havens,' McPherson helped Hood with "the difficult portions of my studies for the day."[54] Hood valued McPherson's assistance in getting through the academic rigors at the military academy. In their time together, the two men formed a bond of brotherhood, learning that duty included assisting your fellow cadets in finding success.

Yet, the two had not seen each other since West Point, with their post-academy lives going in different directions. Hood stated, "Neither the lapse of years, nor the difference of sentiment which led us to range ourselves on opposite sides in the late war, had lessened my friendship." Hood thought the bonds of friendship had been strengthened over time, particularly with his "admiration and gratitude for his conduct toward our people in the vicinity of Vicksburg." Hood saw McPherson as a bright example of the noble and caring officer, a rarity, in his opinion, among the Federal ranks. Hood concluded, "His acts were ever characterized by those gentlemanly qualities which distinguished him as a boy. No soldier fell in the enemy's ranks, whose loss caused me equal regret."[55]

Neither initial failure nor the loss of McPherson could deter Hood. He issued an order to his troops, commanding, "Safety in time of battle consists in getting into close quarters with your enemy. [The capture of] guns and colors are the only unerring indications of victory." Hood further warned, "If your enemy be allowed to continue the operation of flanking you out of position, our cause is in great peril." Furthermore, Hood made command changes, including firing General William Mackall, the chief of staff, after Mackall refused to shake Bragg's hand when Bragg returned on a headquarters visit on July 24. Mackall loathed Bragg, especially because he blamed him for Johnston's removal. Furthermore, according one colonel, Mackall always "was opposed to fighting—always predicted disaster [and] he had been aptly termed the 'owl of the army.'" With Francis Shoup taking his place, Mackall left to join Joseph Johnston in Macon, and took with him all the war records he had kept as chief of staff. Bragg and Hood also shifted troops around and reorganized corps to prepare for future battles. Finally, Bragg wrote to Jefferson Davis that William Hardee had to go. If Richard Taylor, who had effectively caused the Union army under Nathaniel Banks problems along the Red River in February, joined the army in Hardee's place, it "would be invincible," according to Bragg. Hardee remained, but the seeds of doubt in Richmond about William Hardee began to sprout.[56]

On July 28, 1864, Hood began making plans to order another attack near Ezra Church. Hood requested that Stephen D. Lee entrench his soldiers and wait for Alexander Stewart's corps to flank and rout a group of the Union flanking force. Again, the day did not go as expected. When Lee arrived to entrench his soldiers, he found Union troops in the position he planned to occupy. Instead of telling Hood, Lee launched his soldiers piece by piece into the Federal trenches. When Stewart heard the sound of guns, he rushed his men to the field and joined Lee in the attack throughout the day. Stewart fell wounded and Benjamin Cheatham replaced him. The battle proved ineffective and Hood lost another three thousand men. One Ohio soldier noted that he "never saw the dead lying so thick," seeing them "almost in piles—looking as though they had been swept down whole ranks at a time." In nine days of battle, Hood suffered twelve thousand casualties, more than Joseph Johnston had lost in the previous six months. The failure once again depleted the shrinking army and sent morale plummeting, prompting one major to say, "Hood has about enough left to make two killings." As for his adversary, Sherman stood poised to continue the pressure. A Union captain remarked, "We are in excellent spirits, and propose to take Atlanta whenever Sherman wants it."[57]

Despite the losses, Hood excited the Confederate home front by attacking Sherman. On August 7, Robert Kean wrote, "Hood has held his own at Atlanta pretty well and has delivered some good blows." One report in Richmond stated, "Everybody is applauding Gen. Hood and his noble army." Yet, this fleeting moment of glory dissipated under the mighty force of Sherman's army and his relentless devotion to capturing Atlanta. At the same time, soldiers noted the heavy casualties and the lack of fresh recruits to fill their shoes. J. P. Cannon wrote, "Since General Hood took command (within the past eight days) we have fought three battles with a loss of at least 10,000 men and have gained nothing, so far as I am able to see. No doubt the enemy's loss has been as great as ours, but we cannot afford to swap man for man."[58]

Throughout August, Hood continued to maneuver and face off against Sherman, finding some success with his cavalry. On August 2, Hood sent a telegram to Jefferson Davis, explaining, "Since our late success over the enemy's cavalry I hope now to be able, by interrupting Sherman's communications." Wheeler's cavalry had recently broken up a raiding party and captured 1,000 Union soldiers. When Davis received word, he wrote back to Hood, stating, "I concur in your plan, and hope you[r] cavalry will be able to destroy the railroad bridges and depots of the enemy on the line to Bridgeport so as to compel the enemy to attack you in position or retreat. The loss consequent upon attacking him in his entrenchments requires you to avoid that if practicable." Davis hoped Sherman could be "forced to retreat for want of supplies" and thus would succumb to Hood's pursuing force. Davis drew Hood's attention to the fact that Sherman could use his soldiers to forage the Confederate home front.[59]

Though the cavalry had found some success, the rest of the army was restless, especially with their time now spent in siege mode. Private Samuel King Vann, a member of the Nineteenth Alabama, wrote, on August 25, "Well, Lizzie, if you could have seen me night before last when I cam off picket, you would have thought . . . well I don't know what you would have thought for I was a sight sure, for we had to lie in the ditches, in the mud, over knee-deep for 24 hours." The picket duty proved costly, as Vann pointed out how "we get somebody hurt every day" and that "every time we go on picket, which is every three days, and tonight is our time again and who will get wounded this time or killed." With the picket lines about fifty yards apart, according to William Honnell, a soldier from Mississippi, every soldier had to remain alert. "It is work, work every day and there is very little rest here or sleep either but we must put up with it," said Honnell.[60]

While Hood dealt with Sherman, he also assisted in strengthening his army and the citizens of Atlanta. Hood ordered his men not to converse with the enemy, or they could face being negative retaliation from any men in the area. Rations did pour in to feed the city in early August, but they eventually had to undergo reduction to conserve supplies throughout what could be a long siege. One soldier noted, "We are living tolerably well at this time and get plenty of bacon and corn bread and sometimes [a] mess of peas." The rations could not completely eradicate the outbreaks of disease in the army camps. "There is much sickness among us," wrote one soldier to his wife. Shells flew from the

Union artillery every few minutes, with the Confederate artillery only firing intermittently, in hopes of conserving the depleting stockpile of ammunition. "The Citizens tell us that some were killed every day. One young man was walking along with his girl, when a shell came in and cut them both right in two. Another man and his wife and child were in the street when a shell exploded and killed the wife and child," wrote a Union soldier. Hood ordered the citizens to "move their hogs and cattle from the immediate flanks of the army." Otherwise, he would have to confiscate them in order to prevent Union soldiers from acquiring them.[61]

On August 25, 1864, Sherman maneuvered to the south of the city. When Sherman moved, the shelling of the city ceased. The severity of Sherman's artillery barrages cannot be understated. The *Augusta Constitutionalist* wrote, "Shells all night, shells all day, shells for breakfast, dinner and tea, shells for hours and sorts of weather." Many of the buildings in the northwest section of the city had been struck at least once by an artillery shell. Furthermore, a correspondent from Mobile reported "497 people have been killed and 651 wounded" from the shelling. While the newspapers exaggerated the reports of destruction, Sam Richards, in his diary, declared, "It is said that about twenty lives have been destroyed by these terrible missiles, since the enemy began to throw them into the city." Whatever the number of casualties, the shelling brought continual fear, with the possibility of anyone being struck down at any moment. Thus, when the shelling ended, Atlanta breathed a sigh of relief and crowded into church the following Sunday to give thanks that the reign of terror from the skies had ceased.[62]

The shelling and hunger, as well as the aftermath of earlier defeats, prompted more soldiers to abandon the ranks of the Confederacy. Lieutenant Robert Gill wrote, "There is much demoralization in the army—desertions are numerous, some of the best soldiers are leaving. The duties are very heavy indeed and the troops are getting tired of it. I never complain but endeavor to build up spirits. I meet with such little success that I am much disheartened." In order to curb desertions, Hood took action, issuing an order on August 13 that any soldier communicating with the enemy could be "fired upon by all parties in reach." Furthermore, any officers participating in fraternization could be put on trial immediately. Also, Hood requested that a pardon be issued for any troops missing from the ranks "if they will rejoin their commands on this side of the river."[63]

Hood decreased the number of wounded in city hospital beds because he urged surgeons to send able-bodied men to battle, showing clear "evidence of Gen. Hood's determination to increase the strength and efficiency of the army." Furthermore, Hood secured black wagon drivers to take over for soldiers in order to add more men to the battlefield. The *Macon Telegraph* wrote, "The General Commanding wants in the front every man able to handle a musket, and has called upon me to procure two thousand negroes to supply the places of soldiers at present used as teamsters, who can be placed in the trenches by the side of their comrades now struggling on the bloody field." Calls also went out to absentee soldiers asking their return to the trenches to assist soldiers "toiling and weary" at the front lines.[64] Morale rebounded, not only through Hood's actions, but also through news of Union setbacks in Virginia, Sherman's inactivity, and the prospect of Democratic victory in the oncoming election. Thus, John Bell Hood clearly hoped to gain the respect and trust of his soldiers in order to press and continue a campaign against a superior force at the Confederacy's most critical junction.

Hood continued to utilize his cavalry to raid Sherman's rear and strike the railroad to disrupt communications and supplies. During the raid, Sherman again shifted his army and abandoned part of the Union left. Hood believed that the cavalry had worked to the point of forcing Sherman to prepare for a retreat. Captain Thomas Key, who observed the old Union position filled with "bowls, chairs [and] ammunition boxes," declared, "The scales have turned in favor of the South, and the Abolitionists are moving to the rear toward their own homes." William Bowden, a member of the Fifth Tennessee, wrote, "We are all in full confidence of driving the Yankees out of Georgia or at lest I don't think that Sherman will go any [further] in Georgia." Hood and his army stood on the precipice of victory.[65]

Feeling confident, Hood ordered Hardee to march and attack Sherman on August 31 and drive the Union into and then across the Flint River. Hood said, "You must not fail to attack the enemy so soon as you can get your troops up." Hood implored a quick and decisive march, and the attack would commence "with bayonets fixed." Yet, for Hood to have success, Hardee needed to move quickly. He did not. Hood issued orders at 3:10 a.m. Hardee's attack did not take place until the following afternoon and produced minimal results. Cleburne arrived later than expected because of a "false report that Union forces were occupying the direct road from East Point, which caused it to take nearly twelve hours to traverse what should have been a mere twelve miles." When word arrived that Hardee had failed to act in accordance with orders, Hood cried "My God!" Instead of pulling Hardee back after the failed attack, Hood ordered him to remain in place at Jonesboro and warned, "There are some indications that the enemy may make an attempt on Atlanta tomorrow."[66]

Hood's warning came to fruition when Sherman attacked Hardee the next day. Initially, some Texas troops had success. One Southern soldier noted, "They [are] running for life." Though Hardee held his ground for most of the day, his line eventually snapped and many Confederates were taken as prisoners. The remnants of Hardee's army fell back. Hood later reported to Bragg, "I can with justice blame no one with this failure. It seems the troops had been so long confined to trenches and had been taught to believe that entrenchments cannot be taken, so that they attacked without spirit and retired without proper effort." The battle had been such a disaster that Union commander Philip Sheridan in West Virginia, noted, "The rebels report that Hood has been killed, and that Longstreet is in command at Atlanta." Another report indicated that Hardee had been killed, which proved false. Sherman now controlled all the railroads in the Atlanta area. Now, it was only a matter of when Sherman would march into the city.[67]

Outnumbered and with the threat of being surrounded, Hood ordered the evacuation of the city at midnight, September 1. As Hood evacuated the city, he ordered six trainloads of ammunition to be destroyed, essentially to keep them out of Union hands. Robert Patrick heard the "terrible roar" and said, "I could see how to walk for a long distance by the light of the shells and the burning cars. My road lay parallel with the track, and as I approached nearer and nearer the burning train, the sound became perfectly deafening, and the fragments of shells, hurtled through the midnight darkness over my head with an ominous rushing sound." A Union soldier who later marched into the city, wrote, "These they had blown up the night before, also destroyed whole trains of cars . . . I have never seen anything like it. The ground was literally covered for some distance around with bits of shell, machinery, shot, grape and canister, railroad iron, car wheels and smashed up engines."[68]

On September 2, the Union army captured Atlanta. Confederate soldiers throughout the Army of Tennessee reacted to the fall of the city. Captain Samuel T. Foster wrote, "He [Hood] had near 10,000 men murdered around Atlanta trying to prove to the world that he was a greater man than Gen. Johnston—Because Johnston said that Atlanta was untenable, and could not be held with the men he had against the men that Sherman had." In Foster's mind, Hood tried to prove Johnston wrong by defending the "untenable" city.[69]

However, the words of Foster did not hold unanimous among the ranks. J. P. Cannon, on September 4, 1864, realized the situation Hood had been put in. He wrote, "Although Gen. Johnston would probably have given up Atlanta, we believe he would have held it longer with much smaller loss and inflicted a heavier loss upon the enemy. Our army would now be stronger and in better condition." Yet, Cannon did not blame Hood. He stated, "We do not censure General Hood, for he is a brave and gallant officer and was placed in command for the express purpose of making a desperate struggle to hold the 'Gate City.'" Cannon shot his displeasure not at Hood but at the Confederate president, who, when removing Johnston, "made a fatal mistake." For others, such as William Chambers, the removal of Johnston lingered, and Hood's failure to hold Atlanta did not retard any intense anger. Chambers said, "On the contrary, it seemed to be intensified, and hence it was with distrustful glances we looked upon our brave but rash commander-in-chief."[70]

Opinion from other Confederate soldiers back in Virginia also did not bode well for Hood. Thomas Goree had praised Hood after Sharpsburg and even sent a photo of the general home, along with one of Lee, Johnston, and Jackson, whom he called "our distinguished Generals." Now, Goree questioned if Atlanta even ranked in the South as a place "of vital importance." Goree thought otherwise, but noted that President Davis believed this to be true and thus, "Johnston was removed because his policy was to give it up rather than run too great a risk in holding it. Hood was appointed because his policy was to hold it at all hazards." Yet, Hood had lost irreplaceable men. Goree concluded, "He captures a few strands of colors and pieces of artillery. He whips on one part of the field and is whipped on another. What is gained? Nothing, but ground is lost. So much for a change of policy and commanders."[71]

Goree needed to place blame in the change of commanders that now made him "angry to even think on this subject." He thought "somebody should be *hung* for a change which has resulted so disastrously to our cause." First, Goree pointed at Davis, who clearly held a grudge against Johnston and let that "influence him in a matter of such *vital* importance." Next, Goree blamed Hood for maneuvering "to get Johnston out and get himself in." Yet, Goree paused and decided to save the hangman's noose for Braxton Bragg. He scowled, "*His* misrepresentations, *his lies,* induced the removal of Genl. Johnston."[72] As Goree sat bogged down in Petersburg, he continued to vent his frustrations on the failure of the Confederate cause outside Virginia.

General Gustavus Smith wrote after the war, "As an army commander his orders were judicious and well-timed in the operations around Atlanta." Smith believed that Hood commanded as well as anyone could around Atlanta. However, he did hint that some may question Hood's manhood and blame the loss of Atlanta on his injuries. Although Smith confessed that Hood's activity level had declined since the onset of the war, he wrote, "But he was an excellent horseman and could ride nearly as well as most men who have two legs and two arms." Yet, Smith thought that some mistakes made in the campaign could have been avoided if Hood had the ability to ride to meet his subordinates and been more "'at home on horseback' as he was before he was so badly maimed." Despite Smith's analysis, there remains no substantial evidence that Hood had been overly medicated on laudanum to deal with the pain of his injuries. No one who had spent time with Hood following his injuries ever reported it, including Bragg or Davis.[73]

Others throughout the South looked to the corps commanders as the reason behind failure. In a letter to his sister, J. H. Buford wrote, "If we had held Atlanta, which we could have done if Hood old corps [commanded by S. D. Lee] had done their duty they I think are to blame for Atlanta." Buford pointed out that every time Hood gave Stephen Lee orders, his men "moved like slugs," and when Hood wanted them to fight, "they fought like cowards." Buford thought that Lee had received censure for his actions at Atlanta. Winfield Scott Featherson noted a similar situation on July 28, 1864, when Lee's corps "was ordered to march out and attack the enemy on his right flank and dive him back." Yet, Lee failed to drive the enemy back.[74] Lee's and Hood's friendship would be tested and eventually undermined by a debate between the two over military actions throughout the remaining war. Furthermore, their relationship would be pivotal as Hood sought to reconstruct his memory of his tenure as commander of the Army of Tennessee.

The southern press reported the doom evident from the fall of Atlanta. The *Charleston Mercury* originally criticized the removal of Johnston but pledged to support Hood for the sake of striving for victory. The paper reported that the Army of Tennessee "must be far weaker than it was under Gen. Johnston." When assessing why Atlanta fell, the paper wrote, "General Hood's egregious failures, it appears to us, have proved, beyond question, that what was wanted by our army at Atlanta, was not a change of Generals, but reinforcements." The paper demanded that General Beauregard, accompanied by reinforcements, should be sent to Georgia immediately. Beauregard appeared as a logical choice, "as he is of a higher rank than any of the officers in that army."[75]

When Hood offered a report to Jefferson Davis, he exclaimed, "According to all human calculations, we should have saved Atlanta had the officers and men of this army done what was expected of them. It has been God's will for it to be otherwise. I am of good heart and feel that we shall yet succeed." Hood blamed Hardee for failing to attack in the morning and even blamed Joseph Johnston for the way he conducted warfare, which hindered the army's ability in battle. "I am officially informed," Hood wrote to Bragg on September 4, "that there is a tacit if not expressed determination among the men of this army, extending to officers as high in some instances as colonel, that they will not attack breastworks."[76]

The Union victory at Atlanta helped usher in a second presidential term for Abraham Lincoln. When Atlanta fell, the door opened for Sherman to disrupt munitions production at Macon, Columbus, and Augusta, Georgia. Many of the trains destroyed when Hood evacuated Atlanta contained vital ordnance supplies that could not be replaced at this late stage. G. P. Hardwick, who wrote on the Atlanta campaign for the *Confederate Congressional Record,* stated, "Hood thought at Atlanta he'd have a better chance. But Sherman's boys with forty rounds soon made the Johnnies dance. We fought four heavy battles and won the Citadel. Hood could not stand such fighting men, and from it ran pell mell." Thus, Hood, with the loss of Atlanta, hampered his own ability to engage in warfare with a declining amount of armaments.[77]

Even though the loss of Atlanta damaged Hood's ability to engage in warfare and tarnished his reputation that he worked so hard to build, all was not lost. Hood still had his army, and many of his men still had the resolve to continue the fight. With Lee still holding on to Petersburg, Hood had enough time to orchestrate another ambitious and grand campaign that could produce the victory he wanted at Atlanta. This time, the campaign would be of his choosing.

Chapter 6

"Playing Hell in Tennessee"

Still no soldiers' heart but warms when talking of Hood, men love the man and officer while condemning his system of Tactics. Hold in your heart my son a warm place for the noble generous and brave Hood whatever verdict the future shall pass upon him.
—*Confederate Soldier R. M. Gray*

It was a black day for the Army of Tennessee, the day the command was taken from General Johnston and conferred on General Hood; a brave man it is true, and an excellent division commander, but a man wanting in ability, as everybody at all acquainted with him will be ready to testify. General Hood was soon flanked, beaten, and compelled to abandon Atlanta. He then stepped out of the way, hat in hand, and asked Sherman to walk through Georgia. He himself moved up to Tennessee, where he has got beaten, and this time, we fear, badly enough.
—*Richmond Whig*

Captain Alex Erskine Spence, a member of the First Arkansas regiment, spent the latter part of the Civil War with the Army of Tennessee and witnessed the actions of John Bell Hood from a perspective among the rank and file. Spence wrote several letters home to his parents, noting the satisfaction men had with Hood. Yet, Spence's fate changed on November 30, 1864, a pivotal day for both Alex Spence and John Bell Hood. Spence's body lay among thousands of others outside the city of Nashville. As Lieutenant M. M. Sanders remembered, "At the dreadful battle of Franklin, Tenn., the fearful loss of life here, beyond the most terrific scenes of battle array, almost forbids us to call it a battle.... The destruction was so great, yet it must be remembered, our dear old company did not lose many men in this, of all battles, the most terrible. The crimson from chivalrous sons simply stained the field with color so hear rendering it can never be forgotten by those present."[1] The battle of Franklin, an unmitigated disaster, helped bring about the end of the Army of Tennessee and the military career of John Bell Hood.

The tragic conclusion in the closing days of 1864 for the Army of Tennessee could not be predicted when Atlanta fell. The army remained a formidable force, but the overall circumstances for the Confederacy's fortunes had changed. Jefferson Davis had replaced the strategic withdrawal tactics of Joseph Johnston with a fighter in John Bell Hood. Hood fought horrific and bloody battles over the course of ten days to prove to his superiors, to the Confederate populace, and to himself that he would not give up Atlanta without a fight. Yet, the overwhelming numbers swept the Confederacy from the city. Lee was besieged at Petersburg. Union General Philip Sheridan prepared to embark on a ride through the Shenandoah Valley that could elevate the destruction of the Civil War to unprecedented levels.

In the days following Atlanta, John Bell Hood stood at a crossroads. The fighting general needed a plan. He needed to orchestrate a military maneuver so bold that it could eradicate the failure at Atlanta not only from the minds of the Confederate citizens, but also alleviate pressure Lee felt as he stood trapped within Petersburg. Hood decided to leave Atlanta to Sherman and turned his eyes northward, toward Tennessee. If Hood found success, the Confederacy might achieve a stunning victory to prolong the war to the point of northern disillusionment. Yet, if Hood failed with his dwindling army, any hopes for Confederate success in the West would likely vanish permanently.

In the hours following the fall of Atlanta, Hood had sent forward a white flag to Sherman, an officer with whom Hood made acquaintance on his journey to join the Second Cavalry in the years preceding the Civil War. Hood wanted to discuss prisoner exchanges as well as the fate of the civilians inside the city of Atlanta. On September 7, Sherman wrote to Hood. He insisted that the city be evacuated and burned. He offered to "provide food and transportation" for any citizens inside Atlanta who wished to travel north into Tennessee, Kentucky, and even farther north. Hood would be responsible for taking care of the families who wanted to move south, with Sherman assisting them to "Rough and Ready." The Union commander found the city of Atlanta "no place for families or non-combatants." Sherman offered to declare a truce to move the citizens if each side would provide "wagons, horses, animals or persons" as well as a guard unit of one hundred soldiers to see through the city's proper evacuation.[2]

Two days later, Hood responded. He said, "I do not consider that I have any alternative in this matter. I therefore accept your proposition to declare a truce of two days, or such time as may be necessary to accomplish the purpose mentioned." With Hood agreeing to Sherman's proposed stipulations, he took a moment in the letter to consider the magnanimity of Sherman's offer. He wrote, "Sir, permit me to say that the unprecedented measure you propose transcends, in studied and ingenious cruelty, all acts ever before brought to my attention in the dark history of war." Hood proclaimed, "In the name of God and humanity, I protest, believing that you will find that you are expelling from their homes and firesides the wives and children of a brave people."[3]

Hood awaited a response from Sherman. Sherman agreed to begin the evacuation but challenged Hood on his philosophy of war. He reminded Hood, "You yourself burned dwelling-houses along your parapet, and I have seen today fifty houses that you have rendered uninhabitable because they stood in the way of your forts and men." Furthermore, Hood had placed a battle line so close to Atlanta that "every cannon-shot and many musket-shots from our line of investment, that overshot their mark, went into the habitations of women and children." It was not Sherman's purpose to accuse Hood of "heartless cruelty" but to make apparent Hood's hypocrisy in his correspondence to Sherman. Sherman implored Hood to use some "common-sense."[4]

Yet, Sherman did not rest satisfied in only mentioning civilian deaths. Sherman next turned to lambasting Hood for the whole Confederate purpose of engaging the nation in a "dark and cruel war." Sherman declared that the Confederacy had "plunged a nation into war" and that they had "insulted our flag, seized our arsenals and forts," as well as having "expelled Union families by the thousands, burned their houses, and declared, by an act of your Congress, the confiscation of all debts due Northern men for goods had and received." Sherman proposed, "If we must be enemies, let us be men, and fight it out as we propose to do, and not deal in such hypocritical appeals to God and humanity. God will judge us in due time, and he will pronounce whether it be more humane to fight with a town full of women and the families of a brave people at our back, or to remove them in time to places of safety."[5]

Two days later, Sherman received a response from Hood. Hood had not planned on continuing his correspondence with Sherman, but remarks in the last letter prompted him to write again. First, Hood defended his predecessor,

General Joseph Johnston, for actions in northern Georgia. Hood declared, "He depopulated no villages, nor towns, nor cities, either friendly or hostile. He offered and extended friendly aid to his unfortunate fellow-citizens who desired to flee from your fraternal embraces." Next, Hood turned to his own conduct. He regretted the loss of civilian life at Atlanta but declared it simply "an ordinary, proper, and justifiable act of war." In fact, the culprit manifested himself as none other than Sherman, who proceeded to shell the city on a regular basis. Hood did not criticize the act but merely offered, "there are a hundred thousand witnesses that you fired into the habitations of women and children for weeks, firing far above and miles beyond my line of defense."[6]

Turning to Sherman's discussion of the war's causes, Hood found the question inappropriate. He said, "I am only a general of one of the armies of the Confederate States . . . and I am not called upon to discuss with you the causes of the present war, or the political questions which led to or resulted from it." Yet, Hood did not hesitate to go through Sherman's laundry list of complaints one by one, offering that the Confederacy acted only after the northern government had acted upon a "mission of subjugation." Thus, Sherman's declaration of evacuating Atlanta added insult to injury. Hood said, "You order into exile the whole population of a city; drive men, women, and children from their homes at the point of the bayonet, under the plea that it is to the interest of your Government, and on the claim that it is an act of 'kindness to these families of Atlanta.'" Hood noted Benjamin Butler had done the same act in New Orleans, but only as a form of punishment. "And, because I characterize what you call a kindness as being real cruelty," said Hood, "you presume to sit in judgment between me and my God; and you decide that my earnest prayer to the Almighty Father to save our women and children from what you call kindness, is a 'sacrilegious, hypocritical appeal.'"[7]

Hood also returned to Sherman's call to fight like men. Hood exclaimed, "We will fight you to the death! Better die a thousand deaths than submit to live under you or your Government and your Negro allies." Hood used the term "Negro allies" because of his explanation to Sherman about the southern principles. He declared, "You came into our country with your army, avowedly for the purpose of subjugating free white men, women, and children, and not only intended to rule over them, but you make negroes your allies, and desire to place over us an inferior race, which we have raised from barbarism to its present position." To end the correspondence, Hood declined Sherman's offer to evacuate Atlanta. He declared this letter the final correspondence and word on the matter, because Hood believed he had adequately addressed Sherman point by point. Hood concluded, "Notwithstanding your comments upon my appeal to God in the cause of humanity, I again humbly and reverently invoke his almighty aid in defense of justice and right."⁸

Sherman stood unwilling to allow Hood the last word. He wrote again on September 14, but with a brief note. Sherman declared that the correspondence between the two had been "profitless," but pointed the finger at Hood for "characterizing an official act of mine in unfair and improper terms." The general asserted that the Union army had "no negro allies." Furthermore, he had not been bound by any laws of war to "give notice of the shelling of Atlanta, a 'fortified town, with magazines, arsenals, foundries, and public stores;' you were bound to take notice." Sherman got in the last word, declaring this to be the true conclusion to their letter writing and ended the series of conversations "with satisfaction."⁹

The correspondence between Hood and Sherman over the evacuation of Atlanta twisted and turned in many thoughtful and interesting directions. What began as an agreement between the two officers on evacuating all the city's citizens evolved into a heated debate on the philosophy and rules of war, the causes of war, and ultimately, the underlying racial tensions further exposed by the advent of civil strife. The intelligent and insightful banter between the opposing commanders shed light on Sherman's belief that the South must pay for causing the horrific war. The correspondence also allowed both men to debate the principles of humanity in warfare and how both men had to put the interests of victory before saving lives and property. The correspondence came to a close with the citizens remaining within Atlanta.

At the same time, Hood acquiesced that both sides deserved blame, but the South simply acted to defend its property, its families, and its own political best interests. Hood expressed his personal views on a lesson learned at West Point: duty to country. He came to the defense of the southern cause as he expressed his belief about remaining an honorable defender of the country he called his own. With his recent baptism, Hood also turned to God in his correspondence, who now served as a point of inspiration and peace in the midst of chaos. Hood took the time to respond to Sherman point by point in order to come to terms with his own sense of duty and honor, as well as to defend the Confederate citizens who ended up caught in the crossfire.

The loss of Atlanta not only hindered the war effort but also devastated the morale of the South and left Hood searching for the next step. Sarah Louis Wadley wrote, "We have just heard of the fall of Atlanta, but know no particulars. This is indeed a great misfortune, and we feel it deeply. Father had expected it but nevertheless it depressed him much; we hope that Hood has saved his army." Wadley's father later met a gentlemen on his way from Macon, who told her father that the loss of Atlanta "was not considered a very serious loss to us, and that it was there confidently expected that we should have peace in a few months."[10] Wadley wanted peace sooner rather than later.

Despite the loss of the city, the army did not collapse under military failure. According to the *Daily Picayune,* "When we come to Georgia, where we are told Hood's army is only a debris of the past, a demoralized mob, we find a large, compact, tried and patriotic army, which, despite all its misfortunes, is still game." Hood decided to harass Sherman in the vicinity of Atlanta, engaging the Union forces at nearby Allatoona Pass. Jefferson Davis attempted to reinforce Hood's army with "all available troops" and called out "the reserves, detailed men and militia." Yet, the number of reinforcements available remained negligible. Hood even requested that Lee "send him his old division." Sherman did agree to exchange recently captured prisoners from the Atlanta campaign, increasing Hood's army by 128 officers and 1,204 enlisted men.[11]

Robert Kean remembered, "Hood telegraphed that he had adopted a very bold purpose—nothing less than to turn Atlanta on the west . . . and falling on Sherman's communications. This is extremely hazardous. . . . If it is successful, it will be a very great success as it will compel him [Sherman] to evacuate Atlanta or come out and fight on Hood's own ground." Sherman became irritated with Hood, stating, "Hood is eccentric and I cannot guess his movements as I could those of Johnston, who was a sensible man and only did sensible things." As Hood moved north of the city, he attempted to break the railroad and disrupt Union supply lines to Sherman's forces in Atlanta.[12] Despite effective destruction of the railroad, Hood needed a bolder plan to reach the goal of removing Sherman from the Deep South.

Hood decided to invade Tennessee, with hopes of defeating the Union forces stationed within Nashville. By capturing Nashville, Hood would force the Union army out of Tennessee and reunite the state that had been split by U. S. Grant's invasion in early 1862. With Tennessee secured, Hood would then continue northward into the state of his birth, "plant their flag on the Ohio before they stopped," and cross into Ohio. Finally, Hood would then continue eastward with his army until he could reunite with General Lee, which would provide some assistance in driving Grant out of Petersburg, Virginia. A northern invasion might also force Sherman to retrace his steps and give up Atlanta. With the possibility of forcing Sherman away from Atlanta, the *Daily Picayune* wrote, "In either event, Hood's movement is as promising as it is bold and daring." Actually, Hood had conceived part of this plan as far back as the spring of 1864. In a letter to Jefferson Davis, dated April 13, 1864, Hood wrote, "My heart was fixed upon our going to the front and regaining

Tennessee and Kentucky. . . . To regain Tennessee would be of more value to us than a half dozen victories in Virginia."[13]

Hood's plan received accolades from Confederate civilians. George Phifer Erwin wrote to his sister, "Everybody seems to be taking the movement of Hood very quietly, though it appears to me that it is one of the most important movements that has been made since the war." Ella Thomas, residing in Georgia, wrote in her diary, "The deep gloom which hung over us just after the fall of Atlanta has been lifted from our midst and the movement of Gen. Hood has brightened both the army and the people." William Stillwell, in a letter to his wife Molly, wrote, on October 15, 1864, "I think General Hood will have the Yankees driven out of Georgia soon." M. Hill Fitzpatrick, near Petersburg with Lee's army, wrote in a letter to his wife, "The spirits of the army are reviving now, though they have never been at a low ebb. . . . [W]e have high hopes that with the aid of [Forrest] in the rear that Hood will be enabled to drive Sherman from Ga. soil."[14]

In the aftermath of Atlanta, Hood proclaimed a day of fasting on September 15, 1864. Hood also called the army for a review two days later. As John Saucier stated, "Our whole corps was on the field and was reviewed by our Lt. Gen. and Genl Hood." Despite the hardships of the recent campaign, Saucier said, "They were both much pleased with the appearance and condition in general of the troops." The *Daily Picayune* reported, "Gen. Hood has, with great promptitude and with celerity of perception which promises well, made his disposition to suit the emergencies as they rise." Alex Spence noted, "Now we are living fine and expect better times when we get into Tenn." He believed that Hood would winter the army near Corinth, Mississippi. Yet, Hood spent his days making plans for battle. To place more men in line for battle, according to his chief of staff, Brigadier General Francis A. Shoup, "General Hood ordered all white teamsters except ordinance to rejoin their command and Negroes to be used in their stead." Hood worked to gather shoes and clothing throughout September, resulting in the state of the army as "in excellent spirits." Spence reported to his parents, "I am pretty well fixed for the trip 'a new pair of boots and a good suit of clothes.' Genl Hood has got the Army in good fighting trim 'marching trim.'"[15]

The loss of Atlanta did not deter Hood from displaying his personal characteristics of leadership. He formulated a plan that caused great excitement, both among the ranks as well as among the citizens whose support continued to wane behind the lines. By calling teamsters to join the fight, Hood orchestrated the expansion of his army. He also wanted to make sure his army would not stand demoralized following the defeat at Atlanta, by gathering supplies for the soldiers. Though Hood would never be able to replicate the close relationship he had with his Texans on the Peninsula in 1862, he did consciously give orders that would show his soldiers how much he cared about their well-being. By actively attempting to form a close bond with the men of his army, Hood wanted to achieve the same result he had earlier in his career: have a group of soldiers who would fight with sufficient tenacity to achieve all military goals.

However, the loss of Atlanta still caused consternation with the Confederate government, particularly the president. Jefferson Davis arrived in Palmetto, Georgia, on September 25 to personally inspect the Army of Tennessee and meet with General Hood. Two days prior to his visit, Davis stopped in Macon to address an audience at the First Baptist Church. The speaking engagement, where Davis had discussed amputees, as noted earlier, also afforded him the opportunity to defend his own military decisions concerning Hood and Johnston. In terms of Johnston, Davis questioned, "If I knew that a General did not possess the right qualities to command, would I not be wrong if he were not removed?" For Hood, he remarked, "I thus put a man in command who I knew would strike an honest and manly blow . . . and many a Yankee's blood was made to nourish the soil before the prize was won." Despite the fall of the city, the war remained far from over. Davis declared, "Our cause is not lost. Sherman cannot keep up his long line of communications, and retreat, sooner or later, he must."[16]

After injecting the Confederate churchgoers with a shot of optimism, Davis moved directly to see the army that could transform that optimism into reality. Rumors abounded in Confederate society that "Beauregard is with him and that he is going to take over command of this army." Newspapers reported, "It is said that Beauregard will be appointed to the command of this army, with whom his popularity is as great as it is with the country at large." One southerner, a supporter of Beauregard, remarked, "Poor devil. They always give him the leftovers."[17]

The presidential visit prompted one Texas soldier to write, "This army is going to do something wrong—or rather it will undertake something that will not be a success." The soldier felt confident that Davis's presence among the troops signaled an effort "to concoct some other plan for our defeat and display of his Generalship." In terms of the visit, Hood's chief of staff, General F. A. Shoup, noted, "The President and General Hood with their respective staff's rode out to the front today, and were enthusiastically received by the troops." Shoup recalled that Davis had been "serenaded by the 20th Louisiana band" and responded by giving a "short and spirited speech" that received "loud and continued cheering." Davis spoke to the soldiers and said, "Be of good cheer for within a short while your faces will be turned homeward and your feet pressing the soil of Tennessee." While the Tennessee soldiers cheered, some soldiers shunned any display of enthusiasm for their president. As William Chambers noted, "As the presidential party passed in front of our brigade, Colonel Clarke, who was a small man with a thin voice, cried out, 'Three cheers for President Davis and General Hood!' Waving aloft his sword, he, with one or two others, raised a feeble yell." At that moment, someone in the crowd cried out, "Three cheers for General Joe Johnston." Chambers noted, "They were given with a will, the other regiments caught on and in twenty-five seconds the whole line of Sears brigade was 'making the welkin ring' with the regular 'rebel yell.'" Chambers noted that for once, Jefferson Davis looked back to see where "this unseemly demonstration originated."[18]

With the visit concluded, Davis decided to reorganize the department and Army of Tennessee. He wrote a letter to John Bell Hood, dated September 28, 1864. Davis stated, "I have anxiously reflected upon the subject of our closing conversation and the proposition confidentially mentioned. It seems to me best that I should confer with General Beauregard, and if quite acceptable to him, place him in the command of the Department, embracing your army." Davis did let Hood know that if Beauregard arrived with Hood, then he would "command in person." Before Davis made a final decision, he gave Hood the luxury of time "to communicate with me [Davis], and I shall be glad to have your views. In the mean time you will of course proceed as though no notification of existing organization was contemplated."[19]

Davis did not hesitate for long after his correspondence to Hood. First, the Confederate president dealt with the apparent drama between William Hardee and Hood. Historian Steven Woodworth called the ranks of high command among the Army of Tennessee "a pit of vipers." The *Charleston Mercury* reported as early as August 20, 1864, that Hardee intended to resign if not relieved from command. The newspaper stated, from a credible source, "He feels that great injustice has been done him." Some in the Confederacy credited Hardee with trying to save Atlanta. One paper reported, "Hardee and his corps are the theme of universal admiration in this army. . . . It was one of the most brilliant actions of the war. The more I hear of its details, the more I am convinced of the fact."[20]

Despite the views of the southern press, the report read by Jefferson Davis came directly from John Bell Hood. Immediately following the fall of Atlanta, Hood wrote to Davis, "According to all human calculations we should have saved Atlanta had the officers and men . . . done what was expected of them." Hood later clarified himself on September 13, when he wrote to Davis, "In the battle of July 20, we failed on account of General Hardee. Our success on July 22 [was] not what it should have been, owing to this officer. Our failure on August 31, I am now convinced was greatly owing to him. . . . It is of the utmost importance that Hardee should be relieved at once." Hood recommended Richard Taylor or Benjamin Cheatham as willing replacements.[21]

Hardee, angered over Hood resting the fall of Atlanta upon his shoulders, offered an ultimatum to Jefferson Davis that either he or Hood needed to go. Thus, Davis had to honor the request. Previously, Davis had informed Hood of his desire to elevate Beauregard to a position of authority over Confederate forces in the West. Beauregard still had value as a commander and could help balance out Hood's command decisions. With the recent loss of Atlanta, Davis now placed Beauregard as Hood's superior, as he earlier hinted to Hood, effective October 16. The *New York Herald* reported the reshuffling of the department as restoring "the old order of things as they existed under Johnston in the fall of 1863." Davis sought to consolidate the armies under General Hood and General Richard Taylor "to secure the fullest co-operation of the troops without relieving either of you [Hood and Taylor] of the responsibilities and powers of your special commands." Davis acknowledged that if Beauregard happened to be present with either army, then he would have the ability to command in person.[22]

With Beauregard leaving the coastal command of South Carolina and Georgia, a convenient opening arose for William Hardee, who departed for the coast. Benjamin Cheatham took over his corps with the Army of Tennessee. When Hood received word, he told Davis, "I am very hopeful of good results." Hood had been able to meet with Beauregard in October to propose his operational plan. Beauregard agreed as long as Hood would move rapidly and send Joseph Wheeler's cavalry to harass Sherman. Hood wrote to Jefferson Davis, "I think it would be the best thing that could happen for our general good." Hood also proclaimed Beauregard's endorsement, saying, "Beauregard agrees with me as to my plan of operation." Although his superior, Beauregard never rode with the army and joined it long after the plans had come to view.[23]

Hood's ambitious plan arose as the best course of action for the Army of Tennessee at this juncture. The general's force was simply not strong enough to stay in the Atlanta area and attack Sherman again. By posing a legitimate threat to the security of Nashville, Hood would force Sherman to consider abandoning any plans of moving southward, especially if Hood could take Nashville and threaten the North. Grant, when writing to Sherman about Hood's intentions, noted, "Hood would probably strike for Nashville, thinking that by going north he could inflict greater damage upon us than we could upon the rebels by going south. If there is any way of getting at Hood's army, I would prefer that." Ultimately, Grant left it up to Sherman to decide the best course of military action, which, for Sherman, entailed going on an offensive maneuver into the heart of Georgia.[24]

Despite such promise, there were deep anxieties. As Hood's men prepared to disembark, Mary Gay visited with General Granbury from Texas. An ardent reader of Federal newspapers, Gay told the general and the soldiers present how the newspapers had reported, "Hood was working to their hand precisely in going back to Tennessee, as Thomas was there with an army that was invincible, and would whip him so bad that there would not be a Johnnie Reb left to tell the tale." The news startled some of the men, and they inquired on the state of the Federal army and if the reports contained any validity. Gay noted how she had seen the "vindictive spirit" of the Federals and their "implacable feeling towards the South." A wave of sadness passed "over the noble faces of all present." A question shot forth, inquiring, "Have you lost hope of the ultimate success of our cause?" Gay thought for a moment and then responded with her own inquiry, wanting to ascertain the number of men and supplies available for the campaign. But the daunting question rose again, "But have you lost hope?" Gay failed to respond to the vexing question, and wrote later that her only answer was "silence and tears" that "were interpreted to mean what my tongue refused to speak."[25]

Captain William V. Davis, on October 18, 1864, wrote in his diary, "Gen. Hood passes, says we are off for Tennessee." An assistant quartermaster, Captain George Erwin, described the spirits of the Army of Tennessee as "buoyant." In fact, according to Captain Samuel T. Foster, "The whole army are in high spirits," as the troops moved in mid-October. Reports came of "one continued shout for miles. The men cheer Gen. Hood when he comes about them, and say if he will only take them back to Tennessee, they will be perfectly satisfied and fare well on one ear of corn apiece per day." As Hood departed, he issued orders to his troops. In response, William Berryhill stated, "And General Hood issued an order to the troops when we started on this raid saying that he would not force them to charge any strongly fortified positions."[26] Time would surely tell if Hood lived up to his promise.

Hood moved northward, retracing the steps from the previous months of campaigning. He arrived at Resaca and demanded the Union forces there surrender immediately. Hood fervently declared to the Federal occupants, "If the place is carried by assault no prisoners will be taken." The Union troops refused to capitulate. Clark Weaver, the Union commander at Resaca, replied to Hood, "In my opinion I can hold this post; if you want it come and take it."

Hood decided not to attack the garrison. In his memoir, Hood wrote, "No officer should allow his soldiers to burn and pillage after victory has been secured." Instead of recklessly hurling his troops at the garrison, Hood decided simply to observe the enemy and then move northward, destroying the railroad between Resaca and Tunnel Hill throughout mid-October.[27]

The Army of Tennessee prepared to cross the Tennessee River at Guntersville, Alabama, in late October. However, without Nathan Bedford Forrest's cavalry, as well as a lack of provisions for the army to move on their own, Hood moved farther west to Decatur, Alabama, to cross the river. Private Charles S. Coleman, when describing the army, said, "They looked sad and low-spirited. Some of the men were nearly barefoot and had few clothes, but the weather being warm they could stand it. Rations were scarce also, but they were ready to do or die in the attempt." The *Charleston Mercury* noted, "Whole regiments are barefooted, while blankets with any of the men is rather the exception to the rule. And there are some regiments who have not been paid in fifteen months!" The waning support for the war effort throughout the Confederacy hampered supplies, yet the newspaper hoped that "the country promptly forwards these supplies, or Gen. Hood goes into Tennessee and Kentucky and captures them, [or] there will be great suffering among his troops."[28]

Robert Patrick, longing for a return of Joseph Johnston, wrote, "I have no confidence in Hood's abilities. He is a good, rough fighter, but when that is said, all is said. He hasn't the knowledge of military affairs that Johnston possesses." Champion Duke, in a letter to his wife, predicted, "Hood will fail of his object in my opinion." Even with Beauregard doing the planning and Hood doing the fighting, he would fail because of "the force of the enemy," according to Duke. Private John Johnston offered his own assessment, noting, "They were very hardened, ill-clothed, dirty-looking set of fellows—but were laughing and jeering and cursing as if there were nothing serious in life—or death." A Louisiana private noted, "Nothing works right. The trains are all mixed pell-mell. Nobody knows where to find anything or anybody. There are no bread rations." The problem with food led Private E. G. Littlejohn from Texas to write, "We have suffered more for the want of something to eat on this campaign than on any other previous one, having been compelled to eat parched corn right ahead."[29]

Hood's soldiers had to dine on corn and acorns because of the delay in crossing the Tennessee River. Furthermore, Nathan Bedford Forrest still had not arrived. Hood requested, "When can I expect you here or when can I hear from you? I am waiting for you." The Federal forces did have an "aggressive, spirited" defense and Hood also had to consider the dwindling supply of rations. North Alabama simply did not have the food resources to feed the army beyond corn and acorns. Thus, Hood avoided attacking. One colonel remarked, "General Hood's 'slight demonstration' against Decatur occupied him four days. It would appear that he had a great deal of respect for the small force at Decatur, or he would not have taken the trouble he did merely to get his army safely by." Though the colonel believed that the army could have made a successful attack, Hood decided to hold back.[30]

Even with the supply difficulties, optimism remained intact. The *Charleston Mercury* wrote, "Gen. Hood enters upon this campaign at the head of the finest army ever marshaled this side of Virginia. It is larger in number, has better Generals, and is in better spirits than was ever known before." The paper admitted that the army lacked some shoes and blankets, "but the men all believe that they are going to a land where an abundance of all these, and many things more, will be obtained." The newspaper also reported the prospect of adding "twenty thousand men recruits in twenty days." Thus, the army that headed into Tennessee left "in glorious spirits with confidence in their General commanding, and eager to wipe out the invader." The army had a moment to pause in Florence, Alabama, and found a crowd of "ladies lined the streets in every direction" and cheered "the army, with tender words and gentle looks."[31]

The crowds of Confederate spectators could not alter Mother Nature's grip on the Tennessee River. The roads in the region were described by Brigadier General Tyree Bell as "the worst roads on earth." Rain swelled the rivers and horses drowned amid the speeding current. Forrest did not arrive until November 16. Hood had spent weeks trying to get into Tennessee. He explained to Jefferson Davis that "high water, and the fact that I had to draw supplies from and through a department not under my command, involving delay in their reaching me, have retarded my operations." Because of the delay, he wrote Beauregard on November 17, "I have now seven days' rations on hand and need thirteen days' additional. Please use every effort to have these supplies pressed forward." Hood finally crossed on November 20, as the river level fell. He moved the army ahead into Tennessee and prepared to face off against Union commander John Schofield, whom Sherman had detached from Atlanta to deal with Hood's Tennessee invasion. With Union commander John Schofield at Columbia, Tennessee, Hood declared to Chaplain Quintard, "The enemy must give me fight or I'll be in Nashville before tomorrow night." Hood sent a telegram to Jefferson Davis on November 28, stating, "The enemy evacuated Columbia last night and are retreating towards Nashville. Our army is again moving forward. I have no difficulty about supplies and anticipate none in the future."[32]

As Schofield pulled out of Columbia and moved northward, Hood continued his pursuit. He told his army after they had crossed the Tennessee River, "You march to-day to redeem by your valor and your arms one of the fairest portions of our Confederacy. This can only be achieved by battle and by victory. Summon up in behalf of a consummation so glorious all the elements of soldiership and all the instincts of manhood, and you will render the campaign before you full of auspicious fruit to your country and lasting renown to yourselves."[33] At Spring Hill, on November 29, 1864, Hood had the opportunity to outflank the Union army and trap General John Schofield. If Hood could eliminate Schofield's army, he would have a clear path into Nashville and prevent additional Union troops from arriving to further solidify the city's defenses. In order to catch Schofield, someone had to block the main pike to trap the Union commander.

Hood ordered Cheatham to attack and block the pike, supported by Alexander Stewart's corps. However, Cheatham's men, especially those led by Patrick Cleburne, did not know where the Union defensive position was located, because Forrest's cavalry had never scouted the ground. When Cheatham rode to meet with Hood, he found the general quite irritated. Hood remarked, "General, why in the name of God have you not attacked the enemy, and taken possession of that pike?" Cheatham did not take the pike because he had waited for Stewart, who was to assist in the endeavor. However, Stewart never arrived, for Hood had ordered him to remain at Rutherford Creek. Hood remarked, "The men have had a hard day's march, and I do not wish you [Stewart] to march your whole corps up to the right. It will be too far for the men to march." Thus, with men being shuffled about in a confusing fashion, with little knowledge of the precise location of the Union force, no one attacked or moved to block the pike. The opportunity to capture Schofield slipped away into the night.[34]

The next day, November 30, 1864, Hood, disappointed with the missed opportunity at Spring Hill, attended a tense breakfast of "fried ham, hot biscuits and steaming coffee," where the accusations over the failure at Spring Hill flew faster than the biscuits. Hood had alleviated the blame from Stewart, telling him, "I wish you and your people to understand that I attach no blame to you for the failure at Spring Hill; on the contrary, I know if I had had you there the attack would have been made." Despite his own mistakes, Hood blamed Cheatham, and his attitude at breakfast was "wrathy as a rattlesnake." A few days following Spring Hill, Hood would rescind his recommendation to the Confederate government to promote Cheatham. Hood had every right to be angry, for he realized that Schofield had escaped to join Thomas at Nashville, making his campaign now ten times harder. Furthermore, the soldiers in the army realized a tactical error had been committed. J. P. Cannon wrote, "Every private was impressed with the idea that a fearful blunder had been made, and many remarks were made uncomplimentary to those in command. Of course, we were not in position to know who was responsible for the failure."[35]

The lack of clear communication between Hood and his corps commanders had prompted some historians to claim that Hood had been drugged up or drunk at Spring Hill. Historians look at Confederate scout John Gregory's claim that a few hours before the Spring Hill engagement, "there had been a good deal of drinking among the officers." Gregory claimed that Cheatham had been drunk and other subordinate officers also reached the point of intoxication. John Johnston, a soldier with Nathan Bedford Forrest, claimed whiskey as the root of failure at Spring Hill. Other historians have suggested that because Hood had been strapped to his horse since 3 a.m., it may have placed the general in a state utter physical exhaustion, resulting in his ingestion of painkillers, especially if Hood's horse had taken a fall on the "muddy, badly rutted Davis Ferry Road."[36]

Any analysis that bases failure at Spring Hill on alcohol and drug usage is problematic, particularly with the limited amount of evidence. Though it is documented that drinking took place among the officers, there are no specific references to Hood being drunk. Furthermore, there are no sources indicating that Hood had taken any painkillers to alleviate the constant pain from his injuries. Thus, until evidence appears directly indicating that Hood had been drunk or under the influence of narcotics, they cannot be included in the analysis of why the Army of Tennessee failed at Spring Hill. The failure to know the precise location of Union forces, coupled with Hood's inability to effectively communicate with his officers, resulted in failure.

Even with failure at Spring Hill, the Confederacy remained hopeful that Hood would "relieve our oppressed country." Hood later remembered, "I hereupon decided, before the enemy would be able to reach his stronghold at Nashville, to . . . overtake and rout him . . . since I could no longer hope to get between him and Nashville." The afternoon following the tense breakfast, Hood decided to send his nearly twenty-thousand-man army forward against an entrenched position at the town of Franklin. Formulating a plan from the William Harrison house outside Franklin, Hood surveyed the open stretch of field and announced, "We will make the fight!" Hood said, "Moreover, the highest perfection in the education of troops well disciplined, can only be attained through continued appeals to their pride, and through incitement to make known their prowess by the substantial test of guns and colors captured upon the field of battle. Soldiers thus educated will ever prove a terror to the foe." Hood planned for the attack to take place that afternoon around 4 p.m.[37]

Regarding the battle at Franklin, one Union soldier commented, "It was worth a year of one's lifetime to witness the marshalling and advance of the rebel line of battle. Emerging from the woods in the most perfect order, two corps in front and one [division] in reserve, nothing could be more suggestive of strength and discipline, and resistless power than was this long gray advancing over the plain." The grand scene of the soldiers marching in line in the late autumn afternoon turned chaotic, as the Confederates attacked again and again to the point where "blood actually ran in the ditch and in places saturated our clothing where we were laying down," according to one Confederate soldier. Bullets shot across the landscape with "one unceasing volley." Confederate General Patrick Cleburne led an assault that briefly broke the Union's easternmost position, near the Gin House. Hood ordered Cleburne at the start of the battle, commanding, "General, form your division to the right of the pike . . . I wish you to move on the enemy. Give orders to your men not to fire a gun until you run the Yankee skirmish line from behind the first line of works in your front, then press them and shoot them in their backs as they run to their main line; then charge the enemy works." Hood spoke on the importance of Cleburne's task by emphasizing, "Franklin is the key to Nashville and Nashville is the key to independence." Even though he thought the charge a mistake, Cleburne remarked, "General, I will take the works or fall in the attempt."[38] Union reinforcements under General Emerson Opdycke halted the Confederate advance, resulting in the death of Cleburne.

The continual, two-mile frontal assaults against the Union army failed to dislodge Schofield from his entrenchments. The Confederate army had early success in smashing a hole in the center of the line, but Union troops rushed forward to close the gap. In the attempts to break the Union line, the Confederate dead and wounded piled up quickly. Sergeant Major Arthur Fulkerson, of the Nineteenth Tennessee, had his body torn by sixteen bullets during the battle. Private Wolsham, also of the Nineteenth Tennessee, declared, "Oh! This one scene of butchery will go down the ages in history as a blank page in the memory of our lost cause." Among Cleburne's men stood General Hiram Granbury, who led Texas soldiers forward only to be struck in the cheek with a ball. An eyewitness wrote, "Throwing both hand to his face as in the impulse of the instant to find where the pain was he sank forward on his knees, and there, half sitting, half crouching, with his hands over his face [he remained] rigid in the attitude in which the bullet with its blow and its swift coming of death had left him."[39]

General Henry Clayton, commanding his division, came later to the field. He recalled, "Moving rapidly up the road to Franklin we came up with the balance of the army at Spring Hill, and all soon moved on to Franklin. . . . We found that bloody and disastrous engagement begun, and were put in positions to attack, but night mercifully interposed to save us from the terrible scourge which our brave companions had suffered." The brutal fighting moved a private in the Eleventh Tennessee, to write, "Two men on each side of me and the one behind me were shot dead. We would drop and load and rise and fire. The second man [on] my right while I was down was shot through the head and fell dead across my body." One of Abraham Buford's men, part of the Confederate cavalry, remarked, "Our whole line would have been swept away had we not been ordered to throw ourselves on the ground, not daring to raise our heads nor crawl forward even a few rods to give succor to the wounded and dying."[40]

During the battle, General Hood decided not to use the artillery to its fullest capacity because "of the women and children remaining in the town." The correspondence with Sherman following Atlanta, when the two commanders discussed the necessity of firing artillery into civilian populations, must have influenced Hood's decision regarding his own batteries. Hood did recall that he planned to use artillery the following day, if another attack commenced. W. L. Truman, a member of the First Missouri Field Battery, wrote, "General Hood . . . gave orders that not a cannon should be fired. . . . We cannoneers begged our officers to let us go into battery. . . . They told us they wanted to do it as bad as we did, but could not disobey orders." With the Confederate artillery remaining silent, Truman saw the impact of Union shells, stating, "I saw one shell from this battery explode immediately in front of our advancing line, and at least ten men fell in a heap and never rose again, but the line never lost step."[41]

With the mounting number of casualties, color bearers still alive remained a rarity. Colonel M. D. L. Stephens, from the Thirty-first Mississippi, recalled that nine members of the color guard had been shot down. When another bearer fell, he took the flag "with some misgivings, feeling that I would be shot, but I could not refuse to take it." Stephens charged forward as the sun set. Suddenly, a Federal soldier leapt over the works and called, "You are bleeding to death. I must stop it." The Yankee soldier placed the tourniquet on the injured color bearer, and he remained on the field wounded as the battle raged around him. Eventually, "one dear fellow from Iowa pulled off a pair of thick blankets" and placed one under and on top of the wounded colonel. Stephens survived mostly because a Union soldier recognized him to be a colonel and made sure Stephens received care, as a captured prisoner, on the journey to Nashville. One Irish soldier came up to Stephens and said, "Colonel, I have something good for you, something to help you. Help yourself." The soldier handed Stephens a canteen of whiskey, and Stephens took a "good swallow, which warmed me up."[42]

Firing slowly died off in the late evening hours. Schofield decided to retreat to Nashville, giving the Confederates control of the field and, therefore, a victory. It came at a bloody price. The Eighteenth Alabama lost almost its entire regiment, of which the majority ended up captured. Hood claimed that the loss "in killed, wounded, and prisoners was 4,500" and that "The number of dead left by the enemy on the field indicated that his loss was equal or near our own." In reality, Hood lost more than seven thousand irreplaceable soldiers, and among the officers lost five generals dead and several more wounded. His battlefield report stated, "About 4:00 p.m. November 30, we attacked the enemy at Franklin, and drove them from their centre line, of temporary work, into their inner lines, which they evacuated during the night, leaving their dead and wounded in our possession, and retired to Nashville, closely pursued by our cavalry." Hood concluded his field report to the secretary of war, stating, "Our troops fought with real gallantry. We have to lament the loss of many gallant officers and brave men." At the same time, Hood justified his attack, explaining how he had no other choice with the lost opportunity at Spring Hill. He later recalled, "The attack which entailed so great sacrifice of life, had, for reasons already stated, became a necessity as imperative as that which impelled General Lee to order the assault at Gaines's Mills, when our troops charged across an open space."[43]

Colonel Stone, a Federal staff officer, wrote an account of the Battle of Franklin that General Edward Porter Alexander later reprinted in his memoir to explain the contours of battle. Stone wrote, "More than one color-bearer was shot down on the parapet. It is impossible to exaggerate the fierce energy with which the Confederate soldiers, that short November afternoon, threw themselves against the works." Hood's soldiers fought with "what seemed the very madness of despair." Stone recalled the lack of wind and abundant dense smoke that "after the first assault, it was impossible to see at any distance."[44] As the smoke eventually cleared from the field of battle, the grim reality of death and destruction began to settle into the hearts and minds of the soldiers.

The next morning, Hood surveyed the field. William Berryhill stated, "They say that it is horrible to behold. They are laying men in piles, some across others, and in some places the Yankees and Confederates are piled up together." Bowers, a member of Ferguson's Battery, said, "Gen. Hood stopped close to where I was standing and took a long . . . view of the arena of the awful contest. . . . His sturdy visage assumed a melancholy appearance, and for a considerable time he sat on his horse and wept like a child." "I distinctly remember seeing General Hood riding down through the street of Franklin with his one wooden leg and his long, tawny mustache and whiskers," wrote fifteen-year-old Franklin resident Hardin Figures. Before seeing Hood in person, Figures had a preconceived notion of what Hood would look like as a gallant and honorable commander. Now, the young man saw Hood in a moment of reality following a disastrous battle and concluded, "I . . . was much disappointed."[45]

The aura of Hood's celebrity crashed in the mind of Hardin Figures, as he witnessed a distraught and defeated general. Destruction and failure altered Hood's usual jovial and noble appearance. When Hood received word reporting the death of Cleburne, he "then took the cigar out of his mouth, lowered his head, and wept for half an hour." As the residents of Franklin began to clean up, eight-year-old Alice McPhail Nichol said that "We saw a man sitting in a chair in the yard. He looked so sad, and grandpa told me that was Gen. Hood." Moscow Carter, a resident of Franklin, recalled that "Although Hood was said to be a rash fighter, it was hardly thought he would be reckless enough to make a determined assault on the formidable works in front of him."[46]

Immediately after the battle, Captain Samuel T. Foster gave vent to frustration and anger. On December 1, 1864, Foster wrote, "Gen. Hood has betrayed us. This is not the kind of fighting he promised. . . . This was not a fight with equal numbers and choice of the ground by no means." Foster, a supporter of Johnston, criticized Hood's inability to fulfill promises made at the beginning of the campaign. His most telling words against Hood followed. He wrote that "the wails and cries of widows and orphans made at Franklin Tenn. Nov 30th 1864 will heat up the fires of the bottomless pit to burn the soul of Gen J. B. Hood for Murdering their husbands and fathers at the place that day. It can't be called anything else but cold blooded Murder." His continual emphasis of the word murder, capitalized with each reference, reverberates the deadly effects of casualties on the heart and soul of an army. Foster concluded that Hood had "sacrificed those men to make the name Hood famous." In the end, however, "it will make him *infamous.*"[47]

Because Hood declared the battle a victory, many of the soldiers stood dumbfounded on how a victory could be declared in the midst of thousands of horrific casualties. One Mississippi soldier stated, "God grant I may never again behold our victorious band so deeply dyed in blood—the blood of the noblest and bravest men who battled in freedoms cause." The bodies on the field held a look with "ghastly faces and glassy eyes," according to one soldier. The dead, according to one Mississippian, "expressed supreme fear and terror." He described the "mental agony they had endured before death released them." Fred S. Hewes, also a Mississippi soldier, stated, "We had so many wounded that all could not be removed, and an intelligent humanity became necessary." When the search party reached a friend of Hewes who had been hit by grape shot, a "blanket was drawn over him and he was left in his blood alone to die, not one word of spiritual comfort, not even a friendly touch to ease his pain, the only sounds the groans of the wounded and murmurs of the dying." As his friend perished from the earth, Hewes noted the temperature drop and declared, "The Blessed Merciful God sent the cold to freeze his blood that his pains might cease and he pass in peace."[48]

By dislodging the Union army, Hood claimed victory and continued to push onward toward Nashville. The *Cincinnati Commercial* viewed the battle in a different light, in terms of failure of victory, writing, "What once was threatened to be a disastrous defeat was turned into a glorious victory, by the courage of our officers and the desperate bravery of our men." Yet, despite the claims of Union victory, Hood persevered. He issued word to his soldiers and officers, offering congratulations for success achieved through "heroic and determined courage." Hood acknowledged, that although the soldiers would "lament the fall of many gallant officers and brave men," his army still had sent the Union forces "in disorder and confusion to Nashville."[49]

The Confederate force, despite some misgivings, regrouped and marched to Nashville. Joseph Cumming recalled, "We had an abundance of good food, beef, mutton, pork, flour and potatoes." Despite the food, Franklin weighed heavily on the minds of the men. One Missouri captain remarked, "Our army was a wreck. I can safely say that just two such victories will wipe out any army the power of man can organize." As they filed out of Franklin, one soldier noted, "Nothing better calculated to affright and demoralize an army could have been devised than by the exhibition of the dead, as they appeared to those who viewed them there in marching past the gin house that morning." Captain Henry Clay Weaver, of the Sixteenth Kentucky, wrote in a letter to his sweetheart, "Franklin taught me the horrors of war, and remember darling, that while I cannot consent to call myself a base coward, I cannot even yet, think of some incidents witnessed on that bloody field without a cold chill running over me."⁵⁰

As the remnants of the Army of Tennessee moved into position around Nashville, Hood decided to order his men to throw up earthworks and awaited an attack. Hood had told Chaplain Quintard on December 12, "There will be no more great flanking operations . . . the enemy will have to seek our armies and fight them where he can find them . . . there will be more blood spilled in 1865 than in 1864—but . . . the losses will be on the side of the Federals." Yet, one southern critic later stated, "If he had taken another course and struck boldly across the Cumberland, and settled himself in the enemy's communications, he would have forced Thomas to evacuate Nashville and fall back towards Kentucky." Yet, that maneuver could have proven risky, as the winter weather and the strength of Thomas's army proved a formidable task. As the *Charleston Mercury* reported, "Our commander, who, though impetuous and dashing, is not by any means reckless, instantly saw the needlessness of sacrificing so many valuable lives as would be necessary in making a direct assault."⁵¹

As the army waited in the entrenchments, the weather, which had been reasonably mild for December in Tennessee, drastically changed on December 7, with a blast of cold air, followed by five days of ice and sleet. With several soldiers lacking shoes, clothing, and blankets, and with food rations declining, the weather proved a formidable opponent as the men awaited attack. As Hood waited, he wired for more supplies. His telegram stated, "Maj. Pridewell at Augusta has fifty bales of blankets belonging to this army. Please have them sent forward at once in charge of some officers who will push them through. The weather is severe, the ground covered with snow and the men stand much in need of them." Hood also called for "ten thousand sets of clothing and all the additional blankets that can be spared to this army." However, many soldiers had to leave the ranks to search for "whatever leather could be found, and the troops learned that they could build a surprisingly warm shelter by scooping out a hole in the ground large enough for three men to lie in and two or three feet deep." The soldiers covered the hole with twigs, branches and the few blankets on hand.⁵²

But things were not much better on the Union side. The Union did have a numerical advantage, with eighty thousand soldiers compared to Hood's thirty thousand. However, Union General George Thomas, an old friend and comrade of Hood from Fort Mason, Texas, who had been under continual pressure from General Grant and President Lincoln, also had to deal with the weather. Grant wrote to Thomas in early December, commanding "Attack Hood at once, and wait no longer for a remount of your cavalry. There is great danger of delay resulting in a campaign back to the Ohio River." Grant's panic may have rested on a report from Major General George Stoneman, who said, "Bristol papers say Hood has whipped Thomas badly, and that Hood is on his way into Kentucky, where he will be joined by Longstreet." If Thomas could not attack, Grant urged him to call upon the local governors to have an army ready to meet Hood at Louisville. Thomas had to hold Nashville, especially with Sherman uninterested and unavailable to pursue Hood. Thomas sent Grant another note on December 11, which said, "The whole country is covered with a perfect sheet of ice and sleet, and it is with difficulty the troops are able to move about on level ground. It was my intention to attack Hood as soon as the ice melted, and would have done so yesterday had it not been for the storm."[53]

By December 13, the temperatures warmed and rain, rather than ice, fell the next day. With the weather changing, Hood knew the attack stood on the horizon. He not only again wired for supplies, but also for reinforcements. Hood heard a report of fifteen thousand Confederates landing near Memphis. He relayed a telegram to Beauregard, stating, "I respectfully request that all men belonging to this army or any reinforcements that can be spared be sent forward as soon as possible." The men never arrived.[54]

Thomas attacked on December 15, 1864, advancing all along the Confederate position. Soldiers from Texas protected the far right of the Confederate line. Hood declared, "Texans, I want you to hold this hill regardless of what transpires around you." Hood trusted in the soldiers to protect the flanks of the line. The Texas troops, sensing hesitation, unleashed a volley of lead and then stampeded the Union troops, halting any further attacks on the Confederate right during the day. Union commander George Thomas remained confident after the first day's action. He wrote, "Our troops behaved splendidly, all taking their share in assaulting and charging the enemy's breastworks. I shall attack the enemy again tomorrow if he stands to fight, and if he retreats during the night, I will pursue him, throwing a heavy cavalry force in his rear to destroy his trains if possible." During the night, Hood ordered the soldiers to dig in at a new line two miles back toward the south and prepare for the next day.[55]

The next morning, Joseph Cumming recalled, "We were in the saddle by daybreak of the 16th, and while we waited at the house for the General to limp out and mount, the ladies appeared at the upper windows." Cumming noticed that the women had recently awoken, for "they held the curtains across their persons up to their chins, and over those breastworks gave us their wishes and blessings." However, the first rays of daylight gave way to war again, when Thomas attacked and opened the battle with a two hour bombardment, followed by an assault with "heavy double lines" against the Confederates at Overton Hill, where Thomas believed the Confederate line most vulnerable. The attack, including Colonel C. R. Thompson's brigade of African American troops, stormed "up a slope," only to be swept away "by musketry and grape shot." The Federals regrouped and charged again thirty yards from the Confederate lines, only to be shattered by the Confederate defenses. At some locations, "dead men in blue lay five-deep."[56] Thirty percent of all Union casualties occurred at the assaults made at Overton Hill.

Meanwhile, along the rest of the Confederate line, matters worsened. At Shy's Hill, Union artillery delivered a deadly cross fire against the Tennessee troops, prior to soldiers from Illinois, Indiana, Ohio, and Minnesota charging the hill, supported with continual artillery fire. The heavy numbers of Union soldiers overcame the Confederate positions and stormed forward. Basil Duke stated, "A major on General Hoods staff told me that after the men commissioned leaving the line of works 'that every breathing thing, man, horse, jack mules and dogs all turned their faces towards the Franklin Pike and ran as hard as they could; everything frightened to almost to death.'" William Dudley Gale, while witnessing the retreat, wrote of a woman named Mary Bradford. Bradford "ran out under heavy fire and did all she could to induce the men to stop and fight." Bradford appealed and begged to the men to stand and fight, even after Confederate hopes of victory faded into the evening hours.[57]

With the Confederate line broken beyond repair, the Union army continued forward and drove Hood from the city of Nashville, forcing the Confederates to abandon fifty-four artillery pieces. Hood lost 4,462 men killed, wounded, or missing, again suffering irreplaceable casualties. Furthermore, the Union, suffering only 3,057 soldiers, had won a clear victory, and staved off disaster, had Hood won the day. After the war, Henry Stone, a staff officer to General Thomas, remembered, "At so small a cost, counting the chances of war, the whole Northwest was saved from an invasion that, if Hood had succeeded, would have more than neutralized all Sherman's successes in Georgia and the Carolinas." Gideon Viars, a Union soldier, stated, "We have drove the rebels all the time and cut them up terribly. They are the worst demoralized army that I ever heard of." The *Charlottesville Chronicle,* reflecting on all that was lost at Nashville, wrote, "Suppose we had taken Nashville—what then? Mr. Davis . . . gave out that some terrible plan was on foot which would annihilate Sherman as the French were destroyed in the Russian campaign." As the Confederates departed Nashville, Hood called out to his men, "Boys, the cards were fairly dealt at Nashville and Thomas beat the game." Sergeant

James Stevenson of the Nineteenth Tennessee replied, "Yes General, but the cards were [damned] badly shuffled."[58]

The plans that Davis and Beauregard had approved for the Army of Tennessee and the success of the Confederate independence movement collapsed on the frozen ground along the Cumberland River. Nothing could replace the thousands of dead and dispirited soldiers who had endured Hood's Tennessee campaign, resulting in what war clerk John Jones called an "irretrievable disaster." Hood seriously considered the idea of forming a defensive position along the Duck River. However, Nathan Bedford Forrest arrived on December 19 to tell Hood to immediately withdraw the army south of the Tennessee River. Hood agreed and discarded any ideas of remaining within the Volunteer State. Hood's guilt emerged on the retreat, as Chaplain Charles Quintard noted in his diary, that Hood "had so set his heart upon success—had prayed so earnestly for it—had such a firm trust that he should succeed." Yet, during the retreat, Hood described himself to Chaplain Quintard, stating, "I am afraid that I have been more wicked since I began this retreat than for a long time past. I had so set my heart upon success, had prayed so earnestly for it." Hood trusted in the idea that success would come his way, but "his heart has been very rebellious." Thus, all Hood could do was declare that his soldiers sing hymns as they departed Tennessee.[59]

Immediately after the battle, Hood began working to explain the military failure in a way that would not necessarily damage his reputation any more than the military loss already had achieved. Hood reported after the battle that, "At Nashville, had it not have been for an unfortunate event which could not justly have been anticipated, I think we would have gained a complete victory." He definitively stated, "It is my firm conviction that, notwithstanding that disaster, I left the army in better spirits and with more confidence in itself than it had at the opening of the campaign. The official records will show that my losses, including prisoners, during the entire campaign do not exceed 10,000 men." In retrospect, Hood would "make the same marches and fight the same battles, trusting that the same unforeseen and unavoidable accident would not again occur to change into disaster a victory which had been already won."[60]

After Hood died in the postwar era, an obituary writer reexamined the movement into Tennessee. The author acknowledged that in the postwar period he had many conversations with General Hood. When he asked Hood to comment on the Tennessee campaign, Hood responded with a question, asking, "Do you know what a forlorn hope is, and what the duty and position of the officer who leads it?" When the author acknowledged he knew, Hood "impressively" stated, "Then, I have nothing more to say." In the postwar period, Hood reflected on his assignment commanding the Army of Tennessee as a forlorn hope, or an impossible situation. If Hood secured victory, the rewards would have been unimaginable.[61]

The Army of Tennessee had become a ghostly resemblance of its former moments of glory. Joseph Cumming remembered, "Our horses had nothing to eat for 24 hours, and they fairly staggered over the rough roads. Finally, after a ride of 52 miles we got a scanty supply of forage for them. The country was desolate and barren, and everything near the road in the way of the horse feed had been consumed by our army of invasion." The Army of Tennessee, now disillusioned to the point of despair, complained about their commander and longed for a return to the days under Joseph Johnston. John Forsyth wrote, "Hood's army is not worth the value of a regiment if that officer is retained in command.... It is a shattered debris of an army and needs careful yet vigorous handling to hold it together." Most important, Hood's plan of reuniting with Lee vanished in the midst of fire and lead. A few soldiers of the Army of Tennessee changed the lyrics to the popular tune, "The Yellow Rose of Texas." The new version critiqued Hood: "So now we're going to leave you, our hearts are full of woe; We're going back to Georgia to see our Uncle Joe. You may talk about your Beauregard and sing of General Lee, But the gallant Hood of Texas played hell in Tennessee."[62]

As the disasters at Franklin and Nashville reverberated throughout the South, a cloud of gloom seemed to settle over the general populace. One citizen simply noted, "It is truly a gloomy time." Henri Garidel called the loss at Nashville "very disturbing," and with Hood beaten, he noted, "This miserable war drags on and on." In a letter to his wife Malinda, Grant Taylor wrote, "As to going to the cavalry I have no idea I can get a transfer. I know I cannot get one to go with Jack and if I could get one to go with Wick I would have to go to the Army of Tenn. and be under old Hood and I do not like that." Taylor knew that as a member of the cavalry, he would not only avoid the bloody engagements the infantry had faced in recent weeks, but he would also get to ride a horse, especially after the hard travel many of the soldiers had endured on the Tennessee campaign.[63]

Captain Foster once more took an opportunity to reflect on the sacrifices made by the Army of Tennessee under Hood's leadership. He wrote, "Those men who fell in 1864 even in Dec. 64 sacrificed their lives as freely as did the very first that fell in the war. There was no cooling down, no tapering off, no lukewarmness in those men, but they would brave danger when ordered as fearless of Yankee bullets." Once more, Foster praised Johnston and condemned Hood, stating, "At Franklin Tenn. Dec. 1st or Nov. 30/64 was the most wholesale butchery of human lives ever witness[ed] by us. Those brave men had been taught by Gen. Johnston to fear nothing when he made a fight, and expecting the same thing of Hood, were betrayed into a perfect slaughter pen."[64] Foster continued the live with the bitterness of defeat and continued to blame Hood. Yet, Foster could only begin to understand the complicated circumstances and perilous situation that faced Hood when he embarked on this campaign. No officer could have lived up to Foster's expectations at this stage in the war.

Others looked to blame Hood not only for the loss in Tennessee, but also the ease with which Sherman ransacked the state of Georgia. William Pitt Chambers stated, "The campaign inaugurated by General Hood in September has proven the most disastrous of any we have yet sustained." Chambers looked at the dual consequences of the campaign, saying, "In addition to the loss of an army and its equipments, a way was opened for Gen. Sherman to march through the entire state of Georgia, which he promptly did, leaving a broad trail of desolation behind him."[65]

The same level of criticism came from other soldiers. David Pierson wrote a letter to his father, William, dated January 11. The letter read, "I presume you have heard all the bad news that was on hand about a week ago about Sherman's taking Savannah and Hood's defeat in Tenn. It was the worst of the war, and spread gloom and dismay hereabouts." Pierson wrote that "Men of sense and position were freely talking on the streets of our being whipped." He concluded, "Such has never been the case before, and it clearly shows the ominous state of affairs. We are in a bad fix, and everybody knows and feels it. If something is not done and that speedily, all must be lost." Sarah Wadley said, "Hood is defeated, Lee threatened, and the Yankees exult; the Insurrection, they say, is about to collapse." Thomas Goree, writing from Virginia to his brother, asserted that "Hood has again been badly whipped near Nashville." He wrote, "I have only hoped that we might get his *army* back again from Tenn. Now I very much fear that it will be entirely destroyed. *It is too bad!*"[66]

Basil Duke wrote, "General Hood is very unpopular at present but a great many officers say if his orders had been carried out or obeyed Tenn. would have been ours today." Duke pointed the finger at Cheatham, who "disobeyed an order at Spring Hill." He proclaimed that Cheatham had been "ordered to attack at that place and did not do it but let the enemy pass a short distance of him." Even though the army failed at Nashville, Duke observed that "the enemy were repulsed several times with great slaughter." Robert Kean, horrified by the nearly three thousand wounded Confederates left at Nashville, observed that, "disasters have come thick and fast." He pointed out that the "fearful loss" left Hood "fleeing with the shattered remains of that unfortunate army, which has never yet fought under a general nor gained a victory except the sorrowful one of Chickamauga."[67] Heavy casualties at Franklin and Nashville shattered the optimism of Robert Kean, and hope seemed to vanish like the flash of gunpowder.

Despite the heavy casualties suffered by Hood, General Grant remained concerned because he had repeatedly urged Thomas to "attack Hood at once" and "speedily dispose" of the Confederate force threatening Nashville. In a letter to Sherman on December 27, 1864, Grant described his present feelings about Hood: "Hood is now retreating, with his army broken and demoralized. His loss in men has probably not been far from twenty thousand, besides deserters. If time is given, the fragments may be collected together and many of the deserters reassembled," Grant wrote. He knew it was crucial to stop Hood immediately, even in the aftermath of a terrible defeat. George Thomas reassured Grant, writing, "With the exception of the rear guard, [Hood's] army had become a disheartened and disorganized rabble of half-armed and barefooted men." Yet, Grant assigned a section of Sherman's army to make sure Hood did not regroup.[68]

Even with Grant's concerns, the Army of Tennessee did not seem to be in a condition where it could threaten northern ambitions. James Phelan, in a letter to Jefferson Davis on January 17, 1865, described the "present unhappy condition of General Hood's army," noting that the "physical wants" had been satisfied but the emotional state of the army remained in shambles. As Phelan noted, "It's spirit and morale are gone." The Army of Tennessee had been reduced to a "mere mob, without spirit but that of mutinous anger and without hope or care for the future." Even with this conclusion regarding the condition of the army, Phelan did not take the opportunity to lash out at Hood. Instead, he called Hood a "gallant, true man!" "Deeply do I sympathize with him in his misfortunes, and earnestly do I labor to sustain his palsied arm and defend his noble character," stated Phelan. Hood continued to believe that the morale of the army had not fallen to devastating levels, as witnessed by Phelan. Instead of placing the blame on Hood for the failure of the campaign, Phelan concluded, Hood "is only human, and we can well appreciate the causes which prompt him to hope and believe 'better things' than appear to every impartial eye and mind. . . . Truth, when terrible, is hard to bear; but safety abides only in its utterance."[69]

At the same time, Phelan, like Foster, remained adamant in his request that Johnston be returned to command of the army. He said, "I fully approved his removal when displaced by General Hood. I am now as earnestly desirous for his restoration. Apart from all question of his capacity as a Commander, there is a depth of popular feeling and a degree of public clamor which the best policy demands shall be respected." The bond between Johnston and his men did not fade after Hood took the reigns of command. Instead, Phelan observed, "I have not seen a single officer or man who does not declare that it furnishes the only hope for the salvation of the army." Phelan even claimed that Johnston's return would create "a depth of feeling and an intensity of expression" and a "fanatic faith" in all "classes and ranks in the sublime consequences that would result from the restoration of that [Johnston] officer." If Johnston did not get the opportunity to once more command his army, "it will furnish a *pretext* for every failure or disaster that may befall our arms."[70]

With failure dashing all efforts of the Tennessee campaign and a rising sentiment against his ability to command, Hood contemplated his next move. The Confederacy was relieved that Hood had escaped safely. The *Charleston Mercury* wrote, "We have now four months of rest and recuperation before us. Enough strength and enough spirit are left in the country to ensure our independence, if that strength be not wanted and the spirit be kept alive." But his soldiers grew in despair as they realized the current state of affairs. J. P. Cannon wrote, "The future seemed almost hopeless. Our armies were constantly retreating before innumerable, fresh and fully equipped troops. Worn out with hardship and fatigue, hunger and cold, we were in poor condition to bear the vicissitudes of the winter, which was upon us."[71] Hood's weakened force now had to face a harsh winter with an increasing decline in food and clothing available, as they limped farther into the Deep South.

As the army moved back to Corinth, Mississippi, the *Montgomery Appeal* stated, "Hood is in a much better position for defense at Corinth than he would be at Palmetto or Lovejoy's Station in Georgia." Though the failure of the Tennessee campaign remained disheartening, the paper stated, "The heart of the Confederacy is at least free from the presence of the enemy and the tread of hostile armies, and by proper vigilance on the part of our authorities and the people it may be kept so." One citizen, Ellen House, heard that "Gen. Hood certainly died of pneumonia." The origin of the rumor remains unclear, but apparently House used it to vent her frustration over the state of the Confederate war effort. Although her diary had gone unwritten during Sherman's march to the sea, she again made notations in 1865. House noted her hopes on several occasions that Johnston would return to command. On January 1, 1865, she wrote, "Gen. Johnston is to take command of the army of Tenn. once more." By the end of the month, she wrote, "We are to have a Commander-in-chief of our army. I hope Gen. Lee will be he, and Gen. Johnston is to take the field again."[72]

With Hood's army no longer threatening to prolong the war, Lincoln spoke with his cabinet in Washington and told a parable about a man named Slocum and his bulldog. Slocum, "a certain rough, rude and bullying man" possessed the same characteristics as his bulldog, or vice versa. The two terrorized a small community in Illinois. One day, a neighbor came up with a plan. Lincoln said, "Seeing Slocum plodding along the road one day, his dog a little ahead, this neighbor took from his pocket a chunk of meat, in which he had concealed a big charge of powder, to which he had fastened a Deadwood slow-match." After the match had been lit, the neighbor threw the chunk on meat onto the road. The bulldog saw the meat and "gave one gulp at it." After enjoying the morsel of meat, the dog took a few steps forward and then suddenly "blew up in fragments—a forequarter lodging in a neighboring tree, a hindquarter on the roof of a cabin, his head in one place, his tail in another, and the rest scattered along a dusty road." When the dog's master, Slocum, came to view the remains, he cried out, "Bill was a good dog, but as a dog, I reckon his usefulness is over." Lincoln then offered the moral of the story: "Hood's army was a good army. We have been very much afraid of it. But, as an army, I reckon its usefulness is over."[73]

Of note, the bulldog story seemed to echo among the ranks of the Confederacy. William George Pirtle, in his own memoir, said, "The backbone so to speak of the army was broken, and all had lost their bulldogishness to a great extent." Hood, with no fear, "dashed at the yanks, with a whim that cost him more than was possible for him to ever recover." Yet, the failure at Nashville had taken something out of Hood. Pirtle concluded, "Now another fact is that a bull dog is a bull dog, and is hard to conquer but when beaten at his own game, he becomes as docile as a lamb."[74]

Defeat, and political and societal pressure, now engulfed the bulldog, John Bell Hood. Robert Patrick said, "Taken all together the aspect of affairs is anything but encouraging to say the least. If the government allows Hood full swing, he will soon terminate his army." Hood continued to command, issuing a general order on January 15, 1865, granting furloughs to men to "remain at home [no] longer than 15 days" in hopes that they would return to the army with absentees and recruits. He wrote to Jefferson Davis, stating, "If I am allowed to remain in command of this Army I hope you will grant me authority to reorganize it and relieve all incompetent officers. If thought best to *relieve me,* I am ready to command a Corps or Division or do anything that may be considered best for my country." Hood wrote to Stephen Dill Lee on the same date, saying, "I am of course much annoyed at the abuse of my countrymen." Hood now placed his confidence in Stephen Lee, even with the tension between the two commanders during the Atlanta campaign. Hood relayed the message to Lee that he had informed Beauregard that he wanted to be relieved of command, and wanted to either command a corps "or whatever is best for my country."[75]

In a scathing letter to Braxton Bragg, John Forsyth wrote, "Hood's army is not worth the value of a regiment if that officer is retained its command. The men have no confidence in him, and it cannot be inspired. I do not believe the army can be revived under him. It is a shattered debris of an army now, and needs careful, yet vigorous, handing to hold it together." Forsyth noted a unanimous call from the men for Johnston to return to command. He continued, "Men have been taught to look upon the President as a sort inexorable, self-willed man, who will see the country to the devil before giving up an opinion or a purpose. This sentiment is producing alarming consequences of despondency and despair. The President should cultivate the popular feeling, emerge from his shell, and disabuse the public mind." Two days later, January 19, General Richard Taylor arrived in the Tupelo area, and Hood could see his tenure at command had come to a close.[76]

On January 23, 1865, Hood officially resigned and ended his role as commander of the Army of Tennessee. In his official report to President Davis, Hood noted finding "so much dissatisfaction throughout the country." Hood asked to be removed "with the hope that another might be assigned to the command, who might do more than I could hope to accomplish." Hood separated from the Army of Tennessee at Tupelo, Mississippi, and returned to Richmond. He departed with a farewell address. Hood said, "In taking leave of you accept my thanks for the patience with which you have endured your many hardships during the recent campaign. I am alone responsible for its conception and strived hard to do my duty in its execution." Hood concluded by insisting that the army give their "entire support" to General Richard Taylor, son of Zachary Taylor, whom Hood called a "distinguished soldier." Taylor now took command of what remained of the Army of Tennessee.[77]

Yet, even with the mountain of failure that had arrived in Hood's career path, he remained devoted and committed to commanding Confederate armies. Before leaving for Richmond, he wrote Jefferson Davis, stating, "I wish to cross the Mississippi River to bring to your aid twenty-five thousand troops. I know this can be accomplished and earnestly desire this chance to do you so much good service. Will explain my plan on arrival."[78] Hood had let Davis down with the failure of the Tennessee campaign. He wanted to again prove his worth, and his honorable manhood, as a prominent Confederate commander with a strong desire to change the tide of war, and he sought to do so in the West.

Rumors and news spread quickly of a new Confederate commander replacing John Bell Hood. When word of Hood's resignation reached Confederate citizen Kate Stone, she noted in her journal, "[It is said] that Hood is relieved from command and Gen. Johnston reinstated, a rumor that gives general satisfaction." Rumor reached the city of Columbia, South Carolina, that Hood had been killed, sending some citizens into the streets to celebrate. The *Daily Picayune* wrote, "The whole country will be rejoiced, and the army electrified by the telegraphic announcement that Gen. J. E. Johnston has been restored to the command of the Army of Tennessee." The writer observed that Jefferson Davis "has never yet appreciated the full force of the shock produced both upon the army and the people by the unexpected, unnecessary and uncalled for removal of Gen. Johnston from the command of the army, in whose love, confidence and esteem he held an exalted, if not, the very first, place." The author concluded, "It was an evil day for the country and the cause that witnessed his [Johnston] removal from its command, but now that the wrong has been righted, let us hope that all will again move on smoothly, zealously and energetically."[79]

In fact, Hood remained alive and returned to Richmond, staying at the Spotswood Hotel to construct his report of the campaign. To no surprise, Hood's report blamed Joseph Johnston for his early conduct during the Atlanta campaign, and he blamed William Hardee for failure in the battles once Johnston had been removed. Hood said, "I was placed in command under the most trying circumstances which can surround an officer when assigned to a new and most important command." He argued that he moved to take Nashville under the belief that "our people to have harassed, and, in a great measure, destroyed that portion moving to the coast." Yet, Hood noted, "Sherman, however, succeeded in marching to Savannah with but little annoyance, and we failed to gain Nashville." After reviewing the report, Governor Isham Harris asked Hood to make some changes, particularly removing the volley fired at Johnston. Hood said, "You are right, Govr. I wish to God, I had seen you sooner—but it is too late. I cannot change it now." Harris later alleviated Hood of blame by stating, "Hood was a puppet in the hands of others who were sacrificing him to gain their own ends—and striking through him a blow at Gen'l Johnston."[80]

When word reached Confederate military personnel of Hood's campaign report, a flurry of angry correspondences erupted. In particular, a few anonymous reports appeared in southern papers that resonated with the tone and language of Hood's official report. Joseph Johnston wrote to Hood, "After reading your report as submitted, I informed General Cooper by telegraph that I should prefer charges against you as soon as I have leisure to do so, and desired him to give you the information." Hood wondered if he would stand trial for the charges, but Cooper ordered him to proceed to Texas immediately. Hardee wrote to John Breckenridge to refute the report, stating, "It is well known that I felt unwilling to serve under General Hood upon his succession to the command of the Army of Tennessee, because I believed him, though a tried and gallant officer, to be unequal in both experience and natural ability to so important a command." He questioned Hood's failure to be on the field of battle at crucial times, and further asserted that Hood "allowed an enemy superior in numbers to pass unmolested around his flank" and that he failed to attack "with his whole army." Furthermore, Hardee wrote Hood directly, noting, "I cannot say that I am much surprised at its character. My question certainly indicated that I at least suspected you to be capable of attempting to thrust another between yourself and responsibility." Hardee accused Hood of committing slander toward "a brother officer." Hood replied that Hardee's correspondence had been "filled with insults and imputations" and demanded "a retraction of them." After a few more correspondences that eased in tone, the matter appeared to be dropped, as Hardee and Hood continued to battle for how they would be remembered in the postwar years.[81]

General Beauregard also chimed in to dispute portions of the report. For him, Hood's failure to issue the report to Beauregard before other Confederate officials caused the most angst, for Beauregard could have prevented "several errors and inaccuracies in the report," which he could not "leave unnoticed." Beauregard had met with Hood at Cave Spring, Georgia, not Gadsden, Alabama, as Hood had noted. Beauregard spent the rest of his letter going over troop movements and numbers throughout the early part of the Tennessee campaign, drawing constant attention that he constantly worried about "the safety of the troops." Beauregard did defend the plan to approve Hood's invasion of Tennessee, instead of turning around and pursuing Sherman, because Sherman had more soldiers, better roads, a several-week head start, and that Hood's pursuit would have been delayed because of the destruction of several bridges. However, even though the plan had been approved, Hood failed to execute the campaign "without undue delay and modifications and with vigor and skill." With Hood changing where he wanted to cross the Tennessee River, his army had been delayed three weeks, giving Sherman enough time to protect his supply lines.[82]

Furthermore, Beauregard assessed the attacks at Franklin and Nashville. He wrote, "It is clear, also, to my mind that after the great loss and waste of life at Franklin, the army was in no condition to make a successful attack on Nashville—a strongly fortified city, defended by an army nearly as strong as our own, and which was being re-enforced constantly by river and railroads." Hood should have "marched, not on Nashville, but on Murfreesborough, which could doubtless have been captured, with its garrison of about 8,000 men." Beauregard concluded his report by praising the soldiers, stating, "The heroic dead of that campaign will ever be recollected with honor by their countrymen, and the survivors have the proud consolation that no share of the disaster can be laid to them, who have so worthily served their country, and have stood by their colors even to the last dark hours of the republic."[83]

Hood's report received abundant criticism in certain newspapers. One editor hoped that the Confederacy could simply forget the horrific failures of the Atlanta and Tennessee campaigns. However, he wrote, "But General Hood would not have it so. A great part of his Report consists of polemical controversy against General Johnston. . . . It must now be at least admitted, that if General Hood cannot conduct a campaign, he can write a pamphlet." The editor did not necessarily blame Hood for the failures of the campaign, but instead, blamed Davis for naming him to the position in the first place. He wrote, "It will be admitted further that General Hood is a brave and patriotic officer, and in his proper sphere has done good service—in fact that in all this transaction he was not so much criminal as unfortunate—but then his countrymen were more unfortunate still." Though Hood's name had been "dear" to his Texas brigade when he led them "through storms of fire," everything changed when he had been named by Davis to command the army "in an evil hour." The editor concluded, "The country sympathizes with General Hood on that sinister promotion; but desires for the future, if possible, to be permitted to forget his name."[84]

Besides dealing with a barrage of angry correspondence, Hood received another task from Jefferson Davis. Hood was to "procure reinforcements from the Trans-Mississippi" and "gather together all troops willing to follow [him] and move at once to the support of General Lee." Hood had pitched the idea to Davis in January and followed up in March, suggesting that the troops could also "make a movement into Missouri from the other side." Before his departure, Hood wrote a letter to Jefferson Davis. He said, "Before leaving for Texas allow me to say that I more than appreciate all of your kindness to me. Please never allow anyone to cause you to think for one moment, that I did not know that you were ever more ready to assume all responsibility naturally belonging to you." Hood alleviated Jefferson Davis of the responsibility for the Tennessee campaign's failure by offering that he knew Davis was "in no way responsible for the operations whilst commanding the Army of Tenn." Yet, he concluded by defending his own actions, proclaiming, "I am more content and satisfied with my own work whilst in command of the army of Tenn., than all my military career in life." Hood had only begun to do his recruiting in Texas when word came of Lee surrendering to Grant at Appomattox Court House on April 9, 1865. May 31, 1865, marked Hood's final day as an officer in the Confederate army, when he surrendered to Union forces commanded by General John W. Davidson at Natchez, Mississippi.[85]

In a letter to Jefferson Davis, Governor Isham Harris reflected on Hood's career and the reason for failure in Tennessee. He wrote, "I have been with General Hood from the beginning of this campaign, and beg to say, disastrous as it has ended, I am not able to see anything that General Hood has done that he should not, or neglected anything that he should have done, which it was possible to do." Harris not only justified Hood's action but also justified his inactions as well, commenting, "Indeed, the more that I have seen and known of him and his policy, the more I have been pleased with him." Harris concluded, "If all had performed their parts as well as he, the results would have been very different."[86] Harris anticipated the fury of blame that would be placed on Hood's subordinates and their actions at Franklin and Nashville in stunning clarity. These phases of blame would emerge over the next several decades, as a war of words began to explode upon the print landscape.

Chapter 7

Staring into the Fire of Glory and Memory: Hood, New Orleans, and the Construction of Civil War Memory

> *Mr. Davis's favor was no less fatal to its object than his animosities. That young man had a fine career before him until Davis undertook to make him what the good Lord had not done—to make a great general of him. He had thus ruined Hood and destroyed the last hope of the Southern Confederacy.*
> *—Senator Louis T. Wigfall*

In January 1865, John Bell Hood visited with Mary Chesnut and the family of his recent but fading love interest, Sally "Buck" Preston. As Hood sat with the Preston family in conversation, stories filled the room pertaining to the Civil War. Hood described the battles at Franklin and Nashville as a "defeat" and declared, "My army is destroyed." The conversation changed subject to add a more jovial aura to the occasion, but Hood simply sat and did not listen. Jack Preston, who offered his residence as a place for Hood to stay, pulled Mary Chesnut aside to have a brief conversation. Preston remarked, "He did not hear a word she was saying. He had forgotten us all. Did you notice how he stared in the fire, and the livid spots which came out on his face, and the huge drops of perspiration that stood out on his forehead?" "Yes," Chesnut replied, "He is going over some bitter hours. He sees Willie Preston, with his heart shot away. He feels the panic at Nashville, and its shame." Willie Preston, the brother of Sally, had been killed during one of the battles around Atlanta. Jack Preston pushed further, "And the dead on the battlefield at Franklin, they say that was a dreadful sight." He concluded, "And that agony in his face comes again and again. I can't keep him out of those absent fits. It is pretty trying to anyone who looks on. When he looks in the fire and forgets me, and seems going through in his own mind the torture of the damned, I get up and come out as I did just now."[1]

Hood's behavior at the fireplace coincides with historian Eric Dean's understanding of the soldier's response to war's negative effects. Many soldiers suffered from posttraumatic stress disorder, exhibited through episodes of rage, guilt, flashbacks, panic, nightmares, and depression during and after the Civil War. Participating in war produced both mental and physical stress, as the toil of combat and disease wore down the body. As soldiers returned home, they brought with them the daily reminders of war. To cope with their own personal trauma, some soldiers performed acts of racial violence against African Americans. Others became delinquents or utilized morphine addiction to deal with their war memories. Unemployment rose among Civil War veterans, as the former soldiers retreated into their own private hell.[2]

Communities did try to assist their veterans through the pageantry of commemoration. Arthur Neal argues, "The act of commemoration is a formal means of giving recognition to the importance of past events and designating them as worthy of collective remembrance." Citizens tried to help soldiers by decorating graves, offering speeches, and building monuments in dealing with the horrors of war. With emphasis placed on the glorious acts of the soldier, "the horror of war is displaced," and southerners joined with northerners to emphasize those who were "willing to make personal sacrifices for promoting the collective good."[3]

Though commemoration may help soften the pain of the daily reminders of war, it could not completely obliterate memories. As Arthur Neal points out, "In effect, the psychological and physiological responses to traumatic events add up to feelings of helplessness and a crisis of meaning in the personal lives of individuals." Any event that alters how a person lives in society cannot be ignored, and "the traumas of the past become ingrained in collective memories and provide reference points to draw upon when the need arises." As participants during the Civil War came to grips with the experience they had just endured, many resolved to "take an active part in determining what their collective memories will be." However, for the South, the formation of a collective memory about the Civil War would not be easy. Southerners, because of the horrific nature of the war, dealt with two distinct types of social disruptions: an acute crisis and a chronic crisis. The acute crisis emerges "upon the normal course of events in an abrupt and dramatic fashion." The chronic crisis becomes one that is "enduring and long lasting." Although the chronic crisis "lacks the dramatic beginning of an acute crisis," it builds "in intensity with the passing of time."[4]

With the Civil War beginning in a dramatic fashion, southern society faced a situation encompassing a traumatic social disruption. Battles that suddenly erupted on the landscape created a shockwave, without a large amount of preparation to deal with the crisis. In some instances, within twenty-four hours, entire communities transformed from the rigors of daily life to dealing with thousands of wounded and dead individuals, as well as the destructive toll of war. As the war concluded, southerners now had to come to grips with facing the reality of defeat. Though the acute crisis may have faded into the pages of history, the southern populace had to steer their postwar lives through a chronic crisis of living with defeat. In essence, they became prisoners of constantly remembering the Civil War.

In order to deal with the reality of defeat and the memory of failure, the South embraced the Lost Cause as a public and social manifestation that would channel memory in important ways. I choose to define the Lost Cause as the South's reaction to preserve honor while facing the humiliation and loss that accompanied defeat in the Civil War. Southerners sought to explain defeat, seek outlets to blame certain generals for failure, and cope with the unthinkable reality that God had abandoned the southern populace. Within the Lost Cause, women emerged as the primary caretakers to assist in the rehabilitation of returning men. To cope with the financial and psychological stress inflicted through the Civil War, women joined various Ladies' Memorial Associations and participated in the United Daughters of the Confederacy. Through their personal efforts, women could "reassure defeated Confederates about their honor, courage and manhood and to bury the pain of failure by redefining it as noble sacrifice and ultimate moral victory."[5]

No direct historical evidence hints that Hood suffered from any of the afflictions discussed above. Furthermore, the details of his postwar life remain sketchy, with only occasional bits of solid evidence. Yet, it is apparent that the memories of destruction and death in battle impressed Hood with lasting significance. In the aftermath of several battles ranging from Gaines' Mill to Nashville, Hood had gazed upon the dead and wounded with genuine feelings of remorse. Hood not only dealt with witnessing the trauma of the war, but he also possessed a daily reminder of that very trauma: a missing leg and a useless arm. Thus, apparent conditions of trauma for Hood grew from both his injuries and his witnessing the horrible destruction of life throughout the war.

Hood relived the horrible memories of death and destruction. However, he did not have the full benefit of the Lost Cause to supplant his personal trauma. Hood returned from the war with his honor and manhood shattered, both in terms of his physically altered body and his inability to achieve victory in the final stages of the war. He had no clear prospects for a romantic relationship and no clear avenue for returning to an ambitious career path. In the era of the Lost Cause, the defeat at Franklin and Nashville served as the ultimate failure, rendering difficult and controversial any attempts to make the losses honorable. Unfortunately, for Hood, part of the construction of social memory required the assignment of blame. In many ways, Hood served as a scapegoat for Confederate defeat, inhibiting any possibility of quickly resurrecting his honor in the postwar years. Therefore, while dealing with his own personal memories, he became the target of everyone else's.

With the war over, Hood needed to find a place to live in order to begin reconstructing his lost honor. He had once said, "I am a Texan at heart and expect to live, die, and be buried in Texas." After he surrendered in Natchez, Mississippi, in May 1865, Hood traveled down the Mississippi River to New Orleans. The *Daily Picayune,* on June 4, noted that Hood arrived in New Orleans with his staff and was "at the St. Charles Hotel." From New Orleans, Hood decided to make good on his promise to live in Texas following the war and traveled there in the summer of 1865. Louly Wigfall, who accompanied Hood on his journey, said, "He sat opposite, and with calm, sad eyes looked out on the passing scenes, apparently noting nothing." Wigfall deduced that Hood sat "overwhelmed with humiliation at the utter failure of his leadership—his pride was wounded to the quick by his removal from command."[6]

When Hood arrived in San Antonio on July 3, 1865, the newspaper conveyed the public's excitement for the return of their adopted citizen. "It does our heart good to welcome back to San Antonio, after an absence of over four years, this truly great, good and gallant officer, soldier and gentleman. His history is well known to our readers." The paper offered a brief review of Hood's military career, ignoring the details of battle. Instead, the newspaper focused on Hood's injuries, writing, "His manly form has been hacked and pierced until it is now shorn of some of its fair proportions." Yet, the writer continued, "the General is in fine spirits and the full enjoyment of his health," and he no longer suffers from "rheumatic pains caused by cold and camp exposure." Despite the warm reception, Hood did not find permanent settlement financially feasible in Texas. He spent the latter months of 1865 traveling back to New Orleans, Washington, D.C., and Canada to visit Confederate exiles, as well as his mother in Kentucky.[7]

In the few months after the war, Hood began to consciously reconstruct his own memory of the American Civil War. While in Mt. Sterling, Kentucky, visiting his mother, Hood wrote to Stephen D. Lee, one of his former corps commanders during his command of the Army of Tennessee, on November 29, 1865. The two commanders had remained in touch. Now, Hood wrote, "I am anxious to see you before I return to Texas and hope to be able to call and see you en-route to New Orleans, probably in January next." He recalled that every time he heard Lee's name, it called "to mind most happy reminiscences." As Hood complimented Lee, he also knew the stakes his reputation would face in the coming years, writing, "The war is over and the time has come for facts to take the place of falsehoods. In my shattered condition I may before I die write my own memoirs of this great struggle just ended." Hood sought out Lee to get his "military opinion" and knew that his assessment would be "more than one hundred soldiers who were not in position to judge."[8]

Hood needed key allies on his side if he was going to resurrect his shattered reputation following the war. He wanted Lee to write back as quickly as possible. Yet, the two men did not end up meeting. On January 9, 1866, Hood, writing from Louisville, noted the poor condition of the railroad, which forced a delay in his travel plans. Any memory reconstruction would allow Hood, as he stated, "to be able to forgive all who wronged me." Hood expected to "die more proud" of his military actions in "defense of Atlanta" and the Tennessee invasion than of anything else in his entire "career as a soldier."[9]

Hood continued to travel in search of assistance in solidifying his vision of the war. On a visit to Palestine, Texas, in the summer of 1866, John H. Reagan, the Confederate postmaster general, saw Hood and wanted to invite him to his home. Reagan confessed that his house was not "fit to take him to," but Hood insisted that he would go anyway. Reagan recalled, "He spent several days with me, during which time we discussed a number of subjects of mutual interest; and among others his last campaign in Tennessee, in which he showed to my satisfaction that it was the only military move then available." Reagan noted that the problems Hood discussed included the high water of the Tennessee River that prevented crossing at Decatur to beat Thomas back to Nashville, and the missed chance at Spring Hill. Hood arrived back in New Orleans in 1866, where he settled permanently, confident that Lee and Reagan would assist him in the coming years in reconstructing his Civil War memories.[10]

New Orleans offered a place where Hood could find employment behind a desk, which would make his life easier as an amputee. The city would also engage in a constant flurry of memory activities that would assist Hood in coming to grasp with his own memory of the Civil War. Just as the setting of Kentucky created an environment important to Hood's youth, now New Orleans, in turn, created a suitable environment for the final years of his life. The city experienced the war in an extraordinary way, with the ramifications of a blockade that sent commerce values tumbling throughout the latter part of 1861 into early 1862.[11]

Union occupation, which began on April 25, 1862, allowed Lincoln to end the blockade of the city, and food and supplies returned throughout the course of 1862. Federal troops remained in place, censoring newspapers and inflicting discipline upon unruly citizens throughout the city. By the time of Lincoln's second inauguration in 1865, the city had resumed several traditional and valued public events, including Mardi Gras, and held a parade to honor Lincoln's second term of office. However, the celebratory atmosphere over the inauguration ended abruptly with an assassin's bullet on April 14, 1865. News of the assassination hit New Orleans "as if a black pall had descended upon the city," and the citizens displayed "universal expression of unfeigned sorrow, mingled with a very natural feeling of indignation." In honor of the late president, according to newspaper accounts, "Business was suspended, stores and places of amusement were closed, the public offices shut their doors, flags draped in mourning weeds, were hung at half mast from all public and many private buildings, and from the vessels in the harbor, of whatever nation." The city displayed a sense of grief "that lies too deep for expression, as yet, by pen or by voice."[12]

With the war over, New Orleans serves as a prime example of a southern community dealing with the personal and public tragedies inflicted through warfare and failure. The city not only had to deal with personal loss, but also with changes to the southern infrastructure left behind in the war's shadow. To come to grips with the terrible burden of loss, citizens turned to charitable acts, hoping that through acts of charity and acts of "kindness or benevolence to a fellow-being," an individual could gain "satisfaction with self from the practice of this virtue." Three groups became the focus of much of this virtuous activity: disabled and poor veterans, the women who had endured the horrors of war in their own way, and the soldiers who had died in the conflict.[13] Furthermore, with the Reconstruction politics of Congress extending the presence of Union troops, the city had to find a way to construct a Lost Cause memory while simultaneously working toward reconciliation with their occupiers. Though the task appeared daunting, the city reestablished prewar celebrations, particularly commemorating the Battle of New Orleans and Independence Day, as a means of constructing a reunion mentality among the city populace.

As the citizens worked to solidify an appropriate memory of the Civil War, John Bell Hood lived and maneuvered through the tangled web of memory formation in the city of New Orleans. He not only contributed to caring for the disabled, the women, and the dead, but also dealt with how he personally wanted to remember the war and how he wanted to be remembered. A delicate reciprocal relationship, therefore, emerged in New Orleans after the war. Hood assisted the city's citizens in their postwar memory construction and they in turn resolidified Hood's honorable reputation as more than a military figure, and sought to convey that message after his death.

The three groups vital to memory construction in New Orleans drew recognition in a poem, entitled *The Confederate Dead,* that appeared in the New Orleans newspapers on a few different occasions. Published anonymously, the poem set the tone as to how the city of New Orleans would deal with the postwar struggles that war had left behind:

> The Confederate Dead! How quiet they lie
> In the fields they defended, 'neath their own summer sky,
> Here the hearts that once so exultingly flushed
> With the fury of battle, are silent and hushed.
>
> The Confederate Dead! They are strong in their graves,
> They rest like an army of yet valiant braves;
> There's a thrill of emotion that come at the view,
> And a moisture bedims the eye with its dew.
>
> The Confederate Dead! Under "Stonewall" and Lee—
> They taught the pale Northman in terror to flee,
> They fought and they lost, yet the cause they deemed just,
> And memory retains her old love for such dust.
>
> The Confederate Dead! Like the heroes of old,
> Their names will be to posterity told;
> To the places on which they fought and they fell,
> With memory refuse to breathe a farewell.
>
> The Confederate Dead! The spring has come back,
> And sowed her sweet flowers on War's savage track;
> And the rose and the violet sweetly have bloomed
> O'er places beneath which lie heroes entombed.

> The Confederate Dead! Let us cherish them deep
> In our heart, wherever their relics may sleep,
> Let us plant o'er their graves the flowers each year,
> And enshrine in our hearts the dust once so dear.
>
> The Confederate Maimed! With heart and with hand.
> Let us welcome them back to their own native land,
> Let us give them the best our power can reach,
> And be a sister or brother to each.
>
> The Confederate Girls! God bless them; they're true,
> And pure as a gem of early May dew,
> The fairest of women, the chastest of wives,
> Let us love them, protect them, and fight for their lives.
>
> The Confederate flag! Let us fold it away
> In heart like a memory that lived out its day!
> We still have our dead, our girls and our past,
> And these will be true to us e'en to the last.[14]

The poem conveys to the readers of New Orleans exactly how the Lost Cause would function in the city. The soldiers who fought and died, described as strong and valiant, displayed their courage in a losing effort. However, despite military failure, the soldiers endured the strains of battle in order to maintain a cause they saw as honorable. More important, society would remember their fight and work hard to make sure their names would not be forgotten and their deeds would never go unrecognized. To cherish their memory, the citizens would decorate the graves each year as a mutual task of both displaying appreciation outwardly through flowers and displaying appreciation internally through personal memory.

Yet, not every individual met death through the course of war. The wounded soldiers should be welcomed back with open arms. To appreciate their sacrifices, members of society would have to work extra diligently in order to ensure that the wounded would be recognized as men who fought honorably for the same cause that cost some men their lives. A bulk of the people who would welcome back the wounded men and decorate the graves would be the women, who also suffered through four years of warfare. The Lost Cause would work to make sure that each woman also received the equal protection and notice that their male counterparts faced in the Reconstruction era.

Poems can only display sentiments. It would take action from both the government and the average citizen to turn any ideas into reality. With many soldiers returning home in the aftermath of war, the needs of the disabled soldiers would have to be addressed first. The surgeon general of the United States recommended the establishment of asylums and homes throughout the South for "disabled soldiers of the Confederate armies." Many veterans returned to New Orleans with little money. As the *Daily Picayune* stated, "There are numbers of poor Confederates amongst us looking for work. Many of them are disabled for laboring at ditching, or such hard work, but can paint signs or houses, do plastering, or white-washing, put up a very respectable job of carpentry, or bricklaying, and perform many an odd job which a stranger is called upon to do."[15]

The state of Louisiana also had to come up with a comprehensive policy to assist Confederate amputees in securing artificial limbs. With North Carolina being the first state to offer limb provisions, Louisiana waited several years after the war to address this need among their citizenry. In 1873, the General Assembly adopted a limb program for the disfigured veterans of the War of 1812. Finally, in the 1879 constitutional proceedings that would go into effect January 1, 1880, a resolution found acceptance by a vote of ninety-seven to ten. The amendment called on Louisiana to "remember its citizens dismembered as soldiers in the Confederate armies, by supplying them with artificial arms and limbs." Both black and white Republicans agreed to the provision overwhelmingly, despite the possibility that Republicans could use the measure as "another charge against the Southern people of disloyalty and rebellion." One observer stated, "No crippled Union soldier will sneer at the loyalty of a State which provides for its wounded brave, and which in order to do so more effectually provides only for those who are not aided from another quarter." Southern soldiers needed the states to offer limb assistance, owing to no compensation coming from the federal government.[16]

Not only did the disabled veterans serve as a tangible reminder of the devastation of war, but at the same time, the large number of new graves as a direct result of the war drew notice. The city tried to establish "homes and business" for the famed Louisiana Brigade, who had engaged in battle alongside "Stonewall" Jackson. Furthermore, "the graves of nearly all are properly marked, recorded and known." To provide for the marking of graves, funds had to be gathered, either from the brigade or from the "generous people" of the city. Grave marking expanded beyond the city limits to the final resting places of soldiers across America. For Major Wheat of the Louisiana Brigade, his grave, located in Richmond, had the inscription, "Louisiana has not forgotten her lost brothers." Samuel Weaver, a citizen of Gettysburg, Pennsylvania, provided New Orleans with a list of all marked graves located in the Gettysburg area of soldiers who were from Louisiana, Alabama, and

Mississippi. Weaver proclaimed that he would "cheerfully give any information and assistance in his power to the relatives of the deceased."[17]

The city of Winchester, Virginia, changed hands more than seventy times during the course of the war, and several nearby battlefield engagements left many scattered graves in the vicinity of the city. Many had been moved to the old Episcopal graveyard, but at a tremendous financial cost to the citizens of Winchester. To aid these efforts, each Confederate state donated funds to assist the grave situation. Every state had contributed, that is, except Louisiana. A call went out, "Each State has a separate lot in the cemetery, and contributions have been received from all except Louisiana. The enclosure has not been completed and the funds are exhausted, hence this appeal to all in Louisiana, who may wish to render assistance." The citizens of New Orleans contributed to the effort in order to make sure they assisted in "recording deeds of fame."[18]

One of the most fitting tributes came through Memorial Day observances used to undertake a "demonstration of respect to the honored dead." The local newspaper hoped that during the proceedings, "noble women will bow in tender memory over the graves of the fallen patriots whom they honored while living." The same deference and devotion that women were to show their husbands during marriage should be duplicated even after they died. Yet, as the Memorial Day festivities commenced, the events also marked a moment when the citizenry of New Orleans could look toward a future where reconciliation had been completed. One writer longed for when the "Blue and Gray may join hands in honorable and cordial reconciliation, and stand shoulder to shoulder to maintain the honor of a common country." Yet, even if reconciliation took place sooner rather than later, "the South will honor the dead who died fighting in their behalf." Memorial Day offered the South a chance to avoid forgetting the sacrifice of war and "bring fresh tokens of gratitude and affection."[19]

With efforts undertaken to protect the wounded and remember the dead, the final group, the women, emerged as the most prominent on the cityscape of New Orleans. As another writer professed, "Never for one moment did the women of the South, from the highest to the lowest, fail to support the arms of the soldier, and hold them up until the sinking of the sun." No one should dare jeer the women of the South, for "women are worthy of the respect of the world, and will receive a sneer only from cowards and brutes!" The South faced a period of extensive mourning, as women walked around in the years after the war "in deep black, and veiled with deepest crape." Women only appeared briefly in public and then went back "to the seclusion of their home," because, as a northern letter writer stated: "They are utterly broken down by the war. They cannot face the world with their old-time splendor, and hence they will not face it at all."[20]

Any northern observation of southern womanhood was bound to draw a vigorous defense. In New Orleans, the Chicago writer who declared all women in mourning only saw six women attend the theater one evening and extrapolated the above statements. Several women attended the theater, according to a southern respondent, and if the Chicago carpetbagger had not seen them, he must either be "blind, or unable to recognize a lady when he sees her." Yet, the southern voice admitted that the women of the South did stand in mourning, but he challenged the city to find "as many pretty, graceful, sweet-faced girls and handsomely dressed ladies as Canal Street can boast." The women of New Orleans, setting the highest standard for "taste in dress and genuine lady-hood" would always be defended against "some petty scribbler" from Chicago who called them "servants and courtesans."[21]

To assert their womanhood and protect the memory of the South, the women of New Orleans gathered and formed the Ladies Benevolent Association of Louisiana. Originally, the women wanted to call their organization the Ladies' Confederate Memorial Association, but the northern occupants of the city during Reconstruction summarily rejected the name. Men had the opportunity to become honorary members, but had to pay a fee of $50. The association, "prompted by goodness of heart," sought "to furnish artificial limbs to Southern soldiers, and to mark and protect the graves of the Confederate dead." It also needed to "provide for the wounded and cherish the memory of the dead" because of "patriotic service" and the defense of "their people and their homes."[22]

The Ladies Benevolent Association expanded their duties beyond soliciting donations and advertising their fund-raising events. The association immediately targeted orphans and the poor and destitute, as well as Confederate widows. Also, as the city of New Orleans expanded, some streets reopened where soldiers had been buried in shallow graves during the war. The association sought to "procure a place to which their bodies can be removed and their graves nearly marked and properly protected." Sensitive to the presence of military occupiers, no monuments would appear. Simply, the women wanted to "see that their [veterans'] graves have the protection demanded by Christianity and humanity." The added tasks called for another membership drive to both genders. Women, encouraged to be "an active or life member," also asked for more "gentlemen who can afford to give fifty dollars to a noble object" to join as honorary members.[23]

The association raised funds through membership fees, donations from within and from other organizations, and from the sale of clothing and other items at local bazaars. The women collected $20,002.58 and used the money to purchase artificial limbs for twenty-seven soldiers, and to transport twenty-nine soldiers and seven widows to their homes. They also paid rent for 142 widows and offered financial assistance to 295 orphans. The benevolence also allowed for the hiring of a nurse for a sick widow, provided medicine for sick veterans, covered funeral expenses, and even purchased a new cooking stove for one Confederate widow. In addition to food, clothing, and rent payments, the Louisiana chapter also donated funds to the Richmond Bazaar and the Spotsylvania Cemetery and gave a donation to the Firemen's Charitable Association to pay for expenses incurred in burying Confederate soldiers. The women spent close to $11,765.34 in the above-mentioned benevolent acts.[24] Yet, the fund-raising did not cease and the women continued to collect funds for other memorial activities.

On Friday, April 10, 1874, a dedication ceremony for a Confederate monument in Greenwood Cemetery in New Orleans commenced. The women, through their labor and their ability to "still cling to the golden memories" of the past, allowed for an unveiling occasion that served as "a tribute" to the memory of the fallen soldiers. The monument, costing $11,385 for construction, contained the remains of six hundred Confederate soldiers encased in a tomb, with a granite soldier on top, as well as busts of Leonidas Polk, Robert E. Lee, Thomas Jackson, and Albert Sydney Johnston. The inscription read, "In commemoration of the heroic virtue of the Confederate soldier, this monument is erected by the Ladies Benevolent Association of Louisiana."[25]

During the ceremony, H. N. Ogden offered "an elegant speech most appropriate to the occasion." Ogden said, "This very monument, beneath which rests the dust of those who died in our cause, is twice an honor, a glory to Louisiana, for it tells two stories." Not only did the monument exhibit the sacrifices of the brave soldiers buried beneath the marble, but also told of the women who "struggled on in their pious cause, through the dark days that have followed our defeat." As the smoke lifted from the battlefield, revealing the scars of war, the women of New Orleans arrived at the forefront to deal with the tragedies of war, including the "weary, sick or wounded" that arrived at their homesteads defeated. Ogden, after a brief discussion of how the Confederate cause remained alive in the chaos of Reconstruction, concluded by again looking to the image of Robert E. Lee. He said, "It behooves us now in these times to learn the lesson taught by Lee, whose face you see there; Lee is a chain, a tie between the living and the dead, who taught us the great lesson in war and in peace, patience and duty."[26]

As the men and women dealt with the personal tragedies of war through charity and memorialization, the city ushered in a new era designed to forge a reunion with their northern counterparts. In 1866, the city's citizens remembered the Battle of New Orleans from 1814, an event that stood "as not only one of the most valuable jewels in the coronet of our national glory, but as one of the strongest links of a common patriotism, nationality and fraternal affection." The fifty-second anniversary of Andrew Jackson's national triumph afforded New Orleans an opportunity to look away from the recent events of American history and return to remembering "this great triumph of American heroism and patriotism."[27]

However, patriotic celebrations did not serve as enough of a catalyst to fuel a patriotic reunion. Citizens all over the South wondered how best to facilitate and foster goodwill between the sections. The *New York Herald* suggested that Grant and Lee should attend a soldier convention in order to "engender an abiding spirit of union and fraternity amongst all classes of people throughout the country." The writer guaranteed that a national meeting, with Lee and Grant forging the trail, "would send a thrill of joy through the heart of the nation," as well as present a clear image to the world in the form of "a spectacle more sublime and impressive than ever marked." Although Lee and Grant never attended such an event, the *Herald* continued to remain hopeful for any gesture "which constitute such strong guarantees of permanent union and fraternity."[28]

Yet, many in New Orleans felt betrayed by northern sentiment about Decoration Day. The federal government did declare a Decoration Day to take place on May 30, 1873, and the graves at Chalmette Cemetery underwent a ceremony that was "impressive and solemn." Of course, both sides intended such holidays to decorate the graves of their own dead. In particular, a New Orleans newspaper reported, "The grand army of the Republic has ordered that on Memorial Day, no decorations shall be put upon the graves of the Confederate dead at Arlington." Some assumed that the GAR made the preceding decision for the purpose of keeping up "the sectional antagonism and hate which the late war inspired." In 1879, Union veterans decorated the graves in Chalmette, while the southern veterans decorated graves and the newly constructed Confederate monument in Greenwood Cemetery, when John Bell Hood served on the reception committee that greeted patrons paying respects to the honored dead.[29]

During this time, John Bell Hood was involved both as an object of memory and as an active participant. Hood issued a circular to the newspapers to collect as much information as he could about the war and those men who served under his command. He showed no interest in writing a history of the war, but wanted "to collect facts with regard to military operations." Hood argued in the circular, "It will remain for the historian, who shall aspire to draw a truthful picture of the eventful and interesting epoch, with which I was somewhat connected, to assign to the facts embraced in these memorials their proper place and just significance." An editorial writer in Arkansas championed Hood's request, particularly because he felt that without these historical contributions, future historians would construct narratives that would not "do justice to a noble people."[30]

In 1867, the remains of Albert Sydney Johnston, killed in the first day's Battle of Shiloh five years earlier, were disinterred for shipment to his native Texas. The funeral, taking place on January 23, drew several thousand participants and spectators, including P. G. T. Beauregard, Braxton Bragg, and John Bell Hood, the officers who at various times commanded his army after Johnston died. Owing to his injuries, Hood did not serve as a pallbearer, but other Confederate officers, including Richard Taylor and James Longstreet, assisted in carrying Johnston's remains to a steamer bound for Texas. The tribute, fashioned out of "love, homage and respect," created "one of the most remarkable [processions] that has ever been seen in this city." With the pallbearers, "four or five hundred ladies, from the highest circles of society in the city" participated in the procession. A female presence prompted one writer to note, "When the fair ladies of the city treads the rugged streets to do honor to the dead, it carries with it an impressive solemnity that must touch even the soul of a quondam foe."[31]

The Lost Cause imagery dominated New Orleans. The local baseball clubs that played games at the Delachaise Grounds carried the names Southern and Robert E. Lee. The city paused on each anniversary of May 10 to commemorate the death of "Stonewall" Jackson. As one writer noted, "It is fortunate for Americans from any State that they may gather around Jackson's grave with one thought of admiration and reverence for the memory of the most illustrious dead." Announcements in the city newspapers reminded readers of the impending anniversary, stating, "All who esteem purity, generosity and simplicity of character, combined with exemplary piety and exalted talent, will pause in their busy thoughts to remember with sorrow the Christian, the soldier, the scholar and the hero." Jackson possessed a "love of country" and he used his heart to fight "with strong mind, firm will, steady hand and changeless purpose, yet overflowing with all charity and benevolence towards his fellowmen and with a pure devotion towards his Creator."[32]

In the midst of the construction of a Lost Cause ideology and memory in New Orleans, John Bell Hood entered into life and business, thanks to a gift of $10,000 by friends in Kentucky. With no real experience in cotton, Hood selected a job where he could work despite his war injuries. He started J. B. Hood and Co., a cotton commission business, and sought cotton from his old wartime comrades, in particular Stephen D. Lee. Hood wrote Lee on February 9, 1866, stating, "As commission merchants need cotton and that cotton must come from friends and as I take you to be one of my best, I without any reserve ask that you will thro' your many friends in Miss. and elsewhere turn in the direction of this house all the cotton you can." One merchant report saw Hood as being "well spoken of as upright hon[ora]ble and relia[ble]." However, the cotton commission business, despite an early profit of $5,000–$8,000, went sour, owing to high competition, bad weather, plummeting prices, and skyrocketing taxes. In 1869, Hood left the cotton business to become president of Life Association of America, an insurance venture, taking over from his wartime associate, James Longstreet. Even as president, Hood paid an annual premium of $865.90 to his own insurance policy.[33]

The Life Association of America expanded through 1870, when the company held "assets over $2,000,000, and with outstanding policies amounting to more than $36,000,000." Thus, the corporation reported record business that had "never been equaled before in the history of life insurance." The "gentlemen" working for the Life Association received notice for being "high-toned, honorable men, and also men of great business capacity." Hence, as one writer concluded, "Gen. J.B. Hood is the President of the Louisiana and Texas Department, and this fact alone should inspire everyone with confidence."[34]

Despite the late failures in war, Hood's societal reputation and even national renown garnered him high remarks among the insurance purchasing populace of New Orleans. His flexibility not only increased the number of insurance policies but also allowed for expansion of the New Orleans Cotton Exchange. Hood spoke at the meeting of the New Orleans Cotton Exchange to "aid the Exchange in the purchase or erection of a suitable and appropriate building for their use." If members of the exchange agreed to purchase new insurance premiums, to the sum of $143,000, then Hood agreed to offer an advance on the insurance premiums, up to $100,000, consisting of a 25 percent donation as well as a ten-year loan for the exchange to get a new building. Hood saw the Cotton Exchange as an opportunity to expand his business and secure "policies outside of the membership, and to make the same disposition of the premiums as of those acquired from the members or through their influence."[35]

Yet, as Hood engaged in business throughout the city, New Orleans continued to undergo the ramifications of the Civil War, especially the congressional policies of Reconstruction. Hood spoke on the topic of Reconstruction, agreeing to an interview with an editor of the Brownsville *Ranchero,* a newspaper from Texas. The editor also spoke to Gen. James Longstreet, who said, "The duty and safety of the South demanded submission on the part of the Southern people." Though Hood may have agreed with Longstreet, he kept his opinion to himself. In one conversation, Hood warned Longsteet, "The Southern press and the Southern people will vilify you and abuse you."[36] Hood wanted a rapid reconciliation between the North and South, but remained contingent on the prevailing public opinion.

For Hood to have a successful postwar life, he needed assistance as an amputee. Behind the scenes, a woman nurtured both his success in business and his dealings with the memory of the Civil War. However, that woman was not Sally Preston, who ultimately rejected Hood for good. Preston, a Richmond socialite, never loved him and ended the one-sided courtship in 1865. Thus, Hood's chivalric relationship with Preston ended as the Civil War drew to a close.

Three years later, Hood married Anna Marie Hennen, a European-educated daughter of a prominent Louisiana attorney, on April 13, 1868. Hennen, a Catholic, joined in matrimony with Hood, an Episcopalian, who had been baptized by General Leonidas Polk in 1864. At the wedding service, General Simon Bolivar Buckner served as Hood's best man. One observer stated, "It was a touching sight to see the tall, slender form of the maimed soldier move slowly up, by help of crutches or cane, to the altar rail, where he knelt, with the poorest and humblest, to partake of the most solemn rite of his faith, the Communion." Over the course of their married life, the couple produced eleven children in the span of a decade, including three sets of twins. Lydia, the first daughter, arrived in 1869, before Annabel and Ethel Genevieve, the first set of twins, born on May 29, 1870. John Bell Hood Jr., the first son, was born September 23, 1871, with Duncan Norbed, the second son, coming into the world January 25, 1873. Following the two sons, two more sets of female twins arrived: Marion Maude and Lillian Marie on March 6, 1874, and Odile Musson and Ida Richardson, born October 19, 1876. Oswald, born July 11, 1878, followed close behind, with Anna Gertrude the final child, arriving on August 4, 1879. Thus, "Hood's Brigade," as the children were affectionately known, consisted of eight girls and three boys. Legend has it that when traveling, "ever mindful of logistics, Hood had to telegraph ahead in order for milk to be secured for his little troops."[37]

Hood had found some success at restoring his honor through his growing reputation as a businessman. However, restoring his honor also required a strong support structure. Masculine identity, as historian Jane Dailey suggests, is "grounded in personal relations and could be strengthened as well as put at risk through social and political interactions." Masculine honor rested in the ability of a man to provide for and protect his wife and children. In this case, a reciprocal dependency relationship grew as Anna Hood now had the task before her, as with so many other Confederate women, to rehabilitate her husband in the war's aftermath. Hood clearly needed a support structure to assist him in resurrecting his shattered honor, ruined by ultimate failure through the course of the war. In other words, the love of a wife could begin to heal and ultimately repair any honor lost through the loss of a limb.[38]

With his marriage as an anchor and his business reputation soaring, Hood also reasserted his honor through his participation in several charitable endeavors. Shortly after arriving in New Orleans, Hood participated in and eventually served as president of the Southern Hospital Association for Disabled Soldiers, which sought to care for "diseased and maimed soldiers." As noted in one newspaper description, "The beneficiaries are the maimed and crippled of our noble army, who are utterly unable to earn a support, many of them with wounds still unhealed, and without the means to procure the necessary medical attention." With a group consisting of "ladies and gentlemen of the highest standing in our home circles," Hood led weekly meetings designed to discuss ideas and plans for upcoming fund-raising opportunities for maintaining the health and welfare of New Orleans' wounded soldiers.[39]

Annually, the Southern Hospital Association held a ball and a bazaar to raise funds for disabled soldiers residing within the city. Notices appeared in the newspaper notifying volunteers about committee meetings in preparation for the ball, held January 25, 1867. Hood served as chairman of the floor managers. The committee of twenty-two members met at Hood's office at 100 Common Street two evenings prior to the ball. General P. G. T. Beauregard chaired the reception committee, with General James Longstreet serving as a committee member. The ball received assistance from the Hackman's Benefit Association, which offered "the use of their carriages on the occasion of the ball . . . at half price." The ball, "beautifully lighted," gathered together "the elite of the city and of the Southern country, and arrayed on the ballroom floor, they presented a beautiful sight." "A thousand hearts beat happily; and when music arose with its voluptuous swell, soft eyes looked love to eyes that spake again, and all went merry as the marriage bell," reported the *Daily Picayune*. The ball, beginning before 10 p.m., consisted of twenty promenades and twenty dances before breaking for supper at midnight. The menu included roast turkey, pork, veal, beef, a variety of patés made of game and veal, duck, cold tongue, chicken mayonnaise, and a variety of deserts, including sherbet, pineapple, vanilla ice creams, chocolate, raspberries, and strawberries, as well as assorted fancy cakes. The beverages of choice for the evening included "wines of the most excellent vintage." Following the meal, the dancing continued into the morning hours, as the dancers twirled throughout the opera house with "renewed spirit."[40]

The ball presented an opportunity for John Bell Hood to be seen in public participating in a worthy cause. Despite his physical injuries, Hood attended an event that would require men to prove their physical prowess through dancing. Even if he could not dance, the ball provided opportunities for Hood to engage in pleasant conversation with his peers. The citizens who attended would recognize Hood's generosity and make note of his desire to assist fellow veterans who had been injured in the war. By participating in charities that reflected Hood's concerns for the wounded soldiers, he reasserted his honor in front of elite New Orleans residents, who would come to recognize him as one of their own.

After the ball, the Southern Hospital Association held a bazaar on February 18, 1867. To attend, a patron had to purchase a ticket for one dollar. The ticket, with John Bell Hood's signature, contained the image of a Confederate soldier, his arm in a sling, leaning against a tree. His musket rested along his inner left leg. Next to the soldier stood a southern woman, in an elegant dress, with her hair in a ponytail. In her right hand she offered a tin cup to the soldier, with the soldier extending his left arm to reach the cup. In her left hand, the woman held her hat. Behind the two figures, a small farmhouse protected by a white fence with a gate, smoke chugging from the chimney, dotted the landscape. Tickets sold rapidly for the bazaar, as the association advertised for patrons to buy tickets to win "over two thousand prizes." The drawing took place the second week of March.[41]

The success in the sale of the bazaar tickets resulted directly from the groups working to resurrect the lost honor of New Orleans. First, the ticket showed images of a wounded soldier and a southern woman, the two living entities for whom the citizens of New Orleans worked in order to secure their place in Confederate memory. Second, the ticket had the signature of John Bell Hood, who was growing in reputation as a man committed to securing the welfare of the destitute. By using images that would remind the citizenry of their need to protect women and the wounded, the bazaar served as a direct way people could participate in the Lost Cause.

Furthermore, the Southern Hospital Association for Disabled Soldiers also recruited a group of female visitors to visit the disabled soldiers at their hospital. Hood called on "the ladies of the city, and the public generally," to "visit the Hospital." The thirty-five women received the honor on June 25, 1867. During their visit, they were told by one patient, "We have lost arms, and legs, and hands, but we have not lost our love for our country and the first prayers of our hearts are that a merciful God may raise her to her feet, and allow her to stand before the world disenthralled." The situation looked bleak at the hospital, as the patient said, "The graves that refused to receive us in many battles, and through a long war, now seem inclined to draw nearer, and before another year we may be reposing in the tomb." A possible cure, according to the patient, was for the citizens of the city to come and shake hands and visit the "diseased and maimed soldiers."[42]

Significantly, Hood's charitable works extended beyond the hospital. In 1869, Hood agreed, along with Braxton Bragg and P. G. T. Beauregard, to collect funds for the orphan's home in Lauderdale, Mississippi. Laura Reed, who began taking care of fatherless southern children shortly after the Battle of Shiloh, had 250 girls and boys under her watchful eye. Furthermore, many "destitute mothers" also needed care. Hood and his military colleagues used their role as Confederate heroes to command donations of "food, clothing, implements and money." The call for donations sought "any article that can be afforded, in aid of housekeeping, mechanical pursuits and farming, of food, bedding or tools, and we hope they will respond as fully as their means will justify."[43] Hood assisted the South in gathering donations for orphan children. The region would return the favor to General Hood in due time.

With more than two hundred orphans in 1870, the Lauderdale home decided to send twenty girls and eight boys on the road to present benefit concerts for fellow orphans. "They left Lauderdale on the 1st of September, and have visited the principal places in Kentucky, Tennessee, Alabama and Mississippi, entertaining large audiences with their simple but heart-touching songs, and meeting everywhere with a warm reception and generous liberality," reported the *Daily Picayune*. When the children stopped in New Orleans, inclement weather prevented a large attendance. Yet, the children performed another concert the following day, when better weather blessed the city. One writer urged, "Let [the performance] be largely attended. Let our citizens contribute liberally toward alleviating the burden under which the Lauderdale Orphans' Home labors, so that its inmates may not again be compelled by stern necessity to travel from one place to another in search of charity."[44]

As Hood assisted war orphans, the memories of the dead and wounded drove him to continue displaying his compassion for wounded countrymen. He served as an honorary vice president for the Bazaar Association for the Benefit of the Victims of the War in France.[45] By serving as president of the

Southern Hospital Association for Disabled Soldiers and agreeing to collect funds for the Lauderdale orphans, Hood found a clear path through his personal memories of the Tennessee battlefields littered with casualties. Hood moved his genuine interest and compassion for the wounded from the battlefield to the hospital, as well as caring for the widows and orphans left behind from the chaos of war. He may have found an avenue to deal with his own feelings of guilt over the dead at Franklin and Nashville as he reasserted his honor through charitable endeavors. Furthermore, Hood did not simply select a charity for the purpose of enhancing his reputation. He settled on a cause to which he could relate: an organization that cared for wounded, disabled, and amputated men. At the same time, the city of New Orleans used donations to the hospital and orphan funds as outlets to deal with reestablishing any honor the city may have lost during the Union occupation. In caring for both the wounded and the orphans, the city continued fostering the Lost Cause along the banks of the Mississippi. By making sure that those who had been affected by the ravages of war remained secure, the city and John Bell Hood created an atmosphere to effectively deal with the reality of wartime failure.

John Bell Hood and the populace of New Orleans had equally taken steps to secure a citywide collective memory of the Civil War through the care of the maimed, the disabled, the orphaned, the widowed, and the dead. Yet, despite acts of benevolence, the city grew restless with how the story of the war would be told in the postwar period. As early as 1866, local newspapers called for war veterans to offer biographies, descriptions, sketches, anecdotes, incidents, and narratives for the purpose of forging a "sacred memory." In fact, some articles and reminiscences could win a cash prize, with $100 going to poets who best described the sacrifice of the dead, the valor of the soldiers, and even the current incarceration of Jefferson Davis.[46]

With politicians and veterans recording their war experiences, it was important for New Orleans to collect and record all information as part of their concerted effort to remember southern soldiers as heroes rather than failures. In early May 1869, citizens gathered on Camp Street in New Orleans "to organize a permanent society for the purpose of collecting and preserving records and memoranda of the Confederacy." By examining the Civil War from a "Southern stand point," the Southern Historical Society sought to collect "only such data as is perfectly reliable and correct." According to the society, "The movement is one which must receive the endorsement of all right minded men, as it emanates from a desire which exists in the hearts of all true Southern men that their actions and motives may be handed down to posterity, divested of the clouds by which ignorance and misrepresentation have obscured them." To get at the true southern story, the society hoped to collect information from individuals who held knowledge of the "interior workings of the government." The society invited commentaries from "Davis, Johnson, Beauregard, Breckinridge, Gen. Cooper, Bragg, Maury, Toombs, Benjamin, Mallory, Hood, Wigfall, Judge Campbell and a host of others."[47]

The Reverend Dr. B. F. Palmer served as president and Braxton Bragg as the society's first vice president. Each southern state selected its own vice president to represent the state, including Robert E. Lee in Virginia and John Breckinridge in Kentucky. Lee accepted the position "with pleasure," writing, "It is highly important to collect and record reliable historical information, especially in periods of rapid change, such as the present; and I will cheerfully render the society any service that may aid this object in Virginia." Wade Hampton, selected vice president from South Carolina, offered similar sentiments, writing, "I appreciate highly this mark of consideration on the part of the society, and I beg you to express to them, not only my gratification, but to give them the assurance of my cordial cooperation."[48]

To demonstrate appreciation and reverence to the new vice president of the Southern Historical Society from Virginia, a group of citizens, including Hood, Beauregard, and Bragg, commissioned a local artist, E. B. D. Julio, to paint a portrait of "Genls. Lee and Jackson together upon the field." The painting, to be presented to Lee "as a token of regard by his friends and admirers," remained on exhibit on Canal Street for public viewing, to entice donations toward the costs of the painting and shipping it to Lee. Donors also received a lithograph of the painting as a token of remembrance.[49]

Lee responded to receiving a photograph of the painting, writing, "The case in which it was enclosed was broken and the photograph marred and injured. It did not, therefore, give a good representation of your picture; but, as far as I could judge, the effect is spirited and the execution good." Unfortunately, Lee would never get a better glimpse of the portrait, as he passed away on October 12, 1870. Lee, who had served since the war as president of Washington College, was laid to rest in the campus chapel. The southern populace paused to show "the profound love and veneration which they entertain for the great soldier and good man," in the midst of a general gloom cast "over the entire country." Collections were now applied to the task of sending the painting to hang in the chapel, even more appropriate because Jackson's remains lay nearby. Richmond closed their businesses on October 13 and Lexington prepared for a funeral on October 15, where former Confederate General John B. Gordon would present the eulogy.[50]

The city of New Orleans reacted to Lee's death in a similar fashion as the rest of the South. Hundreds of businesses, including banks, theaters, insurance companies, as well as saloons and stores, closed their doors on

October 14. Baseball games had to be rescheduled, as the streets filled with pictures of Lee and black bunting. Word spread quickly of Lee's death, and building after building displayed an aura of sorrow on "balconies, show windows, hall doors [and] verandahs." Churches, draped in mourning cloth, dotted the city, as the fruit vendors who passed by had set up tributes to Lee on their stands. "No one seemed [too] poor to make some exhibition of the love and veneration entertained for the honored dead," reported one local newspaper. The reporter remarked, "Every man, woman and child in the city seemed to be profoundly impressed with the solemnity of the occasion and while they united in giving outward expression to their sorrow, the imagination pictured the form of the beloved leader of the South as it lies in mournful state in Lexington."[51]

The city's residents gathered at the St. Charles Theater on October 18 to hold a memorial service for Lee. The scene encapsulated the picture of mourning, with the theater "draped in flags, and with mourning wreathes and immortelles entwined." Yet, citizens gathered only to remember Lee. One editor wrote, "The display of mourning emblems appeared to have little or no political signification, certainly, no political importance for many joined in the manifestation who cannot be suspected of sympathizing with the 'Lost Cause,' with which the deceased warrior was identified." With the theater packed, it appeared that Lee's life "has left a legacy of goodness to the world which no time can obliterate and destroy."[52]

"All classes and conditions of people" attended the event, complete with music and a eulogy by magazine editor William M. Burwell, who used the moment to defend the legality of secession. Several vice presidents were named for the meeting, including John Bell Hood. The keynote speaker, Benjamin M. Palmer, utilized his speaking opportunity to place Lee on the same pedestal as George Washington. Lee and Washington, he remarked, had both been great because of the supremacy of the white race. "Unquestionably, there is in this problem the element of race, for he is blind to all the truths of history . . . who does not recognize a . . . select race as we recognize a select individual of that race, to make all history," declared Palmer.[53]

With the passing of General Robert E. Lee in 1870, the South and New Orleans sought to immediately secure the memory of its beloved leader. Hood served as vice president of the Lee Memorial Association, created on October 24. He signed a statement, with Bragg, Beauregard, and a host of Confederate veterans, to meet on November 1 to testify "our profound regret for his decease, and our great respect and veneration for his memory." The meeting, held at Old Fellow's Hall, also appeared draped "with the somber insignia of mourning for the occasion." Numerous men and women attended the event. Beauregard offered an address calling for the construction of a monument. He said, "It would not alone perpetuate the memory of the illustrious dead, but to its base the women of the South would take their children and teach them the history of their country and the story of their fathers who fought and died for the cause he so gloriously sustained. The monument would be a shrine at which the followers of the 'Lost Cause' may worship." Organizers wished the monument would prove "an honor and an ornament to our city and State."[54]

Beauregard's speech not only brought notice to Lee's place in history and memory, but also the importance of constructing a narrative of the Confederate story to preserve the Lost Cause for future generations. The Monument Association, which sought to collect funds to construct the Lee monument in New Orleans, announced in 1871 that they intended to go throughout the city garnering money. A large sum would be needed, for the association had set its sights high: "Even as Lee towered above ordinary mortals in the majesty of his character, so should the pile our affections rears to his memory rise far above the monuments to other men."[55]

New Orleans wanted to construct one of the grandest monuments to Lee. The monument would be placed at Tivoli Circle, "the centre of the city and the most prominent and conspicuous place." The towering image of Lee would rest upon "a large mound" and be surrounded "with walks, flower beds, etc." The statue of Lee, fifteen feet high, would stand on a shaft 106 feet, 8 inches above the city streets on a base twelve feet high, atop a twelve-foot-high mound. In the newly named Lee Park, funds from various entertainment events at the Opera House assisted in the monument's construction. The events drew large crowds with "bewitching ladies in charge of refreshment tables" and "handsome men of the reception committee were on the alert." Not only did the opera house offer musical productions geared toward an older audience, but they also offered a production of *Cinderella,* featuring a cast of seventy-five children, making the Lee fund raisers a multigenerational event.[56]

As the city of New Orleans dealt with their memory of Lee, John Bell Hood began to work more diligently in securing the legacy of his Texas Brigade. Despite living in New Orleans, his connection to Texas remained strong. On October 28, 1868, Hood received an honorary membership in the Texan Club of New Orleans, made up of expatriots living in that city. The gentlemen's club sought to create an organization that could serve as a "nucleus" where visiting Texans could gather.[57]

On June 27, 1871, a few surviving members of Hood's Texas Brigade gathered in Barton Springs, Texas. The reunion celebrated the ninth anniversary of the Battle at Gaines' Mill. During the gathering, the small group felt it necessary for all surviving members of the Texas Brigade to begin meeting on a yearly basis. Thus, the call went out for all veterans to gather on May 14, 1872, in Houston. Sixty-six members, including Hood, met and established the annual proceedings of the Memorial and Reunion Association of Hood's Texas Brigade, Army of Northern Virginia. No more than four hundred attended the first reunion. The Texas Brigade had gone from twenty-four hundred members in 1861 to 617 at Appomattox in 1865, and now "400 at the reunion in 1872." As Henry Thomas wrote, "Every seat was filled with a 'war worn' veteran of the brigade, their beloved commander, Gen. Hood, occupying the chair of honor at the head." After an opening prayer by former Chaplain Nicholas Davis, General Robertson called that John Bell Hood should be elected president and, without hesitation, "the motion was adopted by acclamation."[58]

Hood spoke at the meeting to accept the presidency, endorsing the association, and said, "Comrades in arms—I thank you for the honor you have conferred upon me. It is useless to attempt to express the happiness I feel in meeting those upon whose countenances so much is pictured in the past. Time has done its work leaving only a few brave hearts to stand as sentinels over precious memories." Hood urged the present members to not forget the Eighteenth Georgia and Third Arkansas, who had not attended the event but had been valued members of Hood's command. He then stated: "Hereafter, next to my own family, the survivors of that body with whom I passed through so many trials and dangers are nearer and dearer to me than all others upon earth. Since coming into your midst, recollections have rushed through my brain that almost stagger me, of incidents that transpired from 1861 to 1865. I stand, as it were, in your midst with a tear and a smile—a tear of sadness for memories of the past, and a smile of hope for the future."[59]

Hood concluded, "Comrades, you have done your duty nobly as soldiers, continue to do your duty as nobly as citizens, trusting that God will some day give you that liberty which you claim as an inheritance from your forefathers." Because he lived in New Orleans, Hood agreed to serve as temporary chairman but declined the post of president. After Hood's speech, the association passed several resolutions, including perpetuating "remembrance of widows and orphans of comrades who had died in the defense of the cause." The chief objective of the society, the "friendly and social reunion of the survivors," sought to "collect and perpetuate all incidents, anecdotes, history and everything connected therewith and to succor the needy among its members." The meeting concluded with a brief address by General Robertson and then the reading of a poem, entitled "Greetings to Hood's Brigade," by Mrs. M. J. Young, from Texas. At the conclusion of the poem, the veterans raised a silent toast to pay tribute to "Gen. Lee and their dead comrades." "This scene was most affecting and many a tear trickled down many a veteran cheek during the solemn ceremony, which concluded by each passing silently out, extending their hands to the poetess of the occasion in a final adieu," noted one observer.[60]

Hood's caring demeanor and friendship during the war remained imprinted upon the memory of the Texas Brigade well beyond the close of battle. Major J. W. Ratchford remembered, "Few brigades have had the personal love and care as the Texas Brigade had from Hood. He knew every man in the brigade, could call him by his name. . . . He never ordered them to go where he would not lead them." Hood's comrades felt a sense of disappointment when their beloved leader could not attend every reunion. Hood wrote in 1874, "I regret extremely that I cannot be present. My heart goes forth to every member of my old brigade. May God bless you all." The following year, Hood again declined the invitation, writing, "My long and fatiguing journey renders it impossible for me in my maimed condition to be with you, although to meet the members of my old brigade would afford me one of the greatest pleasures of my life. May God's blessing rest upon you all."[61]

Membership in a group that commemorated the achievements of the Texas Brigade arose as an important moment in the postwar life of John Bell Hood. Hood gathered to remember the days of victory with his Texans, as opposed to the memories of defeat, still fresh in his mind following the war. Though many soldiers had been killed, their deaths had resulted in victory or in staving off defeat, as opposed to military disaster. When Hood visited with veterans of the Texas Brigade, he would never hear disparaging remarks about his failure to win as head of the Army of Tennessee. Any moment when Hood could remember his command with the Texas Brigade helped create a lasting set of memories that he wanted and needed to remember, as he continued to come to grips with failure.

Owing to his physical impairment and the distance to Texas, Hood only attended one other reunion. On June 27, 1877, he arrived in Waco to reminisce about the glorious career of his fellow Texans. Hood reviewed the brigade's history, beginning with the engagement at Eltham's Landing, of which Hood said, "True in that fight [we] were only engaged with the skirmish line, but it was [your] first baptism of fire, the place where [I] first knew [you] and [you me]." Hood spoke fondly of the action at Gaines' Mill, calling it "one of the grandest battles of the revolution." Hood recalled the regiment taking "the bit in their teeth" and forcing "themselves ahead, capturing and driving everything before them." Beyond the glory, Hood also recalled the "groaning and crying" of the wounded men who called out "Hood! Oh, Hood!"[62] Here, Hood paused during his celebratory address to reflect on the dead and dying that remained with him well into the postwar period.

Hood continued his historical review, examining how the Fifth Texas "took the reins in their hands, and faster than [I] could keep up with them, had strewn the field with red breeches (Zouaves) and were crowding fast into the very vitals of the enemy" at Second Manassas. At Sharpsburg, a regiment went into the fight, "whipping and driving everything they found" and came out with only "40 men." When Hood fell wounded at Chickamauga, he saw it as "fortune to fall into the arms of [my] old Brigade and by [you] to be borne from the field." Hood recalled, "Could anyone wonder then, after having shared together such perils and privations, that [our] hearts were knit together as with great hooks of steel." He concluded with a discussion of his love for his old command and "thanked his comrades for meeting him." According to Waco newspaper accounts, the speech had been interrupted numerous times to the sound of thunderous applause.[63]

However, the Texans did not stand alone in gathering to commemorate and write the history of the war. In the wake of Lee's death, a new battlefield for memory construction emerged. Since its inception, the Southern Historical Society struggled to gain momentum among the southern populace outside New Orleans. Secretary-Treasurer Joseph Jones stated the "movement has as yet met with no general or material support from the Southern people." Yet, everything changed when Robert E. Lee died. Interest in the society proliferated over the course of a few years as lectures took place every two weeks. The first, presented by Dr. Palmer, the president of the society, took place on February 16, 1872. In a speech entitled "The Tribunal of History," Dr. Palmer offered an assessment of history and discussed the importance of presenting an accurate historical picture for future generations.[64]

Furthermore, the Southern Historical Society published articles in local newspapers to chronicle the details of battle. The society began by discussing the early years of the war and occasionally made reference to John Bell Hood. For his actions on the Peninsula, the SHS wrote, "The Texas troops, under Gen. Hood, especially distinguished themselves. These, followed by their comrades, charged the Federal left on the bluff, and in spite of a desperate resistance, carried the position." In discussing the action at Gettysburg, the SHS author made note of Hood's wounding and further stated, about the second day at Gettysburg, "Whether Hood advanced at the same time that McLaws did, the present writer does not know; but he does know that Hood became engaged with the enemy several hours before, and that his musketry had ceased before he made his attack. Hood's division may have advanced on McLaws's right, but it had made an attack long before this advance near Round Top Mountain."[65]

As the articles poured forth, the Southern Historical Society still faced the difficulty of maintaining interest because of their location away from the heart of the former Confederacy. Furthermore, according to the society, "The country has been flooded with partisan histories, in many of which the pretended historian has wandered as far from the truth as if he had been writing a work of fiction." To diagnose and cure flagging interest in the society, the organization sponsored a convention at White Sulphur Springs, Virginia, on August 14, 1873. General Jubal Early addressed the convention. Louisiana selected a number of gentlemen to represent the state, including John Bell Hood. Yet, his injuries prevented Hood from traveling the distance to Virginia, and other gentlemen took his place.[66]

Early addressed the meeting and "alluded to various misrepresentations on the part of Northern historians." The general criticized several northern accounts and even sarcastically "wondered that some Northern men did not claim that Lee outnumbered Grant at Appomattox." Thus, Early called for a more stringent policy in Confederate historical record keeping. During the convention, members called for it to "be removed from New Orleans to a locality more within reach of those members who reside near the borders." Instead of moving the headquarters to Alabama or the Carolinas, the attendees decided that Richmond, Virginia, served as a more central location. Significantly, Virginia dominated the voting by having the largest representation at the meeting, with twenty-one members. To conclude the proceedings of the second day, the society named officers for the coming year and elected John Bell Hood to serve as vice president representing Louisiana.[67]

New Orleans responded to the Virginia hijacking of the SHS with dignity. In a newspaper report, the writer noted how New Orleans created the SHS and now the society had "on its rolls of membership most of the influential and leading men who took a prominent part in the late struggle from every state." Though the city may have been disappointed by the change of venue, they did not let the decision deter their support for the society. "The pen of the future historian, through the valuable services of the Southern society, will be better able to calmly and without prejudice present the events of the past than if it had been left to the loose and partisan publications which deluge the literary world." With Early now in charge, the SHS sought a more aggressive strategy to further the southern story of the war and agreed to start publishing the papers of the society in its own journal, in 1876.[68]

The Southern Historical Society, which began as an organization to collect the histories of the Civil War, had been stolen away from the city of its birth. Upon moving to Virginia, within the course of a year, the SHS transformed itself into the definitive voice interpreting the Civil War. Part of interpreting the war would unfold through a debate over who or what was ultimately responsible for the honorable failure of the Confederacy. The drama spilled into the society's pages for the public to read and understand as the definitive history of the war. A key question emerged: who should receive blame for the failure of the Confederacy? The society, through lengthy tactical addresses, explained the technical elements of each Confederate defeat. In the world of the Virginia-dominated Southern Historical Society, the "truth" became difficult to locate with a series of conflicting memories. Two appropriate targets, according to the society's membership, emerged: one a former corps commander under Lee, and the other, one of New Orleans' most prominent citizens.

The SHS would lead the way in how the South would remember the Civil War. As former commanders and soldiers spoke before the society, men also sat down to inscribe their memoirs, to be published for the entire world to read. With accusations flying quickly from both the memoirs and the speeches, a memory war broke out between competing factions over who failed at critical junctures during the war. Because John Bell Hood commanded an army during a critical moment of failure, he would now stand as a clear target in the memory wars. Although he had solidified his reputation with his family and the city of New Orleans, with the SHS now in Virginia, Hood now had to defend his honor from afar when he felt jaded and misrepresented by his critics.

One of the first officers to offer a memoir attacking Hood during the memory wars was General Joseph Johnston. As Stephen Vincent Benét noted about Johnston in his poem *John Brown's Body*, "He [Johnston] had to write his reminiscences, too." Described by a newspaper writer as "A distinguished officer—a finished scholar—an able writer—and a military critic of the first grade," Johnston enjoyed access to Confederate records in Washington, D.C. He had been actively gathering information since the close of the war, mostly to respond to Hood's official report that accused him of demoralizing the Army of Tennessee. Before the work went to press, one writer noted, "Gen. Johnston, in defending himself, must necessarily be aggressive. He must criticize very freely the actions and motives of military men and politicians wielding, for the time, the armies and authority of the Confederacy; and it is probable this will draw out many replies." Citizens in New Orleans looked forward to the publication "impatiently" and expected "an immense sale."[69]

Prior to the 1874 publication of General Joseph Johnston's memoirs, *Narrative of Military Operations, Directed, During the Late War Between the States*, an advance review of the work appeared in the *New Orleans Daily Picayune*. The reviewer did not share the enthusiasm among some of the expectant citizens. He wrote, "But it seems that amity and concord cannot exist among our people, even upon the subject of their misfortunes and there are hyenas in human form who stand ready to tear open the grave of the buried past and whet their insatiate appetites for revenge upon the slain heroes of the late war, and spit their venom on those who survive." Johnston received abundant criticism for procuring "testimonials damning to his brother officers." Through the writing of his memoir, the reviewer asserted, Johnston "attempts to set himself up by accomplishing the downfall of others." The reviewer took Johnston to task for opening old wounds, writing, "Shame upon that spirit which would seek to scatter any of the ashes of its noble slain, or attempt to blacken the fame of the illustrious living."[70]

In particular, Johnston aimed much of his criticism directly at Hood. However, Johnston first needed to establish his own credibility. He used his memoir as a medium to counter the reasoning behind his removal as commander of the Army of Tennessee. Johnston began by noting the many reasons for his removal presented by Jefferson Davis and General Braxton Bragg. Johnston, according to Davis and Bragg, had "disregarded the President's instructions," "would not fight the enemy," "refused to defend Atlanta," and "refused to communicate with General Bragg in relation to the operations of the army." Johnston, in his view, worked diligently to protect Atlanta, and he even called for the addition of extra rifled cannon from Mobile, Alabama.[71]

Johnston disputed reports that Hood issued asserting he had made "gross official misstatements of the strength of the army and its losses." Johnston also countered Hood's claim that Johnston had lost a large number of prisoners during the Atlanta campaign. He wrote, "The only prisoners taken from us during this campaign . . . were a company of skirmishers of Hardee's corps, and an outpost of Hood's (some two hundred men)." Johnston devalued Hood's own critical analysis by calling into question Hood's generalship during the Atlanta campaign. Clearly, Johnston had made mistakes. However, because Hood was in command when the defenses around Atlanta collapsed, Johnston could alleviate any blame if he could cast Hood as the scapegoat.[72]

Hood's main attack on Johnston in the official war reports described a declining state of morale throughout the Army of Tennessee. Johnston refuted this claim by pointing out the "admirable conduct of those troops on every occasion." As he departed command, Johnston remembered that the soldiers were "full of devotion to him who had commanded them, and belief of ultimate success in the campaign." The morale Johnston had instilled brought "courage and discipline" to the army, even during the "useless butchery at Franklin" and when the men barely "survived the rout and disorganization at Nashville." Here, Johnston brought up that because he had been replaced by Hood, the army underwent a horrific period of unnecessary deaths that he, as a commander, would have avoided.[73]

Johnston also quoted a letter from Lieutenant General Alex P. Stewart, which stated, "I do not know that its *morale* was ever before equal, certainly never superior, to what it was when the campaign opened in Georgia in 1864, under your command. *You* were the only commander of that army whom *men* and *officers* were disposed to trust." Stewart concluded, "That army *surrendered to you;* they gave you their love and *unlimited* confidence, were willing to follow you, advancing and retreating, and you could have led them wherever you chose." Johnston used the letter to point out that he had done all he could to instill a high level of morale with the Army of Tennessee, especially after the problems they faced at Chattanooga. If anything, Hood's own mismanagement of the troops led to a decline in morale throughout the army.[74]

Throughout his memoir, Johnston established the tone of Hood criticism. Johnston made the first public statement in the realm of the Lost Cause about the failure at Atlanta. Some noticed that Johnston seemed to be starting the memory war over the actions there. As one observer stated, "To the great credit of Gen. Hood, be it said that though conscious of much undeserved criticism and disparagement, he had always refrained from any intrusion of his private grievances before the public, or from any attempt to reopen the old disputes. If he has been forced from this position, it has been by the aggressive observations of Gen. Johnston." Furthermore, by bringing up the memories of failure, Johnston also put pressure on the soldiers who fought. The slippery slope the former commanders descended allowed for other soldiers, still dealing with the trauma of war, to face the horrors of the past again and again in print. "There is enough of sorrowful association and reminiscence connected with that event, without adding new griefs and irritations by exposures of the alleged faults, errors and mistakes of their chieftains, thus dividing into new parties those who ought to be bound together in bonds of fraternity and good will by a common calamity," wrote a newspaperman.[75]

Despite the strong stance against Hood, the memoir did not convince everyone that Johnston should be alleviated of any blame. Senator Benjamin Hill of Georgia, in an interview to a Philadelphia newspaper, said, "The difficulty with General Johnston is that he is suspicious, self-willed and over bearing. Davis never had any ill will toward Johnston and removed him with great regret. He regarded Johnston as a good general and one of the best fighters in the army if he would only fight." One book critic came to Hood's defense, calling him "a young, daring and skilled officer" who accepted command of the Army of Tennessee in a circumstance "full of embarrassment and difficulty," and that Hood "did the best that could be done." Hood took over an army that had experienced demoralization brought by "constant retreat." Although Hood failed to succeed, he did not deserve blame because his "military life has been crowned with glory." The Johnston critic concluded by providing a reprinting of letters from Davis, Jackson, Longstreet, and Bragg that recommended Hood's promotions throughout the war and lauded him for his valor and military prowess on the battlefield.[76]

The publication of Johnston's memoir sought to rectify the southern position in the North, not open up old wounds, according to one reviewer. When Johnston had been asked if he was a bit critical of Hood, Johnston responded, "No! nothing of the kind." Not only did the memoir publication create a feud between Johnston and Hood, but it also brought to light other issues from the war. Essentially, a line had been drawn in the realm of Civil War memory, and officers and soldiers had to decide whom they supported: Johnston or Hood. For instance, Wade Hampton asserted in the *Daily Picayune* that Robert E. Lee had never advised the removal of Johnston from command of the Army of Tennessee. According to Hampton, Lee had expressed "regret" over the situation and had "his entire confidence in him." Lee "urged the Secretary of War not to remove him [Johnston], as no better officer could be found to take his place."[77]

The memoir produced by Joseph Johnston serves as the onset of Hood's postwar memory construction. Since the close of war, Hood returned to the private sector and engaged in charitable and memorial activities to reassert his honor. Furthermore, he attended meetings to preserve a heroic memory of Lee and his Texas brigade. Now, Joseph Johnston changed the terms of memory construction, forcing Hood to take a stand and fight for his memory and reputation. Johnston, to secure his own place in memory, made Hood the scapegoat, ridiculed his military actions, and deflected any possible blame for his own failure at Atlanta. Furthermore, Johnston emphasized Hood's horrible defeats at Franklin and Nashville to mask his own inability to pursue a more aggressive strategy against Sherman outside Atlanta. Johnston's overly technical, dry memoir sought to justify his reputation at the expense of Jefferson Davis and John Bell Hood.

Johnston's memoir, although it sold poorly, angered Hood. He began at once to construct a reply to Johnston that would take the shape of a personal military autobiography and memoir. Hood began publishing attacks at once, calling into question Johnston's reporting of the technical details of the war's latter half. However, any response from Hood would, in turn, draw a response to again assert Johnston's side of the story. Lieutenant Charles G. Johnston, who served with the Washington Artillery as part of the Army of Tennessee, wrote, on June 12, 1874, "I have carefully read Gen. Johnston's narrative of the campaign from Dalton to Atlanta and I believe in every particular it is strictly correct." Charles Johnston further sought to discredit Hood's analysis and memory, writing, "Gen. Hood seeks to convey the idea that the army was demoralized by Gen. Johnston's policies and its morale restored by his own. The contrary is the fact. Gen. Johnston had the unlimited confidence of the army."[78]

Joseph Johnston also found Hood's initial attack problematic. In a letter to Kinloch Falconer, Johnston stated, on June 4, 1874, "General Hood is publishing a series of attacks. I think I'll try to point out the absurdity of his figures and the difference between the authority of your records and statements." General Johnston further discarded Hood's blatant assertions that he had consistently recommended retreat. "He [Hood] says that a meeting of the Lt. Genls at night, in my quarters near New Hope church, I proposed the abandonment of the position and retreat to Macon." Johnston fervently argued that Hood called for the "necessity of abandoning the ground that night."[79]

Johnston looked everywhere for those willing to support his side of the story. In a letter to Benjamin Cheatham, Johnston referred to Hood's statements about Johnston's careless use of the army, and said, "I can only meet this accusation now, but [with] the testimony of the most prominent men in that army—and therefore beg you to write me (for publication)." Hood claimed that Johnston carelessly left behind nineteen thousand small arms. Johnston wanted Cheatham to give his opinion of the army "that always held the ground on which it fought, and therefore could secure the arms of its few dead, wounded and prisoners." Johnston knew Cheatham would offer assistance, for in addition to his long-standing loyalty, Cheatham had even named one of his sons Joseph Johnston Cheatham.[80]

Thus, as the fallout from Johnston's memoir reverberated throughout the South, Hood took to the task of writing his autobiography. Hood not only replied to Johnston, but he also made sure that his personal memory would not fade. With the pressure of the Southern Historical Society and the autobiography of Joseph Johnston, Hood sat down, with pen in hand, to reconstruct his own personal memory. He determined to forge ahead, even if it meant not fitting within the collective memory being constructed across the South.

As Hood wrote, "Although I feel by reason of injustice done me in the past that I have good cause to demand of our people the privilege of a hearing upon certain matters little understood by them, I would, nevertheless have left the work of vindication to the unbiased historian of the future." Historians could not do Hood any justice because his "words and actions [had] been so strangely misrepresented" by the memoirs of Johnston. Hood had no choice but to bring forth "a reply to the erroneous and injurious statements in my regard, brought forward by General Johnston." He felt he needed to protect his character against "derogatory statements" through self-defense, "or otherwise admit by silence the charges brought forth."[81]

Yet, to reconstruct the details of his memory, Hood needed help. He once again turned to his friend Stephen D. Lee, and in the late summer of 1875 asked him to travel to New Orleans to talk about the war. If Lee could not travel, Hood stood willing to go to Mobile to meet. Hood's desperate ploy came when he examined another memoir, this one by General William T. Sherman, who had faced Hood at Atlanta. Sherman published the first edition in 1875 but reworked and expanded his argument in 1885, well after Hood's untimely death. Yet, the original version produced another reason for Hood to commence his writing at once. Hood wrote to Lee, "Since the appearance of Sherman's book I have determined to give a full account of the siege of Atlanta and the TN campaign."[82]

Sherman had written, "[I] Learned [Hood] was bold even to rashness, and courageous in the extreme; I inferred that the change of commanders meant fight." However, a fighter was exactly what Sherman wanted. He wrote, "Notice of this important change was at once sent to all parts of the army, and every division commander was cautioned to be always prepared for battle in any shape. This is what we wanted, viz., to fight in open ground, on any thing like equal terms, instead of being forced to run up against prepared entrenchments." Sherman got his wish, as Hood relentlessly attacked at Atlanta, to no avail.[83]

In Johnston's version, according to Sherman's memoir, Hood and General Polk had been continually bombarded by Union artillery and had not been able to hold the position at Cassville, Georgia. Johnston argued that Hood, who criticized Johnston's usual tactic of retreat, now sought for the Confederate forces to do just that. In contrast, Hood argued that he only wanted Johnston to pursue an "offensive-defensive" game, as opposed to the traditional "pure defensive" offered by Johnston. Under Hood's advice, Johnston decided to withdraw elsewhere to pursue an offensive strategy.[84]

Sherman had the opportunity to communicate with General Johnston and General Hood in the postwar period. Friendly visits with the commanders allowed Sherman to hear both sides of the debate over Confederate actions at Atlanta. In this instance, Sherman's memoirs conveyed the tension between Hood and Johnston. It also reveals how their conflicting memories offered two drastically different interpretations of a strategic troop withdrawal from Cassville. The benefit of Sherman's memoir rests in his balanced approach, allowing the opinions of two postwar friends to be shared equally in his autobiography.

The writings of both Sherman and Johnston provided Hood a provocation to undergo his own memoir writing. Hood's memoir, aptly titled *Advance and Retreat: Personal Experiences in the United States and Confederate States Armies*, began with his military background prior to the war. Hood recounted his days at West Point and fighting in the Indian wars that had raged across the American frontier. D. E. Twiggs, an officer in the United States Army, observed Hood's early military engagements and noted, "Lt. Hood's affair was a most gallant one, and much credit is due to both the officer and the men." Self-consciously seeking to establish his reputation even before the Civil War, Hood used the frontier discussion to establish his military credentials and bolster his reputation as a gallant soldier. He remembered that, "When Kentucky failed to act, I entered the Confederate service from the State of Texas, which thenceforth became my adopted land."[85] From that moment forward, Hood acquired a Texas identity, which suited him just fine.

After a brief introduction, Hood explored his Confederate military career, acknowledging the bravery and devotion of his Texans. Hood managed in just sixty-eight pages to cover his military career from March 1862 through the end of 1863. A discussion of his wounds and the process of recovery dominate the sections on Gettysburg and Chickamauga. Hood also included many letters and reports from Thomas Jackson and Robert E. Lee, detailing his numerous promotions and the high regard the commanders had held for Hood and his comrades. Of note, Hood reprinted a lengthy letter to Longstreet, justifying Longstreet's actions during the Gettysburg campaign. Hood not only sought to rescue his own reputation but those of officers he considered close friends during the years of campaigning.[86]

The rest of the memoir receives the title of *Reply to General Johnston*. Hood began to chip away at the "misrepresented" moments by responding point by point to Johnston's memoir and then giving his own commentary. Through countless letters and numerical figures, Hood sought to justify that he was not in error, essentially accusing Johnston outright, as he had in his earlier article, of making "gross official misstatements of the strength of the Army and its losses" in the vicinity of Dalton and Atlanta. Hood also blamed Johnston for adhering to the "Joe Johnston mode of warfare," which, according to Hood, "depresses, paralyzes, and, in time, brings destruction." Instead, Johnston needed to follow the examples of Jackson and Lee, whose aggressive boldness "elevates" and "inspirits" the troops to successful fighting.[87]

Hood worked to prove that the Army of Tennessee suffered a demoralizing tenure under Johnston because he could only "render them of but little service in a pitched battle." Hood came to command the Army of Tennessee under "embarrassing circumstances," considering the state of morale among both officers and the troops. Johnston's decisions while commanding in the Atlanta campaign seemed inappropriate and allowed morale to plummet, according to Hood. Hood inquired, "Was it General Johnston's policy to retreat till he had demoralized the enemy?" Johnston had argued skilled retreat as the appropriate tactic in the Atlanta campaign. Johnston had even further criticized Hood, charging him "with recklessness, and exposure of my troops to 'useless butchery'" in the battles following Johnston's removal. Hood shrugged off this analysis and pointed out that Johnston's name would only be associated with one "single glorious victory in the annals of our four years' struggle."[88]

Hood continued his defense: he had not attacked at Cassville because of pressure from Federal cavalry on May 19, a dangerous force for infantry to confront. Johnston claimed in his memoir that Hood and Polk arrived and urged him to retreat immediately and head southward. Hood stated, "I do this day and hour, in the name of truth, honor and justice, in the name of the departed soul of the Christian and noble Polk, and in the presence of the Creator, most solemnly deny that General Polk or I recommended General Johnston at Cassville, to retreat when he intended to give battle."[89] Hood's use of Polk, his baptizer and fellow officer, evoked majesty of the fallen and the name of the Lord to justify his position against Johnston's memory.

After responding to Johnston's criticism, Hood concluded his memoir with a heartfelt but historically distorted discussion of the Tennessee campaign. Hood stated that the mishap at Spring Hill had produced "a sudden change in sentiment" among the soldiers, who now expressed a "general feeling of mortification and disappointment." Despite this, the soldiers still attacked. Hood justified the attack, "which entailed so great sacrifice of life" at Franklin, writing that the charge "became a necessity as imperative as that which impelled General Lee to order the assault at Gaines' Mill." When it failed, Hood had to acknowledge the lost opportunity to crush Schofield. For the Tennessee campaign to have any remaining chance of success, Hood decided "to take position, entrench around Nashville, and await Thomas's attack." Hood owed it to his army to engage in "a last and manful effort to lift up the sinking fortunes of the Confederacy."[90] Here, by referring to the Tennessee campaign as a "manful effort," Hood used his memoir to further assert his manhood, resurrect his honor, and deal with the reality of defeat. In fact, securing his honor became more important than ensuring each detail of the memoir maintained factual accuracy. Hood had no choice but to respond and hope to silence the ever-growing chorus of criticism.

In Hood's assessment, three reasons produced the failure in Tennessee: the debacle at Spring Hill, the short amount of daylight during the engagement at Franklin, and the failure of reinforcements to arrive from the Trans-Mississippi region, nearly all of which he would consider beyond his control. Hood addressed his critics by concluding with a medical metaphor. He painted the image of a doctor who had received ample education in the medical sciences. However, Hood questioned, "Who would employ a surgeon who had never used a knife?" And, could the inexperienced doctor be considered "an eminent man in his profession?" Hood used this illustration to characterize Johnston, writing that, "No man is justly entitled to be considered a great General, unless he has won his spurs." Hood asserts that, "Had General Johnston possessed the requisite spirit and boldness to seize the various chances for victory, which were offered him, he never would have allowed General Sherman to push him back one hundred miles in sixty-six days, from one mountain stronghold to another, down into the very heart of the Confederacy." To the bitter end of his memoir, Hood argued that although he was not perfect, he certainly was no Joe Johnston.[91]

In the midst of his memoir writing, Hood sought counsel and encouragement from people he considered friends. In a letter to Stephen D. Lee on April 10, 1879, Hood declared his disdain over a story that appeared in the *New Orleans Times* discussing Hood's conduct during the battle of Franklin. Hood declared, "The reporter of the times made a great blunder." He goes on to discuss the details of Franklin in the letter and stated, "My book will overcome all such misfortunate mistakes as those made by the reporter of the times." Stephen D. Lee asked for a copy of the official reports on the Battle at Franklin. Hood offered to send them but also told Lee he could read them himself in Hood's forthcoming book.[92]

Yet, Lee must have agreed with the reporter, even though he never told Hood so. In a letter to J. Francis H. Claiborne, written June 12, 1878, Lee said, "My opinion is, that Hood with his leg off at his hip, and maimed arm, was physically exhausted from his long forced night and day march on horseback over the rough . . . country roads in getting to Spring Hill. It is a matter of doubt . . . that any soldier so maimed should have such an important command."[93] Lee knew that the publication of Hood's memoir would bring further criticism to his own actions during the war. Thus, Lee, a man whom Hood counted on for assistance in memory construction and reconstruction, privately criticized Hood and may have personally undermined Hood's reputation among other former Confederates.

In addition to his written work, Hood also spoke as often as he could in defense of his honor. In 1879, in a speech before the Louisiana Division of the Army of Tennessee Association, Hood offered a forceful rebuttal to his critics who had blamed him for the loss of life at Franklin. Hood affirmed, "They charge me with having made Franklin a slaughter-pen, but, as I understand it, war means fight and fight means kill." This remains the only surviving excerpt from Hood's speech. This tidbit, nevertheless, reveals Hood's daily emotional struggle against being cast as the chief scapegoat emerging within the Lost Cause.[94]

Though Hood began the journey to see his private memories get into print, the Southern Historical Society continued to hold meetings in Richmond to come to terms with failure and determine who should bear the brunt of the responsibility. The *SHS Papers* sparked several moments of finger pointing and debate as to who or what led to the Confederacy's downfall, particularly in the aftermath of Hood's memoir. Yet, Hood's memoir came forth into publication without the general available to defend it. Hood died in 1879 from the yellow fever epidemic that struck New Orleans before his memoirs could be published. Hence, General P. G. T. Beauregard secured the memoir's publication, which will be discussed in the next chapter. The memory wars would continue to rage, with Hood's memoir having to stand on its own merits to defend the reputation of the late general.

The attacks from the SHS were critical and fierce. Captain W. O. Dodd stated that although Hood's "patriotism and courage were recognized by all," his "ability to command the entire army was much questioned." Of note, Dodd's papers are referred to as "one of the valuable series of papers" held by the Louisville branch of the Southern Historical Society. Dodd dissected Hood's memoirs to reveal what he believed were the inherent falsehoods. In particular, Dodd asserted the inaccuracies of the description of the Spring Hill debacle. He stressed that the soldiers of the Army of Tennessee were willing to fight, in contrast to Hood's claim that "the soldiers were unwilling to fight except behind breastworks." Dodd also looked at the terrain and weather conditions at Spring Hill. Hood's statements that "it got dark about 4 o'clock" and that "there were . . . many shade trees" are falsehoods in Dodd's eyes. Dodd points out, "It was a clear day. . . . [T]he battle would have been largely in a corn-field and an open piece of woodland."[95]

General Benjamin Cheatham, who served under Hood in the Tennessee campaign, also used the Southern Historical Society as an outlet to improve his own reputation and counter the claim that failure at Spring Hill rested on his shoulders. Cheatham attacked Hood in order to bring "truth, and justice" to his reputation by arguing that Hood's memoir provided several examples of places where his "memory proved treacherous," especially when discussing events that unfolded at Spring Hill. Cheatham utilized a letter from Isham G. Harris to Governor James D. Porter, dated May 20, 1877. In the letter, Harris stated that "General Hood, on the march to Franklin, spoke to me, in the presence of Major Mason, of the failure of General Cheatham to make the night attack at Spring Hill, and censured him in severe terms for his disobedience of orders." In private, Mason confided to Harris that he had not sent Cheatham the orders from Hood to attack. Harris demanded that Mason relay this information to Hood because "it is due General Cheatham that this explanation should be made." Hood later told Harris that "he had done injustice to General Cheatham" and held him "blameless for the failure at Spring Hill." On December 13, 1864, Hood wrote to Cheatham, stating, "I do not censure you for the failure at Spring Hill. I am satisfied that you are not responsible for it." Hood concluded, "I now have a higher estimate of you as a soldier than I ever had. You can rely upon my friendship." By having all the facts, including the pertinent information that Mason failed to deliver the orders to Cheatham, Hood, during the war, changed his mind. Yet, in his memoirs, Hood, to secure his honor, once again blamed the Spring Hill debacle on Cheatham.[96]

Cheatham, angry at the publication of Hood's memoir, received support from Colonel T. B. Roy, a member of General William J. Hardee's staff, who attacked Hood. Roy deemed it his "privilege and duty to contribute what I can towards the right and the truth" concerning Hood blaming Hardee for failure during the Atlanta campaign. Roy, in his lengthy report, saw three key issues to address from Hood's memoir: First, Hood's accusation that "Hardee failed to push the attack as ordered" on July 20, 1864. According to Roy, "It would have been folly to throw troops in detail and without concert." In reality, said Roy, it had been Hood who ordered the troops to "be withdrawn to their former positions," leaving Hardee blameless for any failure to attack. Hood decided to withdraw Hardee's division, which "prevented the pushing of the attack."[97]

Second, Hood argued that on July 22, Hardee "failed to entirely turn the enemy's left, as directed." Roy counters this claim by highlighting the fact that Hardee's troops, fatigued after a long and swift march, were not ready to attack after having engaged Union forces all day on July 21. Hood, when blaming Hardee, according to Roy, had not taken into account "the actual distances involved," "the real condition of the troops," and "the respective positions of the opposing forces." Third, at Jonesboro, Georgia, on August 31, 1864, Hardee did not attack the enemy "vigorously," resulting in 1,400 casualties and a failure to dislodge the Union force. Roy again pointed out the critical situation of Hardee's soldiers, "how gallantly the troops fought, how boldly and skillfully they were handled," and how "narrowly the corps escaped capture or destruction," thanks only to the actions of Hardee. Significantly, according to Roy, Hood had to lean on Hardee during this moment of crisis, despite his earlier criticism of Hardee during July 20 and 22. Roy calls the action at Jonesboro one that "towers above all." With the passing of both Hood and Hardee prior to the publication of Roy's address, the issue of blame rested only on this final report from Roy.[98]

On May 30, 1881, General Samuel G. French, who had served in the Army of Tennessee under Hood, wrote a letter to explore further discrepancies in Hood's memoir, particularly pertaining to the battle that took place at Allatoona Pass and other catastrophes in the Tennessee campaign. French claimed that Hood had "departed so unnecessarily from the truth to vindicate himself." By presenting letters that countered Hood's argument that he had been ordered to take a garrison at Allatoona, French presented evidence that the reader could "analyze and construe" and fail to "find one word to sustain the assertion of General Hood, that he ordered me to move to Allatoona, 'capture the garrison if practicable and gain possession of the supplies.'" French also took issue with a report blaming him for withdrawing his force on October 6, 1864, when he received false information that a large Union force was moving in the vicinity. French used Sherman's memoirs and a history of the

Army of the Cumberland to prove that a Union force was on the move and that French had no choice but "to withdraw, after due deliberation, to save my command—left entirely unsupported by the army of General Hood."[99]

As noted, the main task before the society was to explain Confederate defeat. In particular, Hood's role at Gettysburg dominated conversation for several decades following the war. Hood wrote a letter to General Longstreet on June 28, 1875, which the *SHS Papers* published. The letter explained Hood's actions at Gettysburg because he had been physically unable to offer a report of the battle. Hood stated, "These severe wounds in close succession, in addition to the all-absorbing duties and anxieties attending the last year of the war, prevented me from submitting, subsequently, a report." Hood offered a "brief sketch from memory" of the actions of July 2, 1863. He confirmed, "The scenes and events of that day are as clear to my mind as if the great battle had been fought yesterday." Hood established his wishes to attack Round Top and acknowledged Longstreet's insistence that Lee's orders be obeyed, which Hood ultimately achieved. He also remembered his own soldiers as he was wounded, stating, "As I was borne off on a litter to the rear, I could but experience deep distress of mind and heart at the thought of the inevitable fate of my brave fellow-soldiers." Hood also responded to his critics on the potential importance of attacking Round Top, writing, "I shall ever believe that had I been permitted to turn Round Top mountain, we would not only have gained that position, but have been able finally to route the enemy."[100]

General C. M. Wilcox, angered by the letter, blamed Hood for the failed attack on July 2. He said, "I have stated that General Hood did not partially envelop the enemy's left; had this been done, it would have been *driven in* as had been ordered by General Lee." Hood continually sought to attack Round Top and felt it "could be turned." Wilcox pointed out that Hood requested three times to Longstreet to attack at Round Top. Longstreet replied each time, "General Lee orders us to attack up the Emmitsburg road." With respect to Hood's idea of attacking at Round Top, Wilcox writes, "Had Hood been permitted to carry out his plan, it would have been in violation of the spirit or even the letter of General Lee's orders."[101] According to Wilcox's analysis, Hood's inquiries about a change of attack delayed the entire advance of the Confederate force. Because the Confederate attack ultimately stalled on July 2, Wilcox attributed this failure directly to Hood.

In addition to Gettysburg, Hood also received blame for Sherman's March to the Sea. Further speeches in the historical papers stated, "The . . . movement of General Hood, ill-advised and pregnant with disaster, left the State of Georgia fairly open to a Federal advance." The Army of Tennessee had been "far too weak to do more than skirmish in a desultory manner with his [Sherman] powerful army of invasion."[102] In this case, the *SHS Papers* presented a clear set of contradictions that highlighted the problem of conflicting memories. Because Hood withdrew to Tennessee, the state of Georgia laid at the mercy of Sherman. However, even if Hood had remained in Georgia, he never could have defeated Sherman's superior force. In both instances, Hood was reportedly responsible for Confederate failure.

The society, while blaming Hood, further inflated the reputation of other Confederate commanders in the Army of Tennessee. In particular, General J. R. Chalmers of Mississippi offered a biographical sketch of General Nathan Bedford Forrest, generally praised in the *SHS Papers,* in an address before the society. Chalmers stated, "I think I risk nothing in saying if Forrest had been in command of our army, General Schofield would never have marched by Spring Hill, and the disastrous battle of Franklin, where the gallant Cleburne and so many brave men fell, would never have been fought." Chalmers declared Forrest a better commander than Hood and, in his opinion, suggested he could have saved the Army of Tennessee from failure. In this description, Chalmers failed to see the reality of the superior numerical force held by the Union army at Nashville or even to acknowledge Hood's thoughts about the campaign. Despite this, Chalmers continued to assert that Forrest had remained "determined" to do his duty "to the last" and "stood out faithfully to the end." Furthermore, Chalmers made the assumption that Forrest could have properly motivated the subordinate commanders to flank Schofield at Spring Hill, thus preventing the battle of Franklin.[103]

The SHS continued to publish their commentary to further the Lost Cause, including publishing the *Confederate Congressional Record* from the war in 1959. The records reveal that in 1865, the Confederate Congress had been engulfed in partisanship for Johnston and used Hood as a scapegoat for the various problems facing the war effort. In 1865, Tennessee Congressman Henry Foote offered the most biting remarks against Hood to echo throughout the halls of the Confederate Congress. He said, "The Army of Tennessee had been rudely deprived of its noble and gallant leader, General Johnston, there had been nothing in that quarter but an avalanche of misfortune. From the day General Hood was given command of that army he had shown a dire, ruinous want of judgment. See the battle of Franklin." Foote's reflection stained Hood's reputation in the *Confederate Congressional Record.* Letters were also read in congressional sessions describing the dire state of the Army of Tennessee under Hood. One letter, submitted after Hood's resignation, pointed out that "the troops had no confidence in General Hood, would never fight under him, and were clamoring for Johnston." "The evil of the times," the letter stated, "was incompetence in command." The letter concluded with thanks to God that "we had now at the head of our military affairs a man [Johnston] of ability."[104]

From first to last, despite context of personalities and politics that had shaped memories, the SHS remained derisive toward Hood. Although these "attacking" voices dominated, from the publication of Johnston's memoir through individual SHS addresses forged by the Virginia contingency, other voices are available that soften the portrait, or at least provide more detail. Other private memories emerged beyond the official records of the SHS, particularly when yellow fever struck and killed members of the Hood family, including the general, in 1879.

Chapter 8

"A Suitable Monument": Securing the Memory of John Bell Hood

Tombstones and statues crumble and decay, and, even while they stand, their inscriptions fade from sight. . . . But living monuments are worth more than all.
—Clark Howell, editor of the *Atlanta Constitution*

In late November 1879, former President Ulysses S. Grant traveled to Portland, Oregon. Grant's presence in the region inspired a reception "which nearly every man, woman and child in the county" attended. Coincidentally, on the same evening of the reception, the Portland Theater held a charitable performance of *Ours,* of which half of the proceeds would be donated to a charitable cause. Grant, described as an "old Roman and Hero" by a local reporter, "deserted his own reception at a very early hour." The hero of the Union during the Civil War went instead to the theater. The former military commander "sat conscientiously through a long and rather dreary performance." Owing to the large number of empty seats, the Portland Theater raised only a small sum for the charity. However, an observer declared that the funds raised are "better than nothing, and shows at least that everybody's heart is in the right place." The proceeds went directly to the Hood Orphan Fund, a newly created charitable organization formed to care for the orphaned children John Bell Hood and his wife left behind when yellow fever struck New Orleans in August 1879. Thus, Grant attended the performance not only to escape the reception but also "in the hope of helping dear old Hood's little one's."[1]

Grant's charitable actions in Portland came late in an autumn marked by an outpouring of philanthropic endeavors within New Orleans. In September,

D. M. Hollingsworth, a prominent resident of the city, placed an advertisement in the *Daily Picayune*. Hollingsworth announced that he would "take one of my Light Spar Spring no top buggies and put it up for raffle or lottery." For the proposed lottery to take place, Hollingsworth would "have the tickets printed, numbered and stamped, and furnish them to the President, officers and members of the Associations of Armies of Tennessee and of Northern Virginia." Hollingsworth pleaded with the citizenry of the city, as well as former Confederate soldiers and officers, writing, "I would request them to aid and assist in keeping those little ones from actual want. Soldiers, Christians, friends of the lamented Hood, you know your duty, do it, and God will bless you."[2]

Hollingsworth was not the only individual willing to sacrifice for the benefit of John Bell Hood's legacy. The citizens of Laredo, Texas, and Montgomery, Alabama, each auctioned off a bale of cotton to raise money for the Hood orphans. An unnamed woman in Lowndes County, Alabama, raised money from "an abundant and beautiful growth of hair clipped from her own head." The description put forth by the Hood Orphan Fund stated, "She is poor in the world's goods, but rich in the finer and gentler impulses, so characteristic of Southern womanhood. She shrinks from notoriety, and is only solicitous to do her duty in rendering such help as she can to the Orphans."[3] Although not able to contribute financially, the anonymous donor gave away a prized possession, her beautiful hair, to help secure the future of ten orphaned children she never personally knew.

The outpouring of generosity, at a time when the southern states continued to rebuild from the horrors of the American Civil War, came from across the nation, as well as Europe, for a general who failed to secure Confederate victory during the war's final months. The dramatic symbol of ten orphaned children who managed to survive a yellow fever epidemic rallied donations to secure the health and well-being of "the little ones." At the same time, knowingly and unknowingly, the men, women, and children who gave their money, their time, their hair, their baked goods, their bales of cotton, and their buggies all worked toward a larger goal of securing the memory of a Confederate general. Hood had risked life, and lost two limbs, for the possibility of victory. Now, the citizens of New Orleans, the former Confederacy, and beyond would sacrifice part of their financial means to secure an everlasting memorial to John Bell Hood: the health and welfare of his children. Donations, accompanied by a plethora of testimonials, speeches, and written tributes reformulated the collective memory of Hood following a decade of criticism. The tributes did more than avoid speaking ill of the dead: they sought to silence Hood's critics and attempted to remove, at least partially, the burden of blame for Confederate failure from Hood's shoulders. Ultimately, the death of John Bell Hood facilitated a recalculation of how Hood should be remembered and allowed his orphan children to rise above any marble or granite monuments as the ultimate form of memory construction.

To understand how Hood's children served as a way to remember the late general, it is vital first to examine how Hood's untimely death set the wheels in motion. Yellow fever had made its presence felt earlier in the summer of 1878. With the city as well as much of the South gripped in panic, the cotton exchange closed and the city wharves stood bare. Insurance investments also faltered. With Hood still holding personal investments in the cotton market, the yellow fever epidemic practically bankrupted the Hood family by the early part of 1879. A new year brought new opportunities but also brought a continual fear of more yellow fever. Yet, the Board of Health declared that "yellow fever has totally disappeared from New Orleans. In fact, there is no more danger of taking yellow fever in New Orleans than of taking the plague in Chicago. There is no danger of taking any epidemic disease." The Board of Health concluded that New Orleans "is perfectly healthy. It is as healthy as any city in the world. It is not only as healthy as any city in the world, but, we venture to say, it is by far the pleasantest place in the civilized world." Visitors received invitation to come to New Orleans and enjoy the "clear skies, a genial temperature, the balmy airs of spring, the odors of violets and roses, and all the delights of the opening spring." With the Hood family finances in shambles, the family had to remain within the city for the summer of 1879, instead of moving north, as was urged to escape the heat and humidity.[4]

Yet, the Board of Health could not permanently stop the fever outbreaks. Hood, his wife, and eldest daughter Lydia died of yellow fever during the epidemic summer of 1879 that struck the Mississippi River region and flared again in New Orleans on July 22. By September 1, seventeen cases, including four within the Hood residence, had been reported in the city, fifteen of which had "occurred in eleven houses, in a parallelogram of three blocks by six."[5] The symptoms of attack normally came on suddenly, accompanied with a chill, and pain in the back, head, loins, and limbs, as well as soreness all over the abdomen. Nausea and vomiting occurred as the skin turned yellow and "the pulse was generally frequent, full, hard and burning; sometimes so rapid as to reach 120 to 130 beats" per minute. Head and back pain intensified, as the eyes appeared red and the body gave off "the appearance of having been thoroughly smoked."[6]

The symptoms continued to increase over a period of twenty-four to thirty-six hours, with increased pain, fever, sighing, moaning, and tossing, as well as "weakness, faintness, dizziness and dimness of vision [which] made the slightest attempt to rise or move difficult." Despite the worsening symptoms, the patient could enter remission, as "the pulse fell," "the skin cooled," and "the active flush disappeared," allowing for a temporary intermission of disease symptoms that could easily be mistaken for a sign of remission. However, the danger could again rear its ugly head rather quickly, as vomiting increased from a "colorless" solution with increasing "specks like snuff," followed by "threads of mucus, like hairs," "larger and darker particles, like coffee grounds" that resulted in "the fearful black vomit." The previous symptoms returned and the victim "complained of burning heat in the stomach and bowels." As physician William T. Wragg noted, "The mind was gone, and, in his delirium, he would scream or groan in frightful fury from the intolerable anguish of his suffering." At this point, the patient gave up "his strength to the violence of the disease, passed away quietly or in a storm of mortal anguish."[7]

Large doses of quinine and calomel fashioned some success in the treatment of yellow fever. The patient "was made to drink warm teas, keep well covered under several blankets, the room closed, and the drinking of cold water strictly prohibited." Some physicians found a "cold douche upon the head" an effective way to relieve headache and restlessness and to quiet the thundering pulse. To apply the cold douche, the patient's head and shoulders had to be turned "over an empty tub at the side of the bed," and cold water flowed from the pitcher "over the whole head, taking care to guard the ears and eyes." The treatment, repeated at short intervals, also could be used when the patient requested it.[8]

As a way to avoid the debilitating symptoms of yellow fever, citizens took precautions to prevent infection. A Commission of Experts from the National Board of Health in Washington, D.C., published a series of recommendations on August 28, 1879. The commission recommended that the towels and linens used by someone who contracted the disease needed to immediately be placed in a pail of a zinc and salt solution, "boiling hot if possible." All unnecessary furniture should be removed from the patient's room in hopes of avoiding a later disinfection from a sulphur solution. To properly fumigate a room, which would include furniture, the structure of the house, and any large blankets and clothes that could not be doused with the zinc solution, a set of careful procedures must take place. First, "sulphur in iron pans supported on bricks contained in tubs containing a little water" were placed in a room, then closed as tightly as possible. Next, the solution, "set on fire by hot coals or with the aid of a spoonful of alcohol," began the twenty-four-hour fumigation process, which required "at least two pound of sulphur" for a ten foot room. Although the committee recommended burning articles that came in contact with the patient, valuable linens could be boiled in the zinc solution for half an hour, beaten, shaken, and hung in the open air to dry.[9]

Whether or not the Hood family followed the protocol for dealing with yellow fever remains unclear. If the family had taken any precautions, they failed to prevent a family tragedy when Anna Marie Hood contracted the fever on August 22, 1879. When she died two days later, Walter B. Crouch, a personal friend of General Hood, who was with the general from the death of his wife until the death of Hood himself, wrote a poignant letter that described the toll of yellow fever on the Hood family. He wrote, "I never saw a man so completely crushed in my life. . . . He said he'd rather God had taken every one of his children in one day than to have lost his wife, that he was completely ruined and now without his wife he had nothing to live for." The children, or, as Crouch referred to them, the "precious little lambs," woke to the sad news that their mother had passed away in the night, a scene that Crouch "never wanted to witness again."[10] Hood made his final public appearance at the funeral the afternoon of August 25.

The *New Orleans Democrat* announced the "Death of Mrs. J. B. Hood," writing, "A very profound sensation of sorrow and of sympathy" came from "the intelligence of the death of Mrs. J.B. Hood, born Anna Marie Hennen, the wife of that heroic chieftain and mutilated veteran, Gen. John B. Hood." In death, she "departed to join her sister in the spirit world, leaving their mother a grief-stricken invalid, departing from a noble and devoted husband" inflicted with "the most debilitating wounds and mutilations, received in the late war." The obituary concluded, stating, "Surely the cup of affliction and sorrow of this interesting family has been filled to overflowing. If sympathy and condolence can lighten the burden of their grief and alleviate the bitterness . . . they are . . . profoundly felt and expressed by our whole community."[11]

The day after Anna Hood's funeral, August 26, Lydia, the eldest daughter, exhibited signs of the disease. Lydia, described as a child "of uncommon intelligence and amiability," had, even at the age of ten, developed a taste for "literature of a description not usually relished by young persons." She enjoyed the works of Washington Irving as well as "histories, biographies and books of the poets." The following day, General Hood fell ill.[12]

On August 27, 1879, Dr. S. M. Bemiss declared Hood's symptoms a case of yellow fever, and on the same day, members of Hood's Texas Brigade sent a letter of sympathy to the general in response to the death of his wife. The veterans wrote, "This affliction which has befallen you, revives in us anew the sufferings and sorrows of the ill-fated past. When we were but as your children and comrades in arms, you guarded our well being and honor, and to your devotion to the cause which we had espoused, we are indebted for whatever fame we achieved." The soldiers had "watched with pleasure every turn of fortune that has brought you [Hood] success and happiness." From Fort Worth, the veterans concluded, "Your marriage to your accomplished wife excited in us hopes that your last years might be freighted with happiness and love; that your children and ours might mingle and recount the deeds of their fathers. But the pall of sadness has fallen on you and yours. Your old comrades share your poignant grief."[13]

In a few brief paragraphs, the Texas Brigade survivors captured not only what Hood's wife meant to Hood, but also what the Hood family meant to his war comrades. The bonds of brotherhood forged in war remained unbroken, as the former soldiers stood ready to help in any means possible, even if many of the men now lived poor but "with the knightly honor which belongs to such men." They possessed a "sacred trust" and promised the trust would be "discharged with that fidelity which he [Hood] anticipated."[14] Devoted to their commander, the men watched Hood's postwar life with earnest zeal, even if it meant Hood could not join them for every reunion because of his wounds. Yet, even as Hood attempted to grieve the loss of his wife, the threat of yellow fever remained within the doors of the Hood home.

The day before his death, Hood remained "very much depressed" and told a nurse that "he was no better." By 11 p.m. on Friday, August 29, he realized "that his end was near, and to those with him seemed extremely solicitous concerning the fate of his children." Hood's dying wish called for the children to be cared for by the veterans of the Texas Brigade, who, Hood thought, "would not fail to respond when appealed to by their dying commander." In his mind, the relationship Hood forged with the soldiers fulfilled the qualities needed for those who would care for his orphaned children. As the general made his request, he experienced "fearful nausea," "black vomit," and "an interval of exhaustion followed, with heavy breathing, and suddenly his face stiffened, its lines were sharply defined, and J. B. Hood was a corpse."[15] Hood had breathed his final breath and died on Saturday, August 30, 1879, at 3:30 in the morning. His eldest daughter Lydia died later the same day.

Walter Crouch, who had remained at Hood's bedside throughout his ordeal, served as one of the pallbearers during Hood's funeral. The body, quickly and quietly buried, came to rest at 3 p.m., the same day of his death. The Association of the Army of Northern Virginia and Army of Tennessee offered to perform the last rites, but this act was declined by the family, "who desired that his obsequies should be as private and unobtrusive as possible."[16] Hood's body initially came to rest at Lafayette Cemetery, often called Washington Cemetery, but his body was later placed in his wife's family tomb in Metairie Cemetery, in March 1880. The crypt lacked a separate, definitive marker well into the twenty first century.[17] Furthermore, no elaborate memorial to recognize Hood appears on the grounds, most likely owing to the enormous cost the orphaned children would have had to bear. Instead, a simple inscription reads, "John Bell Hood General in the Late Confederate Army, Born June 1, 1831 in Owensville, Kentucky. Died August 30, 1879." Crouch reflected on the burial, writing, "A detachment of Continentals fired a salute over his grave and the last sad tribute was paid to our brave, generous and Christian friend. . . . I think it is altogether the saddest death I have ever known." Immediately upon Hood's death, Crouch showed deep signs of concern for the orphaned children that now remained behind. Mrs. Hennen, the mother-in-law of the general, remained as the children's primary caretaker. But, Crouch noted before the death of Hood's eldest daughter, "Old Mrs. Hennen can only live but a few months and there are eleven little lambs left fatherless and motherless. Oh how much better if God in his providence would take them all."[18]

The day after Hood's death, Rev. A. J. Witherspoon, who served as pastor of the Second Mission Church and had been chaplain of the Twenty-first Alabama Regiment with the Army of Tennessee, offered a sermon in tribute to the late general. Witherspoon had borne witness to Hood's military failures, yet this did not influence his remarks. He said, "There died in this city, on yesterday, a battle scarred warrior whose name will ever rank among the bravest and most dashing of the leaders on one side of the late lamentable war." The minister confessed that he "never looked into the face of General Hood" but that he "felt an inspiration coming upon [him] always to act out the true, the brave and the right thing." Witherspoon lamented the loss of Hood's "honorable" presence in the city. Hood held the balance of being "as gentle as a lamb and as brave as a lion," "as soft and gentle and blushing as a woman," yet, in battle, "he was always at the head of his division" and died "the death of the righteous and his last end was peace."[19]

Witherspoon also offered more details from Hood's deathbed. He remembered that Hood spoke to his physician, Dr. Bemiss, stating, "Doctor, if you cannot overcome the enemy by the regular method do not try any experiments." When his condition improved, Hood believed "we have routed the enemy." While still maintaining his fighting sensibilities, Hood confessed that "I will fight this fight as long as there is a shot left in the locker." Rev. M. Dow, an Episcopal clergyman, offered a final communion with the general. Mrs.

Hennen threw herself upon the bed and exclaimed, "Oh son! How can we give you up. What will your poor mother and these eleven children do!" Hood replied, "Do not weep for me, dear mother. I am prepared to die, and trust in God, dear mother. He will provide for you and my little ones." According to Witherspoon and Dow, the heavenly premonition served as Hood's final words.[20]

The news of Hood's passing reached newspapers throughout the country. The *New York Times* wrote simply, "Gen. J. B. Hood died of yellow fever at 4 o'clock this morning." The *Memphis Commercial Appeal* acknowledged the "thousands of ex-Confederates who remember his brave deeds during the war between the sections." The *Chicago Tribune,* reporting on the deaths attributed by the fever striking New Orleans, elaborated on Hood's character, stating, "At dawn this morning, Gen. John B. Hood, the distinguished Confederate chieftain, breathed his last. . . . Gen. Hood's malady was the result of over-anxiety and care, watching at the bedside of his devoted wife. He truly dies of a broken heart." The *Tribune* looked to Hood's death as the result of his crippling war injuries, as well as "late financial difficulties" and a broken spirit. Hood simply could not muster enough strength to fight the disease while coming to terms with his beloved wife's passing. Now, in the aftermath of his death, New Orleans experienced "gloom on account of the sad event."[21]

Appropriately, a lengthy obituary appeared in The *New York Herald,* a newspaper with Democratic leanings throughout the course of the war. The *Herald* obituary stated, "Hood's thorough knowledge of the 'trade of war,' and his force of character and courtesy and judgment, however, soon impressed officers and men alike with a sense of his fitness to command." The *Herald* echoed the critics, not the remembrances of Hood's friends, through acknowledging the faults in the career of Hood: "He had a high place as a brave and skillful division commander, but did not possess the military genius necessary for the successful conduct of the broader operations of an entire army." However, the *Herald* did acknowledge the success of Hood commanding his Texas Brigade, writing, "General John B. Hood [was] one of the most prominent of the Confederate officers, a brave soldier even though fighting in defense of a mistaken principle." With the wounding at Chickamauga, Hood's "bravery and dash were again conspicuous, but resulted in a serious misfortune to the gallant officer." Despite the "bravery" and "knowledge of the 'trade of war,'" Hood still received the *Herald*'s final analysis as being promoted beyond his ability when conducting "the broader operations of an entire army."[22]

The *New Orleans Times* declared the "death of this distinguished chieftain and admirable citizen" tragic but not unexpected. The obituary writer went on to give a brief account of Hood's military career and also addressed Hood's critics. He wrote, "It has been said of him [Hood] that he led his men into appalling perils, but, on the other hand, it must be remembered that it was his fortune to participate in battles which were essentially desperate and that the humblest of his soldiers was never asked to go where he could not see his general also." "Whenever the tide of battle rolled most fiercely," he wrote, "wherever death and carnage held their wildest orgie, there General Hood was always to be found serene and fearless but blazing like a wargod." Beyond the battlefield, according to the writer, Hood had emerged as a "good citizen" and an "honorable businessman" who had as much worth and integrity in his civilian life as had been displayed with "splendid and chivalrous bravery in war." The obituary concluded with a reflection on what Hood's death might mean for his orphaned children and the obligation now facing the citizenry of the South. "The eldest of these bereaved and desolate creatures is yet too young to understand its loss," the writer stated, "and if the South be true to her traditions, as Gen. Hood was—or only half as true—the full realization of their calamity may never come home to them in all its awful force."[23]

Without doubt, the most laudatory obituary appeared in the *Daily Picayune,* the main newspaper of New Orleans. "It is with the profoundest regret that the *Picayune* chronicles the death of the accomplished gentleman and distinguished soldier, whose name in every chronicle of the gigantic struggle between the North and the South will always rank among the bravest and most chivalric of the Confederate leaders," the paper stated. The obituary offered many details of the "brilliant career of the deceased" and backed the decision to appoint Hood as commander, stating, "Hood's splendid field record was eminently that of a fighting general, and that was what the department deemed was needed—fighting." Nevertheless, Hood, "with characteristic nobility of spirit," accepted blame for the defeat, and said, "I strove hard to do my duty in its execution." The obituary acknowledged, "To do his duty: that was this splendid soldier's rule of conduct."[24]

The obituary concluded with a glorious character analysis and tribute, seeking a "sincere tribute to his memory." Hood "was known to everyone in this city, and by everyone respected and admired." He possessed a "quiet, dignified manner," an "amiable expression of countenance," a "genial disposition," and a "well-informed mind." "The very soul of honor and knighthood lived in that shattered frame," the obituary affirmed. In closing, the author wrote: "Neither wounds, nor sickness, nor danger, nor poverty, nor the defeat of the cause he fought for so heroically, could shake that dauntless spirit or ruffle the composure of the polished and modest gentleman. His little motherless children, whatever betide them in the hereafter, will never have aught to remember him by save what did him honor. His peer in the highest qualities of a man was not easy to find. In death, his rare virtues are consecrated in the memory of a host of mourning friends, who will join with us in this sincere tribute to his memory."[25] To provide support for the orphaned children, the obituary writer suggested, the citizens of the former Confederacy must now bear the weight of an unexpected burden and fulfill it to the same standard as the late general. He believed that Hood's conduct in New Orleans would guarantee a positive collective memory about the general. Despite his critics, Hood still held the "highest qualities of a man" that memory would most assuredly have to secure. Upon his death, Hood's friends had to pick up the torch and continue to reassert and now preserve his honor and reputation for future generations.

On September 9, 1879, the Association of the Army of Tennessee, with General P. G. T. Beauregard as president, issued a telling memorial that reflected on Hood's military career "as one of the most remarkable known in our day." When Hood arrived with the army in 1864, "his towering form and gallant bearing, no less than the martial appearance of his veteran division, inspired us with fresh courage." As Hood led his corps into battle, he "emerged from its smoke and carnage, a maimed trunk, which, inspired by a less lofty son had then sought the retirement of the rear or of the grave." Hood had earned his position as corps commander because of his "unexampled valor and devotion."[26]

Even when Hood received command of the entire army, the association recalled, "He delivered staggering blows against the immense army that encircled us at Atlanta, well nigh throwing it back in disastrous fight. Finally, as leader of the 'forlorn hope of the Confederacy,' in his brilliant and rapid movement of 400 miles into the enemy's rear he achieved the signal victory of Franklin." Of note, the veterans of the Army of Tennessee had now reconfigured Hood's Tennessee campaign from an unparalleled disaster in the memory of the Confederacy to Hood trying to achieve a "forlorn hope." At Nashville, Hood "spent the expiring but unavailing force" in an effort that "staked all on a final effort, and lost all, save honor." To sum up the discussion of their commander, the memorial stated "That, having in four years of constant warfare, borne himself with a courage, a devotion, and a heroism that have never been excelled; having sacrificed his body, limb by limb, to the cause he held dear; having never despaired, but ever stood firm and steadfast, stoutest when most assailed, strongest when maimed; that in these things John B. Hood has earned the name of hero, and has endeared himself to his survivors in that affectionate regard and respectful homage which are only felt for the noble and the great."[27] The association even compared Hood to other leaders of the Confederacy and ranked him fourth, after Lee, Albert Sydney Johnston, and "Stonewall" Jackson. Hood deserved this place in history because of "his great personal prowess, when the hour of battle was approaching," as well as possessing "a greater mind" and a "master spirit." "If there was any commander who, riding into the smoke and roar of battle, could carry into the ranks a greater sensation of relief, or almost supernatural influence, it was Hood, who rode forward a maimed prodigy of most desperate valor," the writer stated. Hood, with "eminent skill" and "unselfish patriotism," emerged in military history as a "brilliant star" that "had suddenly sunk below the horizon." In the history of the war, "there will always remain one bright, shining page, which neither criticism nor calumny can tarnish or obliterate, on which has been inscribed with his own good sword and trusty right arm, the autograph of John B. Hood."[28]

Although they would not go so far as to vindicate Hood's strategy, even the Southern Historical Society, always willing to castigate Hood for the destruction of the Confederacy, offered a few words of tribute. The society papers stated, "The death of General John B. Hood . . . is announced just as we are going to press, and we have only space to say that another gallant soldier, true patriot and highly atoned gentleman has fallen at the post of duty." The society assured that Hood "will be universally lamented by his old comrades" and wished "peace to his ashes" and "all honor to his memory." In November 1879, General Jubal Early, at a meeting of the SHS, gave a speech that provided "a feeling and appropriate tribute to the memory of General John B. Hood." This tribute was never printed in a more permanent form in the next volume or any future printed volume of the *Southern Historical Society Papers*.[29]

Yet, Confederate veterans did not need the SHS in order to offer their own tributes to John Bell Hood. Texas, which Hood had declared his adopted state to justify his resignation from the U.S. Army, held a memorial service for the late general on September 12, 1879, at the Episcopal church in Houston. Some citizens had placed their Lone Star flags "with accompanying mourning at half-mast in a few hours after the death of our beloved Hood," remarked Captain A. C. McKeen in Galveston. For the funeral, the church, with a large attendance, was "draped in mourning. Rev. G.J. Clemmens read scripture, a choir sang hymns and the Honorable John H. Reagan delivered a memorial address, stated as to be both lengthy and very eloquent" that was "befitting the solemn occasion and the dead hero whose name was so intimately associated with the most brilliant deeds of the Texan soldiery in the civil war."[30]

Appropriately, Reagan discussed Hood's career in Texas with laudatory remarks. Yet, he did not stray from the topic of controversy: Hood in command of the Army of Tennessee. Hood came to command because he was someone "who would give battle rather than abandon Atlanta." Yet, "Soon after this Gen. Hood fought the important, but unsuccessful battle of Atlanta, and was compelled to retire before superior numbers." Reagan also defended the Tennessee campaign, pointing out that Hood failed "not for want of a broad, far-seeing plan, or for want of skill and courage in the attempt to execute it, but because of insufficient force, and the exhaustion of the Confederacy in men and supplies." He noted Hood received support "whether in victory or defeat" and his soldiers always "loved him and had confidence in him." He concluded, "I do not doubt that impartial history will approve and justify his action in this campaign."[31]

Reagan argued that criticism could be cast aside because of "the honorable scars he bore to his grave in a way of such magnitude." Criticism aside, Reagan turned to examine Hood in the postwar period. Hood accepted his defeat and left the war both "maimed and in poverty and without a profession as he was with a cheerful fortitude and at once applied himself diligently and earnestly to commercial and other pursuits to earn an independent livelihood by honorable means." In the postwar era, Hood encapsulated "an honorable competence" and remained a man "of strong manly frame and heroic mould, he was as courteous as any knight, and as soft and gentle in his manners and as pure as a woman; beloved and respected by all who knew him, and lived and died without the stain of one breath of calamity." Hood passed away as "a faithful, brave, honest man, and a true Christian gentleman."[32]

Granted, obituaries tend to include laudatory remarks to bring out the highest qualities of any individual suffering a tragic death. Yet, with Hood, his obituary writers and speakers did not ignore his military failures. Instead, they glossed over them, reconfiguring Hood's memory and pointing out a host of reasons for failure that stretched beyond the late general. Moreover, the obituaries brought to light a body of voices that represented a clear force in shaping Hood's collective memory, ones that have long fallen by the wayside within the annals of history. Nevertheless, many obituary writers and eulogies offered a similar conclusion to the one presented by John Reagan: "To have known Gen. Hood in lifetime was to love and respect him. To remember him in death is to esteem his character and to venerate his virtues."[33]

Despite the body of praiseworthy sentiments offered about John Bell Hood following his death, more pressing matters faced the remaining members of the Hood family: the health and welfare of his children. The mayor of New Orleans received offers from families desiring to adopt the orphaned children. Friends and colleagues gathered to begin collecting funds, for securing the Hood family welfare in memory of their father. A committee, appointed by members of the Association of the Army of Northern Virginia and the Army of Tennessee, would gather any funds donated on behalf of the Hood children. In a statement issued to newspapers throughout the South, the newly formed Hood Orphan Fund stated that "To no man more than to Gen. Hood do we owe gratitude for the fame he won for us as a people of soldiers; to no man greater admiration for his exalted character, a courage never surpassed, a purity never stained even by the breath of envy or of slander." The group reminded the South how yellow fever had invaded the home of "a gallant soldier and Christian patriot." Now, "the helpless innocent children remain stricken in the midst of disease and death, orphaned and destitute."[34]

Such a fund was necessary because the Hood estate did not furnish sufficient revenue to support the remaining ten children. The Hood family assets included a set of china, two chandeliers, one small Victorian bed stand, one small rosewood Victorian bed stand, a miniature rosewood bedroom set, and the land, 133 feet 10 inches long and 124 feet wide, located at the corner of Camp and Third, which stood valued, perhaps generously, at $15,000.00. With cash holdings of $1,221.30 in the bank and a Life Association of America policy worth $2,500.00, the Hood family had, on paper, an asset total of $19,021.53. Yet, when the items went up for sale, only $17,489.57 came out of the auction, including the insurance policy and funds from the State National Bank.[35]

Why the Hood estate failed to garner the appraisal price remains unknown. Perhaps the items had been generously appraised beyond their real value. It is possible that citizens making purchases feared paying a hefty sum for items that had been exposed to yellow fever. Furthermore, the bulk of the donation arrived from average soldiers, who may not have been able to afford many of the items auctioned in the estate sale. In any case, no matter the reason, the estate sale failed to raise the appraised value.

Despite the setback, the home and furnishings did produce a large amount of capital that could help the Hood children pay for burial and entombment. On March 6, 1880, J. F. Birchmeyer received $91 to cover the previous seven months' costs for renting the tomb in Lafayette Cemetery. The removal of Hood's body to the Hennen tomb at Metairie Cemetery alleviated any future payments the children would have had to make to Birchmeyer. Other mortgage costs for the home totaled $12,702.25. After all the expenditures, including insurance, stenographer fees, and taxes, the descendants were left with only $3,638.15, a seemingly small amount when balanced against the costs necessary to sustain the well-being and education of all ten orphaned children.[36]

With little funds available for the Hood children, the supporters of John Bell Hood decided that in order to secure the memory of their fallen comrade, they would memorialize him through the creation of living monuments fostered through the care of his children. "Let the sons and daughters of these two great States [Texas and Louisiana] accept the gift thus bestowed, and with a mighty voice proclaim it to the world," declared an editorial in the *Daily Picayune*. The most suitable, and lasting monument to Hood "as a soldier and as a man," would come through the "education and the maintenance of the orphaned ones." The citizens did not want to raise money to build a monument of marble that "in time would discolor and crumble to dust." In a time of distress, the "living monuments," in which Hood's legacy of manhood and honor thrived, could serve as a representation of how much Hood meant as a gentleman of "courage" and "pleasing countenance." Thus, on September 8, 1879, Margaret Haughery, a citizen of New Orleans, donated a United States bond for $500, marking the first financial donation to a more suitable monument to the late general.[37]

The urge to protect the children extended far beyond New Orleans. The *Atlanta Constitution* pleaded with the white citizens of Georgia, stating, "He leaves a nest of little ones, helpless. . . . They are penniless and almost friendless. Are not these children sacred wards of the South? Does not every honest man of the South stand pledged to contribute to their welfare and protection?" The paper reminded Georgians that Hood "lost a leg in defense of Georgia's soil and he fought desperately to save Atlanta." The children could not turn to the federal government because their father fought for the Confederacy. "But shall they suffer for this reason? Is there not manly gratitude enough in the entire South to raise a fund that shall put these little ones above the reach of want? We hope so," the newspaper declared. The *Atlanta Constitution* wanted to make sure that Georgia "take[s] the lead in this noble movement."[38]

The newspaper's supplication rallied a large number of Georgia donors. The bulk of contributions came from Confederate veterans scattered across the state. As a letter written to the paper declared, "Let every old soldier who reads this paragraph put his hand in his pocket and bring out a dollar for Hood's children. Do it right now, old fellow, before you forget it." One older veteran gave a contribution at the newspaper office and stated, "He was the bravest fighter that ever went into a fight." Mr. Bose Adair also donated funds and said, "I was one of Hood's old soldiers, and here are four dollars for his babies." Mrs. Norma Webb, the wife of the general superintendent of the Selma, Rome and Dalton Railroad, offered to adopt the youngest female twins. H. C. Mitchell gave $2 for the children of his old division commander, "the most genial and heroic Major General I ever knew." The contributors in Atlanta heeded the call that "Gen. Hood's children are the children of the South." By September 13, just two weeks after John Bell Hood died, the fund had collected $2,508.10. A week later, the Relief Committee had collected $3,861.25.[39] The donations had only just begun.

Assistance came in a variety of ways and in a variety of forms. College Temple from Georgia offered tuition for one year for one of the children. W. D. Chipley, from Pensacola, Florida, offered $5 and wrote, "It will be a burning shame upon our people if the little band of babies ever want for a comfort or an advantage that money will procure." Two small children "toddled" into the offices of the *Columbus* (GA) *Enquirer* and each held out a silver dollar. One of the children said, "We want to div two dollars to de Hood children." An Arkansas veteran of the Army of Tennessee, who fought under Johnston and Hood, offered a small sum and wrote, "Allow me to contribute towards the support and education of the orphans of the noble, true, brave Gen. Hood. A man never recreant to duty, of spotless character, unquestioned integrity, true to himself, his family, his country and his God. His offspring should be cherished and nourished by his fellow-countrymen."[40]

Support also came in the form of northern donations. G. F. Moody, a Union veteran, offered $5 with a note, stating, "All good men must sympathize with the family of a good and brave soldier overtaken by misfortune." Colonel L. P. Bradley, presently serving in the Thirteenth Infantry with the United States Army, offered his regimental band to perform "in aid of the fund for Gen. Hood's children." He said, "I shall be happy if this small service adds to the success of your noble efforts in behalf of the orphans."[41]

The most sympathetic notes and donations came from Hood's comrades in arms during the war, who essentially adopted his children as the children of the Confederate cause. Some also offered money, even with their own well-being in question. One soldier gave a dollar, and offered his regrets that "I have but little to give, but I divide with these poor children." J. S. Todd, who lost an arm while serving with Hood, gave $5. The plight of the Hood children garnered notice not only from across the Confederate veteran spectrum but from overseas as well, from the wealthy to the destitute. An unnamed Englishman offered $5 because he was "touched with pity for the poor children, and has an unbounded admiration for the . . . Confederate army."[42] Each donation, no matter what the financial amount, helped secure the Hood children as living monuments to the late general.

Several of the donations came with a letter or brief note expressing gratitude toward the general and insisting on the maintenance of his family. Most of the letters collected by the Relief Committee ended up "carefully pasted in a file book, with the intent that the little orphans shall keep them as an heir-loom." The letters arrived, according to the committee, from "men who fought just as desperately against him and his boys in grey; letters from men and women, North and South, old and young, rich and poor—all eager to do something for these little ones, so suddenly and painfully bereft of both mother and father." The orphans deserved sympathy because their father had given "his sword to his country, the flower of his life to its service, a leg to Georgia, an arm to Virginia and his children to the soldiers of the Confederacy." Robert Burns, the secretary of Hood's Texas Brigade, asked the veterans to contribute because the orphans could now be categorized as "the children of the Texas Brigade."[43]

Funds for the children were to be immediately remitted to Colonel Isaac W. Payton, the current mayor of New Orleans and Hood's former business associate. The Hood Relief Fund Committee, made up of various prominent citizens and friends of the late general, included the following: Captain W. R. Lyman, the president of the Crescent Insurance Company; General F. T. Nicholls, an ex-governor of Louisiana; Captain James Chalaron, the president of Hope Insurance Company; General P. G. T. Beauregard, commander of several endeavors for the Confederacy during the war; Major S. D. Stockman, a cotton factor; General Fred Ogden, a merchant; Major Walter V. Crouch, the representative of the Army of Tennessee and secretary of the Carrollton Railroad Company; John H. Murray, the representative of the Army of Northern Virginia and a cashier for D. H. Holmes; David R. Calder, a sugar factor; Colonel Samuel Flower, assistant treasurer of the United States at New Orleans; and Captain James Buckner, a cotton factor. The Hood Orphan Fund encouraged the women of the South to adopt the children, both figuratively and literally, by graciously giving to their "maintenance and education." Also, it suggested that "an association for this purpose be formed in every county and town, and that subscriptions be raised not to exceed one dollar from every child in the family."[44]

The Orleans Dramatic Association, which had held benefit performances earlier for Civil War orphans, decided to hold an event of "the most popular plays of the day while presented by the best amateur talent New Orleans boasts." The association decided that all proceeds would be used "to increase the growing fund for the support of the ten children of the distinguished chieftain." The production, entitled *Ours,* the same one performed in Portland, Oregon, attended by Ulysses S. Grant, consisted of "a full military band and a battalion of troops on the stage." There would be no better way to receive gratification than that of a "pleasant evening under such auspices" and the association hoped the performance would "result in their [citizens of New Orleans] filling the theatre with such an audience as rarely if ever gathered within its walls."[45]

To make sure they were doing their part, as well as to coincide with the Dramatic Association presentation, the Spanish Fort and Lake Railroad Company decided that on Wednesday, September 10, the same day as the dramatic performance, all proceeds from the day would go to the Hood fund. A special fund-raising concert would take place at 4:00 p.m., and all patrons would be returned to the city in time for the performance. The Railroad Company thought that "ladies and children without escorts, who wish to contribute to the fund, will find it a pleasant place to spend a portion of the day." The fare, fifteen cents, would go toward the Hood fund, although patrons were welcome to pay twenty-five cents or more in honor of John Bell Hood. To donate even more, the patron could simply say "Extra" when purchasing the ticket from the ticket clerk or conductor. "Extra" would be interpreted as meaning "Do not want the change." Attending the concert or riding the railroad emerged as a suitable way to "do an act of benevolence without seeing one's name in the papers or letting one hand know what the other doeth is thus afforded."[46]

Theatrical events proved a vital financial cornerstone in the fund-raising efforts. An event at the New Orleans Opera on September 24, 1879, raised $714.70. On October 10, the Hood Relief Fund presented an event at the Grand Opera House in New Orleans, conducted by members of the Shakespeare Club. The performance raised further funds and the city was thanked for "their generous effort in behalf of the orphaned ones." Furthermore, a photograph of the orphaned children taken by Theodore Lillienthal would be available for sale. By October 25 the committee had gathered $6,317.60. By November 8, the number increased to $6,594.20.[47]

Yet, the benefit concerts and performances were simply not enough to raise the full amount needed for the Hood children. General P. G. T. Beauregard, who had once been frustrated with Hood during the Tennessee campaign, now sought to support the orphaned children. Beauregard organized the Hood Memorial Association, which eventually secured the publication of Hood's memoirs, left unpublished at the time of his death. If the memoir sold well, the funds would assist the efforts to raise the needed capital.[48]

Unfortunately, sales from Hood's memoir did little to ease the children's financial burden. Their primary care giver, Eleanor Hennen, Hood's mother-in-law, grew ill, and a suitable guardian would be needed as soon as possible. One prominent woman from Austin, Texas, offered to adopt the children. Yet, the woman's reputation preceded her. E. H. Cunningham, a lessee of the State Penitentiary at Rusk, Texas, questioned the woman's social status in Austin and pleaded for the children to end up elsewhere, noting, "Bob Robinson told me some very damaging things in regards to her." Thus, Eleanor Hennen had no choice but to dictate a different guardian in her last will and testament shortly before her death. Written on January 7, 1880, Hennen left the grandchildren "to my brother-in-law, John A. Morris, husband of my late husband's sister, Cora Hennen. I wish him to have sole control of the children and all property they have at my death." Hennen reiterated at the end of the will that Morris, who had Mrs. Hennen's "full confidence," would "act for them with judgment and conscientiousness."[49]

Hennen wanted to keep the children together. Yet, despite the moderate success of the fund-raising efforts, in her deteriorating condition she could not care for all of the children, and had to entertain at least some of the countless adoption offers from separate families. Again, Hennen had the benefit of General Beauregard and other veterans from the Texas Brigade, who arranged for the mass production of the Lillienthal photograph of the Hood children. The Hood Relief Committee utilized the photograph as an advertisement seeking the adoption of the children to prominent families throughout the country, a dramatic step considering that the children would now be divided. However, the committee wanted the sets of twins to remain together, if at all practicable. The stirring description of the photograph, published in newspapers and the records of the Hood Relief Committee, deserves to be quoted at length:

> The two little girls on left, Odile Musson and Ida Richardson, (twins) three years old; Odile is on the extreme left in the act of trundling a doll's carriage, while Ida is seated with the doll in her arms. Little Ida looks pale and like an invalid, having only recently recovered from the fever when her picture was taken; the third from the left is Duncan Norbet, seven years old, and next to him stand with one hand on Duncan's shoulder, John Bell, Jr., eight years old; both of these boys have bright, beautiful faces, the latter resembling his father. Next

to John Bell sits cunning little Oswald, thirteen months old, whose chubby bare legs and arms many a childless mother will long to dimple with kisses. Next in the order in which they are named, are Ethel Genevieve and Annabel, (twins) nine years old, in whose sweet faces the features of the mother are plainly discerned. Next and in the order of naming are Lillian Marie and Marion Maude, (twins) six years old. In front of the group, and reclining on a miniature sofa, is the little baby fast asleep, Anna Gertrude, only two months old. A vacant chair on the extreme right speaks eloquently but sadly of the missing Lydia, the sweet girl, the eldest of all the children, who, taken sick just before her father, died a few hours after he ceased to be. The portrait of the General is on the left and that of Mrs. Hood on the wall.[50]

The description, published on October 12, 1879, reveals a romanticized portrait of the Hood children, who now relied on the South to secure their financial and emotional well-being. The gentle tone also emphasized the effects of yellow fever on the entire family, not just the three members who passed away. The description notes that the sons resembled their father, inferring that the adoption of the Hood boys would be an adoption of John Bell Hood. By offering an appropriate and endearing description of the children, the society hoped to ensure their adoption. The children served as a living connection between Hood and the present. By securing the welfare of the family, Hood's friend and colleagues shaped and ultimately secured a share of the collective memory pertaining to John Bell Hood.

Included with the portrait was a letter from J. A. Chalaron, the secretary of the Hood Relief Committee. It stated, "The Hood Relief Committee herewith hand you a copy of the smallest size picture of the Hood children. The committee places this in your hands for a double purpose." Chalaron hoped that recipients of the picture would keep it, pass it on, or assist in securing someone to sell the pictures. "We desire to save all we can for the children, and so wish to avoid commissions on sales," Chalaron stated. Various sizes of the picture were available, ranging from fifty cents to $5, which could be sold by some "reliable, self-sacrificing man or woman."[51]

By the summer of 1880, prominent families of the North and South had adopted all of the children. Twins Annabel and Ethel, not officially adopted, resided with their uncle, John Morris, in New Orleans and later traveled to Hanover, Germany, for their education. John Bell Hood Jr. lived with Mr. and Mrs. David M. Russell in Jonestown, Mississippi, while his twin sisters, Odile Musson and Ida Richardson, lived with Mr. and Mrs. George Thomas

McGehee in Woodville, Mississippi. In faraway New York City, Duncan went to live with Miss Clemtina Furness, and twin sisters Marion and Lillian went to live with Mr. and Mrs. Thatcher Adams, also in New York. Oswald resided with Mr. And Mrs. Charles H. Harney in Scarsdale, New York, and Anna Gertrude, the youngest, ended up with Mr. and Mrs. M. E. Joseph in Augusta, Georgia. The association had secured homes for "Hood's entire brigade." The remaining money in the orphan fund would be evenly divided among the children when they turned twenty-one years of age.[52]

Table 3 shows the sources of the children's funds in the months following their father's death.[53] The calls from newspapers in Louisiana and Georgia allowed those two states to lead in the fund-raising efforts. To no one's surprise, Hood's adopted state of Texas, where many of the survivors of the Texas Brigade lived, sent several donations. Yet, the widespread desire to help the children resulted in donations from across the North and South. With Hood's involvement in fund raising for the victims of the Franco Prussian War, it comes as no surprise that Poland and France donated funds for the Hood children. The appeal of donating to a cause protecting the orphaned children of John Bell Hood sent many individuals reaching into their pockets.

A newspaper notice stated, "The generous heart of the country has already been moved to the grateful recognition of the virtues, the chivalry and self-sacrificing devotion of the departed hero, and to an active and giving sympathy of the living." Despite the generosity of the public thus far, the committee called for more "cooperation and assistance in raising a sum which shall be sufficient for the support, maintenance and education of these orphans." The photos continued to sell, raising another $425.00 by July 31, 1885. The committee invested the money into bonds, accounting for, by 1885, an additional $4,809.67. Furthermore, the committee spent very little to promote the collection of funds, with $10 spent on advertisements, $11 on telegrams and postage, and a safe-deposit vault rented for five years at the cost of $25. Donations continued to roll in, as well as the steady sale of Hood's memoir and the family photo. These sources, combined with shrewd investing and little expense, allowed the fund to reach $74,663.20 on May 25, 1895.[54]

Prior to age twenty-one, the children had to ask permission from the fund's chairman to access money for necessities. In one instance, John Bell Hood Jr. requested $25 on May 6, 1892, to acquire new clothing. He purchased a suit, scarf, six pairs of socks, four pairs of drawers, four shirts, two hats, one vest, four pairs of cuffs, and one pair of cuff buttons.[55]

By 1895, Duncan followed in the footsteps of his father and attended the U.S. Military Academy at West Point. Lillian, recently married, resided in

TABLE 3
Funds Collected for the Hood Memorial Fund through 1880 by Geographic Area

Louisiana	$5,282.15
Georgia	$3,580.97
Texas	$1,772.62
New York	$1,605.00
Alabama	$1,466.08
Kentucky	$1,017.62
California	$888.00
Maryland	$848.10
South Carolina	$810.81
Virginia	$709.47
Pennsylvania	$501.00
Mississippi	$492.80
Missouri	$325.90
Arkansas	$137.80
Poland	$120.00
North Carolina	$111.34
Washington, D.C.	$67.50
Oregon (Portland)	$55.25
Tennessee	$43.15
France	$40.00
Total	$19,875.56

New Jersey. Annabel and Ethel eventually left Germany for Liverpool, England, while Odile and Ida remained in Woodville, Mississippi. Before moving to Germany, Annabel served as the queen's maid of honor for the carnival celebration in New Orleans on February 1, 1891. She was dressed in heavy gros grain white silk entrain, with lace garniture held in place by silver butterflies. The corsage from shoulder to waist was crossed by a rich and heavy satin scarf of purple, green, and gold, the royal colors for the 1891 celebration. Oswald had moved to Lexington, Kentucky, and John Bell Hood Jr. stayed in Mississippi. Both Marion and Anna had died by 1895, but the details of their deaths remain unclear.[56]

Though securing the health and welfare of the Hood children emerged as integral in shaping the collective memory of John Bell Hood, charitable actions were not limited to the children. In the fall of 1884, Major Joseph Stewart gathered a group of veterans in Texas to establish the John Bell Hood Camp. The primary function of the camp rested in fund-raising endeavors for purchasing a home for Confederate veterans. In only a year and a half, the camp "purchased a seven-room house and more than fifteen acres atop a high knoll overlooking the Colorado River in Austin." The first physically impaired veterans arrived in November 1886, which officially began operations of the Texas Confederate Home for Men.[57]

However, the private fund-raising efforts to purchase the home were simply not enough to maintain it. The Hood camp transformed itself into a powerful political lobbying organization, vowing to vote against anyone in the 1890 elections who failed to support veterans' benefits. During the 1890 Texas campaign, Attorney General James Hogg voiced his support for the permanent funding of a veterans' home. His subsequent popularity brought him the governorship. During his inaugural address, Hogg stated that when "a state orders her men to fight, it accepts the obligation to care for . . . maimed, tottering helpless men . . . too proud to accept pity." The support of the newly elected governor allowed for $75,000 in public funding for the Hood camp, if the camp agreed to turn over the veterans' home to the state. The measure passed the Texas state legislature 101 to 16, and the governor signed the bill March 6, 1891.[58]

Thus, the memory of John Bell Hood had facilitated not only a guarantee for the health and welfare of his children but also the veterans in Texas he had left behind. Though the image of the late Confederate officer did not appear as statues in town squares, his likeness had been preserved in the faces of his children and his veterans. However, the maintenance of "living monuments" coincided with Lost Cause efforts to continue analyzing the military career of John Bell Hood. Granted, the heated postwar debate over Hood's status in Confederate history paused to pay respect to the general upon his death. A soldier's demise comes as a time for assessment and, in many cases, reassessment, of how that person conducted themselves on and off the field of battle. Without a doubt, obituaries tend to convey laudatory auras, filled with praise and sorrow for the passing of the individual. Yet, with Hood leaving behind orphaned children, both North and South gathered to go beyond obituaries by raising funds and ensuring the health and welfare of his children. By utilizing the name of John Bell Hood, the Confederate veterans in Texas constructed another monument through the maintenance of a home that could care for remaining brothers of the Texas brigade. At the same time, defenders and detractors of Hood's leadership capabilities during the war joined forces to secure his memory. Though the Southern Historical Society had gained momentum in pinning the fall of the Confederacy on Hood, the trickling of memories after his death demonstrated a change in both tone and frequency.

In some instances, however, the defenders gained ground, with glowing tributes, the publication of the memoirs, and leaving behind the surviving Hood children.

With the welfare of the children and many veterans secured, soldiers, friends, and family members continued to offer lengthy tributes to the late general in the form of memoirs, speeches, and published articles. In the aftermath of the U.S. Civil War, memories and reminiscences attempted to make sense of the previous four years of warfare. What historian David Blight has called the "reminiscence industry" served as an outlet for officers, soldiers, and civilians to examine the war from hindsight, exploring how their memory shaped the impressions of wartime experience. Thus, the war participants who decided to construct and even reconstruct their memory on the page of public consciousness not only knew their audience, but had become consciously aware of how their memory would fit into the larger collective. The death of Hood prompted many of his former soldiers and fellow officers to pick up the pen, and probably spurred them to come to the defense of a man who could no longer defend himself. Some wrote full-length memoirs. Others wrote articles and submitted them for publication in large magazines and newspapers. The reminiscences ranged in tone from adulatory to critical, with some settling at the midpoint of indifference. Though each voice may not fit snugly into a perfect puzzle of continuity, each piece remains vital to understanding the power of individual memory and the shaping of the communal, regional, and national collective memory of the Civil War. By working through the war in their own memory, no matter what the publication venue, Americans added their personal reminiscence to the collective experience of war.[59]

Two years after Hood's death, Jefferson Davis published his anticipated memoir *Rise and Fall of the Confederate Government* in 1881. Davis had spent years writing what many hoped would be the definitive work of the Lost Cause. Although Davis's reputation did not rise in the aftermath of war, many hoped his insights as former president of the Confederacy would settle disagreements over the failed war effort, especially regarding his decision to name Hood commander of the Army of Tennessee. Davis, referring to Hood as his "gallant friend," accentuated his "fidelity and gallantry" when he remembered that Hood had "served with distinction under Lee and Jackson, and his tactics were of that school." The Lee and Jackson tactics allowed for Davis to declare that at Franklin, "We had won a victory, but it was purchased at fearful cost." Davis firmly solidified the argument that if Hood had succeeded in destroying Schofield's army, and General Forrest had properly captured the Union supply trains, "we should never have heard complaint because Hood attacked at Franklin." At the end of the campaign, with Hood repeatedly requesting to be removed, Davis felt obligated to honor the request. It came from no "want of confidence in him on my part."[60]

Memoirs not only came from Confederate officials but also Confederate civilians. The voice of civilians when constructing the memory of a Civil War individual remains fundamental, as the actions on the battlefield altered the home front, and vice versa. In particular, one civilian surrounded by the dignitaries of southern society, Mary Chesnut, emerges as the most important link when piecing together the life of John Bell Hood. Not only did Chesnut spend a significant amount of time with Hood, but her memories, offering the voice of an ardent defender, helped shape the collective memory of Hood. Chesnut's diary has been called into question for its historical accuracy, but it remains the only window as a historical source into the private world of John Bell Hood during his moments away from battle.[61]

When Chesnut reconstructed her diaries as a memoir in the 1880s, she remembered Hood, whom she, and others, affectionately called Sam, in a positive light. Upon meeting him, Chesnut recalled his "appearance of awkward strength" and his "face of an old crusader who believed in his cause, his cross and his crown." Hood had the "light of battle shining" in his eyes. Chesnut kept abreast of Hood's activities throughout the war. She noted about Chickamauga, "Hood has won a victory, though now he has only one leg to stand on." General Braxton Bragg, she argued, had achieved victory at Chickamauga, "thanks to Longstreet and Hood." Chickamauga had been the "only real victory we have had since Stonewall Jackson, and this man [Hood] is the hero of Chickamauga."[62]

Chesnut, obviously impressed with Hood's military capabilities, visited him frequently in Richmond following Chickamauga. She even made rice pudding for Hood during his recovery because "he cares for no other dainty." When Hood received his appointment as a corps commander of the Army of Tennessee, Mary Chesnut recalled, "How his eyes blazed" when he told her, "This has been the happiest year of my life, in spite of all my wounds." As Hood continued his military career in Atlanta, Mary Chesnut blamed General Johnston and characterized him as "jealous of the favor shown Hood at Richmond. He hates everybody that Jeff Davis likes." Johnston would not attack. She noted, "Hood and Polk wanted to fight, but [Johnston] resisted their council. All this delay is breaking Hood's heart. So much retreating would demoralize even General Lee's Army." Her own reminiscence adds fuel to the debate on how the flanking maneuvers versus fighting affected morale in the Army of Tennessee under Joseph Johnston.[63]

In the diary, Chesnut presented several assessments of Hood's abilities, offered by her friends and fellow southern society elite. General Taliaferro, who had served with Hood at Second Manassas, recalled, "On the battlefield, Hood has military inspiration!" General James Archer, while not directly criticizing Hood, pointed out his deficiencies, in comparison to Johnston, on an 1864 visit to Mary Chesnut's residence. Archer stated, "He does not compare intellectually with General Johnston, who is decidedly a man of culture and literary attainments, with much experience in military matters." "Hood," he wrote, "has the help of youth, and energy, to counterbalance. He has a simple-minded directness of purpose always." Although Hood may not have been intellectually as capable as Johnston, in Archer's view, he certainly had characteristics important in effective generalship.[64]

During the war, Mary Chesnut, a regular Hood defender, had visitors who offered abundant criticism of Hood and his actions. Mars' Kit asked Chesnut, "How do you like Hood's defeats?" as word leaked about the losses at Franklin and Nashville. Chesnut replied, "They will hardly hurt us more than Johnston's victories." Colonel Carter, a cousin of General Lee, spoke with Chesnut about Hood and said, "Hood's a fine dare-devil of a soldier. I give him all the credit due him. But if he is as smart a man as old Joe [Johnston], I'm a fool, and if there is a braver man than Joe, I have to meet him yet." Louis Wigfall, after the defeat at Nashville, said, "Hood is dead, smashed, gone up forever!" Nevertheless, Chesnut remained a Hood supporter and dismissed Wigfall as having "only been destructive."[65]

In 1865, Hood returned to see Chesnut. She recalled, "How plainly he spoke." He told her, "My defeat and discomfiture! My army is destroyed. My losses!" Chesnut also remembered Hood stating that "he had nobody to blame but himself."[66] This last statement presents yet another quandary in the life of John Bell Hood. After the war, Hood would blame everyone except himself for the disasters of Franklin and Nashville. Yet, in the immediate aftermath of battle, according to Chesnut, he had blamed himself.

Despite the best efforts of Hood defenders who wrote in the months following his death, not all the memories that emerged from the reminiscence industry spun the late general in a positive light. Other voices sought neither to defend nor chastise John Bell Hood. This series of memories provided a more balanced approach, assessing Hood fairly and noting both his strengths and failures. Sam Watkins, who fought in the Army of Tennessee, offered *Co. Aytch,* a personal memoir in 1882, to the body of negative and positive Hood memories. Watkins picked up the pen at the peak of SHS scholarship that critiqued the military abilities of Hood. Watkins, influenced by discussions throughout the South, wrestled with the image of Hood he remembered and the image painted by society.

As Watkins recalled, when Hood was appointed commander of the Army of Tennessee, "It came like a flash of lightning, staggering and blinding everyone. It was like applying a lighted match to an immense magazine. It was like the successful gambler, flushed with continual winning, who staked his all and lost. It was like the end of the Southern Confederacy." In fact, Watkins heard the news initially from a Yankee who called out across the banks of the Chattahoochee, "General Joseph E. Johnston is relieved, and Hood appointed in his place." Watkins responded, "You are a liar, and if you will come out and show yourself I will shoot you down in your tracks, you lying Yankee galloot." Watkins remembered a sense of doom surrounding the army as word of Hood's ascendancy spread like a cautious but vicious wildfire. One fellow soldier even stated, "Then I'll never fire another gun. . . . I've quit, and am going home. Please tender my resignation to Jeff Davis as a private soldier in the C.S. Army." Watkins further asserted that the soldiers viewed Hood as "an over-rated general."[67]

But throughout his discussion of Hood, Watkins presented a wide range of memories, both praising and criticizing Hood. Watkins wrote, "The most terrible and disastrous blow that the South ever received was when Hon. Jefferson Davis placed General Hood in command of the Army of Tennessee. I saw, I will say, thousands of men cry like babies—regular, old-fashioned boohoo, boohoo, boohoo." However, Watkins softened his judgment of Hood and stated that he "meant no disrespect." With his memoir being written after Hood's death, it is possible that Watkins's recant could have resulted from a personal response to both the death of Hood and his orphaned children. He writes, "[Hood] was a noble, brave and good man, and we loved him for his many virtues and goodness of heart. I do not propose to criticize his generalship or ability as a commander." Watkins had "always loved and honored him, and will ever revere and cherish his memory." Hood "gave his life in the service of his country, and I know today he wears a garland of glory beyond the grave."[68]

Although Watkins stated that he did not wish to criticize Hood, his closing remarks pass a final judgment on Hood's abilities as commander of the Army of Tennessee. Watkins stated, "As a soldier, he was brave, good, noble, and gallant, and fought with the ferociousness of the wounded tiger, and with the everlasting grit of the bulldog; but as a general he was a failure in every particular."[69] Here, Watkins echoed a persistent criticism presented in the Confederate Congress and the SHS speeches. Hood did not have the intelligence to lead the army, according to Watkins. Even if he had been mentally capable, Hood's physical condition rendered his military effectiveness impracticable, as Watkins questioned Hood's manhood based on his disfigured physique. Yet, it is reasonable to deduce from this assessment that Watkins's memoir had been influenced by the final assessment offered by both Johnston's and the society's criticism. Hood's critics repeatedly returned to the theme of Hood not being mentally capable to handle the rigors of command. Therefore, despite his high regard for Hood's character, Watkins did not hold a positive memory of Hood's leadership ability or potential.

Despite Watkins's conflicting memories, other soldiers wrote memoirs that did not directly reflect the criticisms of the time. Captain William L. Ritter, a member of the Third Maryland Artillery, assessed the retreat from Nashville and Hood's performance during the battles. Ritter pointed out that Hood had been outnumbered by almost four to one at the Battle of Nashville. Thomas had fifty-five thousand men against Hood's force of fewer than seventeen thousand. Ritter praised Hood, writing, "Hood certainly deserves the credit of saving the remnant of his command against such odds." The balance in Ritter's voice comes with his statement, "[Hood] ought to have withdrawn after the battle of Franklin." According to Ritter, Hood had been aware that the Federal army had been amassing troops in Nashville, and "it was only a question of time when he would be driven back, and then at a disadvantage." Hood had been "rendered powerless to prosecute the campaign any farther" with the loss of 5,500 men at Franklin. In Ritter's eyes, Hood failed for not withdrawing after Franklin but deserved credit for saving his army from capture in the face of superior enemy force.[70]

Others, such a S.A. Cunningham, the editor of the *Confederate Veteran,* offered no assessment of the generalship abilities of Hood. Instead, Cunningham only recalled details about the Battle of Franklin. By not directly blaming Hood for the heavy casualty rate, Cunningham offered an analysis untainted by the direct criticism of the situation at Franklin. He wrote, "No event of the war perhaps showed a scene equal to the charge at Franklin." Cunningham remembered, "The soldiers were full of ardor, and confident of success. They had unbounded faith in General Hood, whom they believed would achieve a victory that would give us Nashville." Contrary to Watkins, Cunningham remembered a body of men who believed in their commander. When the battle ended, Cunningham recalled, "Our spirits were crushed. It was indeed the Valley of Death."[71] Franklin conveyed the realities of battle. In this memory, the soldiers had faith in their beloved commander and believed victory was lingering around the corner. Defeat crushed the spirits of the soldiers. In this instance, however, defeat did not cause Cunningham to lash out against his commander. Instead, he simply reflected on the horrors of war.

General Alexander P. Stewart called the removal of Johnston for Hood a "stupendous blunder" resulting in "the coup de grace of the Confederate cause." Stewart never doubted the essential qualities of John Bell Hood. He wrote after the war, "Hood was a brave soldier, a man of many excellent qualities, and a good subordinate." Philip Daingerfield Stephenson, who had served throughout the Civil War both as a loader for the Washington Artillery and a private in the Thirteenth Arkansas, remembered Hood in 1896 as "reckless, rash, narrow minded, obstinate, a man of no skill, no fertility of resource, no ability, who head had been turned by his rapid elevation and the kindling of unbounded ambition." Stephenson remembered that the battles around Atlanta made the men "demoralized" and they lost confidence in Hood, looking upon their commander "as though he was a madman." Hood tried to save the army by inquiring "into their wants and manifested zeal for their comfort and welfare." Some of the soldiers now even began "to like Hood." Yet, the positive image crashed after the Tennessee campaign, when Stephenson remembered, "He seemed overwhelmed by his defeat and sat on his horse, a picture of despair—his head sunk on his breast, reins dangling loosely, an oil cloth around him."[72]

Sometimes, memories about Hood that emerged long after the war recalled humorous tales that reflected the bond between Hood and his soldiers. Private Jonathan W. Stevens, a member of Company K, Fifth Texas Regiment, reflected on his experience in a memoir published in 1902. Stevens remembered an occasion when the Army of Northern Virginia arrived in the Pennsylvania countryside in June 1863. Stevens had the opportunity to guard General Hood's headquarters, which he called "quite a treat to us." As the soldiers set up camp in the shadow of their beloved leader, Hood called out, "Boys, you are now on the enemy's soil; stack your arms and do pretty much as you please. So you stay close by and prevent any stranger from coming here to kill me, and establish your camp here by my tent." Within five minutes, the troops began to explore the property, grabbing anything that could be eaten. In particular, the men desired chicken. Stevens recalled, "[The chickens] were squalling and halloing in every direction. I guess they thought we were all hungry Methodist preachers." The disturbance upset the lady of the house, who made it a point to visit General Hood and point out the actions of his men. Hood smiled and said, "Yes, madam, I see what my men are doing . . . my men are hungry for chickens. Your people have killed every chicken, and nearly everything else in Virginia, and I guess your people ought to have a little teaching of what war means."[73] In exchange for protecting his headquarters, Hood protected his troops from any possible civilian repercussions for looting the home front.

The most fitting tribute to Hood came from within the Hood family circle. When John Bell Hood died on August 30, 1879, Ida Richardson Hood, one of the ten remaining children, was only three years old. On September 4, 1904, the twenty-fifth anniversary of her father's death, Ida Richardson offered a telling *In Memoriam,* printed in the *New Orleans Picayune,* as well as the *Southern Historical Society Papers.* Adopted by Mr. And Mrs. George Thomas McGehee, Ida grew up with her twin sister, Odile, in Woodville, Mississippi. As she came of age, Richardson must have heard the criticism offered about her late father but was also no doubt nurtured in the kinder memories. Families normally commemorate their own memories, but with the Hood family divided in many directions, each member had to determine how they would remember the actions of their father and mother. Under these circumstances, Ida Richardson had the ability to construct her personal memory of John Bell Hood in the midst of a cult, the Lost Cause, which sought to shape the collective memory of Hood in a particular manner.

Yet, her new family, who had rushed to adopt her and her sister to preserve the Hood memory, may have countered the criticism. Although the Hood family had been separated, the adopting families held a positive view of the Confederate officer and, by passing that knowledge onto the orphaned children, refashioned the family memory in several individual environments. By writing her *In Memoriam,* Ida Richardson Hood solidified her own belief about the reputation of her father, despite the lingering criticisms. Her keen observations and eloquent writing style not only traced the military career of General Hood, but also framed his reputation in the context of the Hood family for future generations. Barely knowing her father, Ida Richardson held onto the positive memories that had been spoken to her as she grew older, thus solidifying the family memory over the resounding critical collective memory.

In the *In Memoriam,* as a plea to have memories of a father she could not possibly remember, she wrote, "Then, when he is resting in his grave, perhaps after a long journey over the thorn-studded path of disappointments . . . then men will rise and outvie each other to do honor to the memory of one to whom they had perhaps denied the barest recognition while he was in their midst." Richardson acknowledged that her father may not have been fully praised during his time on earth. Instead, "the lasting monument of Influence, based on the firm pedestal of the human heart, needs time to anchor and take root.

... Men flock to its foot to find there the inspiration for noble effort or the worthy deed, a sculptured image or the graven word can never give."[74] General Hood's actions and deeds, after they had endured the test of time, serve as the only fitting monument to the memories of glory and defeat that encompassed his military career.

Though Ida Richardson Hood did not offer an assessment of his career, she did offer an analysis of her father's character. She wrote, "But he was one of the bravest, who never spared himself, sharing with his men all the burdens, the joys and sorrows. He was more than merely their general officer commanding, he was their friend; doubly so as they reciprocated his feelings." Of his wounding at Chickamauga, she offered, "His mind—his blood—aye, his life, he has consecrated to the active service at the front. He thought not of his own safety. He thought of his country and its cause." Concerning the mistakes Hood made in battle, she wrote that, "So great was he, indeed, so chivalrous, that, should he have erred deeply, he would not have hesitated, like Cotton Mather, to unbare his head at the corners of the street and ask forgiveness of everybody." To conclude, Ida Richardson elevated his character to a higher plane, offering a description to memorialize his character for the coming generations. She said: "Refined by sorrow, purified by aspirations, strengthened through self-reliance, and made gentle by an earnest faith . . . he was genial, generous and indulgent towards others and severe with himself. His aims were prompted by noble desires, and in politics his ideals for democratic action were high. He knew his powers and also his limitations. And he had his limits as the sun has its spots. Above all, the strong force of his character yielded an influence no oratory can command, and that influence is not ended—nay, it is only just beginning to sprout in our hearts."[75]

Though the tribute by Ida Richardson could not reformulate the Hood collective memory away from a critical phase, it did offer a glimpse into how the Hood family wanted the officer to be remembered. In the midst of the Richardson tribute, more memoirs from soldiers and officers, who considered themselves part of the Hood family, emphasized his positive attributes as both an officer and a human being. Though the transition did not change the overall collective memory, it did provide an audience for numerous anecdotes and humorous memories that continued to emerge in speeches, as the anniversary of the war approached fifty years. After the turn of the century, only the family and former soldiers under John Bell Hood served as the defenders of the late general in the midst of the entrenched criticism that would become the basis for historical analysis into the coming decades.

Captain Mark W. Searcy shared his reminiscences of General Hood in a 1908 article. Searcy remembered that Hood, despite being "shot all to pieces during the war," stood "a thousand times more of a man at that than most of the people we see wearing pants ever dream of being." Captain J. T. Hunter, writing a tribute from Texas for the *Confederate Veteran* in 1916, saw Hood as a man of "nobility, devotion to principle and courage [that] soar[ed] far above earthly comprehension." Hunter declared that not even Hood's injuries could destroy him, and his spirit, will, and vigor of his "powerful mind was unbroken." He emphasized Hood's "wonderful patriotism" and "love for the Confederacy" and declared much "admiration for this great hero." Hood's memory was secured after his death through the "generous heart of the country" that "quickly moved in grateful recognition of the virtues, the chivalry and self-sacrificing devotion" of their departed comrade.[76]

Instrumental in securing the welfare of the Hood children, Hood's Texas Brigade Association remained active well after the passing of John Bell Hood. On June 27, 1885, Mrs. C. M. Winkler, from Corsicana, Texas, delivered an address at the association's annual meeting. Winkler offered several minutes detailing the military career of the late officer but also assessed his character, noting that he possessed "the high sense of honor, the proud record he labored to make for his men and himself, the noble sacrifice of mere personal advancement, the devotion to the cause he followed with such persistence." As a man, Hood stood "refined and cultivated" and possessed elegance and a courtly manner, and was "generous and true, possessing the rare faculty of remembering not only the faces, but the names of every man under his command with whom he ever came in contact." Winkler noted his photographic memory as most impressive, considering the number of promotions and different individuals Hood met in his brief military career, as he had traveled through Texas after the war to spend "a few hours to re-cement the bond of friendship formed in camp."[77]

The Memorial Association continued to assert their vision and memory of the military endeavors of the soldiers. In 1907, they named J. B. Polley to serve as the historian. He would "collect data from every available source, and give to the world a fair and impartial history of Hood's Texas Brigade." Polley saw the appointment as "a great honor," but he needed help. He called on all survivors to provide details and accounts of all the "details of daring, gallant and heroic acts performed by individual members of the brigade." He asked for the material immediately to preserve the memory of the brigade.[78]

In 1911, the association adopted a resolution to ask the state of Texas to "set aside June 27, the anniversary of the battle of Gaines' Mill, as a legal holiday to be called 'Hood's Texas Brigade Day.'" Unfortunately for the society, the Texas legislature never adopted the resolution. In 1924, John Bell Hood Jr., now fifty-two years old, his wife, and three-year-old son, John Bell Hood

III, attended the dwindling Texas Brigade's annual reunion. Hood addressed the reunion, calling it the "proudest moment of [my] life to stand before the comrades of his father's old command." At the end of the address, John Bell Hood III, holding a small Confederate flag, appeared seated on a table before the entire crowd. The association, moved by the moment of Confederate patriotism, adopted John Bell Hood Jr. and his wife as honorary members, and John Bell Hood III as the mascot. The Hood family, cherished by the aging veterans, returned to that command out of love and remembrance time and time again, serving as proud staples of the 1925, 1926, and 1928 reunions.[79]

October 27, 1910, marked the culmination of an important task before the association. That day, a large granite monument, topped with a nine-foot-tall bronze statue of a Confederate infantryman, erected on the capital grounds in Austin, served to forever memorialize the efforts of the Texas Brigade. The monument, "erected by surviving comrades and friends," proudly listed the brigade's regiments and engagements. Quotations and inscriptions, positively reflecting the actions of the brigade, encompassed an important part of the monument. Among the quotations, General Robert E. Lee appears six times, Jefferson Davis three, Hood three times, and General "Stonewall" Jackson, General John Gregg, and General Stephen D. Lee one time each. The overwhelming theme of the quotations conveyed the bravery and sacrifice of the ragtag group of Texans. One of Lee's quotes states that "Their ragged clothes makes no difference, the enemy never sees their backs."[80] The Texas Brigade monument serves as one of the few lasting elements, other than Hood's descendants, memorializing the military actions of John Bell Hood and his courageous troopers. Those who had sought to secure the memory of John Bell Hood had performed their duty.

Notes

Introduction

1. John C. West, *A Texan in Search of a Fight: Being the Diary and Letters of a Private Soldier in Hood's Texas Brigade* (Waco, TX: Texian Press, 1969), 171–89, quotes from 174–75.
2. Thomas B. Buell, *The Warrior Generals: Combat Leadership in the Civil War* (New York: Three Rivers Press, 1997), 425. Buell points out that Camp Hood, established by the U.S. Army in September 1941, was comprised of 158,000 acres and up to eighty-one thousand soldiers during World War II. The army changed the name from Camp Hood to Fort Hood in 1950, and it emerged as a primary training base. Now, Fort Hood consists of 340 square miles and forty-five thousand soldiers, and trains heavy divisions and a combat air brigade. For a history of Fort Hood, see "History of Fort Hood," Thomas Buell Papers, Southern Historical Collection, University of North Carolina at Chapel Hill Manuscripts Department (SHC).
3. For a brief biographical sketch of Hood, examine Robert Wooster, *The Civil War 100: A Ranking of the Most Influential People in the War Between the States* (Secaucus, NJ: Carol Publishing Group, 1998), 105–6, as well as Ezra J. Warner, *Generals in Gray: Lives of the Confederate Commanders* (Baton Rouge: Louisiana State University Press, 1959), 143. Wooster ranks Hood thirty-eighth out of the one hundred most influential Civil War people. For more in-depth biography, see Richard O' Connor, *Hood: Cavalier General* (New York: Prentice Hall, 1949); John Dyer, *The Gallant Hood* (Indianapolis: Bobbs-Merrill Co., 1950); and Richard McMurry, *John Bell Hood and the War for Southern Independence* (Lexington: University Press of Kentucky, 1982) as well as a recent article, Keith S. Bohannon, "A Bold Fighter Promoted beyond His Abilities: General John Bell Hood," in Gary W. Gallagher and Joseph T. Glatthaar, eds., *Leaders of the Lost Cause: New Perspectives on Confederate High Command* (Mechanicsburg, PA: Stackpole Books, 2004), 249–87. A discussion of Hood as military commander of the Army of Tennessee can be found in works pertaining to specific battles. For a discussion of Hood at the battles for Atlanta, see Albert Castel, *Decision in the West: The Atlanta Campaign of 1864* (Lawrence: University Press of Kansas, 1992); David Coffey, *John Bell Hood and the Struggle for Atlanta* (Abilene, TX: McWhiney Foundation Press, 1988), and Anne Bailey, *The Chessboard of War: Sherman and Hood in the Autumn Campaigns of 1864* (Lincoln: University of Nebraska Press, 2000). For a general overview of the entire Tennessee campaign, see Thomas Robson Hay, *Hood's Tennessee*

Campaign (New York: Press of Morningside Bookshop, 1956), and Wiley Sword, *Embrace an Angry Wind: The Confederacy's Last Hurrah: Spring Hill, Franklin and Nashville* (New York: Harper Collins, 1992). James Lee McDonough and Thomas L. Connelly, *Five Tragic Hours: The Battle of Franklin* (Knoxville: University of Tennessee Press, 1983) discussed the battle of Franklin, while Stanley Horn, *The Decisive Battle of Nashville* (Baton Rouge: Louisiana State University Press, 1956), offers keen insights into Hood's actions during the final battle of the Tennessee campaign, as well as a recent work, James Lee McDonough, *Nashville: The Western Confederacy's Final Gamble* (Knoxville: University of Tennessee Press, 2004).

4. Steven Woodworth, ed., *Civil War Generals in Defeat* (Lawrence: University Press of Kansas, 1999), 3.

5. Douglas Southall Freeman, *Lee's Lieutenants: A Study in Command,* vol. 1 (New York: Charles Scribner's Sons, 1942), 196, 198, 199, and 758; Douglas Southall Freeman, *Lee's Lieutenants: A Study in Command,* vol. 2 (New York: Charles Scribner's Sons, 1943), xxx; Douglas Southall Freeman, *Lee's Lieutenants: A Study in Command,* vol. 3 (New York: Charles Scribner's Sons, 1944), 232. Freeman was the first author to analyze Hood. Jacob Cox provided a narrative without keen analysis of Hood's campaign into Tennessee in his work, *The March to the Sea, Franklin and Nashville* (New York: Charles Scribner's Sons, 1882). Furthermore, several early brief biographical sketches appeared about John Bell Hood, but they remained neutral, highlighting his success and his failure on an even keel. See *A Short History of General John Bell Hood.* (New York: Knapp and Co., 1888); Walter Lynwood Flemming, ed., *The South in the Building of the Nation,* vol. 11 (Richmond, VA: Southern Historical Publication Society, 1909), 507–9; Lucian Lamar Knight, ed., *Library of Southern Literature Biographical Dictionary of Authors,* vol. 15 (Atlanta: Martin and Hoyt Co., 1907), 206, and *The National Cyclopedia of American Biography,* vol. 4 (New York: James T. White and Co., 1895), 265.

6. James McPherson, *Battle Cry of Freedom* (New York: Ballantine Books, 1988), 467, 811, and 812. For similar language on the plan to invade Tennessee as being a dream, see McDonough and Connelly, *Five,* 5–18, 40, 64–68, and 171. Some have countered that Hood's plan served as the best outlet at this point in the war. See Frank Vandiver, "General Hood as Logistician," *Military Affairs* 16, no. 1 (Spring 1952): 11, and Woodworth, *Generals,* 2.

7. For specific references to describing Hood's personality, see O' Connor, *Hood,* viii, ix, 10–20, 90, and 277–78; Dyer, *Gallant,* 15, 30, 45, 128, 250, 304, and 319–20; Hay, *Tennessee,* 37–42; Sword, *Embrace,* 6–8, 31, 263, 387, and 430; Wiley Sword, *Southern Invincibility: A History on the Confederate Heart* (New York: St. Martin's Griffin, 1999), 210, 252, 258, 260, 263, 267, and 302–3; McMurry, *Hood,* 23, 24, 52, 55, 59, 84, 123–29, 167, and 190–91. Part of McMurry's analysis deals with Hood's desire to emulate the commanding style of Robert E. Lee. For more on this topic throughout the Hood historiography, see Coffey, *Hood,* 30, 59, 61, 71, and 116; Bailey, *Chessboard,* 6, 8, 24, 84, 123, 129, 167, 190, and 191; Stephen Davis, *Atlanta Will Fall: Sherman, Joe Johnston, and the Yankee Heavy Battalions* (Wilmington, DE: SR Books, 2001), 187–89. The body of Lee scholarship could fill several small warehouses. I have found these works listed here to be particularly helpful in understanding Robert E. Lee: Alan T. Nolan, *Lee Considered: General Robert E. Lee and Civil War History*

(Chapel Hill: University of North Carolina Press, 1991); Thomas L. Connelly, *The Marble Man: Robert E. Lee and His Image in American Society* (Baton Rouge: Louisiana State University Press, 1977), Gary W. Gallagher, ed., *Lee: The Soldier* (Lincoln: University of Nebraska Press, 1996). For more on Hood's personality, see Lieutenant Colonel Harry W. Houchens, "The Making of General John Bell Hood: A Study of Command, An Individual Study Project" (Carlisle Barracks, PA: U.S. Army War College, 1993). Houchens uses a Myers-Briggs Type Indicator to hypothesize exactly what type of personality a modern psychologist would have discovered had they the opportunity to test Hood. Houchens classified Hood as possessing an ESTP personality. First, Hood possessed extroversion (people) over introversion (ideas) based, according to Houchens, on the way he acted at West Point and in Kentucky. Second, Hood displayed sensing (aware of the hard facts) over intuition (imagination of a situation) because he would rather act than think, according to Houchens. Third, Hood displayed more thinking (value impersonal logic) over feeling (value emotions) when making decisions. Finally, Hood, tended to perceive (respond spontaneously) instead of judge (analyze and categorize) in an environment. Of note, this analysis is based on the historiography, which Houchens utilized to form his conclusions.

8. McDonough and Connelly, *Five,* 64–68; Woodworth, *Band,* 119. For wildness, see Sword, *Embrace,* 6–8. For a discussion of Southern values, see Coffey, *Hood,* 14 and 17. A discussion of West Point appears in Bailey, *Chessboard,* 6, 8, and 24.

9. McPherson, *Battle,* 812; McDonough and Connelly, *Five,* 3. Neither McPherson nor McDonough and Connelly provide a citation for the foundation of this statement. For specifics on casualties, see Stephen Sears, *Chancellorsville* (New York: Mariner Books, 1996), 492 and Thomas L. Livermore, *Numbers and Losses in the Civil War in America 1861–1865* (New York: Houghton, Mifflin and Co., 1901), 75, 86, 114–15, and 132. Livermore states Union casualties during the Seven Days' battles total 9,796 (1,734 killed and 8,062 wounded). At Franklin, according to Livermore, Hood suffered 1,750 killed and 3,800 wounded. In this case, the difference in killed is only sixteen, favoring McPherson's assertion. However, McClellan suffered twice as many wounded. There is no clear discussion with McPherson or Livermore as to how many of the wounded eventually died. In the instance of Cold Harbor, however, the numbers tell a drastically different story. At Cold Harbor, Livermore asserts that 5,170 Union soldiers were killed during the assaults on June 1 and 2 and seven thousand killed and wounded on the assault on June 3 for the Union army, totaling approximately twelve thousand killed and wounded over the three days of fighting. To be fair, casualty figures can vary widely, but Livermore is often cited as definitive. In his discussion of Hood, McPherson only cites McDonough's and Connelly's *Five Tragic Hours*. As discussed, McDonough and Connelly do not cite any sources for their arguments, making their work problematic. Elsewhere, McPherson endorses a different set of numbers in Bruce Catton, *The American Heritage New History of the Civil War,* ed. James McPherson (New York: Viking, 1996), 429 and 529. Catton lists the total casualties of Cold Harbor for the Union army as nearly fifteen thousand, while Hood lost only 6,252 men at Franklin. Ulysses Simpson Grant, *Memoirs* (Lincoln: University of Nebraska Press, 1996), 564, quotes General George Thomas's report after Franklin listing the enemy (Confederate) casualties as 1,750 buried on the field, 3,800 in the hospital, and 702 prisoners. According to Grady McWhiney and

Perry Jamieson, *Attack and Die: Civil War Military Tactics and the Southern Heritage* (Tuscaloosa: University of Alabama Press, 1982) 19–21, Hood lost only 5,500 at Franklin, compared to McClellan losing 9,796 during the Seven Days and Grant losing fifty thousand from Wilderness through Cold Harbor. Also, refer to John S. Bowman, ed., *The Civil War Almanac* (New York: World Almanac Publications, 1983), 104, 105, 207, and 237. Union casualties are listed as follows: Gaines' Mill—6,837, the Peninsula campaign—nearly sixteen thousand dead, Cold Harbor—July 1 and 2 at five thousand and July 3 with around seven thousand. Confederate loses at Franklin are listed as 6,252, of which 702 are listed as missing. See Grant, *Memoirs*, 501–4, and Gordon Rhea, *The Battle of Cold Harbor* (Washington, DC: Eastern National, 2001), 49–51. Historian John Neff points out that miscommunication between Lee and Grant at Cold Harbor swelled for more than thirty-six hours following the battle, preventing a truce from being declared in order for the wounded and dead to be collected. See John R. Neff, *Honoring the Civil War Dead: Commemoration and the Problem of Reconciliation* (Lawrence: University Press of Kansas, 2005), 35.

10. McDonough and Connelly, *Five*, 64–68. See also Horn, *Decisive*, 32, 41, and 166 and McDonough, *Nashville*, 210–11, McDonough also reiterates the gambling theme as part of the title. McDonough utilizes the card game example to argue that Hood gambled with the invasion into Tennessee, the assaults at Franklin, as well as the movement forward to Nashville. After the first day of battle at Nashville, Hood decided to gamble once again by staying for another day of battle. McDonough calls this "the final gamble." For more examples on how gambling is used in other connotations to describe commanders, see Steven Woodworth, *No Band of Brothers: Problems in the Rebel High Command* (Columbia: University of Missouri Press, 1999), 93; McPherson, *Battle*, 526. For a case against the gambler label, see Coffey, *Hood*, 14 and 17.

11. McDonough and Connelly, *Five*, 37 and 50; McDonough, *Nashville*, 52 and 76; Bailey, *Chessboard*, 44, 71–72, and 87; David Williamson, *The Third Battalion MS Infantry and the 45th MS Regiment* (Jefferson, NC: McFarland and Co., 2004), 267; Woodworth, *Brothers*, 92. Also see Steven E. Woodworth, *Jefferson Davis and His Generals: The Failure of Confederate Command in the West* (Lawrence: University Press of Kansas, 1990), 364 n.84. Woodworth does not offer the laudanum assertion in his text but does offer, in the footnotes, the historian's claim that Hood took the drug that clouded his decision making abilities.

12. Stephen Davis, "John Bell Hood's 'Addictions' in Civil War Literature," *Blue and Gray Magazine* (October 1998): 28–31. Davis suggests that the rumor came possibly from Percy Hamlin, who referred to Hood as a man so crippled that he became dependent on opium.

13. Ibid. For the most recent reference to Hood's supposed drug usage, see McDonough, *Nashville*, 69. Interestingly, McDonough fails to even reference Stephen Davis's 1998 article in the same magazine anywhere in his recent work.

14. Charles Reagan Wilson defines the Lost Cause as primarily a religious movement in his insightful work, *Baptized in Blood: The Religion of the Lost Cause* (Athens: University of Georgia Press, 1980). Gaines Foster views the Lost Cause as more of a social and cultural phenomenon rather than a religious movement in his helpful work, *Ghosts of the Confederacy: Defeat, the Lost Cause, and the Emergence of the New South* (New York: Oxford University Press, 1987). William C. Davis notes that the losers

in war create more myths than the winners. See his work, *The Cause Lost: Myths and Realities of the Confederacy* (Lawrence: University Press of Kansas, 1996). Other useful works include Nina Silber, *The Romance of Reunion: Northerners and the South, 1865–1900* (Chapel Hill: University of North Carolina Press, 1993), Thomas L. Connelly and Barbara Bellows, *God and General Longstreet: The Lost Cause and the Southern Mind* (Baton Rouge: Louisiana State University Press, 1982), Gary W. Gallagher, *The Confederate War: How Popular Will, Nationalism and Military Strategy Could Not Stave Off Defeat* (Cambridge, MA: Harvard University Press, 1997), and also his edited work with Alan T. Nolan, *The Myth of the Lost Cause and Civil War History* (Bloomington: Indiana University Press, 2000). See also C. Vann Woodward, *Origins of the New South: 1877–1913* (Baton Rouge: Louisiana State University Press, 1971). For literature on the importance of memory in history, see David Thelen, "Introduction: Memory and American History," in his ed. *Memory and American History* (Bloomington: Indiana University Press, 1990); Maurice Halbwachs, *On Collective Memory* (Chicago: University of Chicago Press, 1992); Pierre Nora, "Between Memory and History: *Les Lieux de Mémoire*," *Representations* 26 (Spring 1989): 7–25; Paul Connerton, *How Societies Remember* (Cambridge, England: Cambridge University Press, 1989); Patrick H. Hutton, *History as an Art of Memory* (Hanover, NH: University Press of New England, 1993); and Michael Kammen, "Some Patterns and Meanings of Memory Distortion in American History," in *Memory Distortion: How Minds, Brains, and Societies Reconstruct the Past*, ed. Daniel Schacter (Cambridge, MA: Harvard University Press, 1995), 329–45. Studies of the American Civil War in social memory have been a relatively recent phenomenon. See Carol Reardon, *Pickett's Charge: In History and Memory* (Chapel Hill: University of North Carolina Press, 1997); David W. Blight, "For Something Beyond the Battlefield: Frederick Douglass and the Struggle for the Memory of the Civil War," *Journal of American History* 75, no. 4 (March 1989): 1156–78; and his most recent works, *Race and Reunion: The Civil War in American Memory* (Cambridge, MA: Harvard University Press, 2001) and *Beyond the Battlefield: Race, Memory, and the American Civil War* (Boston: University of Massachusetts Press, 2002). Further useful works dealing with the historical lens of memory include Michael Kammen, *Mystic Chords of Memory: The Transformation of Tradition in American Culture* (New York: Alfred Knopf, 1991); Michael S. Roth, *The Ironist's Cage: Memory, Trauma and the Construction of History* (New York: Columbia University Press, 1995); Jeffrey Herf, *Divided Memory: The Nazi Past in the Two Germanys* (Cambridge, MA: Harvard University Press, 1997); and Edward T. Linenthal, *Sacred Ground: Americans and Their Battlefields* (Urbana: University of Illinois Press, 1993).

15. See Arthur Neal, *National Trauma and Collective Memory: Major Events in the American Century* (Armonk, NY: M. E. Sharpe, 1998), 213–15.
16. Historians who examine the antebellum and Civil War eras have begun to construct new interpretations that are recasting biographies in new cultural lights. For examples, see Eric J. Wittenberg, *Little Phil: A Reassessment of the Civil War Leadership of Gen. Philip Sheridan* (Washington, DC: Brassey's, 2002), Lesley J. Gordon, *General George E. Pickett in Life and Legend* (Chapel Hill: University of North Carolina Press, 1998), and David S. Reynolds, *Walt Whitman's America: A Cultural Biography* (New York: Alfred A. Knopf, 1995).

Chapter 1

1. Hood, *Advance*, 5; McWhiney and Jamieson, *Attack*, 172–74 and 178; Grady McWhiney and Perry Jamieson argue that the South eventually bled itself to death during the war because of the way they approached military tactics. Southerners charged forward during the Civil War because of their Celtic heritage. They view northern culture as part of a transplanted English culture, with southern culture being Celtic, a background of Scottish, Cornish, Welsh, Irish, and Scotch-Irish. Though Hood remembered his ancestry as rooted in English tradition, historian Richard McMurry discovered that Hood is actually a Scottish surname, which would help solidify the Jamieson's and McWhiney's thesis. See McMurry, *Hood*, 1. No matter the origin of Hood's ancestors, his family had been steeped in a rich military tradition.
2. Bertram Wyatt-Brown, *Southern Honor: Ethics and Behavior in the Old South* (New York: Oxford University Press, 1982), 122; James K. Phillabaum, *The Ancestors of John Bell Hood: A Civil War General, 1831–1879* (Miami, OH: Miami University Libraries, 1996), 11–13; McMurry, *Hood*, 2.
3. Hood, *Advance*, 5; John B. Boles, *Religion in Antebellum Kentucky* (Lexington: University Press of Kentucky, 1976), 1; Charles Wilkins Short Papers, Filson Historical Society, Louisville, Kentucky (Filson). There is an extensive body of literature on the experience of living on the frontier of Kentucky, especially with work done on Daniel Boone's exploration of the emerging state. For more on the frontier of Kentucky and its early days of settlement, see Otis K. Rice, *Frontier Kentucky* (Lexington: University Press of Kentucky, 1993); Daniel Drake, *Pioneer Life in Kentucky, 1785–1800* (New York: Henry Schuman, 1948); Hazel Dicken-Garcia, *To Western Woods: The Breckenridge Family Moves to Kentucky in 1793* (Madison, WI: Associated University Press, 1991); William Carlos Kozee, *Pioneer Families of Eastern and Southeastern Kentucky* (Huntington, WV: Standard Printing and Publishing Co., 1957); Arthur K. Moore, *The Frontier Mind: A Cultural Analysis of the Kentucky Frontiersman* (Lexington: University Press of Kentucky, 1957); Joan Wells Coward, *Kentucky in the New Republic: The Process of Constitution Making* (Lexington: University Press of Kentucky, 1979). For narratives on early Kentucky, see Chester Raymond Young, ed., *Westward into Kentucky: The Narrative of Daniel Trabue* (Lexington: University Press of Kentucky, 1981) and especially Ellen Eslinger, ed., *Running Mad for Kentucky: Frontier Travel Accounts* (Lexington: University Press of Kentucky, 2004). For works on Daniel Boone, see W. H. Bogart, *Daniel Boone and the Hunters of Kentucky* (Auburn, NY: Miller, Orton and Milligan, 1854); C. B. Hartley, *Life and Times of Colonel Daniel Boone* (Philadelphia: G. G. Evans, 1869); John Bakeless, *Daniel Boone* (Harrisburg, PA: Stackpole Co., 1965); Reuben Gold Thwaites, *Daniel Boone* (New York: D. Appleton-Century Co., 1940); Lawrence Elliott, *The Long Hunter: A New Life of Daniel Boone* (New York: Reader's Digest Press, 1976); Michael A. Lofaro, *The Life and Adventures of Daniel Boone* (Lexington: University Press of Kentucky, 1978); and Michael A. Lofaro, *Daniel Boone: An American Life* (Lexington: University Press of Kentucky, 2003).
4. Phillabaum, *Ancestors*, 4–10 and 17.
5. William Sudduth, "A Sketch of the Early Adventures of William Sudduth in Kentucky," *Historical Quarterly* 2, no. 2 (January 1928): 47–49 and 52.
6. Sudduth, "Sketch," 53, 60, 61, 64, and 65.

7. Phillabaum, *Ancestors*, 6–8 and 17; McMurry, *Hood*, 2.
8. Hood, *Advance*, 5; Phillabaum, *Ancestors*, 4 and 17; McMurry, *Hood*, 2.
9. Phillabaum, *Ancestors*, 3 and 17; Emma Jane Walker and Virginia Wilson, eds., *Some Marriages in Montgomery County, Kentucky, Before 1864* (Lexington, KY: Society Daughters of the American Revolution, 1961), 52; McMurry, *Hood*, 2–3; Lewis H. Kilpatrick, "Historic Owingsville" in *Kentucky Magazine* (Louisville, KY: Lost Cause Press, 1979), 316. James K. Phillabaum hypothesizes that John married Theodosia around 1823. Emma Walker and Virginia Wilson argue that the marriage occurred somewhere between 1829 and 1835. The later date range of Walker and Wilson raises the issue of Hood being born before his parents were married.
10. McMurry, *Hood*, 5; O'Connor, *Hood*, 13.
11. O'Connor, *Hood*, 13.
12. Robert M. Ireland, *The County Courts in Antebellum Kentucky* (Lexington: University Press of Kentucky, 1972), 20; Boles, *Religion*, 128.
13. Boyd, *History*, 27–28.
14. "Ellen to Hector, October 6, 1833," Green Family Papers, Filson; "William Blackburn to Henrietta, July 2, 1848," Blackburn Family Papers, Filson.
15. Kilpatrick, "Owingsville," 318; J. A. Richards, *A History of Bath Country, Kentucky* (Yuma, AZ: Southwest Printers, 1961), 561; McMurry, *Hood*, 3; Rowena Lawson, *Bath Country, KY 1820–1840 Censuses* (Bowie, MD: Heritage Books, 1986), 23; 1830s Census Records for Owingsville, Kentucky, obtained from http://www.ancestry.com.
16. 1840 and 1850 Census Data for Montgomery County, Kentucky, obtained at http://www.ancestry.com; Rowena Lawson, *Montgomery Country, KY 1810–1840 Censuses* (Bowie, MD: Heritage Books, 1985), 51; Rowena Lawson, *Montgomery County, KY 1850 Census* (Bowie, MD: Heritage Books, 1986), 10; McMurry, *Hood*, 3.
17. Phillabaum, *Ancestors*, 4–5; McMurry, *Hood*, 2–3. For more on Mt, Sterling, see Carl B. Boyd and Hazel Mason Boyd, *A History of Mt. Sterling, Kentucky, 1792–1918* (Carl Boyd Jr., 1984).
18. Phillabaum, *Ancestors*, 4–5; Richard French biography at http://bioguide.congress.gov/scripts/biodisplay.pl?index=F000379. For some of French's most important speeches, see Richard French, *Slavery in the Territories Delivered in the House of Representatives, Thursday, June 29, 1848* (Washington, DC: Congressional Globe Office, 1848), 3–8, and Richard French, *The Right of Members to their Seats in the House of Representatives Delivered in the House of Representatives February 12, 1844* (Washington, DC: Globe Office, 1844), 3–8.
19. Harold D. Tallant, *Evil Necessity: Slavery and Political Culture in Antebellum Kentucky* (Lexington: University Press of Kentucky, 2003), 115–16, 234, and 249n23. For more on the slave culture of antebellum Kentucky, see Tallant, 1–3, 13, 20–21, and 28–30; Boles, *Religion*, 119. For more on the role of gender and abolition, see Bruce Dorsey, *Reforming Men and Women: Gender in the Antebellum City* (Ithaca, NY: Cornell University Press, 2002), 136–94.
20. Craig Thompson Friend and Lorri Glover, "Rethinking Southern Masculinity: An Introduction," in Craig Thompson Friend and Lorri Glover, eds., *Southern Manhood: Perspectives on Masculinity in the Old South* (Athens: University of Georgia Press, 2004), x and xi; Wyatt-Brown, *Southern Honor*, 14 and 34. See also George L. Mosse, *The Image of Man: The Creation of Modern Masculinity* (New York: Oxford

University Press, 1996), 16–20; David Pugh, *Sons of Liberty: The Masculine Mind in Nineteenth-Century America* (Westport, CT: Greenwood Press, 1983); Arthur Brittan, *Masculinity and Power* (New York: Basil Blackwell, 1989) and Rachel Alsop, Annette Fitzsimons, and Kathleen Lennon, *Theorizing Gender* (Malden, MA: Blackwell Publishers, 2002).

21. Friend and Glover, "Rethinking Southern Masculinity," x and xi; Wyatt-Brown, *Southern Honor*, 14 and 34. For more on gender notions in the antebellum South, see Kathleen M. Brown, *Good Wives, Nasty Wenches and Anxious Patriarchs: Gender, Race and Power in Colonial Virginia* (Chapel Hill: University of North Carolina Press, 1996). Of note, some recent historians have challenged the notion that honor and mastery are the twin pillars in defining southern manhood. See John Mayfield, " 'The Soul of a Man!': William Gilmore Simms and the Myths of Southern Manhood," *Journal of the Early Republic* 15 (1995): 477–500; Janet Moore Lindman, "Acting the Manly Christian: White Evangelical Masculinity in Revolutionary Virginia," *William and Mary Quarterly* 57 (2000): 393–416, and Anya Jabour, "Male Friendship and Masculinity in the Early National South: William Wirt and His Friends," *Journal of the Early Republic* 20 (2000): 83–111.

22. Harry S. Laver, "Refuge of Manhood: Masculinity and the Militia Experience in Kentucky," in Friend and Glover, *Manhood*, 1; Lorri Glover, " 'Let Us Manufacture Men': Educating Elite Boys in the Early National South," in Friend and Glover, *Manhood*, 23.

23. Stephen W. Berry II, *All that Makes a Man: Love and Ambition in the Civil War South* (New York: Oxford University Press, 2003), 12; Friend and Glover, "Rethinking," ix; Laura F. Edwards, "The Problem of Dependency: African Americans, Labor Relations and the Law in the Nineteenth-Century South," *Agricultural History* 72, no. 2 (Spring 1998): 315, as well as Laura Edwards, *Scarlett Doesn't Live Here Anymore: Women in the Civil War Era* (Urbana: University of Illinois Press, 2000).

24. Berry, *Man*, 12 and 20–21; Friend and Glover, "Rethinking," xii; Jane Dailey, *Before Jim Crow: The Politics of Race in Post Emancipation Virginia* (Chapel Hill: University of North Carolina Press, 2000), 90–95. For more on how the image of the whole man equated manhood, see Kenneth S. Greenberg, *Honor and Slavery: Lies, Duels, Noses, Masks, Dressing as a Woman, Gifts, Strangers, Humanitarianism, Death, Slave Rebellions, the Proslavery Argument, Baseball, Hunting, and Gambling in the Old South* (Princeton, NJ: Princeton University Press, 1996), 3; Gail Bederman, *Manliness and Civilization: A Cultural History of Gender and Race in the United States, 1880–1917* (Chicago: University of Chicago Press, 1995), 5–8 and 11; E. Anthony Rotundo, *American Manhood: Transformations in Masculinity from the Revolution to the Modern Era* (New York: Basic Books, 1993), 233–34, as well as Christina S. Jarvis, *The Male Body at War: American Masculinity during World War II* (DeKalb: Northern Illinois University Press, 2004), 112–18. For more on honor and southern manhood, see Wyatt-Brown, *Southern Honor*, 34–36, 133–34, 144–59, and 164–70; W. J. Cash, *The Mind of the South* (New York: Vintage, 1991), Kenneth S. Greenberg, *Masters and Statesmen: The Political Culture of Slavery* (Baltimore: John Hopkins University Press, 1985), Steven M. Stowe, *Intimacy and Power in the Old South* (Baltimore: John Hopkins University Press, 1987), Joanne B. Freeman, *Affairs of Honor: National Politics in the New Republic* (New Haven, CT: Yale University Press, 2001), as well as Edward L. Ayers, *Vengeance*

and Justice: Crime and Punishment in the Nineteenth Century South (New York: Oxford University Press, 1984).

25. *Paris (KY) Western Citizen,* October 8, 1831; *Paris (KY) Western Citizen,* October 28, 1838.
26. Boles, *Religion,* 15 and 123; Robert Baldick, *The Duel: A History of Dueling* (New York: Clarkson N. Potter, 1965), 117; Clayton E. Cramer, *Concealed Weapon Laws of the Early Republic: Dueling, Southern Violence, and Moral Reform* (Westport, CT: Praeger, 1999), 60–62. The literature on dueling and the advent of gun violence is rich, particularly regarding the Old South. See Wyatt-Brown, *Southern Honor,* 350–51; Jack K. Williams, *Dueling in the Old South: Vignettes of Social History* (College Station: Texas A&M University Press, 1980); Edward L. Ayers, *Vengeance and Justice: Crime and Punishment in the 19th-Century American South* (New York: Oxford University Press, 1984); J. Winston Coleman Jr., *Famous Kentucky Duels: The Story of the Code of Honor in the Bluegrass State* (Frankfort, KY: Roberts Printing Co., 1953); Michael Bellesiles, ed., *Lethal Imagination: Violence and Brutality in American History* (New York: New York University Press, 1999); W. Eugene Hollon, *Frontier Violence: Another Look* (New York: Oxford University Press, 1974); Malcolm J. Rohrbough, *The Trans-Appalachian Frontier: People, Societies, and Institutions 1775–1850* (New York: Oxford University Press, 1979); Carl P. Russell, *Guns on the Early Frontier* (Lincoln: University of Nebraska Press, 1980); William Oliver Stevens, *Pistols at Ten Paces: The Story of the Code of Honor in America* (Cambridge, MA: Riverside Press, 1940); Harnett C. Kane, *Gentlemen, Swords and Pistols* (New York: William Morrow and Co., 1951); "January 1835, remarks on the Rowan v. Marshall Duel by Annita Beynroth," Charles Exteen Beynroth Papers, Filson. For more on dueling in Kentucky, including the first duel in Kentucky between John Thurston and John Harrison, as well as across the nation before the Civil War, see Hamilton Cochran, *Noted American Duels and Hostile Encounters* (Philadelphia: Clinton Books, 1963).
27. Cramer, *Concealed,* 2, 47–49, 56, and 57. See Ireland, *County.*
28. "Hensh to Mother, July 11, 1858," Gorn Family Papers, Filson; *Paris (KY) Western Citizen,* February 12, 1831. Kentucky, as it did with a movement to end slavery and dueling, also pushed for temperance legislation. For more on the temperance movement, see Boles, *Religion,* 132; Thomas H. Appleton Jr., " 'Moral Suasion Has Had Its Day': From Temperance to Prohibition in Antebellum Kentucky," in John David Smith and Thomas H. Appleton Jr., eds., *A Mythic Land Apart: Reassessing Southerners and Their History* (Westport, CT: Greenwood Press, 1997), 19–28; "Ellen to Hector, October 17, 1833," Green Family Papers, Filson; Dorsey, *Reforming,* 90–135.
29. For more on the contours of manhood on the frontier, see Berry, *Man,* 17–44; Wyatt-Brown, *Southern Honor,* 330, and Craig Thompson Friend, "Belles, Benefactors, and the Blacksmith's Son: Cyrus Stuart and the Enigma of Southern Gentlemanliness," in Friend and Thompson, *Manhood,* 95–97.
30. Wyatt-Brown, *Southern Honor,* 134 and 165–66.
31. McMurry, *Hood,* 5; Woodworth, *Davis,* 266; John Mayfield, "Being Shifty in a New Country: Southern Humor and the Masculine Ideal," in Friend and Glover, *Manhood,* 114.
32. Nicolas W. Proctor, *Bathed in Blood: Hunting and Mastery in the Old South* (Charlottesville: University Press of Virginia, 2002), 1, 38–39, 44, 47–48, 57, and 66.

33. Proctor, *Bathed*, 61, 63–65, and 72. For more on self-control, see E. Anthony Rotundo, "Learning About Manhood: Gender Ideals and the Middle-Class Family in Nineteenth-Century America," in J. A. Mangan and James Walvin, eds., *Manliness and Morality: Middle-Class Masculinity in Britain and America 1800–1940* (New York: St. Martin's Press, 1987), 35–51.
34. *Paris (KY) Western Citizen*, February 12, 1831.
35. Wyatt-Brown, *Southern Honor*, 339–44. For more on horse handling in Kentucky, see "November 19, 1832, W. H. Hursh to William Bodley," Bodley Papers, Filson, and "Letter February 20, 1854," A. C. Williams Collection, Filson.
36. See Linda Lindsey, *Gender Roles: A Sociological Perspective* (Upper Saddle River, NJ: Prentice Hall, 1997), 222–23. Lindsey argues that men often participate in war and soldiering in order to validate their manhood. Participation in war emphasizes qualities such as glory and virtue and often ignores the horror and destruction of war. Men find the battlefield appealing, especially with the ability to witness the mechanics of war and the time they spend in company with their fellow men.
37. Laver, "Refuge," 2–4, 6, and 9–15.
38. Jennifer R. Green, "'Stout Chaps Who Can Bear Distress:' Young Men in Antebellum Military Academies," in Friend and Glover, *Manhood*, 176 and 186; Wyatt-Brown, *Southern Honor*, 191; Hood, *Advance*, 5. See also Donald J. Mrozek, "The Habit of Victory: The American Military and the Cult of Manliness," in Mangan and Walvin, *Manliness*, 220–39.
39. Wyatt-Brown, *Southern Honor*, 190–92. For another possibility on why Hood went to West Point, see O'Connor, *Hood*, 14. O'Connor tells the story of Hood falling in love with a farmer's daughter. Yet, the family insisted that she marry a wealthier gentleman. The young woman agreed, but requested that she could write a letter to Hood, explaining the situation. Yet, the letter served as an opportunity for the young woman to make plans for her and Hood to run away together, before eventually being captured by a family posse. Legend has it that the unhappy woman, after her marriage to a wealthy suitor, placed a curse on anyone who had interfered with her romantic attempts to betroth John Bell Hood.
40. Ellsworth Eliot Jr., *West Point in the Confederacy*. (New York: G. A. Baker and Co, 1941), 1; Stephen E. Ambrose, *Duty, Honor, Country: A History of West Point* (Baltimore: Johns Hopkins University Press, 1966), 128–29.
41. William H. Baumer Jr., *West Point: Molder of Men* (New York: D. Appleton-Century Co., 1943), 2, 5, and 62; Ambrose, *Duty*, 84.
42. Harold B. Simpson, "John Bell Hood," in W. C. Nunn, ed., *Ten Texans in Gray* (Hillsboro, TX: Hill Junior College Press, 1968), 57.
43. Ambrose, *Duty*, 16–17.
44. Kendall Banning, *West Point Today* (New York: Funk and Wagnalls Co., 1937), 29–33; Baumer, *Moulder*, 92; James R. Endler, *Other Leaders, Other Heroes: West Point's Legacy to America Beyond the Field of Battle* (Westport, CT: Praeger, 1998), 10; Ambrose, *Duty*, 73. For more on the history of West Point, see Lieutenant General Sidney B. Berry, *The United States Military Academy: A Fundamental National Institution, West Point: A Special Place* (New York: The Newcomen Society in North America, 1977); George S. Pappas, *To the Point: The United States Military Academy, 1802–1902* (Westport, CT: Praeger, 1993); Ambrose, *Duty*; Theodore J. Crackel, *West Point: A Centennial History*

(Lawrence: University Press of Kansas, 2002); *The Sesquicentennial of the United States Military Academy: An Account of the Observance, January–June, 1952* (Buffalo: Baker, Jones, Hausauer and Savage, 1953); Gerard A. Patterson, *Rebels from West Point* (New York: Doubleday, 1987), 3; Captain Charles King, *Cadet Days: A Story of West Point* (New York: Harpers, 1894).

45. Ambrose, *Duty*, 90. For more on the curriculum and changes made, see Ambrose, *Duty*, 94–105.
46. Crackel, *West*, 121–23.
47. John C. Waugh, *The Class of 1846, From West Point to Appomattox: Stonewall Jackson, George McClellan and Their Brothers* (New York: Warner Books, 1994), 19. See also Ralph Kirshner, *The Class of 1861: Custer, Ames, and Their Classmates after West Point* (Carbondale: Southern Illinois University Press, 1999).
48. Banning, *West*, 285; Pappas, *Point*, 274 and 290. For more on Lee as superintendent, see Pappas, *Point*, 287–307.
49. McMurry, *Hood*, 7–8; Baumer, *Moulder*, 188; Pappas, *Point*, 270–71.
50. Crackel, *West*, 121.
51. Crackel, *West*, 121–22; Ambrose, *Duty*, 154.
52. Ambrose, *Duty*, 130 and 158; McMurry, *Hood*, 7 and 9.
53. Waugh, *1846*, ix and x; Crackel, *West*, 123; Ambrose, *Duty*, 137–39.
54. Ambrose, *Duty*, 149 and 153.
55. Ambrose, *Duty*, 162–63; Waugh, *1846*, 36–38.
56. Crackel, *West*, 123; Ambrose, *Duty*, 162–63. Both Haven and his wife, interestingly enough, hold the distinction of being the only American citizens forbidden to ever step foot on the grounds of West Point, because of Haven's liquor license.
57. Banning, *West*, 50–52.
58. Ambrose, *Duty*, 74. *Official Register of the Officers and Cadets of the U.S. Military Academy*, West Point, NY, June 1850, 19; June 1851, 20; June 1852, 18; June 1853, 21, United States Military Academy Archives and Special Collections, West Point, New York.
59. Cubbison, "Hood," 54.
60. Eliot, *West*, 5; Cubbison, "Hood," 54–55.
61. Ambrose, *Duty*, 132; *Official Register*, June 1850, 16; *Official Register*, June 1851, 14; *Official Register*, June 1852, 10; *Official Register*, June 1853, 8.
62. Banning, *West*, 281–87; Eliot, *West*, xx–xxiv.
63. Pappas, *Point*, 273; Eliot, *West*, 5–6.
64. Banning, *West*, 285–86.

Chapter 2

Epigraphs: U. S. Grant, *Personal Memoirs of U. S. Grant* (Lincoln: University of Nebraska Press, 1996), 120; Harold B. Simpson, "Fort Mason," in Harold B. Simpson, ed., *Frontier Forts of Texas* (Waco, TX: Texian Press, 1966), 141.

1. Martha Doty Freeman, *A History of Camp Cooper, Throckmorton County, Texas* (Albany, TX: Aztec of Albany Foundation, 1997), 21. Item courtesy of Center for American History, University of Texas at Austin; McMurry, *Hood*, 11. Of note, Camp Cooper in Texas, where Hood would serve in the coming years, was named in honor of Samuel Cooper.

2. Anni P. Baker, "Daughters of Mars: Army Officers' Wives and Military Culture on the American Frontier," *The Historian* 67, no. 1 (Spring 2005): 22–23 and 41. See also Allan R. Millett, *Military Professionalism and Officership in America* (Columbus: Mershon Center of The Ohio State University, 1977).
3. McMurry, *Hood*, 11–12; Hood, *Advance*, 6; Cubbison, "Hood," 55.
4. Gilbert W. Davies and Florice M. Frank, eds., *Fort Jones (Ca) 1852–1858 Military Notes* (Hat Creek, CA: History Ink Books, 1994), v, 23, 48, and 355; McMurry, *Hood*, 13.
5. Davies, *Jones*, 22–25, 36, and 46–47.
6. Davies, *Jones*, 19–21.
7. Ibid., 34–35.
8. Ibid., 22.
9. C. M. Winkler, *Life and Character of Gen. John B. Hood*. Address given before Hood's Texas Brigade Association, June 27, 1885, 7, courtesy of Howard-Tilton Memorial Library, Tulane University. Grant, *Memoirs*, 121–22. Hood, *Advance*, 7. Robert Edward Lee Richardson, "Boots and Saddles: The Second Cavalry in Texas, 1855–1861," honors thesis, Austin College, 1995, 30.
10. Lambert, *Hundred*, 8–50; Richardson, "Boots and Saddles," 4–5.
11. Richardson, "Boots and Saddles," 2–4.
12. Lambert, *Hundred*, 51–52; Steven E. Woodworth, *Jefferson Davis and His Generals: The Failure of Confederate Command in the West* (Lawrence: University Press of Kansas, 1990), 48; Simpson, "Hood," 58; Simpson, "Mason," 152.
13. Simpson, "Hood," 58; Simpson, "Mason," 152–53. For a complete listing of all those who served at Fort Mason prior to the Civil War, see Jerry Ponder, *Fort Mason, Texas: Training Ground for Generals* (Mason, TX: Ponder Books, 1997), 57–85.
14. McMurry, *Hood*, 14–15.
15. Bohannon, "Promoted," 251; Winkler, *Hood*, 8; Richardson, "Boots and Saddles," 12 and 15.
16. Winkler, *Hood*, 8; Richardson, "Boots and Saddles," 19.
17. Richardson, "Boots and Saddles," 14–15; Harold B. Simpson, *Cry Comanche* (Hillsboro, TX: Hill Junior College Press, 1979), 28.
18. Richardson, "Boots and Saddles," 19 and 20; Simpson, "Mason," 153–54.
19. T. R. Havins, *Camp Colorado: A Decade of Frontier Defense* (Brownwood, TX: Brown Press, 1964), 11–24; Colin G. Calloway, *First Peoples: A Documentary Survey of American Indian History* (New York: Bedford/St. Martin's, 2004), 259–61 and 265–66. Buffalo robes also served as clothing and bedding, and the bones from the animal could be made to serve various functions as tools or weapons. Yet, most important, the Comanche utilized the meat as their main source of food. When it came time for a buffalo hunt, the men did the killing and the women usually participated in the butchering. The men of the tribe used bows, arrows, and spears for both the killing of buffalo and when needing to engage in warfare with other native parties or white settlers. Comanche women prepared the meat, usually through broiling or drying, or even served the meat raw. For more on the early history of the Comanche, see Thomas Kavanagh, *Comanche Political History: An Ethnohistorical Perspective, 1706–1875* (Lincoln: University of Nebraska Press, 1996); Gerald Betty, *Comanche Society: Before the Reservation* (College Station: Texas A&M University Press, 2002); T. R.

Fehrenbach, *Comanches: The Destruction of a People* (New York: Knopf, 1974); Ernest Wallace and E. Adamson Hoebel, *The Comanches: Lords of the South Plains* (Norman: University of Oklahoma Press, 1952); Calloway, *First,* 145–46; Betty Ballantine and Ian Ballantine, eds., *The Native Americans: An Illustrated History* (North Dighton, MA: World Publications Group, 2001), 108–9, 221–22, and 277–80; Maxwell, *America's,* 155–203. In particular, pages 167–70 deal with the Comanche excellence in horsemanship. The number of buffalo dwindled over the course of the nineteenth century from close to sixty million in 1800 to thirteen million in 1870. Fewer than one thousand buffalo remained by 1900. For more, see Guy Gibbon, *The Sioux: The Dakota and Lakota Nations* (Malden, MA: Blackwell Publishing, 2003), 6–7; Maxwell, *America's,* 199. For more on the idea of the shatter zone and how it altered Native American life, see Eric R. Wolf, *Europe and a People Without History* (Berkeley: University of California Press, 1982); Richard White, *The Middle Ground: Indians, Empires, and Republics in the Great Lakes Region, 1650–1815* (New York: Cambridge University Press, 1991); Brian Ferguson and Neil Whitehead, *War in the Tribal Zone: Expanding States and Indigenous Warfare* (Santa Fe, NM: School of American Research, 1992); Robbie Ethridge, "Raiding the Remains: Indian Slave Traders and the Collapse of the Southeastern Chiefdoms," presented at the Annual Meeting of SEAC, November 14–17, 2001 in Chattanooga, TN; Robbie Ethridge, "Shatter Zone: Early Colonial Slave Raiding and its Consequences for the Natives of the Eastern Woodland Indians," presented at the American Society for Ethnohistory Annual Meeting, November 7–12, 2003 in Riverside, CA; Charles Hudson, "Introduction" in Robbie Ethridge and Charles Hudson, eds., *The Transformation of the Southeastern Indians, 1540–1760* (Jackson: University Press of Mississippi, 2002); Robbie Ethridge, *Creek Country: The Creek Indians and Their World* (Chapel Hill: University of North Carolina Press, 2003); Chief Red Fox, *The Memoirs of Chief Red Fox* (Greenwich, CT: Fawcett Publications, 1971); James A. Maxwell, ed., *America's Fascinating Indian Heritage* (Pleasantville, NY: Reader's Digest Association, 1978); Robert M. Utley, *The Indian Frontier of the American West, 1846–1890* (Albuquerque: University of New Mexico Press, 1984); and Linea Sundstrom, "Smallpox Used Them Up: Reference to Epidemic Disease in Northern Plains Winter Counts, 1714–1920," *Ethnohistory* 44, no. 2 (Spring 1997).

20. Simpson, "Mason," 141–42. For more on the early years of the fort, see Margaret Bierschwale, *Fort Mason, Chapter V from A History of Macon County, Texas* (Mason, TX: Margaret Bierschwale, 1968), 7–14. Manuscript courtesy of the Texas State Library, Austin.
21. Simpson, "Mason," 143–44.
22. Bierschwale, *Mason,* 14 and 22.
23. Simpson, "Mason," 150–51; Robert M. Utley, *Frontiersmen in Blue* (Lincoln: University of Nebraska Press, 1981), 126.
24. Winkler, *Hood,* 9; Hood, *Advance,* 7–8; Freeman, *Cooper,* 27–28.
25. Hood, *Advance,* 7–8; McMurry, *Hood,* 22–23; Simpson, "Mason," 163–64.
26. McMurry, *Hood,* 20–21.
27. Ponder, *Mason,* 89; Richardson, "Boots and Saddles," 34; Hood, *Advance,* 9.
28. Simpson, "Mason," 135–37 and 155; McMurry, *Hood,* 18–19; Hood, *Advance,* 9 and 10. For more on other Native American encounters with the soldiers at Fort Mason, see Simpson, "Mason," 154–59.

29. Hood, *Advance*, 10; Simpson, "Mason," 138–39; McMurry, *Hood*, 18; Winkler, *Hood*, 10. See also O'Connor, *Hood*, 3–9.
30. Simpson, "Mason," 139; Hood, *Advance*, 12–13; George F. Price, *Across the Continent with the Fifth Cavalry* (New York: Antiquarian Press, 1883), 60; Ponder, *Mason*, 91; Richardson, "Boots and Saddles," 45.
31. Simpson, "Mason," 139–40; Ponder, *Mason*, 91; Boyd, *History*, 3; Simpson, "Hood," 55–56.
32. Simpson, "Hood," 56 and 59; "Letter to Colonel Albert Sydney Johnston," Mrs. Mason Barret Collection, Archives Department, Howard Tilton Memorial Library, Tulane University (TU); Ponder, *Mason*, 91.
33. Freeman, *Cooper*, 34, 36–37, and 82; Havins, *Colorado*, 72–73. While stationed at Camp Colorado, if Hood wanted to send or receive mail, he had to rely on a man named Stieler and his mule. The mule made mail runs twice a month from Fort Mason to Camp Colorado and back, in all sorts of weather. Furthermore, the mule had to deal with occasional Indian attacks on the journey. Though several Native Americans attempted to capture the mule, he always got away. Historian Harold Simpson wrote, "The Pony Express may have been faster, but it couldn't have been more dependable or more colorful than Stieler and his brown mule." Simpson, "Hood," 56 and 59; Simpson, "Mason," 161–62.
34. Havins, *Colorado*, 75.
35. Havins, *Colorado*, 77 and 81–83.
36. Simpson, "Mason," 141; Simpson, "Hood," 56 and 59; Cubbison, "Hood," 55; Winkler, *Hood*, 11; McMurry, *Hood*, 22.
37. Patterson, *Rebels*, 8.
38. Lowell H. Harrison and James C. Klotter, *A New History of Kentucky* (Lexington: University Press of Kentucky, 1997), 181–94, quoted from 188–89.
39. Hood, *Advance*, 16.

Chapter 3

1. R. M. Gray Reminiscence Papers (SHC), 64–65.
2. Mary Lasswell, ed., *Rags and Hope: The Recollections of Val. C. Giles, Four Years with Hood's Brigade, Fourth Texas Infantry, 1861–1865* (New York: Coward-McCann, 1961), 112.
3. McMurry, *Hood*, 25–26; Hood, *Advance*, 16–18; Winkler, *Hood*, 12; U.S. War Department, *The War of the Rebellion: A Compilation of the Official Records of the Union and Confederate Armies*, 127 vols. (Washington, DC: GPO, 1880–1901) (OR) 51, part 1, p. 122.
4. McMurry, *Hood*, 25–26; Hood, *Advance*, 16–18; Winkler, *Hood*, 12.
5. McMurry, *Hood*, 26; Hood, *Advance*, 18.
6. McMurry, *Hood*, 28.
7. Winkler, *Hood*, 13.
8. Bohannon, "Promoted," 252; Hood, *Advance*, 18–19.
9. For more on the early military action of 1861, see William C. Davis, *The Battle of Bull Run* (Baton Rouge: Louisiana State University Press, 1977).
10. McMurry, *Hood*, 29 and 33.
11. Lasswell, *Rags*, 53.
12. McMurry, *Hood*, 32; Winkler, *Hood*, 14–15.

13. McMurry, *Hood*, 34–35.
14. McMurry, *Hood*, 36; Nicholas A. Davis, *Chaplain Davis and Hood's Texas Brigade*, ed. Donald E. Everett (Baton Rouge: Louisiana State University Press, 1999), 52–53; Lasswell, *Rags*, 66.
15. McMurry, *Hood*, 37; Lasswell, *Rags*, 67.
16. McMurry, *Hood*, 36.
17. Nicholas Davis, *Chaplain*, 57.
18. Ibid., 12.
19. Stephen W. Sears, *To the Gates of Richmond: The Peninsula Campaign* (New York: Houghton Mifflin Co., 1992), 21–39; McMurry, *Hood*, 37. See also Ronald Bailey, *Forward to Richmond: McClellan's Peninsula Campaign* (Alexandria, VA: Time-Life Books, 1983), 90–92.
20. Sears, *Gates*, 82. For more on Yorktown and the battle at Williamsburg, see Sears, *Gates*, 40–82.
21. Harold B. Simpson, *Gaines' Mill to Appomattox: Waco and McLennan County in Hood's Texas Brigade* (Waco, TX: Texian Press, 1988), 77; Hood, *Advance*, 21; Lasswell, *Rags*, 95–96. See also Sears, *Gates*, 85.
22. Hood Report on Eltham's Landing, James Power Smith Papers, Library of Congress (LOC).
23. Craig L. Symonds, *Joseph E. Johnston: A Civil War Biography* (New York: W.W. Norton and Co., 1992), 156; John W. Spencer, *From Corsicana to Appomattox: The Story of the Corsicana Invincibles and the Navarro Rifles* (Corsicana, TX: The Texas Press, 1984), 16; Lasswell, *Rags*, 98; Simpson, *Gaines' Mill*, 78. See also Sears, *Gates*, 86.
24. OR 11, part 1, pp. 605, 627, and 631; Winkler, *Hood*, 17; Hood, *Advance*, 22; A. L. Drayton Diary, LOC.
25. McMurry, *Hood*, 45.
26. McMurry, *Hood*, 42.
27. McMurry, *Hood*, 42. For more on McClellan's movements after Williamsburg, see Sears, *Gates*, 82–110. Sears also talks at length about the Battle at Seven Pines/Fair Oaks, where Joseph Johnston was wounded, on pages 111–45.
28. For an explanation of Lee taking command, see Sears, *Gates*, 146–77. Sears discusses the Battle of Oak Grove and Mechanicsville (days one and two of the Seven Days) on 181–209.
29. McMurry, *Hood*, 46 and 50; OR 11, part 2, p. 556; Lasswell, *Rags*, 110 and 112; Simpson, *Gaines' Mill*, 85–88; Hood, *Advance*, 27 and 64. See also Warren Wilkinson and Steven E. Woodworth, *A Scythe of Fire: A Civil War Story of the Eight Georgia Infantry Regiment* (New York: William Morrow, 2002), 139.
30. "Peninsula Recollections," John Cheves Haskell Papers, Special Collections, Perkins Library, Duke University.
31. McMurry, *Hood*, 48–50; Winkler, *Hood*, 18; Sears, *Gates*, 240; Patterson, *Rebels*, 20.
32. McMurry, *Hood*, 50; Sears, *Gates*, 241–42.
33. McMurry, *Hood*, 50–51; Nicholas Davis, *Chaplain*, 91.
34. Hood, *Advance*, 29.
35. Patterson, *Rebels*, 28; Hood, *Advance*, 30.
36. Pharris Deloach Johnson, ed., *Under the Southern Cross: Soldier Life with Gordon Bradwell and the Army of Northern Virginia* (Macon, GA: Mercer University Press, 1999), 69.

37. Nicholas Davis, *Chaplain*, 63; Hood, *Advance*, 28.
38. Hood's Texas Brigade, A. L. Drayton Diary, LOC.
39. OR 11, part 3, p. 667; OR 12, part 3, p. 928. For more on the final battles of the Seven Days, see Sears, *Gates*, 277–336.
40. Hood, *Advance*, 32–33.
41. OR 12, part 2, pp. 553, 557, and 605; John J. Hennessy, *Return to Bull Run: The Campaign and Battle of Second Manassas* (Norman: University of Oklahoma Press, 1993), 289–96, 302, and 309–10.
42. Steven H. Stubbs, *Duty, Honor, Valor: The Story of the Eleventh Mississippi Infantry Regiment* (Philadelphia, MS: Dancing Rabbit Press, 2000), 272–73; McMurry, *Hood*, 55; Hennessy, *Return*, 378–90.
43. Wilkinson and Woodworth, *Scythe*, 172; "September 3, 1862," Robert P. Tondee Papers, Duke; Nicholas Davis, *Chaplain*, 116–21; Stubbs, *Duty*, 297; Winkler, *Hood*, 18. See also Hennessy, *Return*, 390–406 and OR, series 1, vol. 12, part 2, p. 605.
44. OR 12, part 2, p. 610; McMurry, *Hood*, 56, 59, and 60–61.
45. Hood, *Advance*, 38; Nicholas Davis, *Chaplain*, 124–25.
46. Stephen W. Sears, *Landscape Turned Red: The Battle of Antietam* (New York: Ticknor and Fields, 1983), 135; Winkler, *Hood*, 19–20; Hood, *Advance*, 39–40; Nicholas Davis, *Chaplain*, 124–25.
47. Stubbs, *Duty*, 298; Robert E. Lee, *Wartime Papers of Robert E. Lee*, ed. Clifford Dowdey (New York: Da Capo Press, 1961), 318–19; Hood, *Advance*, 41; McMurry, *Hood*, 58; Sears, *Landscape*, 177.
48. Sears, *Landscape*, 197–99 and 201; James McPherson, *Crossroads of Freedom: Antietam* (New York: Oxford University Press, 2002), 118.
49. "Sketch of Sixth North Carolina," Alphonso Avery Papers, SHC; McMurry, *Hood*, 58–59.
50. Stubbs, *Duty*, 307 and 321; Hood, *Advance*, 45; Sears, *Landscape*, 214.
51. Jerome B. Robertson, *Touched with Valor: Civil War Papers and Casualty Reports of Hood's Texas Brigade*, ed. Harold B. Simpson (Hillsboro, TX: Hill Junior College Press, 1964), 28–29; Thomas W. Cutrer, ed., *Longstreet's Aide: The Civil War Letters of Major Thomas J. Goree* (Charlottesville: University Press of Virginia, 1995), 100.
52. Hood, *Advance*, 45–46; *New Orleans Daily Picayune*, January 8, 1874.
53. Nicholas Davis, *Chaplain*, 130; McMurry, *Hood*, 61 and 72.
54. "May 24, 1863," Lafayette McLaws Papers, SHC.
55. "May 31, 1863," Lafayette McLaws Papers, SHC; Nicholas Davis, *Chaplain*, 130.
56. "May 31, 1863," and "June 3, 1863," Lafayette McLaws Papers, SHC; McMurry, *Hood*, 73.
57. Nicholas Davis, *Chaplain*, 130; "July 30, 1863," Lafayette McLaws Papers, SHC.
58. Lasswell, *Rags*, 134.
59. McMurry, *Hood*, 62; Lasswell, *Rags*, 140–42.
60. McMurry, *Hood*, 62–64; George Rable, *Fredericksburg! Fredericksburg!* (Chapel Hill: University of North Carolina Press, 2002), 78 and 157.
61. Rable, *Fredericksburg*, 251; McMurry, *Hood*, 65–66.
62. Lasswell, *Rags*, 151–52; Bohannon, "Promoted," 257; General James Longstreet, *From Manassas to Appomattox: Memoirs of the Civil War in America* (New York: Da Capo Press, 1992), 317. See also Rable, *Fredericksburg*, 160 and 220.

63. Simpson, *Gaines' Mill*, 115.
64. McMurry, *Hood*, 67; Roberson, *Touched*, 41.
65. McMurry, *Hood*, 69–70.
66. "Hood to Lee, April 29, 1863," Charles Venable Collection, SHC.
67. "March 18, 1863" and "March 19, 1863," Dr. Lee Papers, Duke; "March 22, 1863 Letter," Virginia Arnett Papers, Duke; Stephen W. Sears, *Chancellorsville* (New York: Houghton Mifflin Co., 1996), 174 and 376; OR 25, part 2, 327, 332, and 477.
68. OR 25, part 2, p. 811; Lee, *Wartime Papers*, 490; Winkler, *Hood*, 20; *New Orleans Daily Picayune*, January 8, 1874. See also Sears, *Chancellorsville*, 449.
69. Woodworth, *Davis*, 212–13. Woodworth argues that Lee made a mistake by not sending at least one division to assist Joseph Johnston, which would have increased his army by 25 percent. However, Lee would have needed several spectacular victories or a possible invasion of Washington to draw Grant away from Vicksburg.
70. Wilkinson and Woodworth, *Scythe*, 213; "June 6, 1863," Robert P. Tondee Papers, Duke.
71. McMurry, *Hood*, 73–74; *Southern Historical Society Papers*, ed. R. A. Brock, vol. 38 (Richmond, VA: Southern Historical Society, 1910), 312–13.
72. John C. West, *A Texan in Search of a Fight: Being the Diary and Letters of a Private Soldier in Hood's Texas Brigade* (Waco, TX: Texian Press, 1969), 89; Arthur James Lyon Fremantle, *Three Months in the Southern States: April–June 1863* (Lincoln: University of Nebraska Press, 1991), 239 and 243; Patterson, *Rebels*, 66.
73. Fremantle, *Three*, 242 and 261; Harry W. Pfanz, *Gettysburg: The Second Day* (Chapel Hill: University of North Carolina Press, 1987), 112.
74. Longstreet, *Manassas*, 361; Pfanz, *Gettysburg*, 158 and 163–65; Lasswell, *Rags*, 186. There is a report that states Hood began his attack at 2 p.m. See OR 27, part 2, p. 608.
75. Pfanz, *Gettysburg*, 167, 172, and 500; Wilkinson and Woodworth, *Scythe*, 235; Bohannon, "Promoted," 260; Simpson, "Hood," 66. See also Robert K. Krick, "'If Longstreet... Says So, It is Most Likely Not True': James Longstreet and the Second Day at Gettysburg," in Gary W. Gallagher, ed., *The Second Day at Gettysburg: Essays on Confederate and Union Leadership* (Kent, OH: Kent State University Press, 1993), 57–86, as well as Longstreet, *Manassas*, 367–68, for more on Hood's argument to shift farther to the right.
76. "Gettysburg Recollections," John Cheves Haskell Papers, Duke.
77. Fremantle, *Three*, 282; Pfanz, *Gettysburg*, 178; West, *Texan*, 96; OR, 27, part 2, p. 364.
78. Hood, *Advance*, 60; Simpson, "Hood," 66–67.
79. Cutrer, *Longstreet's*, 117; Woodworth, *Davis*, 246.
80. Major Joseph B. Cumming Recollections, SHC.
81. Timothy H. Donovan and others, *The American Civil War* (Wayne, NJ: Avery Publishing Group, 1987), 178.
82. Nathaniel C. Hughes, ed., *Liddell's Record: St. John Richardson Liddell, Brigadier General CSA Staff Officer and Brigade Commander, Army of Tennessee* (Dayton, OH: Morningside, 1985), 141; R. M. Gray Reminiscence Papers, SHC; Bohannon, "Promoted," 261. See also Thomas Lawrence Connelly, *Autumn of Glory: The Army of Tennessee, 1862–1865* (Baton Rouge: Louisiana State University Press, 1971), 201–2; OR 30, part 2, p. 32.

83. McMurry, *Hood*, 77; Woodworth, *Davis*, 236; Major Joseph B. Cumming Recollections, SHC; "October 12, 1863, North Carolinians at Chickamauga," Alphonso Avery Papers, SHC.
84. Bohannon, "Promoted," 261; John Cheves Haskell, *The Haskell Memoirs*, ed. Gilbert E. Govan and James Livingood (New York: G.P. Putnam's Sons, 1960), 49; McMurry, *Hood*, 77.
85. Hood, *Advance*, 64–65.
86. Longstreet, *Manassas*, 448; Lee, *Wartime Papers*, 603 and 605; OR 29, part 2, 743 and 749; Simpson, "Hood," 67. See also John Bowers, *Chickamauga and Chattanooga: The Battles that Doomed the Confederacy* (New York: Avon Books, 1994), 130.
87. William Button Bailey Memoir, TU; Jones quoted in Coffey, *Hood*, 13–14; Obituary reprinted in *The American Annual Cyclopedia and Register of Important Events of the Year 1863* (New York: D. Appleton and Co., 1864), 3:717–18.
88. Jones quoted in Coffey, *Hood*, 13–14; *New Orleans Daily Picayune*, October 6, 1863; Robert Garlick Hill Kean, *Inside the Confederate Government: The Diary of Robert Garlick Hill Kean*, ed. Edward Younger (Baton Rouge: Louisiana State University Press, 1957), 106; OR, 29, part 2, p. 753; OR 30, part 2, p. 35.
89. McMurry, *Hood*, 79.
90. Michael Bedout Chesson and Leslie Jean Roberts, eds., *Exile in Richmond: The Confederate Journal of Henri Garidel* (Charlottesville: University Press of Virginia, 2001), 86.
91. Hood, *Advance*, 66–67; *New Orleans Daily Picayune*, January 8, 1874.
92. *Huntsville Daily Confederate*, October 17, 1863; *Atlanta Daily Appeal*, November 4, 1863.
93. McMurry, *Hood*, 79–80.
94. *New Orleans Daily Picayune*, November 16, 1863; Simpson, "Hood," 67.

Chapter 4

1. Mary Chesnut, *A Diary from Dixie* (Boston: Houghton Mifflin Co., 1949), 332.
2. One of the most recent works on the social ramifications of amputation is Frances Clarke, " 'Honorable Scars': Northern Amputees and the Meaning of Civil War Injuries," in Paul A. Cimbala and Randall M. Miller, eds., *Union Soldiers and the Northern Home Front: Wartime Experiences, Postwar Adjustments* (New York: Fordham University Press, 2002). For more on the experience of amputation, see Laurann Figg and Jane Farrell-Beck, "Amputation in the Civil War: Physical and Social Dimensions," *Journal of the History of Medicine and Allied Sciences* 48, no. 4 (1993): 454–75, as well as Ansley Herring Wegner, *Phantom Pain: North Carolina's Artificial-Limbs Program for Confederate Veterans* (Raleigh: Office of Archives and History, North Carolina Department of Cultural Resources, 2004). Wegner mostly offers a brief discussion of the artificial limbs programs in the South as well as offering a listing of all Confederate veterans in North Carolina who applied for an artificial limb in the postwar era. See Lawrence W. Friedmann, *The Psychological Rehabilitation of the Amputee* (Springfield, IL: Charles C. Thomas, 1978), 20, 32, and 43. Although his study looks at modern notions of amputation, Friedmann argues that amputees worried about how their family and friends would view them, as they faced a "loss of self-esteem, loss of completeness of body image, loss of respect for one's appearance and functional ability,

and inability to relate to oneself, one's spouse and one's family, friends and employer in a normal manner." For a look at historians who have asserted that Hood used drugs or alcohol to command, based on his injuries, see McDonough and Connelly, *Five,* 37 and 50; McDonough, *Nashville,* 52 and 76; Bailey, *Chessboard,* 44, 71–72, and 87; and Sword, *Embrace,* 439. For a discussion on the feminizing effects of amputation, see Valerie DeBrava, "The Offending Hand of War in Harper's Weekly" *American Periodicals* 11 (2001): 49–64. Of note, the correspondences of Hood's surgeons have never been located, pointing out the importance of establishing a framework on Southern amputation to fully understand Hood's life and the memory of his life. A notion of amputation causing emasculation seems based on a post–World War I analysis, which saw amputation as having a "feminizing" effect on the male body. For a discussion of how amputation further equated feminization, see Erin O'Connor, "'Fractious of Men': Engendering Amputation in Victorian Culture," *Comparative Studies in Society and History* 39 (October 1997): 744–47, and Lisa Herschbach, "Prosthetic Reconstructions: Making the Industry, Remaking the Body, Modeling the Nation," *History Workshop Journal* 44 (Autumn 1997): 24–35.

3. For more on how the image of the whole man equated manhood, see Greenberg, *Honor,* 3; Gail Bederman, *Manliness and Civilization: A Cultural History of Gender and Race in the United States, 1880–1917* (Chicago: University of Chicago Press, 1995), 5–8 and 11; E. Anthony Rotundo, *American Manhood: Transformations in Masculinity from the Revolution to the Modern Era* (New York: Basic Books, 1993), 233–34; and Mosse, *Image,* 27–28.

4. See Greenberg, *Honor,* 3; Bederman, *Manliness,* 5–8 and 11; Rotundo, *Manhood,* 233–34. Rotundo sees manhood as undergoing a transformation from a communal ideal to a self-made manhood, with values attained from family and society. For many boys, the father was away, placing a heightened emphasis on the mother to build a lasting bond with her son and, eventually instill characteristics of love and moral suasion, resulting in a strong conscience. The mother provided advice against such things as liquor, sex, and gambling, as well as the sins of selfishness, envy, and greed. For more on honor, see Wyatt-Brown, *Southern Honor,* 34–36, 133–34, 144–59, and 164–70. See also Laura F. Edwards, *Gendered Strife and Confusion: The Political Culture of Reconstruction* (Urbana: University of Illinois Press, 1997); Dailey, *Before.* For information on the Union experience, see Clarke, "Scars," 361–94, quoted 365–68, 379, 381–83, and 394. Clarke notes that of the 2.2 million Union soldiers in the service, 21,753 survived amputation of a limb. Because of prewar notions of poverty and the misfortunate, northerners took up the gauntlet to only help the soldiers help themselves. Clarke also points out that although amputated, Northern soldiers remained in the field of battle and continually sought to fight, against all odds. By enduring the pain and relentless anguish of the amputation experience, men proved themselves men just by surviving. Northerners were also further aided by a relatively quick disbanding of the army at the conclusion of war, which allowed an affirmation of manhood in terms of the war experience ending on a high, masculine note (the self-disciplined nature).

5. Sarah A. Dorsey, *Recollections of Henry Watkins Allen* (New Orleans: M. Doolady, 1866), 74, 144–47. For a discussion of the biographical details of his medical history, see Jack D. Welsh, *Medical Histories of Confederate Generals* (Kent, OH: Kent State University Press, 1995), 4–5.

6. For more on scars and the possible ramification of injuries on notions of honor, see Elliot J. Gorn, "'Gouge and Bite, Pull Hair and Scratch': The Social Significance of Fighting in the Southern Backcountry," *American Historical Review* 90, no. 1, supplement (February 1985): 18–43; Daphne Frick, "Soldiers with Empty Sleeves: The Minié Ball and Civil War Medicine," *Proceedings and Papers of the Georgia Association of Historians* 14 (1993): 48; Wyndham B. Blanton, *Medicine in Virginia in the Nineteenth Century* (Richmond, VA: Garrett and Massie, 1933), 286; Estelle Brodman and Elizabeth B. Carrick, "American Military Medicine in the Mid-Nineteenth Century: The Experience of Alexander H. Hoff, M.D," *Bulletin of the History of Medicine* 64, no. 1 (1990): 63–78.

7. Joseph K. Barnes, ed., *The Medical and Surgical History of the Civil War* (Wilmington, NC: Broadfoot Publishing Co., 1991), 11:339; Wegner, *Pain,* ix; The total number of Confederate amputations as an estimate is found in Dixon Wecter, *When Johnny Comes Marching Home* (Cambridge, MA: Houghton Mifflin Co., 1944), 209; The 1861–62 figures are from Joseph K. Barnes, *The Medical and Surgical History of the Civil War* (Wilmington, NC: Broadfoot Publishing Co., 1991), 5:30; Joseph K. Barnes, *The Medical and Surgical History of the Civil War* (Wilmington, NC: Broadfoot Publishing Co., 1991), 12:880 offers the statistics on severe amputation cases; Blanton, *Medicine,* 286, offers the statistics during the Richmond campaign. See also H. H. Cunningham, *Doctors in Gray: The Confederate Medical Service* (Baton Rouge: Louisiana State University Press, 1958), 222–29.

8. James M. Greiner, Janet L. Coryell, and James R. Smither, eds., *A Surgeon's Civil War: The Letters and Diary of Daniel M. Holt, M.D.* (Kent, OH: Kent State University Press, 1994), 37n27; Wilkinson and Woodworth, *Scythe,* 89–90.

9. G. M. B. Maughs, "Thoughts on Surgery, Operations and Conservative, suggested by a visit to the Battlefield and Hospital of the Army of Tennessee," in *Confederate States Medical and Surgical Journal* (Metuchen, NJ: Scarecrow Press, 1976), 130.

10. F. Sorrel, "Gun Shot Wounds—Army of Northern Virginia," in *Confederate States Medical and Surgical Journal* (Metuchen, NJ: Scarecrow Press, 1976), 153–54.

11. Hutson Papers, SHC, available at http://www.unc.edu/lib/mssinv/exhibits/civilwar/hutsonpg.html; Sam R. Watkins, *Co. Aytch: A Side Show of the Big Show* (Wilmington, NC: Broadfoot Publishing Co., 1994), 153–54. Also see Stuart W. Sanders, "The Bishop's Nephew." *Civil War Times Illustrated* 40, no. 1 (2001): 24–30 and 56–60.

12. For a discussion of notions of honor within officer culture or southern society, see Wyatt-Brown, *Southern Honor,* 48–49; Greenberg, *Honor,* 3; Bederman, *Manliness,* 5–8 and 11, and Rotundo, *American Manhood,* 233–34; Anni P. Baker, "Daughters of Mars: Officers' Wives and Military Culture on the American Frontier," *The Historian* 67, no. 1 (Spring 2005): 23; James McPherson, *For Cause and Comrades: Why Men Fought in the Civil War* (New York: Oxford University Press, 1997), 15–16, 80, and 137; Jennifer R. Green, "'Stout Chaps Who Can Bear the Distress': Young Men in Antebellum Military Academies," in Friend and Glover, *Manhood,* 174–76 and 182. There are several examples of Confederate officers rejecting amputation. See Eugene Ferris Collection, University of Mississippi Archives (UM); M. D. L. Stephens Manuscript, UM; McWhiney and Jamieson, *Attack;* Wilkinson and Woodworth, *Scythe,* 90–91; Frank R. Freemon, *Gangrene and Glory: Medical Care*

during the American Civil War (Cranbury, NJ: Associated University Presses, 1998), 157; William A. Fletcher, *Rebel Private: Front and Rear, Memoirs of a Confederate Soldier* (New York: Meridian, 1997), 102–6; Welsh, *Medical,* 15–16; Sam Davis Elliott, ed., *Dr. Quintard, Chaplain in C.S.A. and 2nd Bishop of Tennessee: The Memoir and Civil War Diary of Charles Todd Quintard* (Baton Rouge: Louisiana State University Press, 2003), 79; Joseph K. Barnes, ed., *The Medical and Surgical History of the Civil War* (Wilmington, NC: Broadfoot Publishing Co., 1991), 11:382–83. This volume was formerly part of volume 2 of the original *The Medical and Surgical History of the War of the Rebellion, 1861–65.*

13. Freemon, *Gangrene,* 81–82.
14. Thomas Jackson Arnold, *Early Life and Letters of General Thomas J. Jackson* (Chicago: Fleming H. Revell Co., 1916), 349 and 355; Sears, *Chancellorsville,* 446–47; Wyndham B. Blanton, *Medicine in Virginia in the Nineteenth Century* (Richmond, VA: Garrett and Massie, 1933), 314.
15. Wecter, *Johnny,* 188.
16. Donald C. Pfanz, *Richard S. Ewell: A Soldier's Life* (Chapel Hill: University of North Carolina Press, 1998), 257–58; Welsh, *Medical,* 64; Blanton, *Medicine,* 315.
17. Pfanz, *Ewell,* 261–65.
18. Bertram Wyatt-Brown, *The Shaping of Southern Culture: Honor, Grace, and War, 1760s–1880s* (Chapel Hill: University of North Carolina Press, 2001), 250–51; Drew Gilpin Faust, "Altars of Sacrifice: Confederate Women and the Narrative of War," in Catherine Clinton and Nina Silber, eds., *Divided Houses: Gender and the Civil War* (New York: Oxford University Press, 1992), 175; Victoria Bynum, *Unruly Women: The Politics of Social and Sexual Control in the Old South* (Chapel Hill: University of North Carolina Press, 1992), 132; George Rable, "'Missing in Action': Women of the Confederacy," in Clinton and Silber, *Divided,* 139.
19. LeeAnn Whites, "'Stand by Your Man': The Ladies Memorial Association and the Reconstruction of Southern White Manhood," in Christie Anne Farman, ed., *Women of the American South: A Multicultural Reader* (New York: New York University Press, 1997), 133–49. In gender theory, the image of the "Sturdy Oak" for men means that they are able to handle tasks that seem impossible and do so with confidence and control of the situation. For more on the "Sturdy Oak," see Lindsey, *Gender,* 227. See also Berry, *Man,* 83–160.
20. Laura F. Edwards offers a thorough discussion of gender and politics and how they pertain to the ideas of asserting honor in her work, *Gendered Strife,* 113–29. Edwards dispels the notion that only physique defined manhood, arguing that a man remained complete without a wife or home. For Confederate amputees to be complete, they needed to function as regularly as possible as an integral part and head of the household to maintain a sense of mastery. Also see Dailey, *Before,* 90–95; Drew Gilpin Faust, *Mothers of Invention: Women of the Slaveholding South in the American Civil War* (New York: Vintage Books, 1996), 106; W. L. Kennon, "A Tribute to the Womanhood of the Confederacy, 1934." *SMMSS* 77–73, UM; Janie Smith, located at http://www.rootsweb.com/~nccumber/janlet.htm. The sacrifices of women are also well documented in several works, including Rable, "Missing" and Faust, "Alters" in Clinton and Silber, *Houses,* 134–46 and 171–99.

21. McPherson, *Cause*, 137–38; "Letter from Evangeline to Will dated January 22, 1862," Crutcher-Shannon Papers, Eugene C. Barker Texas History Center, University of Texas at Austin.
22. Bynum, *Unruly*, 149; Elizabeth Fox-Genovese, *Within the Plantation Household: Black and White Women of the Old South* (Chapel Hill: University of North Carolina Press, 1988), 49.
23. "Letter from Evangeline"; also examine Faust, *Mothers* for more on the Confederate war experience for women in the South, as well as the previously noted Faust, "Altars," 171–99.
24. Lynda Lasswell Crist and others, eds., *The Papers of Jefferson Davis: Volume 11, September 1864–May 1865* (Baton Rouge: Louisiana State University Press, 2003), 62.
25. *New Orleans Daily Picayune*, January 15, 1871.
26. Pfanz, *Ewell*, 265; Douglas Southall Freeman, *Lee's Lieutenants: A Study in Command*, ed. Stephen W. Sears (New York: Scribner, 1998), 525–26.
27. Pfanz, *Ewell*, 265; Freeman, *Lee's*, 654–55.
28. Pfanz, *Ewell*, 429.
29. Ibid., 429–31.
30. Again, refer to Gorn, "Gouge, Bite."
31. Pfanz, *Ewell*, 429–31.
32. *Richmond Enquirer*, November 16, 1863.
33. Robertson, *Touched*, 56; O'Connor, *Hood*, 171.
34. Chesnut, *Diary*, 332.
35. Chesnut, *Diary*, 332; *Richmond Enquirer*, January 18, 1864; Hood, *Advance*, 67. Also see Brian Craig Miller, "So Strangely Misrepresented: Rethinking John Bell Hood and the Fight for Civil War Memory," master's thesis, University of Mississippi, 2002, 55–64.
36. Chesnut, *Diary*, 334–36.
37. Ibid., 337–38.
38. Eliot, *West*, 98; Hood, *Advance*, 67; Woodworth, *Davis*, 269.
39. Woodworth, *Davis*, 269; Chesnut, *Diary*, 368–69.
40. McMurry, *Hood*, 68; Mary Chesnut, *Mary Chesnut's Civil War*, ed. C. Vann Woodward (New Haven, CT: Yale University Press, 1981), 430–31; McMurry, *Hood*, 69.
41. Chesnut, *Civil War*, 443, 509–10, 559, and 565.
42. Chesnut, *Civil War*, 555; Chesnut, *Diary*, 370. For more, see McMurry, *Hood*, 82–84.
43. Kendra Lynne McDonald, "The Creation of History and Myth in Mary Boykin Miller Chesnut's Civil War Narrative," Ph.D. diss., The Ohio State University, 1996, 225; Chesnut, *Diary*, 374.
44. Woodworth, *Davis*, 269–70.
45. Chesnut, *Civil War*, 561–62; McMurry, *Hood*, 90–91.
46. Hood, *Advance*, 68.
47. James Grant Wilson and John Fiske, eds., *Cyclopedia of American Biography* (New York: D. Appleton and Co., 1888), 3:247; Chesnut, *Diary*, 326, 332, and 395.
48. Chesnut, *Diary*, 326, 332, and 395.

Chapter 5

Epigraph: Winkler, *Hood*, 37.

1. Lynda Lasswell Crist and others, eds., *The Papers of Jefferson Davis: Volume 10, October 1863–August 1864* (Baton Rouge: Louisiana State University Press, 1999), 26, 32, 137, and 225.
2. OR series 1, vol. 32, pp. 699, 763, 804, and 812; OR series 1, vol. 52, part 2, p. 624; McMurry, *Hood*, 95. See also OR series 1, vol. 38, part 5, p. 1021, and OR series 1, vol. 25, part 2, pp. 784–85.
3. "Letter to Wife, June 27, 1864," and "Letter to Wife, June 9, 1864," Champion Duke Papers, Duke; Bohannon, "Promoted," 264; Williamson, *Battalion*, 176; McMurry, *Hood*, 99. For an analysis on Johnston's mode of warfare, see John Derrick Fowler, "Mountaineers in Gray: The Story of the Nineteenth TN Volunteer Regiment, CSA," Ph.D. diss., University of Tennessee, Knoxville, 2000, 265.
4. Major Joseph B. Cumming Recollections, 71, SHC; Woodworth, *Davis*, 271; "June 10, 1864," Thomas Clayton Papers, SHC.
5. OR, series 1, vol. 32, part 3, pp. 606–7; Hood to Davis, March 7, 1864, Hood Papers, National Archives and Records Administration (NARA).
6. OR, series 1, vol. 32, part 3, pp. 606–8 and 781; "Confederate States of America Army, Department of Tennessee, Message of the President, Confederate Pamphlets #441," Duke; McMurry, *Hood*, 96–97; Castel, *Decision*, 103.
7. Major Joseph B. Cumming Recollections, 54, SHC; McMurry, *Hood*, 101–2.
8. Thomas Robson Hay, "The Davis-Hood-Johnston Controversy of 1864," *Mississippi Valley Historical Review* 11, no. 1 (June 1924): 60.
9. Glenn Robins, *The Bishop of the Old South: The Ministry and Civil War Legacy of Leonidas Polk* (Macon, GA: Mercer University Press, 2006), 189; Castel, *Decision*, 148; Sam Davis Elliott, ed., *Doctor Quintard, Chaplain C.S.A. and Second Bishop of Tennessee: The Memoir and Civil War Diary of Charles Todd Quintard* (Baton Rouge: Louisiana State University Press, 2003), 84.
10. Castel, *Decision*, 58 and 164; "April 25, 1864," Clayton Family Papers, SHC.
11. OR, series 1, vol. 32, part 3, p. 575. More detailed orders can be found on p. 593 of the same volume.
12. Castel, *Decision*, 164; "May 14, 1864," Kinloch Falconer Collection, UM; McMurry, *Hood*, 105. For more on the Army of Tennessee at Atlanta in May, see Castel, *Decision*, 121–254.
13. McMurry, *Hood*, 106–7.
14. Davis, *Atlanta*, 26 and 55; Major Joseph B. Cumming Recollections, 55–56, SHC; McPherson, *Battle*, 747; Woodworth, *Davis*, 276; "May 22, 1864," Burton Butler Papers, UM.
15. Davis, *Atlanta*, 56.
16. Eliot, *West*, 100–101; Castel, *Decision*, 211.
17. OR series 1, vol. 38, part 3, pp. 705 and 724; *Coffey*, 45–46; Davis, *Atlanta*, 67; McMurry, *Hood*, 110.
18. Castel, *Decision*, 242–43.
19. "May 31, 1864" and "June 5, 1864," Sidney Champion Papers, Duke; Major Joseph B. Cumming Recollections, 59, SHC.

20. McMurry, *Hood*, 111; Wynne, *Trip*, 121; Davis, *Atlanta*, 82–83; Castel, *Decision*, 295.
21. Lockwood Collection, UM; Castel, *Decision*, 319. For more on the Atlanta campaign in June 1864, see Castel, *Decision*, 255–326; 309–26 covers the engagement at Kennesaw Mountain.
22. McMurry, *Hood*, 116.
23. "July 3, 1864," Juanita Brown Collection, UM; Hay, "Davis," 60–62.
24. Richard McMurry, *Atlanta 1864: Last Chance for the Confederacy* (Lincoln: University of Nebraska Press, 2000), 140; F. Jay Taylor, ed., *Reluctant Rebel: The Secret Diary of Robert Patrick, 1861–1865* (Baton Rouge: Louisiana State University Press, 1959), 194–95. Interestingly, the *New York Times* reported that Bragg was the best man to command the army and was disliked, because he was a strict disciplinarian, by a group of young men who tended to do as they pleased. The report was reprinted in the *New Orleans Daily Picayune*, August 20, 1864.
25. "JB Hood to B Bragg 14 July 1864," Jefferson Davis Papers (TU); OR series 1, vol. 38, part 5, p. 880.
26. Crist and others, *Davis*, 10:523; Hay, *Davis*, 62–65; OR, series 1, Vol. 39, part 2, p. 713; McMurry, *Hood*, 120.
27. OR, series 1, vol. 51, part 2, p. 691; OR, series 1, vol. 52, part 2, p. 692; Davis, *Atlanta*, 104; Lee, *Wartime Papers*, 821; Eliot, *West*, 72.
28. Lee, *Wartime Papers*, 822. Also see Woodworth, *Davis*, 283, for more on the conversation between Lee and Davis.
29. "Confederate States of America Army, Department of Tennessee, Message of the President, Confederate Pamphlets #441," Duke.
30. Hay, *Davis*, 65; "Ecuador Recollections, 1900," Samuel Wragg Ferguson Papers, Duke; William Pettis Buck, "Headquarters' Staff: Cleburne's Division, Hardee's Corps," in Mauriel Phillips Joslyn, ed., *A Meteor Shining Brightly: Essays on the Life and Career of Major General Patrick R. Cleburne* (Macon, GA: Mercer University Press, 2000), 73; OR series 1, vol. 38, part 5, p. 885.
31. OR series 1, vol. 38, part 5, p. 885; "July 18, 1864," Clayton Family Papers, SHC; Hood, *Advance*, 126; Bohannon, "Promoted," 269; Letter from Halsey Wigfall, August 7, 1864, Louis T. Wigfall Papers, LOC. For more on Johnston's removal, see Connelly, *Autumn*, 391–426.
32. Joseph Johnston, "Opposing Sherman's Advance to Atlanta," in Robert Underwood Johnson and Clarence Clough Buel, eds., *Battles and Leaders of the Civil War* (New York: Thomas Yoseloff, 1956), 4:274–75.
33. OR, series 1, vol. 38, part 5, pp. 887–89; Davis Telegram, July 18, 1864, Hood Papers, NARA; Crist and others, *Davis*, 10:539–40.
34. *New Orleans Daily Picayune*, July 26, 1864; OR series 1, vol. 38, part 5, p. 890; James Cooper Nisbet, *Four Years on the Firing Line* (Jackson, TN: McCowat-Mercer Press, 1963), 206.
35. *Charleston Mercury*, July 22, 1864.
36. Eliot, *West*, 108.
37. Ibid., 109.
38. Coffey, *Hood*, 56; Castel, *Decision*, 364; Telegram to Secretary of War Seddon, July 19, 1864, Hood Papers, NARA; McMurry, *Atlanta*, 144–45.
39. *James Palmer Diary*, Mississippi Department of History and Archives; copy of First Lt. John Henry Marsh letter to Chaplain Charles T. Quintard, July 26, 1864 (Duke),

courtesy of Carter House Archives, Franklin, Tennessee; Mary Miles Jones and Leslie Jones Martin, eds., *The Gentle Rebel: The Civil War Letters of William Harvey Berryhill, First Lieutenant, Company D, 43rd Regiment, MS Volunteers* (Yazoo City, MS: Sassafras Press, 1982), 57–58 and 71.

40. Noel Crowson and John V. Brogden, eds., *Bloody Banners and Barefoot Boys: A History of the 27th Regiment Alabama Infantry CSA: The Civil War Memoirs and Diary Entries of J. P. Cannon M.D.* (Shippensburg, PA: Burd Street Press, 1997), 83–84; *New York Herald*, September 11, 1864; Crabb, *Afire*, 230; Eliot, *West*, 110. For more reactions to the removal of Johnston, see William Pitt Chambers, *Blood and Sacrifice: The Civil War Journal of a Confederate Soldier*, ed. Richard A. Baumgartner (Huntington, WV: Blue Acorn Press, 1994), 156, and Samuel Foster, *One of Cleburne's Command: The Civil War Reminiscence and Diary of Capt. Samuel T. Foster, Granbury's Texas Brigade, C.S.A.*, ed. Norman Brown (Austin: University of Texas Press, 1980), 105–7, 129.

41. Taylor, *Rebel*, 197.

42. James M. McCaffrey, *This Band of Heroes: Granbury's Texas Brigade, C.S.A.* (Austin, TX: Eakin Press, 1985), 114; "July 16, 1864," Sidney Champion Papers, Duke; Mark K. Christ, ed., *Getting Used to Being Shot At: The Spence Family Civil War Letters* (Fayetteville: University of Arkansas Press, 2002), 97–98 and 100.

43. Major Joseph B. Cumming Recollections, 60, SHC; *Richmond Dispatch*, August 3, 1864; "July 31, 1864," John Snow Papers, Duke; Chesson and Roberts, *Exile*, 182.

44. OR series 1, vol. 38, part 5, p. 211; Hay, "Davis," 71–72; *History*, 3; John F. Marszalek, *Sherman: A Soldier's Passion for Order* (New York: Vintage Books, 1993), 276–77; McDonough, *Nashville*, 6; William T. Sherman, "The Grand Strategy of the Last Year of the War," in Johnson and Buel, *Battles*, 253. For more on the reaction to Hood's ability to attack Sherman, see Davis, *Atlanta*, 117 and 131 and the *Charleston Mercury*, July 20, 1864.

45. *Annie Jeter Carmouche Memoirs*, Tulane; Crist and others, *Davis*, 10:547; Castel, *Decision*, 395.

46. OR series 1, vol. 38, part 5, p. 889; *New Orleans Daily Picayune*, July 26, 1864; Hood, *Advance*, 162.

47. "July 27, 1864," Charles Dean Collection, UM; Crabb, *Afire*, 229; Woodworth, *Davis*, 286; Joseph R. Reinhart, ed., *Two Germans in the Civil War: The Diary of John Daeuble and the Letters of Gottfried Rentschler, 6th Kentucky Volunteer Infantry* (Knoxville: University of Tennessee Press, 2004), 145; Winkler, *Hood*, 30; Castel, *Decision*, 368–69.

48. Castel, *Decision*, 369–80, quoted on page 380; OR series 1, vol. 38, part 2, p. 140.

49. Castel, *Decision*, 380–81; Gustavus W. Smith, "The Georgia Militia About Atlanta," in Johnson and Buel, *Battles*, 334; "July 1864," William Penn Davis Papers, Duke; Woodworth, *Davis*, 287; Castel, *Decision*, 382–83.

50. Bohannon, "Promoted," 249; R. M. Gray Reminiscences, 45, SHC; James Palmer Diary, Mississippi Department of History and Archives. For more on July 21, see Castel, *Decision*, 383–94.

51. Major Joseph B. Cumming Recollections, 63, SHC; John W. Fuller, "A Terrible Day: The Battle of Atlanta, July 22, 1864," in Peter Cozzens, ed., *Battles and Leaders of the Civil War* (Urbana: University of Illinois Press, 2002), 5:546; McMurry, *Hood*, 131.

52. *Charleston Mercury*, July 25, 1864; Davis, *Atlanta*, 138; Daniel E. Sutherland, ed., *A Very Violent Rebel: The Civil War Diary of Ellen Renshaw House* (Knoxville: University

of Tennessee Press, 1996), 136; Woodworth, *Davis*, 287. For more on the military details at Bald Hill, see Castel, *Decision*, 395–410. "July 22, 1864," Richard Wharton Papers, SHC; Castel, *Decision*, 410.
53. Chesson and Roberts, *Exile*, 184; *A Short History*, 5; Castel, *Decision*, 412.
54. Hood, *Advance*, 182.
55. Ibid.
56. OR series 1, vol. 38, part 5, p. 909; Castel, *Decision*, 422–23.
57. Woodworth, *Davis*, 287–88; Castel, *Decision*, 434 and 450. For more on the Battle at Ezra Church, see Castel, *Decision*, 424–36.
58. Kean, *Inside*, 168; Davis, *Atlanta*, 147; Crowson and Brogden, *Bloody*, 88.
59. Crist and others, *Davis*, 10:583 and 586; OR series 1, vol. 38, part 5, p. 946; For more on the role of the cavalry around Atlanta, see Castel, *Decision*, 450–52, and "Letter to Jennie, Sept. 3, 1864," Duke Benham Papers, Duke.
60. Castel, *Decision*, 482–83.
61. OR series 1, vol. 38, part 5, p. 965; Castel, *Decision*, 483; Davis, *Atlanta*, 157–58; OR series 1, vol. 38, part 5, p. 9.
62. Castel, *Decision*, 488. More reaction on what the shelling did to the citizens of Atlanta can be found at "Gideon Viars to sister Mary," Viars Family Papers, Filson.
63. Castel, *Decision*, 483; McMurry, *Hood*, 139.
64. Davis, *Atlanta*, 160–62, 165, and 172; Castel, *Decision*, 484.
65. "August 24, 1864," William Bowden Civil War Letter, UM; McMurry, *Hood*, 144–47.
66. OR series 1, vol. 38, part 5, p. 1006; McMurry, *Hood*, 148; Castel, *Decision*, 498 and 509.
67. "McCaffrey, *Band*, 124. McMurry, *Hood*, 149; OR, series 1, vol. 51, part 2, p. 730; OR series 1, vol. 43, part 1, p. 953; OR series 1, vol. 38, part 5, p. 776. For more on Jonesboro see Castel, *Decision*, 509–22. For more on the fall of Atlanta, see Castel, *Decision*, 522–29.
68. Taylor, *Rebel*, 205; "Letter to Jennie, Sept. 3, 1864," Duke Benham Papers, Duke.
69. Foster, *Cleburne's*, 151. For more on the reaction to the fall of Atlanta from Sherman and the Union army, see Donovan, *American*, 212; "Letter to Jennie, Sept. 3, 1864," Duke Benham Papers, Duke.
70. Crowson and Brogden, *Bloody*, 94; Chambers, *Blood*, 168.
71. Cutrer, *Aide*, 134–35.
72. Ibid., 140.
73. Gustavus W. Smith, "The Georgia Militia About Atlanta," in Johnson and Buel, *Battles*, 335.
74. "September 26, 1864," Juanita Brown Collection, UM; Winfield Scott Featherson Collection, UM.
75. *Charleston Mercury*, September 6, 1864.
76. Crist and others, *Davis*, 11:14–15. For more on Hardee, see Castel, *Decision*, 536–39.
77. Frank Vandiver, "General Hood as Logistician." *Military Affairs* 16, no. 1 (Spring 1952): 3–5; G. P. Hardwick, "Sherman's Campaign," Filson.

Chapter 6

Epigraphs: R. M. Gray Reminiscence Papers, 66, SHC; Eliot, *West,* 112.
1. Christ, *Shot,* 117.
2. Sherman, *Memoir,* 486–87.
3. Ibid., 487.
4. Ibid., 488.
5. Ibid., 488–89.
6. Ibid., 489–90.
7. Ibid., 490–91.
8. Ibid., 492.
9. Ibid., 496.
10. "September 16, 1864" and "September 19, 1864," Sarah Louis Wadley Papers, SHC.
11. *New Orleans Daily Picayune,* September 21, 1864; Jefferson Davis, *His Letters, Papers and Speeches,* ed. Dunbar Rowland (Jackson: Mississippi Department of Archives and History, 1923), 6:331; OR series 1, vol. 39, part 2, p. 826.
12. Kean, *Inside,* 175; Marszalek, *Sherman,* 290–93. See also Archer, *Command,* 209.
13. OR, series 1, vol. 39, part 1, p. 612; *New Orleans Daily Picayune,* October 12, 1864; Sword, *Southern,* 249. For more on all of Hood's Tennessee campaign, see Hay, *Tennessee.*
14. "Letter to Sister October 4, 1864," George Phifer Erwin Papers, SHC; Ella Gertrude Clanton Thomas, *The Secret Eye: The Journal of Ella Gertrude Clanton Thomas: 1848–1 880,* ed. Virginia Ingraham Burr (Chapel Hill: University of North Carolina Press, 1990), 239 and 244; Ronald H. Moseley, ed., *The Stilwell Letters: A Georgian in Longstreet's Corps, Army of Northern Virginia* (Macon, GA: Mercer University Press, 2002), 286; Jeffrey C. Lowe and Sam Hodges, ed., *Letters to Amanda: The Civil War Letters of Marion Hill Fitzpatrick, Army of Northern Virginia* (Macon, GA: Mercer University Press, 1998), 173.
15. Civil War Diary of Rev. Jesse L. Henderson, 1844–1940, UM; H. Grady Howell Jr., *To Live and Die in Dixie: A History of the 3rd Regiment MS Volunteer Infantry, CSA* (Jackson, MS: Chickasaw Bayou Press, 1991), 355; *New Orleans Daily Picayune,* October 27, 1864; Christ, *Shot,* 108–9 and 111; Arthur E. Green, *Southerners at War: The 38th Alabama Infantry Volunteers* (Shippensburg, PA: Burd Street Press, 1999), 24; OR, series 1, vol. 39, part 2, pp. 860–65.
16. Castel, *Decision,* 551. Davis offered a similar speech in Greensboro, North Carolina, on October 5, 1864. See Crist and others, *Davis,* 11:91–92.
17. *New Orleans Daily Picayune,* October 1, 1864; Chesson and Roberts, *Exile,* 216.
18. McCaffrey, *Band,* 127; Shoup Diary, September 21, 1864, Hood Papers, NARA; Woodworth, *Davis,* 291; Chambers, *Blood,* 170.
19. "Jefferson Davis to JB Hood, September 28, 1864," Jefferson Davis Papers, TU.
20. Woodworth, *Davis,* 263; *Charleston Mercury,* August 20, 1864; *New Orleans Daily Picayune,* October 1, 1864.
21. McMurry, *Hood,* 152–53; McDonough, *Nashville,* 26.
22. Green, *Southerners,* 29; *New York Herald,* October 19, 1864; Crist and others, *Davis,* 11:71; Jefferson Davis, *His Letters, Papers and Speeches,* 6:345.
23. OR, series 1, vol. 39, part 2, p. 879; Woodworth, *Davis,* 295; Crist and others, *Davis,* 11:71; McDonough, *Nashville,* 40.

24. OR, series 1, vol. 46, part 1, p. 37; vol. 36, part 1, p. 39.
25. Mary A. H. Gay, *Life in Dixie During the War* (Macon, GA: Mercer University Press, 2001), 187–88.
26. Joe and Lavon Ashley, eds., *Oh for Dixie! The Civil War Record and Diary of Captain William V. Davis, 30th MS Infantry, CSA* (Colorado Springs, CO: Standing Pine Press, 2001), 51; "November 6, 1864," George Phifer Erwin Papers, SHC; John R. Lundberg, *The Finishing Stroke: Texans in the 1864 Tennessee Campaign* (Abilene, TX: McWhiney Foundation Press, 2002), 62; Jones, *Gentle*, 104.
27. OR series 1, vol. 39, part 1, pp. 718, 732, and 753; Hood, *Advance*, 242 and 258.
28. OR, series 1, vol. 39, part 1, pp. 796–97; Nathaniel Cheairs Hughes Jr., *Brigadier General Tyree H. Bell, C.S.A.: Forrest's Fighting Lieutenant* (Knoxville: University of Tennessee Press, 2004), 190; *Charleston Mercury*, October 28, 1864.
29. Taylor, *Rebel*, 232; "Letter to Wife, Oct. 13, 1864," Champion Duke Papers, Duke; Bailey, *Chessboard*, 25; Lundberg, *Finishing*, 69.
30. OR, series 1, vol. 39, part 3, p. 879; Cubbison, "Hood," 62–63.
31. Donovan, *American*, 219; *Charleston Mercury*, October 19, 1864; *Charleston Mercury*, November 4, 1864; *Charleston Mercury*, October 31, 1864; *Charleston Mercury*, December 14, 1864; Archer, *Command*, 213. Confederate President Jefferson Davis offered military advice on how Hood could actually strike at Sherman's forces first before maneuvering toward the Ohio River. See Crist and others, *Davis*, 11:145.
32. Hughes, *Bell*, 189–90; OR, series 1, vol. 39, part 3, p. 913; OR series 1, vol. 45, part 1, p. 1215; "November 28, 1864," Confederate States of America Archives, Army of Tennessee, Duke; Woodworth, *Davis*, 298; Donovan, *American*, 219; Elliott, *Doctor*, 95.
33. OR series 1, vol. 45, part 1, p. 1236.
34. Sam Davis Elliott, *Soldier of Tennessee: General Alexander P. Stewart and the Civil War in the West* (Baton Rouge: Louisiana State University Press, 1999), 228–32. Also see B. F. Cheatham, "General Cheatham at Spring Hill," in Johnson and Buel, *Battles*, 438–39; Woodworth, *Davis*, 299; OR series 1, vol. 45, part 1, pp. 657–58.
35. McDonough, *Nashville*, 72–73, 82, and 94. OR series 1, vol. 45, part 1, p. 713, part 2, p. 659; Crowson and Brogden, *Bloody*, 98. For more on Spring Hill, see McDonough and Connelly, *Five*, 36–59.
36. McDonough, *Nashville*, 75–77; Cubbison, "Hood," 70–71; David E. Roth, "The Mysteries of Spring Hill, Tennessee," *Blue and Gray Magazine* 2, no. 2 (October–November 1984): 21–33.
37. "HR Moore to Smith Lipscomb, November 29, 1864," Lipscomb Family Papers, SHC; Hood, *Advance*, 291; Woodworth, *Davis*, 300; Winkler, *Hood*, 29; Cubbison, "Hood," 71. For more on the preparation for battle, see McDonough, *Nashville*, 93–98.
38. McMurry, *Hood*, 175; Thomas Y. Cartwright, "Franklin: The Valley of Death," in Joslyn, *Meteor*, 173.
39. Fowler, "Mountaineers in Gray," 287–88 and 293; Lundberg, *Finishing*, 92–93. For more on the Battle of Franklin, see a Confederate perspective in the *Charleston Mercury*, January 7, 1865; McDonough and Connelly, *Five*, 92–123.
40. Green, *Southerners*, 32; David R. Logsdon, ed., *Eyewitnesses at the Battle of Franklin* (Nashville, TN: Kettle Mill Press, 2000), 41; Hughes, *Bell*, 202.
41. *Daily Morning Chronicle* (Washington, DC), November 3, 1865; OR series 1, vol. 45, part 1, p. 654; Logsdon, *Eyewitnesses*, 49.

42. M. D. L. Stephens manuscript, UM.
43. Thomas W. Cutrer, ed., *Oh, What a Loansome Time I Had: The Civil War Letters of Major William Morel Moxley, Eighteenth Alabama Infantry, and Emily Beck Moxley* (Tuscaloosa: University of Alabama Press, 2002), 141; OR series 1, vol. 45, part 1, p. 654; *Charleston Mercury*, December 17, 1864; "Letter to Seddon," John Bell Hood Papers, Duke; Hood, *Advance*, 296. For more on the battle at Franklin, see McDonough, *Nashville*, 99–112; Sword, *Embrace*, 177–244.
44. Edward Porter Alexander, *Fighting for the Confederacy: The Personal Recollections of Gen. Edward Porter Alexander*, ed. Gary W. Gallagher (Chapel Hill: University of North Carolina Press, 1989), 498–99.
45. Jones, *Gentle*, 124; Logsdon, *Eyewitness*, 83–84.
46. Lundberg, *Finishing*, 100; Logsdon, *Eyewitness*, 83–84. For more on the fallout from the battle, see McDonough and Connelly, *Five*, 124–40; Nathaniel Cheairs Hughes Jr., ed., *The Civil War Memoir of Philip Daingerfield Stephenson, D.D.: Private, Company K, 13th Arkansas Volunteer Infantry, Loader, Piece No. 4, 5th Company, Washington Artillery, Army of Tennessee, CSA* (Baton Rouge: Louisiana State University Press, 1995), 289.
47. Foster, *Cleburne's*, 151. For more reaction to Franklin, see McDonough, *Nashville*, 111; Sword, *Embrace*, 245–57.
48. Howell Jr., *Live and Die*, 388–89; Wynne, *Trip*, 145; Lundberg, *Finishing*, 98 and 103.
49. Woodworth, *Davis*, 294; McDonough, *Nashville*, 136; Cincinnati article reprinted in *New Orleans Daily Picayune*, December 9, 1864; Wynne, *Trip*, 144.
50. Major Joseph B. Cumming Recollections, 74, SHC; Sword, *Embrace*, 262; W. E. Beard, *The Battle of Nashville: The Limit of the Last Aggressive Movement of the Armies of the Confederacy, Hood's Grand Maneuver Designed to Prevent Sherman's March to the Sea, Fought in the Southern Suburbs of Nashville, December 15–16, 1864* (Nashville, TN: Nashville Industrial Bureau, 1913), 3; letter to Cornelia Wylie, December 14, 1864, Henry Clay Weaver Papers, LOC. For a good discussion on the mechanics of the battles of Franklin and Nashville, see Horn, *Decisive*, and editors, *The Battles for Franklin and Nashville* (Harrisburg, PA: Eastern Acorn Press, 1988).
51. McMurry, *Hood*, 178; *A Short History*, 12; *Charleston Mercury*, January 19, 1865; McDonough, *Nashville*, 136 and 141–43.
52. Beard, *Nashville*, 3; "December 13, 1865," Confederate States of America Archives, Army of Tennessee, Duke; McMurry, *Hood*, 177.
53. OR series 1, vol. 45, part 2, pp. 70, 80, 91, 111, and 143.
54. "Hood Telegram December 14, 1864 to Beauregard," William Asbury Whitaker Papers, SHC.
55. McCaffrey, *Band*, 144–45; McDonough, *Nashville*, 149 and 207–8; *New Orleans Daily Picayune*, December 27, 1864; Beard, *Nashville*, 7; McMurry, *Hood*, 179. For more on the opening action, see McDonough, *Nashville*, 180–83; Horn, *Nashville*, 73–107; Sword, *Embrace*, 331–91.
56. Major Joseph B. Cumming Recollections, 75, SHC; Beard, *Nashville*, 5–7.
57. Beard, *Nashville*, 8–9; Basil W. Duke Papers, SHC; "January 19, 1865," Gale and Polk Family Papers, SHC; Woodworth, *Davis*, 301. For more on Shy's Hill, see McDonough, *Nashville*, 252–53; Horn, *Nashville*, 108–53.

58. Beard, *Nashville*, 8–9; Henry Stone, "Repelling Hood's Invasion of Tennessee," in Johnson and Buel, *Battles*, 464; "December 27, 1864," Viars Family Papers, Filson; *Charleston Mercury*, December 31, 1864. The *Mercury* reprinted the *Charlottesville Chronicle* article, originally dated December 22, 1864; Fowler, "Mountaineers in Gray," 305–6. For more details on the Battle of Nashville, see McDonough, *Nashville*, 157–264.
59. Earl Schenck Miers, ed., *A Rebel War Clerk's Diary by John B. Jones* (New York: Sagamore Press, 1958), 463; McDonough, *Nashville*, 270; Elliott, *Doctor*, 108. For more on the debate on why Hood failed in the Tennessee campaign, see Bohannon, "Promoted," 249–50; Herman Hattaway, "The General Whom the President Elevated Too High: Davis and John Bell Hood," in Gabor S. Boritt, ed., *Jefferson Davis's Generals* (New York: Oxford University Press, 1999), 85; Woodworth, *Davis*, 303; *Daily Morning Chronicle* (Washington, DC), November 3, 1865; *New Orleans Daily Picayune*, October 4, 1864. The debate over Hood's demotion in Congress has been reprinted in the *Southern Historical Society Papers*, ed. Frank Vandiver, vol. 52 (Richmond, VA: Southern Historical Society, 1959), 21 and 283. See also McDonough, *Nashville*, 209–10. McDonough argues that Hood had been given a high rank "that called for abilities beyond his capacities." Hood, after the attacks at Nashville, had forced his army, according to McDonough, to a position of bad supplies and morale.
60. OR series 1, vol. 45, part 1, p. 656.
61. *New Orleans Daily Picayune*, August 31, 1879, morning edition.
62. Major Joseph B. Cumming Recollections, 80, SHC; Hay, *Tennessee*, 178; Horn, *Nashville*, 153.
63. "Letter to father, December 26, 1864," William B. G. Andrews Papers, Duke; Chesson and Roberts, *Exile*, 259 and 273; Ann K. Blomquist and Robert A. Taylor, eds., *This Cruel War: The Civil War Letters of Grant and Malinda Taylor, 1862–1865* (Macon, GA: Mercer University Press, 2000), 299 and 325.
64. Foster, *Cleburne's*, 170. Other blame can be found echoed from Howell Cobb, which can be located in Crist and others, *Davis*, 11:283.
65. Chambers, *Blood*, 191.
66. Thomas W. Cutrer and T. Michael Parrish, eds., *Brothers in Gray: The Civil War Letters of the Pierson Family* (Baton Rouge: Louisiana State University Press, 1997), 221–22. Of note, the editors of the volume have this letter dated January 11, 1864. Yet, the details of the letter, including the fall of Savannah and Hood's Tennessee campaign, reveal that the year should be 1865. The mistake originates from the Pierson Family Papers, January 14, 1864, Kuntz Collection, TU; "February 3, 1865," Sarah Louis Wadley Papers, SHC; Cutrer, *Aide*, 141.
67. Basil W. Duke Papers, SHC; Kean, *Inside*, 181 and 231.
68. Grant, *Memoirs*, 566–69; Sherman, *Memoirs*, 598; Horn, *Nashville*, 158.
69. James Phelan, *"For the good of the bleeding land": Being the text of a letter from James Phelan to Confederate President Jefferson Davis* (Louisville, KY: Contre Coup Press, 1999), 1, 9–13. Letter obtained from Filson.
70. Phelan, "Good," 13–17. Emphasized text is how it is emphasized in the letter.
71. *Charleston Mercury*, January 9, 1865; Crowson and Brogden, *Bloody*, 106.

72. *Montgomery Appeal* article reprinted in *New Orleans Daily Picayune,* January 6, 1865; Sutherland, *Violent,* 139 and 142.
73. Buell, *Warrior,* 410–11.
74. William George Pirtle Memoir, Filson.
75. "General Order No. 1, January 15, 1865," John Bell Hood Papers, Duke; Crist and others, *Davis,* 11:330; "Hood to Lee, January 15, 1865," Stephen D. Lee Papers, SHC.
76. OR series 1, vol. 51, part 2, pp. 808–9.
77. Jefferson Davis, *The Rise and Fall of the Confederate Government* (New York: D. Appleton and Co., 1881), 2:579; Taylor, *Rebel,* 248; Sword, *Embrace,* 432; OR series 1, vol. 45, part 2, p. 805.
78. Crist and others, *Davis,* 11:338 and 349; OR series 1, vol. 51, part 2, p. 1047.
79. Kate Stone, *Brokenburn: The Journal of Kate Stone, 1861–68,* ed. John Q. Anderson (Baton Rouge: Louisiana State University Press, 1995), 312–13; *New Orleans Daily Picayune,* January 17, 1865.
80. Hood initial report, January 16, 1865, Louis T. Wigfall Papers, LOC; OR series 1, vol. 38, part 3, p. 636; Symonds, *Johnston,* 340; McMurry, *Hood,* 185–86. The entire report appears on 628–36. The discussion of the Tennessee campaign appears in OR series 1, vol. 45, part 1, pp. 652–56.
81. OR series 1, vol. 38, part 3, pp. 637–38, 697, and 703; Hood to Johnston, April 4, 1865, Hood Papers, NARA, Hood to Cooper, April 5, 1865, Hood Papers, NARA; McMurry, *Hood,* 187–88.
82. OR series 1, vol. 45, part 1, pp. 646–51.
83. OR series 1, vol. 45, part 1, p. 651.
84. Unidentified newspaper editorial, March 1865, Louis T. Wigfall Papers, LOC.
85. Hay, *Tennessee,* 194; Crist and others, *Davis,* 11:449–50 and 489; McMurry, *Hood,* 188; Simpson, "Hood," 65; OR series 1, vol. 47, part 2, p. 698.
86. Crist and others, *Davis,* 11:248–49.

Chapter 7

Epigraph: Patterson, *Rebels,* 122.

1. Chesnut, *Diary,* 474.
2. Eric Dean presents a grim and realistic view of what happened to Civil War veterans once the shooting stopped. See his article, "We Will All Be Lost and Destroyed: Post Traumatic Stress Disorder and the Civil War," *Civil War History* 38 (June 1991): 138–53, for a better explanation. Also see his *Shook Over Hell: Post-Traumatic Stress, Vietnam, and the Civil War* (Cambridge, MA: Harvard University Press, 1997), 46–114.
3. Neal, *National,* 207. See also W. Scott Poole, *Never Surrender: Confederate Memory and Conservatism in the South Carolina Upcountry* (Athens: University of Georgia Press, 2004).
4. Neal, *National,* 3–7 and 202.
5. Faust, *Mothers,* 252.
6. Lasswell, *Rags,* 9; *New Orleans Daily Picayune,* June 6, 1865; McMurry, *Hood,* 192.

7. *San Antonio Herald* article reprinted in *New Orleans Daily Picayune,* July 22, 1865; McMurry, *Hood,* 193.
8. Letters to S. D. Lee, "November 29, 1865," Stephen D. Lee Papers, SHC.
9. Letters to S. D. Lee, "January 9, 1866" and "February 9, 1866," Stephen D. Lee Papers, SHC. Hood also received further correspondence in late 1865 from other Confederate soldiers and officers, including W. S. Featherston, S. G. Marshall, Taylor Beattie, and O. S. Holland, who provided military details to assist Hood in reconstructing his memory of the war. These letters are in the Hood Papers, NARA.
10. John H. Reagan, *Memoirs with Special Reference to Secession and the Civil War* (Austin, TX: Pemberton Press, 1968), 235.
11. For a history of New Orleans during the war, see John D. Winters, *The Civil War in Louisiana* (Baton Rouge: Louisiana State University Press, 1963); McPherson, *Battle,* 421–22; Shelby Foote, *The Civil War: A Narrative, Fort Sumter to Perryville* (New York: Vintage Books, 1986).
12. Winters, *War,* 404; *New Orleans Daily Picayune,* April 20, 1865, 4.
13. *New Orleans Daily Picayune,* March 30, 1873. Though beyond the scope of this study of the life of John Bell Hood, African Americans present another key group in New Orleans that personally dealt with memory construction in the postwar period. In many ways they came into conflict with the white vision of postwar memory constructed through the Lost Cause in New Orleans. The topic of another layer in memory construction would serve as a key piece of historical scholarship when understanding the complicated city of New Orleans. While no single work deals directly with the topic, some works do deal with race in New Orleans. For more, see Blight, *Race and Reunion;* James G. Hollandsworth Jr., *An Absolute Massacre: The New Orleans Race Riot of July 30, 1866* (Baton Rouge: Louisiana State University Press, 2001); Ted Tunnell, *Crucible of Reconstruction: War, Radicalism, and Race in Louisiana, 1862–1877* (Baton Rouge: Louisiana State University Press, 1984), and Alecia P. Long, *The Great Southern Babylon: Sex, Race and Respectability in New Orleans, 1865–1920* (Baton Rouge: Louisiana State University Press, 2004).
14. *New Orleans Daily Picayune,* June 10, 1866.
15. *New Orleans Daily Picayune,* November 14, 1865.
16. Wegner, *Phantom,* 34; *New Orleans Daily Picayune,* June 19, 1879, afternoon edition.
17. *New Orleans Daily Picayune,* May 10, 1866; *New Orleans Daily Picayune,* June 10, 1866; *New Orleans Daily Picayune,* December 16, 1866.
18. *New Orleans Daily Picayune,* May 9, 1868. It is no coincidence that the appeals for grave donations and poetry regularly appeared in the block of time surrounding Decoration Day festivities. For examples, see *New Orleans Daily Picayune,* February 15, 1867, and *New Orleans Daily Picayune,* June 20, 1869.
19. *New Orleans Daily Picayune,* April 5, 1877. For more on the role of Memorial Day, see Neff, *Honoring.*
20. *New Orleans Daily Picayune,* November 28, 1865; *New Orleans Daily Picayune,* January 6, 1877. For more on northern perceptions of southern women, see Silber, *Romance,* 26–28, 34–36, 111–12, 165–66, and 194–96.
21. *New Orleans Daily Picayune,* January 6, 1877.
22. Louisiana Historical Association (LHA): Memorial Associations Papers, TU; *New Orleans Daily Picayune,* May 13, 1866.

23. *New Orleans Daily Picayune,* July 22, 1866.
24. LHA Memorial Associations Papers, TU.
25. "Dedication Announcement," LHA Memorial Associations Papers, TU; *New Orleans Daily Picayune,* March 29, 1874.
26. *New Orleans Daily Picayune,* April 11, 1874.
27. *New Orleans Daily Picayune,* January 7, 1866.
28. *New York Herald* remarks reprinted in *New Orleans Daily Picayune,* September 6, 1866.
29. *New Orleans Daily Picayune,* May 31, 1873; *New Orleans Daily Picayune,* June 1, 1873; *New Orleans Daily Picayune,* May 30, 1878; *New Orleans Daily Picayune,* April 6, 1879.
30. *Weekly Arkansas Gazette,* November 20, 1866.
31. *New Orleans Daily Picayune,* January 23, 1867, afternoon edition; *New Orleans Daily Picayune,* January 24, 1867.
32. *New Orleans Daily Picayune,* November 30, 1869; *New Orleans Daily Picayune,* May 10, 1871.
33. McMurry, *Hood,* 194; Bohannon, "Promoted," 277; *New Orleans Daily Picayune,* May 13, 1869; Simpson, "Hood," 70; McMurry, *Hood,* 194–97, provides a well-documented discussion of Hood's business ventures from 1866 to 1869 in New Orleans.
34. *New Orleans Daily Picayune,* June 26, 1870; *New Orleans Daily Picayune,* February 12, 1876; *New Orleans Daily Picayune,* December 13, 1874. For more on the Life Association, see *New Orleans Daily Picayune,* January 27, 1871 and *New Orleans Daily Picayune,* January 14, 1872.
35. Ibid.
36. Bohannon, "Promoted," 277–78.
37. McMurry, *Hood,* 195–96; Simpson, "Hood," 70; Lasswell, *Rags,* 12.
38. Dailey, *Before,* 90–95.
39. "Terry Letter," LHA: Memorial Associations Papers, TU; *New Orleans Times,* November 22, 1866; *Weekly Arkansas Gazette,* January 22, 1867; McMurry, *Hood,* 197.
40. *New Orleans Daily Picayune,* January 23, 1867; *New Orleans Daily Picayune,* January 25, 1867.
41. "Bazaar Ticket," LHA: Memorial Associations Papers, TU; *New Orleans Daily Picayune,* March 8, 1867.
42. *New Orleans Daily Picayune,* June 26, 1867; *New Orleans Daily Picayune,* January 1, 1869.
43. *New Orleans Daily Picayune,* April 30, 1869.
44. *New Orleans Daily Picayune,* December 17, 1870.
45. *New Orleans Daily Picayune,* October 29, 1870.
46. *New Orleans Daily Picayune,* December 15, 1866.
47. *New Orleans Daily Picayune,* May 12, 1869, 9. For more on the formation of the SHS, see Foster, *Ghosts,* 50 and Blight, *Race,* 78.
48. *New Orleans Daily Picayune,* August 1, 1869; *New Orleans Daily Picayune,* August 22, 1869. In 1869, the society issued an article on the number of casualties lost during the war. That article can be found in the *New Orleans Daily Picayune,* September 28, 1869.
49. *New Orleans Daily Picayune,* February 20, 1870.
50. *New Orleans Daily Picayune,* January 15, 1871; *New Orleans Daily Picayune,* October 14, 1870. For more on Lee's death, see Blight, *Race,* and Thomas Connelly, *The Marble*

Man: Robert E. Lee and His Image in American Society (Baton Rouge: Louisiana State University Press, 1978).
51. Michael A. Ross, "The Commemoration of Robert E. Lee's Death and the Obstruction of Reconstruction in New Orleans," *Civil War History* 51.2 (2005): 141; *New Orleans Daily Picayune*, October 19, 1870.
52. Ross, "Commemoration," 143–44; *New Orleans Daily Picayune*, October 19, 1870.
53. *New Orleans Daily Picayune*, October 19, 1870; Ross, "Commemoration," 145–46.
54. *Southern Historical Society Papers*, ed. J. William Jones, vol. 11 (Richmond, VA: Southern Historical Society, 1883), 390; *New Orleans Daily Picayune*, October 29, 1870.
55. *New Orleans Daily Picayune*, January 29, 1871.
56. *New Orleans Daily Picayune*, May 29, 1877; *New Orleans Daily Picayune*, May 11, 1878; *New Orleans Daily Picayune*, May 16, 1878. For more on the Lee memorial efforts in New Orleans, see *New Orleans Daily Picayune*, April 25, 1876; *New Orleans Daily Picayune*, March 14, 1871. More information can be found at *New Orleans Daily Picayune*, April 25, 1875 on the Lee Memorial Association and also on fund-raising efforts in Baltimore.
57. *New Orleans Daily Picayune*, October 29, 1868.
58. Harold B. Simpson, *Hood's Texas Brigade in Reunion and Memory* (Hillsboro, TX: Hill Junior College Press, 1974), 16–18; *New Orleans Daily Picayune*, June 9, 1872.
59. *New Orleans Daily Picayune*, June 9, 1872.
60. Ibid.
61. Simpson, *Hood's*, 157–59.
62. Ibid., 329–30.
63. Ibid., 330–31.
64. Foster, *Ghosts*, 51–52; *New Orleans Daily Picayune*, February 11, 1872. The *Tribunal* speech appeared reprinted, with some modifications to make it read as an article in *New Orleans Daily Picayune*, June 2, 1872.
65. *New Orleans Daily Picayune*, August 18, 1872; *New Orleans Daily Picayune*, September 22, 1872.
66. *New Orleans Daily Picayune*, July 16, 1873; *New Orleans Daily Picayune*, August 7, 1873.
67. *New Orleans Daily Picayune*, August 24, 1873. Also see Foster, *Ghosts*, 54 and Blight, *Race*, 79.
68. *New Orleans Daily Picayune*, September 27, 1873; Foster, *Ghosts*, 54–57; Blight, *Race*, 151. Both Foster and Blight discuss the deeper motives behind the Virginia domination of the SHS. Foster articulates how the SHS blamed Northern numerical superiority and Longstreet at Gettysburg for failure in the war. Blight shows how the society's Lost Cause vision of historical memory dominated the print landscape in the postwar years.
69. *New Orleans Daily Picayune*, December 9, 1873; Symonds, *Johnston*, 358 and 364–65; "Letter from Joseph Johnston, September 30, 1865," Louis T. Wigfall Papers, LOC; McMurry, *Hood*, 198–99.
70. *New Orleans Daily Picayune*, January 8, 1874.
71. Joseph Johnston, *Narrative of Military Operations, Directed, During the Late War Between the States* (New York: D. Appleton and Co., 1874), 355 and 363.
72. Ibid., 351–54.

73. Ibid., 351.
74. Ibid., 365–68.
75. *New Orleans Daily Picayune,* May 16, 1874.
76. Senator Ben Hill interview, Alfred P. Roman Papers, LOC; *New Orleans Daily Picayune,* January 8, 1874.
77. *New Orleans Daily Picayune,* January 21, 1874; *New Orleans Daily Picayune,* August 29, 1874.
78. "Johnston Letter," LHA, Chalaron Papers, TU.
79. "Johnston to Falconer, June 4, 1874," and "Johnston to Falconer, June 20, 1874," Kinloch Falconer Collection, UM.
80. "June 13, 1874" and "May 7, 1872," Benjamin Cheatham Papers, SHC.
81. Hood, *Advance,* 68–69; See also McMurry, *Hood,* 199–200.
82. "August 19, 1875," Stephen D. Lee Papers, SHC.
83. Sherman, *Memoirs,* 444.
84. Ibid., 415–16.
85. Hood, *Advance,* 14 and 16.
86. Ibid. Letters from Jackson and Lee appear on 28, 43, 45–46, and 52–53. Longstreet's letter appears on 55–59.
87. Ibid. Hood's exploration of strength of army and casualty figures appears on 69–88 and 218–24. See 89–130 for the discussion of Atlanta and Johnston's "mode of warfare."
88. Ibid. See 134–35 and 162 for the discussion of morale in the Army of Tennessee. Page 156 provides the discussion of Johnston's accusation of "useless butchery."
89. Winkler, *Hood,* 27; Hood, *Advance,* 89–116, offers a complete discussion of the details surrounding Cassville.
90. Hood, *Advance,* 292, 296, and 299–300.
91. Ibid., 304, 309, and 316.
92. "April 10, 1879" and "April 14, 1879," Stephen D. Lee Papers, SHC.
93. "Stephen Lee to Claiborne, June 12, 1878," J. Francis Claiborne Papers, SHC.
94. McMurry, *Hood,* 201.
95. *Southern Historical Society Papers,* ed. J. William Jones, vol. 9 (Richmond, VA: Southern Historical Society, 1881), 518 and 521.
96. Ibid., 524–32. Cheatham's discussion offers several memories and contemporary accounts disputing and questioning the actions at Spring Hill.
97. *Southern Historical Society Papers,* ed. J. William Jones, vol. 8 (Richmond, VA: Southern Historical Society, 1880), 337–38, 345, 349, and 353.
98. Ibid., 346, 357, 359, 370, and 374. Roy's entire report, including several letters and memoir excerpts, can be found on 337–87.
99. *Southern Historical Society Papers,* ed. J. William Jones, vol. 22 (Richmond, VA: Southern Historical Society, 1882), 402–6; *Southern Historical Society Papers,* ed. R.A. Brock, vol. 22 (Richmond, VA: Southern Historical Society, 1894), 1–9.
100. *Southern Historical Society Papers,* ed. J. William Jones, vol. 4 (Richmond, VA: Southern Historical Society, 1877), 145–50.
101. Ibid., vol. 6 (1878): 104 and 114–15.
102. Ibid., vol. 12 (1884): 298–99.
103. Ibid., vol. 7 (1879): 482.

104. *Southern Historical Society Papers,* ed. Frank Vandiver, vol. 52 (Richmond, VA: Southern Historical Society, 1959), 21 and 283.

Chapter 8

Epigraph: R. B. Rosenburg, *Living Monuments: Confederate Soldiers' Homes in the New South* (Chapel Hill: University of North Carolina Press, 1993), xiii.

1. "August 1, 1885 Report of the Hood Relief Committee at New Orleans LA," Duke.
2. *New Orleans Daily Picayune,* September 6, 1879.
3. "Hood Family Relief Committee," LHA, TU.
4. Simpson, "Hood," 71; *New Orleans Daily Picayune,* February 13, 1879, afternoon edition.
5. *New Orleans Daily Picayune,* September 1, 1879.
6. William T. Wragg, "Report on the Yellow Fever Epidemic at Wilmington, N.C., In the Autumn of 1862," located in *The Confederate States Medical and Surgical Journal* (Metuchen, NJ: Scarecrow Press, 1976), 33–34. The original article was published in the March 1864 issue of the journal.
7. Ibid.
8. Ibid.
9. *New Orleans Daily Picayune,* September 5, 1879.
10. Photocopied typescript of "The Orphaned Children of Gen. John B. Hood," Hood File, Carter House Archives (CHA), Franklin, Tennessee.
11. *New Orleans Democrat,* August 26, 1879.
12. Ibid.
13. Simpson, "Hood," 71; *New Orleans Daily Picayune,* September 7, 1879.
14. *New Orleans Daily Picayune,* September 18, 1879, afternoon edition.
15. *New Orleans Times,* August 31, 1879. For more on his death, see H. T. Englehardt, "A Note on the Death of John Bell Hood," *Southwestern Historical Quarterly* 62, no. 1 (July 1953): 91–93.
16. *New Orleans Times,* August 31, 1879.
17. "Civil District Court Suit Records," 1880–1925, #8450, New Orleans Public Library (NOPL). On Saturday, August 30, 2003, the day marking the 124th anniversary of the death of John Bell Hood, a small crowd of friends and Hood descendants gathered to witness the unveiling of a new plaque at the site of Hood's tomb. The marker reads as follows:

    John Bell Hood was born June 29, 1831, in Owingsville, Kentucky, and was reared in Mt. Sterling, Kentucky. After graduating from West Point in 1853, he served in the elite U.S. 2nd Cavalry Regiment on the Texas frontier. In 1861, he joined the Confederate Army. He was promoted to brigadier general in 1862 and commanded the renowned Hood's Texas Brigade under Gen. Robert E. Lee at the important Confederate victories at Gaines' Mill (Seven Days Battles) and 2nd Manassas (Battle of 2nd Bull Run). He held the critical Confederate left flank at Miller's Cornfield at Antietam, after which he was promoted to major general by Thomas J. ("Stonewall") Jackson. In July 1863, while serving as a division commander at Gettysburg, he was severely wounded and forever lost the use of his left arm. In September 1863, while leading a decisive Confederate victory at Chickamauga, Georgia, Hood was again severely wounded and lost his right leg. Promoted to Lieutenant general by Gen. James Longstreet, he returned to duty in 1864 in north Georgia under Gen. Joseph Johnston, as corps commander. He succeeded Johnston as commander of the Army of Tennessee and was temporarily promoted to full general in July 1864. In November, in an unsuccessful attempt to draw Union Gen. William T. Sherman from his March to the Sea, Hood led the Army of Tennessee in an invasion of that state. After decisive defeats at Franklin and Nashville, he retreated to Tupelo, Mississippi. In January 1865, he resigned command. He surrendered to Union authorities at Natchez, Mississippi, on May 31, 1865. After the war, Hood set up residence in New Orleans, where on April 30, 1868, he married Anna Marie Hennen, with whom he fathered 11 children. He died of yellow fever on August 30, 1879, within days of his wife and eldest child. Seven families in 5 different states adopted the surviving orphans. Hood was buried in the Garden District's Lafayette Cemetery, but was moved to this location in 1927.

18. Photocopied typescript of "The Orphaned Children of Gen. John B. Hood," Hood File, CHA. Crouch made the remarks prior to the death of Lydia, which explains his reference to the eleven children; *New Orleans Daily Picayune,* August 31, 1879, morning edition; West, *Texan,* 175.
19. *New Orleans Times,* September 2, 1879.
20. Ibid.
21. *New York Times,* August 31, 1879; *Memphis Commercial Appeal,* August 31, 1879; *Chicago Tribune,* August 31, 1879.
22. *New York Herald,* August 31, 1879.
23. *New Orleans Times,* August 31, 1879.
24. *New Orleans Daily Picayune,* August 31, 1879, morning edition.
25. Ibid. For additional remarks on Hood's career, see *New Orleans Democrat,* September 7, 1879.
26. *New Orleans Daily Picayune,* February 6, 1878; "Association of the Army of Tennessee," *LHA,* TU.
27. Ibid.
28. Ibid.
29. *Southern Historical Society Papers,* ed. J. William Jones, vol. 7 (Richmond, VA: Southern Historical Society, 1879), 496 and 585.
30. *New Orleans Daily Picayune,* October 7, 1879; *New Orleans Daily Picayune,* September 18, 1879, afternoon edition.
31. *New Orleans Daily Picayune,* September 18, 1879, afternoon edition.
32. Ibid.
33. Ibid.
34. *New Orleans Daily Picayune,* September 5, 1879, afternoon edition; *New Orleans Daily Picayune,* September 9, 1879; "White Sulphur Springs" letter, *Hood File,* CHA. See also Simpson, *Hood's Texas Brigade,* 157–73. Of note, the announcement in the *Picayune*

that announced the members of the committee ran each day from September 5 to 21, 1879, with a brief pause, returning to run September 26–28 and 30.
35. Civil District Court Suit Records (Successions, Divorces and Related Matters), 1880–1925, #8450, NOPL.
36. Ibid.
37. *New Orleans Daily Picayune,* September 7, 1879; "August 1, 1885 Report of the Hood Relief Committee at New Orleans LA," Duke.
38. *New Orleans Daily Picayune,* September 12, 1879, afternoon edition; "Hood Family Relief Committee," LHA Papers, TU.
39. *New Orleans Daily Picayune,* September 7, 1879; *New Orleans Daily Picayune,* September 21, 1879; "Hood Family Relief Committee," LHA Papers, TU.
40. *New Orleans Daily Picayune,* September 29, 1879, afternoon edition.
41. *New Orleans Daily Picayune,* September 12, 1879, afternoon edition.
42. Ibid.
43. *New Orleans Daily Picayune,* November 2, 1879; *New Orleans Daily Picayune,* September 29, 1879, afternoon edition. The file book of letters compiled would be a worthy historical find, and may be located within the Hood family circle still or in another unspecified location. Nevertheless, the letters surely express similar sentiments as those published in the *New Orleans Daily Picayune.*
44. "August 1, 1885 Report of the Hood Relief Committee at New Orleans LA," Duke; "White Sulphur Springs" letter, Hood File, CHA; *New Orleans Daily Picayune,* September 10, 1879.
45. *New Orleans Daily Picayune,* September 9, 1879; *New Orleans Daily Picayune,* September 13, 1879.
46. *New Orleans Daily Picayune,* September 8, 1879.
47. "August 1, 1885 Report of the Hood Relief Committee at New Orleans LA," Duke; *New Orleans Daily Picayune,* October 10, 1879; *New Orleans Daily Picayune,* October 26, 1879; *New Orleans Daily Picayune,* November 9, 1879.
48. T. Harry Williams, *P.G.T. Beauregard: Napoleon in Gray* (Baton Rouge, Louisiana State University Press, 1955), 320. Williams refers to Hay (215) and to a letter to Jubal Early from Beauregard on September 4, 1879, in the footnotes. The story of the publication process of the memoirs remains unexplored, with the exception that the memoirs were published and that proceeds went to support the orphaned Hood children.
49. Lasswell, *Rags,* 10–11; Winkler, *Hood,* 36.
50. Lasswell, *Rags,* 12; Caption courtesy of the CHA and the Museum at Confederate Memorial Hall, New Orleans, Louisiana; "Hood Family Relief Committee," LHA Papers, TU. Additional information can be found in editors, "What Will Become of the Children: General Hood's Family Faces an Uncertain Future," *Civil War Times Illustrated* (January 1987): 36–37.
51. "Hood Family Relief Committee," LHA Papers, TU.
52. Simpson, *Hood's Texas Brigade,* 163. Additional information on the homes of the children and the division of funds was provided by the Museum at Confederate Memorial Hall, New Orleans, Louisiana.
53. "Hood Family Relief Committee," LHA Papers, TU.
54. "August 1, 1885 Report of the Hood Relief Committee at New Orleans LA," Duke; *New Orleans Daily Picayune,* November 20, 1879, afternoon edition; "Hood Family

Relief Committee," LHA Papers, TU. This figure comes from the bank books for the fund, located in folder 2. This number contradicts the figure presented in the *Confederate Veteran* 22 (March 1912): 123, which states that $30,000 had been raised. Richard McMurry notes that almost $40,000 had been raised for the children (McMurry, *Hood*, 203n33).

55. "Hood Family Relief Committee," LHA Papers, TU.
56. "Hood Family Relief Committee," LHA Papers, TU; *New Orleans Times Democrat*, February 1, 1891.
57. Rosenburg, *Living*, 32.
58. Ibid., 33–34.
59. Blight, *Race*, 164–65 and 171–210. See also Halbwachs, *Collective*, 171; Thelen, "Memory," 1118–26.
60. Jefferson Davis, *Rise and Fall*, 556–57, 573, 575–76, and 580.
61. C. Vann Woodward and Elisabeth Muhlenfeld, eds., *The Private Mary Chesnut: The Unpublished Civil War Diaries* (New York: Oxford University Press, 1984), ix–xxix; McDonald, *Chesnut*, 210.
62. Chesnut, *Diary*, 297, 307, 316, and 372.
63. Ibid., 326, 332, 367, 392, and 416.
64. Ibid., 425 and 428.
65. Ibid., 425, 429, and 467–68.
66. Ibid., 474.
67. Watkins, *Aytch*, 167–69 and 175.
68. Ibid., 170, 174–75, 198, 222, and 225.
69. Ibid., 226.
70. *Southern Historical Society Papers*, ed. J. William Jones, vol. 12 (Richmond, VA: Southern Historical Society, 1884), 171. See also 2–3 and 443 for other memories about Hood's ability.
71. *Southern Historical Society Papers*, ed. R. A. Brock, vol. 24 (Richmond, VA: Southern Historical Society, 1896), 189–92.
72. Elliott, *Soldier*, 201 and 257; Hughes, *Memoir*, 179, 206, 209–10, 225, 241, 278, 334, and 348.
73. Jonathan W. Stevens, *Reminiscences of the Civil War* (Hillsboro, TX: Hillsboro Manor Print, 1902), 106–7.
74. *Southern Historical Society Papers*, ed. R. A. Block, vol. 32 (Richmond, VA: Southern Historical Society, 1904), 151–56.
75. Ibid.
76. *Memphis Commercial Appeal*, October 11, 1908, arts section; *Confederate Veteran* 24, no. 6 (June 1916): 258–59.
77. Winkler, *Hood*, 4.
78. "History of Hood's Brigade," Annie B. Giles Papers, Center for American History, UT, Austin.
79. Simpson, *Hood's Texas Brigade*, 117, 208–9.
80. Ibid., 183–85, 293.

Bibliography

PRIMARY SOURCES

Archive Collections and Materials

Center for American History, University of Texas at Austin
    Crutcher-Shannon Papers
    Annie B. Giles Papers
Carter House Archives, Franklin, Tennessee
    First Lt. John Henry Marsh letter to Chaplain Charles T. Quintard, July 26, 1864
    The Orphaned Children of Gen. John B. Hood
    White Sulphur Springs Letter, Hood File
Chickamauga and Chattanooga National Military Park Archives, Ft. Oglethorpe, Georgia
Gettysburg National Military Park Library, Gettysburg, Pennsylvania
Library of Congress, Manuscripts Division, Washington, D.C.
    Alfred P. Roman Papers
    James Power Smith Papers
    A. L. Drayton Diary
    Henry Clay Weaver Papers
    P. G. T. Beauregard Papers
    Louis Trezevant Wigfall Papers
Mississippi Department of History and Archives
    James Palmer Diary
Museum at Confederate Hall, New Orleans
    Hood Family Photograph and Caption
National Archives and Records Administration, Washington, D.C.
    John Bell Hood Papers
    Samuel G. French Papers
New Orleans Public Library
    Civil District Court Suit Records (Successions, Divorces, and Related Matters), 1880–1925
Rare Book, Manuscript, and Special Collections, Perkins Library, Duke University
    William B. G. Andrews Papers

Virginia Arnett Papers
August 1, 1885 Report of the Hood Relief Committee at New Orleans LA
Duke Benham Papers
Sidney Champion Papers
Confederate States of America Archives, Army of Tennessee
Confederate States of America Army, Department of Tennessee,
    Message of the President, Confederate Pamphlets #441
William Penn Davis Papers
Champion Duke Papers
Paul Hamilton Hayne Papers
John Cheves Haskell Papers
John Bell Hood Papers
Dr. Lee Papers
John Snow Papers
Robert P. Tondee Papers
Louis Tresevant Wigfall Papers

Southern Historical Collection, University of North Carolina at Chapel Hill
Alphonso Avery Papers
Benjamin Cheatham Papers
J. Francis Claiborne Papers
Clayton Family Papers
Thomas Clayton Papers
Major Joseph B. Cumming Recollections
Basil W. Duke Papers
George Phifer Erwin Papers
Samuel Wragg Ferguson Papers
Gale and Polk Family Papers
R. M. Gray Reminiscence Papers
Hutson Papers
Stephen D. Lee Papers
Lipscomb Family Papers
Lafayette McLaws Papers
Raphael Jacob Moses Papers
Charles Venable Collection
Sarah Louis Wadley Papers
Richard Wharton Papers
William Asbury Whitaker Papers

Howard Tillman Memorial Library Archives Department, Tulane University
William Button Bailey Jr. Memoir
"Letter to Colonel Albert Sydney Johnston," *Mrs. Mason Barret Collection*
Annie Jeter Carmouche Memoirs
Jefferson Davis Papers
    Kuntz Collection
Louisiana Historical Association Papers
    Association of the Army of Tennessee Papers
    Chalaron Papers

    Hood Family Relief Committee Papers
    Memorial Associations Papers
  C. M. Winkler, Life and Character of Gen. John B. Hood.
United States Military Academy Archives and Special Collections, West Point, New York
    Official Register of the Officers and Cadets of the U.S. Military Academy,
      West Point, NY, June 1850–53
University of Mississippi Archives
    William Bowden Civil War Letter
    Juanita Brown Collection
    Burton Butler Papers
    Charles Dean Collection
    Kinloch Falconer Collection
    Winfield Scott Featherson Collection
    Eugene Ferris Collection
    Filson Club Historical Society Papers
    The Civil War Diary of Rev. Jesse L. Henderson, 1844–1940
    W. L. Kennon, "A Tribute to the Womanhood of the Confederacy, 1934"
    Lockwood Collection
    M. D. L. Stephens Manuscript

Internet Sources

Census data, http://www.ancestry.com
Richard French biography, http://bioguide.congress.gov/scripts/biodisplay.
  pl?index=F000379
Hutson Papers, http://www.unc.edu/lib/mssinv/exhibits/civilwar/hutsonpg.html
Janie Smith, http://www.rootsweb.com/~nccumber/janlet.htm

Periodicals

Charlottesville Chronicle, Charlottesville, Virginia
Chicago Tribune, Chicago
Civil War Times Illustrated
Confederate Veteran
Charleston Mercury, Charleston, South Carolina
Daily Appeal, Atlanta
Daily Confederate, Huntsville Alabama
Daily Morning Chronicle, Washington, D.C.
Daily Picayune, New Orleans
Daily Times, Columbus, Georgia
Memphis Commercial Appeal, Memphis
New Orleans Democrat, New Orleans
New Orleans Times, New Orleans
New York Herald, New York City
New York Times, New York City
Richmond Enquirer, Richmond, Virginia

Weekly Arkansas Gazette, Little Rock, Arkansas
Western Citizen, Paris, Kentucky

Books

Alexander, Edward Porter. *Fighting for the Confederacy: The Personal Recollections of General Edward Porter Alexander.* Edited by Gary W. Gallagher. Chapel Hill: University of North Carolina Press, 1989.

Ashley, Joe, and Lavon Ashley, eds. *Oh for Dixie! The Civil War Record and Diary of Captain William V. Davis, 30th MS Infantry, CSA.* Colorado Springs, CO: Standing Pine Press, 2001.

Barnes, Joseph K., ed. *The Medical and Surgical History of the Civil War.* Vol. 5. Wilmington, NC: Broadfoot Publishing Co., 1991.

Barnes, Joseph K., ed. *The Medical and Surgical History of the Civil War.* Vol. 10. Wilmington, NC: Broadfoot Publishing Co., 1991.

Barnes, Joseph K., ed. *The Medical and Surgical History of the Civil War.* Vol. 11. Wilmington, NC: Broadfoot Publishing Co., 1991.

Barnes, Joseph K., ed. *The Medical and Surgical History of the Civil War.* Vol. 12. Wilmington, NC: Broadfoot Publishing Co., 1991.

Bearss, Edwin C., ed. *A Louisiana Confederate: Diary of Felix Pierre Poché.* Natchitoches, LA: Louisiana Studies Institute, Northwestern State University, 1972.

Blomquist, Ann K., and Robert A. Taylor, eds. *This Cruel War: The Civil War Letters of Grant and Malinda Taylor, 1862–1865.* Macon, GA: Mercer University Press, 2000.

Brock, R. A., ed. *Southern Historical Society Papers.* Vol. 38. Richmond, VA: Southern Historical Society, 1910.

Chambers, W. P. *Chamber's Confederate Journal.* Carrollton, MS: Pioneer Publishing Co., 2002.

Chambers, William Pitt. *Blood and Sacrifice: The Civil War Journal of a Confederate Soldier.* Edited by Richard A. Baumgartner. Huntington, WV: Blue Acorn Press, 1994.

Chesnut, Mary. *A Diary from Dixie.* Boston: Houghton Mifflin Co., 1949.

Chesnut, Mary. *Mary Chesnut's Civil War.* Edited by C. Vann Woodward. New Haven, CT: Yale University Press, 1981.

Chesnut, Mary. *The Private Mary Chesnut: The Unpublished Civil War Diaries.* Edited by C. Vann Woodward and Elisabeth Muhlenfeld. New York: Oxford University Press, 1984.

Chesson, Michael Bedout, and Leslie Jean Roberts, eds. *Exile in Richmond: The Confederate Journal of Henri Garidel.* Charlottesville: University Press of Virginia, 2001.

Christ, Mark K., ed. *Getting Used to Being Shot At: The Spence Family Civil War Letters.* Fayetteville: University of Arkansas Press, 2002.

Confederate States Medical and Surgical Journal. Metuchen, NJ: Scarecrow Press, 1976.

Cozzens, Peter, ed. *Battles and Leaders of the Civil War.* Vol. 5. Urbana: University of Illinois Press, 2002.

Crist, Lynda Lasswell, Kenneth H. Williams, and Peggy L. Dillard, eds. *The Papers of Jefferson Davis: Volume 10, October 1863–August 1864.* Baton Rouge: Louisiana State University Press, 1999.

Crist, Lynda Lasswell, Barbara J. Rozek, and Kenneth H. Williams, eds. *The Papers of Jefferson Davis: Volume 11, September 1864–May* 1865. Baton Rouge: Louisiana State University Press, 2003.

Crowson, Noel, and John V. Brogden, eds. *Bloody Banners and Barefoot Boys: A History of the 27th Regiment Alabama Infantry CSA: The Civil War Memoirs and Diary Entries of J. P. Cannon M.D.* Shippensburg, PA: Burd Street Press, 1997.

Cutrer, Thomas W., ed. *Longstreet's Aide: The Civil War Letters of Major Thomas J. Goree.* Charlottesville: University Press of Virginia, 1995.

Cutrer, Thomas W., ed. *Oh, What a Loansome Time I Had: The Civil War Letters of Major William Morel Moxley, Eighteenth Alabama Infantry, and Emily Beck Moxley.* Tuscaloosa: University of Alabama Press, 2002.

Cutrer, Thomas W., and T. Michael Parrish, eds. *Brothers in Gray: The Civil War Letters of the Pierson Family.* Baton Rouge: Louisiana State University Press, 1997.

Davies, Gilbert W., and Florice M. Frank, eds. *Fort Jones (Ca) 1852–1858 Military Notes.* Hat Creek, CA: HiStory ink Books, 1994.

Davis, Jefferson. *His Letters, Papers and Speeches.* Edited by Dunbar Rowland. Jackson: Mississippi Department of Archives and History, 1923.

Davis, Jefferson. *The Rise and Fall of the Confederate Government.* Vol. 2. New York: D. Appleton and Co., 1881.

Davis, Nicholas A. *Chaplain Davis and Hood's Texas Brigade.* Edited by Donald E. Everett. Baton Rouge: Louisiana State University Press, 1999.

Delbanco, Andrew, ed. *The Portable Abraham Lincoln.* New York: Penguin Books, 1992.

"Diary of William Joseph Clark being an account of his trip from Clark County, KY to St. Louis to take the deposition of Col. Daniel Boone for the Widow Sweeny in 1804." *Kentucky State Historical Society Register* 25, no. 74 (May 1927).

Dorsey, Sarah A. *Recollections of Henry Watkins Allen.* New Orleans: M. Doolady, 1866.

Early, Jubal A. *Narrative of the War Between the States.* New York: Da Capo Press, 1989.

Elliott, Sam Davis, ed. *Doctor Quintard, Chaplain C.S.A. and Second Bishop of Tennessee: The Memoir and Civil War Diary of Charles Todd Quintard.* Baton Rouge: Louisiana State University Press, 2003.

Eslinger, Ellen, ed. *Running Mad for Kentucky: Frontier Travel Accounts.* Lexington: University Press of Kentucky, 2004.

Fletcher, William A. *Rebel Private: Front and Rear, Memoirs of a Confederate Soldier.* New York: Meridian, 1997.

Foster, Samuel. *One of Cleburne's Command: The Civil War Reminiscences and Diary of Capt. Samuel T. Foster, Granbury's Texas Brigade, C.S.A.* Edited by Norman Brown. Austin: University of Texas Press, 1980.

Fremantle, Arthur James Lyon. *Three Months in the Southern States: April–June 1863.* Lincoln: University of Nebraska Press, 1991.

French, Richard. *The Right of Members to their Seats in the House of Representatives Delivered in the House of Representatives February 12, 1844.* Washington, DC: Globe Office, 1844.

French, Richard. *Slavery in the Territories Delivered in the House of Representatives, Thursday, June 29, 1848.* Washington, DC: Congressional Globe Office, 1848.

Fox, Chief Red. *The Memoirs of Chief Red Fox.* Greenwich, CT: Fawcett Publications, 1971.

Gay, Mary A. H. *Life in Dixie During the War.* Edited by J. H. Segars. Macon, GA: Mercer University Press, 2001.

Grant, Ulysses Simpson. *Personal Memoirs.* Lincoln: University of Nebraska Press, 1996.

Greiner, James M., Janet L. Coryell, and James R. Smither, eds. *A Surgeon's Civil War: The Letters and Dairy of Daniel M. Holt, M.D.* Kent, OH: Kent State University Press, 1994.

Haskell, John Cheves. *The Haskell Memoirs.* Edited by Gilbert E. Govan and James Livingood. New York: G.P. Putnam's Sons, 1960.

Hood, John Bell. *Advance and Retreat: Personal Experiences in the United States and Confederate States Armies.* New York: Da Capo Press, 1993.

Hughes, Nathaniel C., ed., *Liddell's Record: St. John Richardson Liddell, Brigadier General CSA Staff Officer and Brigade Commander, Army of Tennessee.* Dayton, OH: Morningside, 1985.

Hughes, Nathaniel Cheairs, Jr., ed. *The Civil War Memoir of Philip Daingerfield Stephenson, D.D.: Private, Company K, 13th Arkansas Volunteer Infantry, Loader, Piece No. 4, 5th Company, Washington Artillery, Army of Tennessee, CSA.* Baton Rouge: Louisiana State University Press, 1995.

Johnson, Pharris Deloach, ed. *Under the Southern Cross: Soldier Life with Gordon Bradwell and the Army of Northern Virginia.* Macon, GA: Mercer University Press, 1999.

Johnson, Robert Underwood, and Clarence Clough Buel, ed. *Battles and Leaders of the Civil War.* Vol. 4. New York: Thomas Yoseloff, 1956.

Johnston, Joseph E. *Narrative of Military Operations, Directed, During the Late War Between the States.* New York: D. Appleton and Co., 1874.

Jones, Mary Miles, and Leslie Jones Martin, eds. *The Gentle Rebel: The Civil War Letters of William Harvey Berryhill, First Lieutenant, Company D, 43rd Regiment, MS Volunteers.* Yazoo City, MS: Sassafras Press, 1982.

Kean, Robert Garlick Hill. *Inside the Confederate Government: The Diary of Robert Garlick Hill Kean.* Edited by Edward Younger. Baton Rouge: Louisiana State University Press, 1957.

Kirwan, A. D., ed., *Johnny Green of the Orphan Brigade: The Journal of a Confederate Soldier.* Lexington: University of Kentucky Press, 1956.

King, Capt. Charles. *Cadet Days: A Story of West Point.* New York: Harpers, 1894.

King, Spencer Bidwell, Jr. *Ebb Tide: As Seen Through the Diary of Josephine Clay Habersham.* Athens: University of Georgia Press, 1958.

Lasswell, Mary, ed. *Rags and Hope: The Recollections of Val. C. Giles, Four Years with Hood's Brigade, Fourth Texas Infantry, 1861–1865.* New York: Coward-McCann, 1961.

Lawson, Rowena. *Bath County, KY 1820–1840 Censuses.* Bowie, MD: Heritage Books, 1986.

Lawson, Rowena. *Montgomery County, KY 1810–1840 Censuses.* Bowie, MD: Heritage Books, 1985.

Lawson, Rowena. *Montgomery County, KY 1850 Census.* Bowie, MD: Heritage Books, 1986.

Lee, Robert E. *Wartime Papers of Robert E. Lee.* Edited by Clifford Dowdey. New York: Da Capo Press, 1961.

Logsdon, David R., ed. *Eyewitnesses at the Battle of Franklin.* Nashville, TN: Kettle Mill Press, 2000.

Longstreet, General James. *From Manassas to Appomattox: Memoirs of the Civil War in America*. New York: Da Capo Press, 1992.

Lowe, Jeffrey C., and Sam Hodges, eds. *Letters to Amanda: The Civil War Letters of Marion Hill Fitzpatrick, Army of Northern Virginia*. Macon, GA: Mercer University Press, 1998.

Miers, Earl Schenck, ed. *A Rebel War Clerk's Diary by John B. Jones*. New York: Sagamore Press, 1958.

Moseley, Ronald H., ed. *The Stilwell Letters: A Georgian in Longstreet's Corps, Army of Northern Virginia*. Macon, GA: Mercer University Press, 2002.

Nisbet, James Cooper. *Four Years on the Firing Line*. Jackson, TN: McCowat-Mercer Press, 1963.

Phelan, James. *"For the good of the bleeding land": Being the text of a letter from James Phelan to Confederate President Jefferson Davis*. Louisville, KY: Contre Coup Press, 1999.

Pierson, William Whatley, Jr., ed. *Whipt 'em Everytime: The Diary of Bartlett Yancey Malone, Co. H 6th NC Regiment*. Jackson, TN: McCowat-Mercer Press, 1960.

Polley, J. B. *Hood's Texas Brigade: It's Marches, It's Battles, It's Achievements*. Dayton, OH: Press of Morningside Bookshop, 1976.

Reagan, John H. *Memoirs with Special Reference to Secession and the Civil War*. Austin, TX: Pemberton Press, 1968.

Reinhart, Joseph R., ed. *Two Germans in the Civil War: The Diary of John Daeuble and The Letters of Gottfried Rentschler, 6th Kentucky Volunteer Infantry*. Knoxville: University of Tennessee Press, 2004.

Robertson, Jerome B. *Touched with Valor: Civil War Papers and Casualty Reports of Hood's Texas Brigade*. Edited by Harold B. Simpson. Hillsboro, TX: Hill Junior College Press, 1964.

The Sesquicentennial of the United States Military Academy: An Account of the Observance, January–June, 1952. Buffalo: Baker, Jones, Hausauer and Savage, 1953.

Sherman, William Tecumseh. *Memoirs*. Edited by Michael Fellman. New York: Penguin Books, 2000.

Sorrel, F. "Gun Shot Wounds—Army of Northern Virginia." *Confederate States Medical and Surgical Journal*. Metuchen, NJ: Scarecrow Press, 1976.

Souchon, Edward. "Reminiscences of Dr. T. G. Richardson." *New Orleans Medical and Surgical Journal* (June 1896).

Southern Historical Society Papers. Volumes 1–52. Richmond, VA: Southern Historical Society, 1876–1959.

Stevens, Jonathan. *Reminiscences of the Civil War*. Hillsboro, TX: Hillsboro Manor Print, 1902.

Stone, Kate. *Brokenburn: The Journal of Kate Stone, 1861–1868*. Edited by John Q. Anderson. Baton Rouge: Louisiana State University Press, 1995.

Sudduth, William. "A Sketch of the Early Adventures of William Sudduth in Kentucky." *Historical Quarterly* 2, no. 2 (January 1928).

Sutherland, Daniel E., ed. *A Very Violent Rebel: The Civil War Diary of Ellen Renshaw House*. Knoxville: University of Tennessee Press, 1996.

Taylor, F. Jay, ed. *Reluctant Rebel: The Secret Diary of Robert Patrick, 1861–1865*. Baton Rouge: Louisiana State University Press, 1959.

Thomas, Ella Gertrude Clanton. *The Secret Eye: The Journal of Ella Gertrude Clanton Thomas, 1848–1880.* Edited by Virginia Ingraham Burr. Chapel Hill: University of North Carolina Press, 1990.

U.S. War Department. *The War of the Rebellion: A Compilation of the Official Records of the Union and Confederate Armies.* 127 vols. Washington, DC: GPO, 1880–1901.

Walker, Emma Jane, and Virginia Wilson, eds. *Some Marriages in Montgomery County, Kentucky, Before* 1864. Lexington, KY: Society Daughters of the American Revolution, 1961.

Watkins, Sam. *Co. Aytch: A Side Show of the Big Show.* Wilmington, NC: Broadfoot Publishing Co., 1994.

West, John C. *A Texan in Search of a Fight: Being the Diary and Letters of a Private Soldier in Hood's Texas Brigade.* Waco, TX: Texian Press, 1969.

Wragg, William T. "Report on the Yellow Fever Epidemic at Wilmington, N.C., In the Autumn of 1862." *Confederate States Medical and Surgical Journal.* Metuchen, NJ: Scarecrow Press, 1976.

Young, Chester Raymond, ed. *Westward into Kentucky: The Narrative of Daniel Trabue.* Lexington: University Press of Kentucky, 1981.

SECONDARY SOURCES

Alsop, Rachel, Annette Fitzsimons, and Kathleen Lennon. *Theorizing Gender.* Malden, MA: Blackwell Publishers, 2002.

Ambrose, Stephen E. *Duty, Honor, Country: A History of West Point.* Baltimore: John Hopkins University Press, 1966.

*The American Annual Cyclopedia and Register of Important Events of the Year 1863.*Vol. 3. New York: D. Appleton and Co., 1864.

Arnold, Thomas Jackson. *Early Life and Letters of General Thomas J. Jackson.* Chicago: Fleming H. Revell Co., 1916.

Ayers, Edward L. *Vengeance and Justice: Crime and Punishment in the Nineteenth Century South.* New York: Oxford University Press, 1984.

Bailey, Anne J. *The Chessboard of War: Sherman and Hood in the Autumn Campaigns of 1864.* Lincoln: University of Nebraska Press, 2000.

Bailey, Ronald. *Battles for Atlanta: Sherman Moves East.* Alexandria, VA: Time-Life Books, 1989.

Bailey, Ronald. *The Bloodiest Day: The Battle of Antietam.* Alexandria, VA: Time-Life Books, 1984.

Bailey, Ronald. *Forward to Richmond: McClellan's Peninsula Campaign.* Alexandria, VA: Time-Life Books, 1983.

Bakeless, John. *Daniel Boone.* Harrisburg, PA: Stackpole Co., 1965.

Baker, Anni P. "Daughters of Mars: Army Officers' Wives and Military Culture on the American Frontier." *The Historian* 67, no. 1 (Spring 2005).

Baldick, Robert. *The Duel: A History of Dueling.* New York: Clarkson N. Potter, 1965.

Ballantine, Betty, and Ian Ballantine, eds. *The Native Americans: An Illustrated History.* North Dighton, MA: World Publications Group, 2001.

Banning, Kendall. *West Point Today.* New York: Funk and Wagnalls Co., 1937.

The Battles for Franklin and Nashville. Harrisburg, PA: Eastern Acorn Press, 1988.

Baumer, William H., Jr. *West Point: Moulder of Men*. New York: D. Appleton-Century Co., 1943.

Beard, W. E. *The Battle of Nashville: The Limit of the Last Aggressive Movement of the Armies of the Confederacy, Hood's Grand Maneuver Designed to Prevent Sherman's March to the Sea, Fought in the Southern Suburbs of Nashville, December 15–16, 1864*. Nashville, TN: Nashville Industrial Bureau, 1913.

Bederman, Gail. *Manliness and Civilization: A Cultural History of Gender and Race in the United States, 1880–1917*. Chicago: University of Chicago Press, 1995.

Bellesiles, Michael, ed. *Lethal Imagination: Violence and Brutality in American History*. New York: New York University Press, 1999.

Berry, Lt. Gen. Sidney B. *The United States Military Academy: A Fundamental National Institution, West Point: A Special Place*. New York: Newcomen Society in North America, 1977.

Berry, Stephen W., II. *All that Makes a Man: Love and Ambition in the Civil War South*. New York: Oxford University Press, 2003.

Betty, Gerald. *Comanche Society: Before the Reservation*. College Station: Texas A&M University Press, 2002.

Bierschwale, Margaret. *Fort Mason, Chapter V from A History of Macon County, Texas*. Mason, TX: Margaret Bierschwale, 1968.

Blanton, Wyndham B. *Medicine in Virginia in the Nineteenth Century*. Richmond, VA: Garrett and Massie, 1933.

Blight, David W. "For Something Beyond the Battlefield: Frederick Douglass and the Struggle for the Memory of the Civil War." *Journal of American History* 75, no. 4 (March 1989): 1156–78.

Blight, David W. *Race and Reunion: The Civil War in American Memory*. Cambridge, MA: Harvard University Press, 2001.

Bogart, W. H. *Daniel Boone and the Hunters of Kentucky*. Auburn, NY: Miller, Orton and Milligan, 1854.

Bohannon, Keith S. "Wounded and Captured at Gettysburg: Reminiscence by Sgt. William Jones, 50th Georgia Infantry." *Military Images* 9, no. 6 (1998): 14–15.

Boles, John B. *Religion in Antebellum Kentucky*. Lexington: University Press of Kentucky, 1976.

Boritt, Gabor S., ed. *Jefferson Davis's Generals*. New York: Oxford University Press, 1999.

Bowers, John. *Chickamauga and Chattanooga: The Battles that Doomed the Confederacy*. New York: Avon Books, 1994.

Bowman, John S., ed. *The Civil War Almanac*. New York: World Almanac Publications, 1983.

Boyd, Carl B., and Hazel Mason Boyd. *A History of Mt. Sterling, Kentucky, 1792–1918*. Carl Boyd Jr., 1984.

Brittan, Arthur. *Masculinity and Power*. New York: Basil Blackwell, 1989.

Brodman, Estelle, and Elizabeth B. Carrick. "American Military Medicine in the Mid-Nineteenth Century: The Experience of Alexander H. Hoff, M.D." *Bulletin of the History of Medicine* 64, no. 1 (1990): 63–78.

Brown, Kathleen M. *Good Wives, Nasty Wenches and Anxious Patriarchs: Gender, Race and Power in Colonial Virginia*. Chapel Hill: University of North Carolina Press, 1996.

Buell, Thomas B. *The Warrior Generals: Combat Leadership in the Civil War.* New York: Three Rivers Press, 1997.
Burke, James Lee. *In the Electric Mist with Confederate Dead.* New York: Hyperion, 1993.
Bynum, Victoria. *Unruly Women: The Politics of Social and Sexual Control in the Old South.* Chapel Hill: University of North Carolina Press, 1992.
Calloway, Colin G. *First Peoples: A Documentary Survey of American Indian History.* New York: Bedford/St. Martin's, 2004.
Carnes, Mark C., and Clyde Griffen, eds. *Meanings for Manhood: Constructions of Masculinity in Victorian America.* Chicago: University of Chicago Press, 1990.
Cash, W. J. *The Mind of the South.* New York: Vintage, 1991.
Castel, Albert. *Decision in the West: The Atlanta Campaign of 1864.* Lawrence: University Press of Kansas, 1992.
Catton, Bruce. *The American Heritage New History of the Civil War.* Edited by James McPherson. New York: Viking, 1996.
Censer, Jane Turner. *The Reconstruction of White Southern Womanhood, 1865–1895.* Baton Rouge: Louisiana State University Press, 2003.
Chaning, Steven. *Confederate Ordeal: The Southern Home Front.* Alexandria, VA: Time-Life Books, 1989.
Cimbala, Paul A., and Randall M. Miller, eds. *Union Soldiers and the Northern Home Front: Wartime Experiences, Postwar Adjustments.* New York: Fordham University Press, 2002.
Clark, Champ. *Gettysburg: The Confederate High Tide.* Alexandria, VA: Time-Life Books, 1985.
Clinton, Catherine, and Nina Silber, eds. *Divided Houses: Gender and the Civil War.* New York: Oxford University Press, 1992.
Cochran, Hamilton. *Noted American Duels and Hostile Encounters.* Philadelphia: Clinton Books, 1963.
Coffey, David. *John Bell Hood and the Struggle for Atlanta.* Abilene, TX: McWhiney Foundation Press, 1998.
Coleman, J. Winston, Jr. *Famous Kentucky Duels: The Story of the Code of Honor in the Bluegrass State.* Frankfort, KY: Roberts Printing Co., 1953.
Connelly, Thomas L. *The Marble Man: Robert E. Lee and His Image in American Society.* Baton Rouge: Louisiana State Press, 1977.
Connelly, Thomas Lawrence. *Autumn of Glory: The Army of Tennessee, 1862–1865* Baton Rouge: Louisiana State University Press, 1971.
Connelly, Thomas L., and Barbara Bellows. *God and General Longstreet: The Lost Cause and the Southern Mind.* Baton Rouge: Louisiana State University Press, 1982.
Connerton, Paul. *How Societies Remember.* Cambridge, England: Cambridge University Press, 1989.
Coward, Joan Wells. *Kentucky in the New Republic: The Process of Constitution Making* Lexington: University Press of Kentucky, 1979.
Cox, Jacob. *The March to the Sea, Franklin and Nashville.* New York: Charles Scribner's Sons, 1882.
Crabb, Martha L. *All Afire to Fight: The Untold Tale of the Civil War's Ninth Texas Cavalry.* New York: Avon Books, 2000.

Crackel, Theodore J. *West Point: A Centennial History.* Lawrence: University Press of Kansas, 2002.
Cramer, Clayton E. *Concealed Weapon Laws of the Early Republic: Dueling, Southern Violence, and Moral Reform.* Westport, CT: Praeger, 1999.
Cubbison, Douglas R. "John Bell Hood and the Campaign in North Alabama and Middle Tennessee, October–November 1864." *Military History of the West* 34 (2004): 53–54.
Cunningham, H. H. *Doctors in Gray: The Confederate Medical Service.* Baton Rouge: Louisiana State University Press, 1958.
Dailey, Jane. *Before Jim Crow: The Politics of Race in Post Emancipation Virginia.* Chapel Hill: University of North Carolina Press, 2000.
Davis, Stephen. *Atlanta Will Fall: Sherman, Joe Johnston, and the Yankee Heavy Battalions.* Wilmington, DE: SR Books, 2001.
Davis, Stephen. "John Bell Hood's 'Addictions' in Civil War Literature." *Blue and Gray Magazine* (October 1998).
Davis, William C. *The Battle of Bull Run.* Baton Rouge: Louisiana State University Press, 1977.
Davis, William C. *The Cause Lost: Myths and Realities of the Confederacy.* Lawrence: University Press of Kansas, 1996.
Dean, Eric T., Jr. *Shook Over Hell: Post-Traumatic Stress, Vietnam, and the Civil War.* Cambridge, MA: Harvard University Press, 1997.
Dean, Eric T., Jr. "We Will All Be Lost and Destroyed: Post Traumatic Stress Disorder and the Civil War." *Civil War History* 38 (June 1991).
DeBrava, Valerie. "The Offending Hand of War in Harper's Weekly." *American Periodicals* 11 (2001): 49–64.
Dicken, Garcia, Hazel. *To Western Woods: The Breckenridge Family Moves to Kentucky in 1793.* Madison, WI: Associated University Press, 1991.
Donovan, Timothy H., Thomas E. Greiss, Roy K. Flint, Arthur V. Grant, and Gerald P. Stadler. *The American Civil War.* Wayne, NJ: Avery Publishing Group, 1987.
Dorsey, Bruce. *Reforming Men and Women: Gender in the Antebellum City.* Ithaca, NY: Cornell University Press, 2002.
Drake, Daniel. *Pioneer Life in Kentucky, 1785–1800.* New York: Henry Schuman, 1948.
Dyer, John P. *The Gallant Hood.* Indianapolis: Bobbs-Merrill Co., 1950.
Edwards, Laura F. *Gendered Strife and Confusion: The Political Culture of Reconstruction.* Urbana: University of Illinois Press, 1997.
Edwards, Laura F. "The Problem of Dependency: African Americans, Labor Relations and the Law in the Nineteenth-Century South." *Agricultural History* 72, no. 2 (Spring 1998): 313–40.
Edwards, Laura F. *Scarlett Doesn't Live Here Anymore: Women in the Civil War Era.* Urbana: University of Illinois Press, 2000.
Eliot, Ellsworth, Jr. *West Point in the Confederacy.* New York: G.A. Baker and Co, 1941.
Elliott, Lawrence. *The Long Hunter: A New Life of Daniel Boone.* New York: Reader's Digest Press, 1976.
Elliott, Sam Davis. *Soldier of Tennessee: General Alexander P. Stewart and the Civil War in the West.* Baton Rouge: Louisiana State University Press, 1999.

Endler, James R. *Other Leaders, Other Heroes: West Point's Legacy to America Beyond the Field of Battle*. Westport, CT: Praeger, 1998.

Englehardt, H. T. "A Note on the Death of John Bell Hood." *Southwestern Historical Quarterly* 62, no. 1 (July 1953).

Ethridge, Robbie. *Creek Country: The Creek Indians and Their World*. Chapel Hill: University of North Carolina Press, 2003.

Ethridge, Robbie. "Raiding the Remains: Indian Slave Traders and the Collapse of the Southeastern Chiefdoms." Presented at the Annual Meeting of SEAC, November 14–17, 2001, in Chattanooga, TN.

Ethridge, Robbie. "Shatter Zone: Early Colonial Slave Raiding and its Consequences for the Natives of the Eastern Woodland Indians." Presented at the American Society for Ethnohistory Annual Meeting, November 7–12, 2003, in Riverside, CA.

Ethridge, Robbie, and Charles Hudson, eds. *The Transformation of the Southeastern Indians, 1540–1760*. Jackson: University Press of Mississippi, 2002.

Farman, Christie Anne, ed. *Women of the American South: A Multicultural Reader*. New York: New York University Press, 1997.

Faust, Drew Gilpin. *Mothers of Invention: Women of the Slaveholding South in the American Civil War*. New York: Vintage Books, 1996.

Fehrenbach, T. R. *Comanches: The Destruction of a People*. New York: Knopf, 1974.

Ferguson, Brian, and Neil Whitehead. *War in the Tribal Zone: Expanding States and Indigenous Warfare*. Santa Fe, NM: School of American Research, 1992.

Figg, Laurann, and Jane Farrell-Beck. "Amputation in the Civil War: Physical and Social Dimensions." *Journal of History of Medicine and Allied Sciences* 48, no. 4 (1993): 454–75.

Flemming, Walter Lynwood, ed. *The South in the Building of the Nation*. Vol. 11. Richmond, VA: Southern Historical Publication Society, 1909.

Foote, Shelby. *The Civil War: A Narrative, Fort Sumter to Perryville*. New York: Vintage Books, 1986.

Foster, Gaines. *Ghosts of the Confederacy: Defeat, the Lost Cause, and the Emergence of the New South*. New York: Oxford University Press, 1987.

Fowler, John Derrick. *Mountaineers in Gray: The Story of the Nineteenth TN Volunteer Regiment, CSA*. Ph.D. diss., University of Tennessee, Knoxville, 2000.

Fox-Genovese, Elizabeth. *Within the Plantation Household: Black and White Women of the Old South*. Chapel Hill: University of North Carolina Press, 1988.

Freeman, Douglas Southall. *Lee's Lieutenants: A Study in Command*. Edited by Stephen W. Sears. New York: Scribner, 1998.

Freeman, Douglas Southall. *Lee's Lieutenants: A Study in Command*. Vol. 1. New York: Charles Scribner's Sons, 1942.

Freeman, Douglas Southall. *Lee's Lieutenants: A Study in Command*. Vol. 2. New York: Charles Scribner's Sons, 1943.

Freeman, Douglas Southall. *Lee's Lieutenants: A Study in Command*. Vol. 3. New York: Charles Scribner's Sons, 1944.

Freeman, Joanne B. *Affairs of Honor: National Politics in the New Republic*. New Haven, CT: Yale University Press, 2001.

Freeman, Martha Doty. *A History of Camp Cooper, Throckmorton County, Texas*. Albany, TX: Aztec of Albany Foundation, 1997.

Freemon, Frank R. *Gangrene and Glory: Medical Care during the American Civil War.* Cranbury, NJ: Associated University Presses, 1998.

Frick, Daphne. "Soldiers with Empty Sleeves: The Minie Ball and Civil War Medicine." *Proceeding and Papers of the Georgia Association of Historians* 14 (1993): 48.

Friedmann, Lawrence W. *The Psychological Rehabilitation of the Amputee.* Springfield, IL: Charles C. Thomas, 1978.

Friend, Craig Thompson, and Lorri Glover, eds. *Southern Manhood: Perspectives on Masculinity in the Old South.* Athens: University of Georgia Press, 2004.

Gallagher, Gary W., ed. *Antietam: Essays on the 1862 Maryland Campaign.* Kent, OH: Kent State University Press, 1989.

Gallagher, Gary W. *The Confederate War: How Popular Will, Nationalism and Military Strategy Could Not Stave Off Defeat.* Cambridge, MA: Harvard University Press, 1997.

Gallagher, Gary W., ed. *Lee: The Soldier.* Lincoln: University of Nebraska Press, 1996.

Gallagher, Gary W., ed. *The Second Day at Gettysburg: Essays on Confederate and Union Leadership.* Kent, OH: Kent State University Press, 1993.

Gallagher, Gary W., and Alan T. Nolan, eds. *The Myth of the Lost Cause and Civil War History.* Bloomington: Indiana University Press, 2000.

Gallagher, Gary W., and Joseph T. Glatthaar, eds. *Leaders of the Lost Cause: New Perspectives on Confederate High Command.* Mechanicsburg, PA: Stackpole Books, 2004.

Gibbon, Guy. *The Sioux: The Dakota and Lakota Nations.* Malden, MA: Blackwell Publishing, 2003.

Gillett, Mary C. *The Army Medical Department, 1818–1865.* Washington, DC: Center of Military History, U.S. Army, Government Printing Office, 1987.

Glatthaar, Joseph T. *General Lee's Army: From Victory to Collapse.* New York: Free Press, 2008.

Gordon, Lesley J. *General George E. Pickett in Life and Legend.* Chapel Hill: University of North Carolina Press, 1998.

Gorn, Elliot J. " 'Gouge and Bite, Pull Hair and Scratch': The Social Significance of Fighting in the Southern Backcountry." *American Historical Review* 90, no. 1 and supplement (February 1985): 18–43.

Graber, John W. "One Man's Civil War." *Minnesota History* 52 (1990): 144–45.

Green, Arthur E. *Southerners at War: The 38th Alabama Infantry Volunteers.* Shippensburg, PA: Burd Street Press, 1999.

Greenberg, Kenneth S. *Honor and Slavery: Lies, Duels, Noses, Masks, Dressing as a Woman, Gifts, Strangers, Humanitarianism, Death, Slave Rebellions, the Proslavery Argument, Baseball, Hunting, and Gambling in the Old South.* Princeton, NJ: Princeton University Press, 1996.

Greenberg, Kenneth S. *Masters and Statesmen: The Political Culture of Slavery.* Baltimore: John Hopkins University Press, 1985.

Groom, Winston. *Shrouds of Glory: From Atlanta to Nashville: The Last Great Campaign of the Civil War.* New York: Atlantic Monthly Press, 1995.

Halbwachs, Maurice. *On Collective Memory.* Chicago: University of Chicago Press, 1992.

Harrison, Lowell H., and James C. Klotter. *A New History of Kentucky.* Lexington: University Press of Kentucky, 1997.

Hartley, C. B. *Life and Times of Colonel Daniel Boone.* Philadelphia: G.G. Evans, 1869.

Havins, T. R. *Camp Colorado: A Decade of Frontier Defense.* Brownwood, TX: Brown Press, 1964.

Hay, Thomas Robson. "The Davis-Hood-Johnston Controversy of 1864." *Mississippi Valley Historical Review* 11, no. 1 (June 1924).

Hay, Thomas Robson. *Hood's Tennessee Campaign.* New York: Press of Morningside Bookshop, 1976.

Hennessy, John J. *Return to Bull Run: The Campaign and Battle of Second Manassas.* Norman: University of Oklahoma Press, 1993.

Herf, Jeffrey. *Divided Memory: The Nazi Past in the Two Germanys.* Cambridge, MA: Harvard University Press, 1997.

Herschbach, Lisa. "Prosthetic Reconstructions: Making the Industry, Remaking the Body, Modeling the Nation." *History Workshop Journal* 44 (Autumn 1997): 24–25.

Hess, Earl J. *Liberty, Virtue and Progress: Northerners and Their War for the Union.* New York: New York University Press, 1988.

Hollandsworth, James G., Jr. *An Absolute Massacre: The New Orleans Race Riot of July 30, 1866.* Baton Rouge: Louisiana State University Press, 2001.

Hollon, W. Eugene. *Frontier Violence: Another Look.* New York: Oxford University Press, 1974.

Horn, Stanley F. *The Decisive Battle of Nashville.* Baton Rouge: Louisiana State University Press, 1956.

Houchens, Lt. Col. Harry W. "The Making of General John Bell Hood: A Study of Command, An Individual Study Project." Carlisle Barracks, PA: U.S. Army War College, 1993.

Howell, H. Grady, Jr. *To Live and Die in Dixie: A History of the 3rd Regiment MS Volunteer Infantry, CSA.* Jackson, MS: Chickasaw Bayou Press, 1991.

Hughes, Nathaniel Cheairs, Jr. *Brigadier General Tyree H. Bell, C.S.A.: Forrest's Fighting Lieutenant.* Knoxville: University of Tennessee Press, 2004.

Hutton, Patrick H. *History as an Art of Memory.* Hanover, NH: University Press of New England, 1993.

Ireland, Robert M. *The County Courts in Antebellum Kentucky.* Lexington: University Press of Kentucky, 1972.

Jabour, Anya. "Male Friendship and Masculinity in the Early National South: William Wirt and His Friends," *Journal of the Early Republic* 20 (2000).

James, Alfred P. "General Joseph Eggleston Johnston, Storm Center of the Confederate Army." *Mississippi Valley Historical Review* 14 (1927).

Jarvis, Christina S. *The Male Body at War: American Masculinity during World War II.* DeKalb: Northern Illinois University Press, 2004.

Jaynes, Gregory. *The Killing Ground: Wilderness to Cold Harbor.* Alexandria, VA: Time-Life Books, 1986.

Jones, Archer. *Civil War Command and Strategy: The Process of Victory and Defeat.* New York: Free Press, 1992.

Joslyn, Mauriel Phillips, ed. *A Meteor Shining Brightly: Essays on the Life and Career of Major General Patrick R. Cleburne.* Macon, GA: Mercer University Press, 2000.

Kammen, Michael. *Mystic Chords of Memory: The Transformation of Tradition in American Culture.* New York: Alfred Knopf, 1991.

Kane, Harnett C. *Gentlemen, Swords and Pistols.* New York: William Morrow and Co., 1951.
Kavanagh, Thomas. *Comanche Political History: An Ethnohistorical Perspective, 1706–1875.* Lincoln: University of Nebraska Press, 1996.
Kilpatrick, Lewis H. "Historic Owingsville." *Kentucky Magazine.* Louisville, KY: Lost Cause Press, 1979.
Kirshner, Ralph. *The Class of 1861: Custer, Ames, and Their Classmates after West Point.* Carbondale: Southern Illinois University Press, 1999.
Knight, Lucian Lamar, ed. *Library of Southern Literature Biographical Dictionary of Authors* Vol. 15. Atlanta: Martin and Hoyt Co., 1907.
Korn, Jerry. *The Fight for Chattanooga: Chickamauga to Missionary Ridge.* Alexandria, VA: Time-Life Books, 1985.
Kozee, William Carlos. *Pioneer Families of Eastern and Southeastern Kentucky.* Huntington, WV: Standard Printing and Publishing Co., 1957.
Kuhn, Thomas S. *The Structure of Scientific Revolutions.* Chicago: University of Chicago Press, 1996.
Lambert, Major Joseph I. *One Hundred Years with the Second Cavalry.* Fort Riley, KS: Capper Printing Co., 1939.
Lee Takes Command: From Seven Days to Second Bull Run. Alexandria, VA: Time-Life Books, 1984.
Linderman, Gerald F. *Embattled Courage: The Experience of Combat in the American Civil War.* New York: Free Press, 1987.
Lindman, Janet Moore. "Acting the Manly Christian: White Evangelical Masculinity in Revolutionary Virginia." *William and Mary Quarterly* 57 (2000).
Lindsey, Linda. *Gender Roles: A Sociological Perspective.* Upper Saddle River, NJ: Prentice Hall, 1997.
Linenthal, Edward T. *Sacred Ground: Americans and Their Battlefields.* Urbana: University of Illinois Press, 1993.
Livermore, Thomas L. *Numbers and Losses in the Civil War in America 1861–1865.* New York: Houghton, Mifflin and Co., 1901.
Lofaro, Michael A. *Daniel Boone: An American Life.* Lexington: University Press of Kentucky, 2003.
Lofaro, Michael A. *The Life and Adventures of Daniel Boone.* Lexington: University Press of Kentucky, 1978.
Long, Alecia P. *The Great Southern Babylon: Sex, Race and Respectability in New Orleans, 1865–1920.* Baton Rouge: Louisiana State University Press, 2004.
Lundberg, John R. *The Finishing Stroke: Texans in the 1864 Tennessee Campaign.* Abilene, TX: McWhiney Foundation Press, 2002.
Mangan, J. A., and James Walvin, eds. *Manliness and Morality: Middle-Class Masculinity in Britain and America 1800–1940.* New York: St. Martin's Press, 1987.
Marszalek, John F. *Sherman: A Soldier's Passion for Order.* New York: Vintage Books, 1993.
Martin, Samuel J. *Southern Hero Matthew Galbraith Butler: Confederate General, Hampton Red Shirt and U.S. Senator.* Mechanicsburg, PA: Stackpole Books, 2001.
Maxwell, James A., ed. *America's Fascinating Indian Heritage.* Pleasantville, NY: Reader's Digest Association, 1978.

Mayer, Henry. *All on Fire: William Lloyd Garrison and the Abolition of Slavery*. New York: St. Martin's Press, 1998.
Mayfield, John. "'The Soul of a Man!': William Gilmore Simms and the Myths of Southern Manhood." *Journal of the Early Republic* 15 (1995).
McCaffrey, James M. *This Band of Heroes: Granbury's Texas Brigade, C.S.A.* Austin, TX: Eakin Press, 1985.
McDonald, Kendra Lynne. *The Creation of History and Myth in Mary Boykin Miller Chesnut's Civil War Narrative*. Ph.D. diss., The Ohio State University, 1996.
McDonough, James Lee. *Nashville: The Western Confederacy's Final Gamble*. Knoxville: University of Tennessee Press, 2004.
McDonough, James Lee, and Thomas L. Connelly. *Five Tragic Hours: The Battle of Franklin*. Knoxville: University of Tennessee Press, 1983.
McMurry, Richard. *Atlanta 1864: Last Chance for the Confederacy*. Lincoln: University of Nebraska Press, 2000.
McMurry, Richard M. *John Bell Hood and the War for Southern Independence*. Lexington: University Press of Kentucky, 1982.
McMurry, Richard M. *The Road Past Kennesaw: The Atlanta Campaign of 1864*. Washington, DC: National Park Service, 1972.
McPherson, James. *Battle Cry of Freedom*. New York: Ballantine Books, 1988.
McPherson, James. *Crossroads of Freedom: Antietam*. New York: Oxford University Press, 2002.
McPherson, James. *For Cause and Comrades: Why Men Fought in the Civil War*. New York: Oxford University Press, 1997.
McWhiney, Grady, and Perry D. Jamieson. *Attack and Die: Civil War Military Tactics and the Southern Heritage*. Tuscaloosa: University of Alabama Press, 1982.
Miller, Brian Craig. "'A People's Dream Died There': Shatter Zones and the Trans-Mississippi West." *Heritage of the Great Plains* 39 (Summer 2006): 30–46.
Miller, Brian Craig. "'So Strangely Misrepresented': Rethinking John Bell Hood and the Fight for Civil War Memory." Master's thesis, University of Mississippi, 2002.
Millett, Allan R. *Military Professionalism and Officership in America*. Columbus: Mershon Center of The Ohio State University, 1977.
Moore, Arthur K. *The Frontier Mind: A Cultural Analysis of the Kentucky Frontiersman*. Lexington: University Press of Kentucky, 1957.
Mosse, George L. *The Image of Man: The Creation of Modern Masculinity*. New York: Oxford University Press, 1996.
The National Cyclopedia of American Biography Vol. 4. New York: James T. White and Co., 1895.
Neal, Arthur G. *National Trauma and Collective Memory: Major Events in the American Century*. Armonk, NY: M.E. Sharpe, 1998.
Neff, John R. *Honoring the Civil War Dead: Commemoration and the Problem of Reconciliation*. Lawrence: University Press of Kansas, 2005.
Nevin, David. *Sherman's March: Atlanta to the Sea*. Alexandria, VA: Time-Life Books, 1986.
Nolan, Alan T. *Lee Considered: General Robert E. Lee and Civil War History*. Chapel Hill: University of North Carolina Press, 1991.

Nora, Pierre. "Between Memory and History: *Les Lieux de Mémoire.*" *Representations* 26 (Spring 1989): 7–25.
Nunn, W. C., ed. *Ten Texans in Gray.* Hillsboro, TX: Hill Junior College Press, 1968.
O'Connor, Erin. "'Fractious of Men': Engendering Amputation in Victorian Culture." *Comparative Studies in Society and History* 39 (October 1997): 744–47.
O'Connor, Richard. *Hood: Cavalier General.* New York: Prentice Hall, 1949.
Palmer, Michael A. *Lee Moves North: Robert E. Lee on the Offensive.* New York: John Wiley and Sons, 1998.
Pappas, George S. *To the Point: The United States Military Academy, 1802–1902.* Westport, CT: Praeger, 1993.
Patterson, Gerard A. *Rebels from West Point.* New York: Doubleday, 1987.
Pfanz, Donald C. *Richard S. Ewell: A Soldier's Life.* Chapel Hill: University of North Carolina Press, 1998.
Pfanz, Harry W. *Gettysburg: The Second Day.* Chapel Hill: University of North Carolina Press, 1987.
Phillabaum, James K. *The Ancestors of John Bell Hood: A Civil War General, 1831–1879.* Miami, OH: Miami University Libraries, 1996.
Ponder, Jerry. *Fort Mason, Texas: Training Ground for Generals.* Mason, TX: Ponder Books, 1997.
Poole, W. Scott *Never Surrender: Confederate Memory and Conservatism in the South Carolina Upcountry.* Athens: University of Georgia Press, 2004.
Price, George F. *Across the Continent with the Fifth Cavalry.* New York: Antiquarian Press, 1883.
Proctor, Nicolas W. *Bathed in Blood: Hunting and Mastery in the Old South.* Charlottesville: University Press of Virginia, 2002.
Pugh, David. *Sons of Liberty: The Masculine Mind in Nineteenth-Century America.* Westport, CT: Greenwood Press, 1983.
Rable, George. *Civil Wars: Women and the Crisis of Southern Nationalism.* Urbana: University of Illinois Press, 1989.
Rable, George. *Fredericksburg! Fredericksburg!* Chapel Hill: University of North Carolina Press, 2002.
Reardon, Carol. *Pickett's Charge: In History and Memory.* Chapel Hill: University of North Carolina Press, 1997.
Reynolds, David S. *Walt Whitman's America: A Cultural Biography.* New York: Alfred A. Knopf, 1995.
Rhea, Gordon. *The Battle of Cold Harbor.* Washington, DC: Eastern National, 2001.
Rice, Otis K. *Frontier Kentucky.* Lexington: University Press of Kentucky, 1993.
Richards, J. A. *A History of Bath County, Kentucky.* Yuma, AZ: Southwest Printers, 1961.
Richardson, Robert Edward Lee. *Boots and Saddles: The Second Cavalry in Texas, 1855–1861; A College of Leadership.* Honors thesis, Austin College, 1995.
Robins, Glenn. *The Bishop of the Old South: The Ministry and Civil War Legacy of Leonidas Polk.* Macon, GA: Mercer University Press, 2006.
Rohrbough, Malcolm J. *The Trans-Appalachian Frontier: People, Societies, and Institutions 1775–1850.* New York: Oxford University Press, 1979.

Rosenburg, R. B. *Living Monuments: Confederate Soldiers' Homes in the New South.* Chapel Hill: University of North Carolina Press, 1993.

Ross, Michael A. "The Commemoration of Robert E. Lee's Death and the Obstruction of Reconstruction in New Orleans." *Civil War History* 51, no. 2 (June 2005): 135–50.

Roth, Michael S. *The Ironist's Cage: Memory, Trauma and the Construction of History.* New York: Columbia University Press, 1995.

Rotundo, E. Anthony. *American Manhood: Transformations in Masculinity from the Revolution to the Modern Era.* New York: Basic Books, 1993.

Russell, Carl P. *Guns on the Early Frontier.* Lincoln: University of Nebraska Press, 1980.

Sanders, Stuart W. "The Bishop's Nephew." *Civil War Times Illustrated* 40, no. 1 (2001): 24–60.

Schacter, Daniel, ed. *Memory Distortion: How Minds, Brains, and Societies Reconstruct the Past.* Cambridge, MA: Harvard University Press, 1995.

Sears, Stephen W. *Chancellorsville.* New York: Houghton Mifflin Co., 1996.

Sears, Stephen W. *Landscape Turned Red: The Battle of Antietam.* New York: Ticknor and Fields, 1983.

Sears, Stephen W. *To the Gates of Richmond: The Peninsula Campaign.* New York: Houghton Mifflin Co., 1992.

A Short History of General John Bell Hood. New York: Knapp and Co., 1888.

Silber, Nina. *The Romance of Reunion: Northerners and the South, 1865–1900.* Chapel Hill: University of North Carolina Press, 1993.

Simpson, Harold B. *Cry Comanche.* Hillsboro, TX: Hill Junior College Press, 1979.

Simpson, Harold B., ed. *Frontier Forts of Texas.* Waco, TX: Texian Press, 1966.

Simpson, Harold B. *Gaines' Mill to Appomattox: Waco and McLennan County in Hood's Texas Brigade.* Waco, TX: Texian Press, 1988.

Simpson, Harold B. *Hood's Texas Brigade in Reunion and Memory.* Hillsboro, TX: Hill Junior College Press, 1974.

Smith, John David, and Thomas H. Appleton Jr., eds. *A Mythic Land Apart: Reassessing Southerners and Their History.* Westport, CT: Greenwood Press, 1997.

Sonne, Niels Henry. *Liberal Kentucky, 1780–1828.* Lexington: University of Kentucky Press, 1968.

Spencer, John W. *From Corsicana to Appomattox: The Story of the Corsicana Invincibles and the Navarro Rifles.* Corsicana, TX: The Texas Press, 1984.

Stevens, William Oliver. *Pistols at Ten Paces: The Story of the Code of Honor in America.* Cambridge, MA: Riverside Press, 1940.

Stowe, Steven M. *Intimacy and Power in the Old South.* Baltimore: John Hopkins University Press, 1987.

Stubbs, Steven H. *Duty, Honor, Valor: The Story of the Eleventh Mississippi Infantry Regiment.* Philadelphia, MS: Dancing Rabbit Press, 2000.

Sundstrom, Linea. "Smallpox Used Them Up: Reference to Epidemic Disease in Northern Plains Winter Counts, 1714–1920." *Ethnohistory* 44, no. 2 (Spring 1997).

Sword, Wiley. *Embrace an Angry Wind: The Confederacy's Last Hurrah: Spring Hill, Franklin and Nashville.* New York: Harper Collins, 1992.

Sword, Wiley. *Southern Invincibility: A History of the Confederate Heart.* New York: St. Martin's Griffin, 1999.

Symonds, Craig L. *Joseph E. Johnston: A Civil War Biography*. New York: W.W. Norton and Co., 1992.

Tallant, Harold D. *Evil Necessity: Slavery and Political Culture in Antebellum Kentucky*. Lexington: University Press of Kentucky, 2003.

Thelen, David, ed. *Memory and American History*. Bloomington: Indiana University Press, 1990.

Thwaites, Reuben Gold. *Daniel Boone*. New York: D. Appleton-Century Co., 1940.

Tunnell, Ted. *Crucible of Reconstruction: War, Radicalism, and Race in Louisiana, 1862–1877*. Baton Rouge: Louisiana State University Press, 1984.

Utley, Robert M. *Frontiersmen in Blue*. Lincoln: University of Nebraska Press, 1981.

Utley, Robert M. *The Indian Frontier of the American West, 1846–1890*. Albuquerque: University of New Mexico Press, 1984.

Vandiver, Frank. "General Hood as Logistician." *Military Affairs* 16, no. 1 (Spring 1952).

Wallace, Ernest, and E. Adamson Hoebel. *The Comanches: Lords of the South Plains*. Norman: University of Oklahoma Press, 1952.

Warner, Ezra J. *Generals in Gray: Lives of the Confederate Commanders*. Baton Rouge: Louisiana State University Press, 1959.

Waugh, John C. *The Class of 1846, From West Point to Appomattox: Stonewall Jackson, George McClellan and Their Brothers*. New York: Warner Books, 1994.

Wecter, Dixon. *When Johnny Comes Marching Home*. Cambridge, MA: Houghton Mifflin Co., 1944.

Wegner, Ansley Herring. *Phantom Pain: North Carolina's Artificial-Limbs Program for Confederate Veterans*. Raleigh: Office of Archives and History, North Carolina Department of Cultural Resources, 2004.

Welsh, Jack D. *Medical Histories of Confederate Generals*. Kent, OH: Kent State University Press, 1995.

"What Will Become of the Children: General Hood's Family Faces an Uncertain Future." *Civil War Times Illustrated* (January 1987).

White, Richard. *The Middle Ground: Indians, Empires, and Republics in the Great Lakes Region, 1650–1815*. New York: Cambridge University Press, 1991.

Wilkinson, Warren, and Steven E. Woodworth. *A Scythe of Fire: A Civil War Story of the Eight Georgia Infantry Regiment*. New York: William Morrow, 2002.

Williams, Jack K. *Dueling in the Old South: Vignettes of Social History*. College Station: Texas A&M University Press, 1980.

Williams, T. Harry. *P.G.T. Beauregard: Napoleon in Gray*. Baton Rouge: Louisiana State University Press, 1955.

Williamson, David. *The Third Battalion MS Infantry and the 45th MS Regiment*. Jefferson, NC: McFarland and Co., 2004.

Wilson, Charles Reagan. *Baptized in Blood: The Religion of the Lost Cause*. Baton Rouge: Louisiana State Press, 1980.

Wilson, James Grant, and John Fiske, eds. *Cyclopedia of American Biography*. Vol. 3. New York: D. Appleton and Co., 1888.

Winters, John D. *The Civil War in Louisiana*. Baton Rouge: Louisiana State University Press, 1963.

Wittenberg, Eric J. *Little Phil: A Reassessment of the Civil War Leadership of Gen. Philip Sheridan*. Washington, DC: Brassey's, 2002.

Wolf, Eric R. *Europe and a People Without History*. Berkeley: University of California Press, 1982.

Woodward, C. Vann. *Origins of the New South: 1877–1913*. Baton Rouge: Louisiana State University Press, 1971.

Woodworth, Steven, ed. *Civil War Generals in Defeat*. Lawrence: University Press of Kansas, 1999.

Woodworth, Steven E. *Jefferson Davis and His Generals: The Failure of Confederate Command in the West*. Lawrence: University Press of Kansas, 1990.

Woodworth, Steven. *No Band of Brothers: Problems in the Rebel High Command*. Columbia: University of Missouri Press, 1999.

Wooster, Robert. *The Civil War 100: A Ranking of the Most Influential People in the War Between the States*. Secaucus, NJ: Carol Publishing Group, 1998.

Wyatt-Brown, Bertram. *The Shaping of Southern Culture: Honor, Grace, and War, 1760s–1880s*. Chapel Hill: University of North Carolina Press, 2001.

Wyatt-Brown, Bertram. *Southern Honor: Ethics and Behavior in the Old South*. New York: Oxford University Press, 1982.

Wynne, Ben. *A Hard Trip: A History of the 15th Mississippi Infantry, CSA*. Macon, GA: Mercer University Press, 2003.

Index

Adair, Bose, 229
Adairsville, Georgia, 113
Adams, John, 6
Adams, Thatcher, 233
Alexander, Gen. Edward Porter, 156
Allatoona Pass, 114–16, 144, 211
Allen, Col. R. T. P., 45
Allen, Henry Watkins, 89
amputation: xvii, 73, 75, 76, 78, 89, 90–92, 95, 98, 99, 100, 105, 108–9; and artificial limbs, xx, 75, 101, 181, 183–84; numbers, 89–91; views by historians, 87–88
Andersonville, 119
Andries, Tryntje Luykas, 2
Antietam, Battle of. *See* Sharpsburg
Appomattox Court House, 172, 199
Archer, Lt. Col. James, 47, 48, 239
Army of Northern Virginia, xviii, 43, 56, 58, 60, 69–71, 74, 107, 119, 196, 220, 227, 230, 242
Army of Tennessee Association, 216, 220, 224–25, 227; Louisiana Division, 209
Army of Tennessee, xx, xvii, xviii, 74, 75, 87, 91, 105, 107–9, 110–11, 114–21, 123, 124, 126, 134, 136, 139–40, 146–49, 153, 159, 162, 163, 165, 168–70, 177, 197, 200–204, 207, 209–13, 220, 221, 224, 226–27, 229–30, 237–40; crossing the Tennessee River, 150
Army of the Cumberland, 127, 212
Association of the Army of Northern Virginia, 216, 220, 227

Atlanta *Constitution*, 215; and appeal for funds for Hood's children, 228
Atlanta, Georgia, xvi, xvii, 78, 96, 109–11, 116–23, 125–28, 130, 133–37, 139–48, 151, 155, 168,69, 171, 177, 201–7, 211, 224, 226, 228–29, 238, 242; evacuation of, 134, 137, 142; shelling of city, 131–32, 141–42
Atlanta *Daily Appeal*, 77
Augusta *Constitutionalist*, 78, 94, 100, 132
Augusta, Georgia, 120, 137, 159, 234

Bald Hill, 128
Banks, Nathaniel, 130
Barton Springs, Texas, 195
baseball, 186, 194
Baton Rouge, 89
Battle of New Orleans, 179, 185
Beauregard, P. G. T., xvi, 23, 119, 123, 136, 146–48, 151, 160, 163, 168, 170–71, 186, 189, 191, 193–95, 209; as head of Association of the Army of Tennessee, 224; command during Civil War, 148, 150, 162; and Hood Relief, 230–32
Bell, Brig. Gen. Tyree, 151
Bemiss, S. M., 219, 221
Benét, Stephen Vincent, 200
Benica Barracks, 28
Benny Haven's, 19, 129
Berry, Stephen, 8
Berryhill, William Harvey, 124, 149, 157
Binford, Captain George, 112

Birchmeyer, J. F., 227–28
Blair, Gen. Frank, 107
Blight, David, 237
Board of Health, 217–18
Bowden, William, 133
Bradford, Mary, 161
Bradley, Col. L. P., 229
Bragg, Braxton, xviii, 23, 33, 70, 74–77, 107, 109, 111, 117–19, 123–24, 129–30, 134–36, 168, 186, 191, 193–94, 201, 203, 238
Breckenridge, Gen. John, 102, 104–5, 170,
Breckinridge, John, 32, 50, 193
Brown, Campbell, 93
Brown, John, 200
Brown, Lizinka Campbell, 97, 98
Brown, Samuel, 9
Brownsville *Ranchero*, 188
Buckner, Capt. James, 230
Buckner, Gen. Simon Bolivar, 23, 188
Buford, Abraham, 155
Buford, J. H., 136
Burns, Robert, 230
Burnside, Ambrose, 58, 62, 66
Burwell, William, 194
Butler, Benjamin, 142
Butler, Burton, 114
Bynum, Victoria, 95

Calder, David R., 230
Camp Colorado, 39–41
Camp Cooper, 35–36, 39
Camp Wood, 40–41
Cannon, J. P., 124, 130, 134–35, 153, 166
Carmouche, Annie, 125
Carter, Col., 239
Carter, Moscow, 157
Carter, Shirley, 103
Cassville, GA, 113–15, 205–7
Chalaron, Capt. James, 230, 233
Chalmers, Gen. J. R., 213
Chambers, William Pitt, 135, 147, 164
Chambersburg, PA, 71
Champion, Sidney, 115, 124

Chancellorsville, xix, 69, 92
Charleston *Mercury*, 123, 136, 147, 150–51, 159, 166
Charlottesville *Chronicle*, 161
Chattahoochee River, 124, 126, 240
Chattanooga, TN, 74–75, 109–11, 119, 202
Cheatham, Benjamin, 123, 126, 128, 130, 148, 152–53, 164, 210; and correspondence with Joseph Johnston, 204
Chesnut, Mary, xx, 102–5, 114, 173–74; memory of Hood, 238–39; reactions to Hood's amputation, 87, 101
Chicago, IL, 183, 217, 222
Chickamauga, xvii, xx, 74–78, 87, 100–101, 109, 165, 198, 206, 222, 238, 244
Chipley, W. D., 229
chloroform, 91
cholera, 4, 5
Cincinnati *Commercial*, 158
Claiborne, J. Francis H., 209
Clay, Cassius Marcellus, 7
Clayton, General Henry, 155
Clayton, Thomas, 110, 112, 121
Cleburne, Patrick, 123, 133, 152, 154, 157, 213
Clemmens, Rev. G. J., 225
Co. Aytch, 239–40
Coleman, Private Charles S., 150
Columbus, GA, 137
Columbus, Georgia Enquirer, 229
Comanche, 27, 31, 34, 37, 76
Comanche Creek, 35
Confederate Congressional Records, 137, 213
Confederate Veteran, 241, 245
Conner, Colonel James, 98
Cooper, Samuel, 27
Cox, Jacob, 116
Crouch, Major Walter V., 230
Crouch, Walter B., 219–21
Crutcher, Emma, 95–96
cultural biography, xxi, xxii, xxiii, xxiv
Cumming, Joseph, 74–75, 109, 111, 114–15, 125, 128, 158, 160, 163

Cunningham, E.H., 232
Cunningham, S.A., 241–42

Dailey, Jane, 188
Daily Picayune, 76, 78, 144–45, 169, 176, 181, 189, 191, 201, 203, 216, 223, 228
Dalton, GA, 107, 111, 114, 120, 204, 207, 229
Darby, John, 73, 75, 78, 103
Darry, Surgeon, 100
Daughters of the Confederacy, 175
Davis, Capt. William V., 149
Davis, Chaplain Nicholas, 45, 49, 55, 59, 60, 63–65, 196
Davis, Jefferson, xv, xvii, xx, 19, 23, 31–32, 36, 45, 70, 75–77, 107–8, 117–20, 125–26, 130–31, 135–36, 144,148, 151, 161–62, 165, 167–69, 171–72, 174, 192–93, 201, 203–4, 235, 240, 246; appointment of Hood, 120–22; call to women, 96–97; correspondence with Hood about Johnston, 109–11, 114; and Hood's recovery, 102; memory of Hood, 237–38; review of Army of Tennessee, 146–47; speech in Macon, Georgia, 96–97, 99, 146
Davis, Varina, 104
Dean, Eric, 174
death, xvii, xxii, 3, 6, 8, 33, 36, 47, 50, 57, 69, 74–77, 88–9, 90–93, 95, 100, 102, 104, 109, 120, 129, 141–42, 150, 154–58, 161, 175–76, 179–80, 186, 193–94, 197–98, 202, 205, 217, 219, 220–27, 232, 234–37, 239–41, 243, 245
Decatur, AL, 150–51, 177
Decatur, GA, 128–29
Decoration Day, xv, xvi, 185
Delachaise Grounds, 186
Dodd, Capt. W. O., 209–10
Dow, Rev. M., 221–22
Duck River, 162
dueling, 9, 10, 12, 24, 99
Dug Gap, 111
Duke, Basil, 161, 164

Duke, Champion, 150
Dunblane, 94

Early, Jubal, 14, 23; during Civil War, 62, 93; and Southern Historical Society, 199, 200, 225
East Point, GA, 133
Edey, Arthur H., 56–57
Eighteenth Alabama, 156
Eighteenth Georgia, 47–48, 59, 62, 66, 196
Eighteenth Tennessee, 112
elections, 6, 47, 97, 117, 133, 197
Eleventh Tennessee, 155
Eltham's Landing, 50–52, 108, 197
empty sleeve, 96, 106
enfield rifle, 90
Episcopal Church, Houston, TX, 225
Episcopal Graveyard, 182
Erwin, George Phifer, 145, 149
Ewell, Richard, 23, 101; and amputation, 91, 93; perceptions as an amputee, 98–99; recovery from injury, 94, 97–98
Ezra Church, 130

Falconer, Kinloch, 204
Featherson, Winfield Scott, 136
Ferguson, Samuel Wragg, 121
Ferguson's Battery, 157
Fifth Tennessee, 133
Fifth Texas, 46–48, 57, 59, 69, 198, 242
Figures, Hardin, 157
First Manassas, 46–47
First Texas, 48, 62
Fitzpatrick, M. Hill, 145
Flint River, 133
Flower, Col. Samuel, 230
Forrest, Nathan Bedford, 145, 150–53, 162, 213, 237
Forsyth, John, 163, 168
Fort Belknap, 33, 34, 40
Fort Clark, 38
Fort Columbus, 28
Fort Hood, xvi

Fort Huger, 68
Fort Jones, 28–29, 30, 33
Fort Mason, 33–39, 159
Fort Sumter, 41
Fort Vancouver, 30
Fort Washita, 33
Fort Worth, TX, 220
Fortress Monroe, 44, 49
Foster, Capt. Samuel T., 134, 149, 157, 163–65
Fourth Infantry Regiment, U.S., 27
Fourth Louisiana, 89
Fourth Texas, xv, 44–49, 52, 54–57, 59, 62, 71
Fox-Genovese, Elizabeth, 95
Franco Prussian War, 234
Franklin, TN, xvi, xvii, xviii, xix, 51, 158, 163–65, 171–73, 176, 192, 202–3, 208–10, 213, 224, 237–39, 241; battle of, 153–56; horrific casualties, 157; reaction of citizens, 157
Fredericksburg, VA, 47–49, 58, 63, 66–69, 70
Freeman, Douglass Southall, xviii
Freeman's Ford, 58
Fremantle, Lt. Col. Arthur, 71–73
French, xix, 15, 22, 102
French, Gen. Samuel B., 23, 123, 211–12
French, James, 6
French, Rep. Richard, 6, 7, 14, 27
French, Theodosia, 3, 6
Fulkerson, Maj. Arthur, 154
Fuller, John, 128
Furness, Clemtina, 234

Gaines Mill, xvi, 53–57, 59, 61, 120, 156, 175, 196–97, 208, 245
Gale, William Dudley, 161
Galveston, TX, 225
Garidel, Henry, 77, 128, 163
Gay, Mary, 149
Geary, John, 127
Gettysburg, PA, ix, xvi, xx, 22, 56, 71, 73–74, 76, 78, 100, 181, 198, 206, 212
Giles, Val, 44, 46, 48, 50, 65, 67

Gill, Robert, 132
Goree, Thomas, 63, 73, 135, 164
Gordon, John, 193
Gordonsville, 58
Gorn, Elliott, 99
Gorn, Hensh, 10
Granbury, General Hiram, 154
Grand Army of the Republic (GAR), 185
Grand Opera House, New Orleans, 231
Grant, Ulysses S., xix, 22, 27, 70, 109, 110, 121, 144, 172, 185, 199; attending *Ours*, 215, 231; and concern about Hood, 125, 148–49, 159–60, 165; on frontier, 30
Gray, R. M., 43, 74, 127, 139
Green, Duff, 98–99
Green, Ellen, 5
Greenwood Cemetery, 184–85
Gregg, Gen. John, 246
Gregory, John, 153
Groveton, VA, 93
gunshot wounds, 90

Hackman's Benefit Association, 189
Hammond, James Henry, 8
Hampton, Wade, 73, 193, 203
Hardee, William, 23, 32, 147–48, 169–70, 201, 210–11; as a corps commander, 122–23, 126–28, 130, 133–34, 136; passed over command, 119–20, 123–24
Hardwick, G. P., 137
Harney, Charles H., 234
Harris, Gov. Isham G., 169, 172, 210
Harrisburg, PA, 71
Harrison, J. P., 4, 5
Harrison, William, 153
Harrison, William Henry, 14
Harrison's Landing, 57
Haughery, Margaret, 228
Hennen, Ana Marie, 188, 219
Hennen, Cora, 232
Hennen, Eleanor, 221–22, 232
Hewes, Fred S., 158
higher education, 15

Hill, Ambrose Powell, 23, 53, 62, 69
Hill, Daniel Harvey, 23, 51, 53, 64
Hill, Senator Benjamin, 203
hip injuries, 75, 91, 105, 209
Hogg, Attorney General James, 236
Hollingsworth, D. M., 216
Holmes, D. H., 230
Honnell, William, 131
honor, xv, xxi, xxii, 1, 18, 24–5, 28, 40, 44, 47, 51, 54, 56, 60, 64–65, 76, 88–89, 91–96, 98–99, 101, 106, 108, 143, 148, 157, 169, 171, 175–76, 178–80, 182–92, 194–96, 200, 203, 207–10, 220, 221, 223–26, 228, 231, 243, 245; as a marker of manhood, 7–16
Hood Memorial Association, 231
Hood Orphan Fund, 215–16, 227, 230
Hood Relief Fund Committee, 230–33
Hood, Andrew, 2–3
Hood, Anna Gertrude, 188, 233–34
Hood, Anna Marie (Hennen), 189, 219, 283
Hood, Annabel, 188, 233, 235
Hood, Dr. John W., 3, 5, 10, 13, 25, 36; medical practice, 4, 5, 11; slave holding, 5–7; and West Point decision, 14–15
Hood, Duncan Norbet, 188, 232, 234
Hood, Ethel Genevieve, 188, 233, 235
Hood, Ida Richardson, 188, 232–33, 243; and *In Memoriam*, 243–44
Hood, Jasper, 2
Hood, John Bell: address to Hood's Texas Brigade, 194–95, 197–98; and *Advance and Retreat*, 204, 206–9, 232–33; and amputation, 72–73, 75–76, 87–88, 90–91; arrest, 60–61; Atlanta campaign, 17, 111, 113–18, 122–34; baptism, 111–12; biographical sketch, xvi, xvii; bond with soldiers, 24, 43, 48–9, 71, 112; burial, 221, 227–28; at Camp Colorado, 39–40; at Camp Cooper, 36–9; casualty figures, xix, 54–55, 59, 62, 66, 73, 127–28, 130, 134, 156, 161; and charitable work, 185–86, 189–92; at Chickamauga, 74–75; childhood, 9–13; in command of the Fourth Texas, 44–45, 48; conflict with father, 14, 15, 36; correspondence with Stephen D. Lee, 167–68, 177, 187, 205, 208–9, 246; correspondence with William T. Sherman, 140–44, 155; and current position in memory, ix, xvi, xxiii; death, 215–16, 220; as described by historians, xviii, xix, xx, xxi; and discipline, 46–47, 51–52, 65–66, 71; and dispute with Lafayette McLaws, 64–65, 199; at Eltham's Landing, 50–51; employment after war, 186–87; estate value and holdings, 227–28; family lineage, 1–4, 6; fight with Comanche Indians, 36–9; at Fort Jones, 28–30; at Fort Mason, 36–39; at Fredericksburg, 48, 65–67; as a gambler, xix; at Gettysburg, 71–73; and Joseph Johnston, 107–8, 113–14, 116, 121, 122, 200–202; journey after surrender, 172, 176–78; life insurance, 187, 228–29; at Manassas, 58–60; marriage, 188; memoir conflict, 200–214; memorial photograph, 232–34; memory of, 200–214, 221, 224–26, 235–46; plan to invade Tennessee, 140, 144–45, 147–48; physical description, 43, 45, 109–10; and PTSD, 173–75, 192; problems in historiography, xviii, xix, xx; promotions, 44, 48, 63, 77, 118–22; public appearances, 101–2, 104; reaction to dead soldiers, 54, 59, 62, 66, 157; reaction to death of his wife, 219–20; recovery from amputation in Richmond, 73–4, 78, 87, 99, 100–105; relationship with Sally Preston, 73, 101–6, 108; report regarding Atlanta, 136–37; report regarding Franklin, 156; report regarding Tennessee Campaign, 162–63, 169–71; resigns from Army of Tennessee, 166–68; resigns from U.S. Army, 40–41; and

Hood, John Bell (cont.)
    Robert E. Lee, 44–45, 53, 60–61, 63, 65, 67–69, 119–20; rumors about alcohol and drug abuse, xx, xxi, 153; rumors about death, 76–78; service in U.S. Army, 27–30, 32, 36–40; and Seven Days Battles, 52–57; and Sharpsburg, MD, 61–62; and slavery, 5, 6, 141–42; and Tennessee Campaign, 145–47, 149–55, 158–61; winter encampment, 1863, 67–69; and West Point, 13–17; appointment to instructor position, 40; demerits, 17–20; graduation, 23–24; rankings, 22, 24; wounding at Chickamauga, 75, 76, 87; wounding at Gettysburg, 72–73; and yellow fever, 217, 219–21
Hood, John Bell, obituary: Chicago *Tribune*, 222; New Orleans *Daily Picayune*, 223–24; Memphis *Commercial Appeal*, 222; New Orleans *Times*, 223; New York *Herald*, 222; New York *Tribune*, 222; New York *Times*, 222
Hood, Jr., John Bell, 188, 233–35, 246; and Texas Brigade, 245–46
Hood, III, John Bell, 246
Hood, Lillian Marie, 188, 233–34
Hood, Lizzie, 4
Hood, Lucas, 2–3
Hood, Lydia: birth, 188; death, 217; and yellow fever, 219–20, 233
Hood, Marion Maude, 188, 233–35
Hood, Odile Musson, 188, 232–35, 243
Hood, Oswald, 188, 233–35
Hood, Thomas, 2
Hood, Thomas Jefferson, 3
Hood's Minstrels, 46–47, 68
Hood's Texas Brigade, 57, 219, 230, 245; and holiday, 245; monument, 246; memorial organization and meetings, 195–98
Hooker, Joseph, xix, 61, 69–70
hospitals, 28, 39, 55, 89–91
House, Ellen Renshaw, 128
Howard, Oliver Otis, 125

Howard, Volney, 31
Howell, Clark, 215
Hunter, Captain J. T., 245
Hunting, 1, 10–13, 30, 34
Hutson, Charles, 91

Jackson, Andrew, 185
Jackson, Joshua, 39
Jackson, Thomas J. "Stonewall," ix, xi, xvi, 23, 62, 65, 70, 77, 120, 135, 181, 184, 186, 193, 203, 206–7, 225, 237–38, 246; amputations, 92–93; death, 93; thoughts on Hood, 56, 63
Jefferson Barracks, Missouri, 33
John Bell Hood Camp, 235
Johnson, Herschel, 107
Johnston, Albert Sydney, xvi, 23, 30–36, 38, 77, 225; and reburial, 184, 186
Johnston, Joseph E., xvi, xvii, 23, 70, 107, 127, 134–35, 139–40, 142, 144, 146, 148, 150, 157, 163–65, 167–71, 208, 213–14, 229, 238–42; and Atlanta campaign, 107–9, 111–19, 130; bickering with Jefferson Davis, 117, 119–21; as commander in Virginia, 46, 49, 50–52; and memoir, 114, 201, 203–8; relieved of duty, 121–24; review of memoir, 200–201
Johnston, Lt. Charles G., 204
Johnston, Pvt. John, 153
Johnston, Richard, 34, 38
Jones, John B., 76, 162
Jones, Joseph, 198
Jonesboro, GA, 133, 211
Joseph, M. E., 234
Julio, E. B. D., 193

Kean, Robert, 76, 77, 130, 144, 164–65
Kennesaw Mountain, 116–18
Kentucky, xvi, xxii, 27, 32, 36, 111, 140, 145, 150, 158–60, 176, 178, 186, 191, 193, 221, 235; and antebellum culture, 1, 7–10, 11–13, 24; as border state, 40–41, 206; cholera epidemic,

4–5; and dueling, 9–10; and frontier communities, 2–3; and militia, 2–3; and Native Americans, 2–3; and religion, 9; slavery, 7
Key, Thomas, 133
Kit, Mars, 239
Knighthood, 100, 233
Kolb Farm, 116

Ladies Benevolent Association of Louisiana, 183–84
Ladies Confederate Memorial Association, 183
Ladies Memorial Associations, 175
Lafayette Cemetery, 221, 227
Laredo, TX, 216
laudanum, xx, 5, 136
Lauderdale Orphan's Home, 191–92
Lee Memorial Association, 194; and monument at Tivoli Circle, New Orleans, 195
Lee, Robert E., ix, x, xvi, xvi, xvii, xviii, xx, 20, 23, 51–53, 56–58, 62, 64, 66, 71–72, 74, 76, 93, 110, 115–19, 123–24, 126, 135, 137, 140, 144–45, 156, 163–64, 167, 171–72, 179, 184–86, 193, 199, 200, 203, 206–8, 212, 225, 237–39, 246; at Camp Cooper, 32, 34–36, 39; death of, 193–95, 197–98; as head of West Point, 17, 22; relationship with John Bell Hood, 44–45, 53, 60–61, 63, 65, 67–69, 119–20; response to death of Stonewall Jackson, 69–70
Lee, Stephen, 23; and Atlanta Campaign, 130, 136; correspondence with Hood, 167–68, 177, 187, 205, 209, 246
Life Association of America, 187; and Hood, 227
Lillienthal, Theodore, 231–32
Lincoln, Abraham, 41, 137, 159, 167, 178
Lipan-Apache Indians, 34, 37, 76
Littlejohn, Pvt. E. J., 150
Lockwood, Dr. T. P., 116

Longstreet, James, 22–23, 58, 63, 66–68, 70, 72–77, 134, 160, 186–89, 203, 206, 212, 238
Lost Cause, ix, xiii, xvi, 88, 93, 154, 175, 178, 180, 186, 190, 192, 194–95, 237; and Hood's memory, xxiii, 176, 202, 209, 213, 236, 243
Louisiana Brigade, 181
Lowndes County, AL, 216
Lyman, Capt. W. R., 230
Lyon, Nathaniel, 129

Mackall, William, 129–30
Macon *Telegraph*, 133
Macon, GA, 96, 130, 137, 143, 146
Magruder, John B., 23, 44–45
manhood, ix, xxii, 1, 7–10, 15, 18, 25, 109, 135, 169, 175–76, 208, 228, 241; and alcohol consumption, 10; altered by amputation, 88–89, 92–95, 98–99, 106; dueling, 9–10, 12; and horse racing, 11–12; and hunting, 11–12; mastery of animals, 11; military experience, 13, 28, 44, 47; military leadership, 18, 100, 152; and relationships, 97, 105
Mansfield, J. F. K., 28, 35
Marietta, GA, 116
Marsh, John Henry, 124
Marshall, John, 48
Maughs, Dr. G. M. B., 90
McClellan, George B., xix, 22, 46, 49–50, 52–53, 56–57
McDowell, Irwin, 46, 49
McGehee, George Thomas, 243
McGuire, Hunter Holmes, 92–93
McKeen, Captain A. C., 225
McLaws, Lafayette, 23, 63–64, 199; and dispute with Hood, 63–65
McPherson, James B., 125, 128; death, 129; at West Point, 20, 23
medicine, 24, 36, 89–91, 184; on the frontier of Kentucky, 3, 5, 10
Melton, Samuel, 56
Memorial Day, 182, 185

Index 313

memory, x, xvi, xxi–iv, 19, 154, 174–79, 180, 182–84, 186, 190, 192, 194–95, 198, 237; collective memory, xxiii, 174, 192, 205, 216, 224, 226, 233, 235, 237–38, 243–44; dispute between Hood and Johnston, 200–208; dispute between Hood and McLaws, 64–65, 199; pertaining to John Bell Hood, xxiii, xxiv, 65, 87, 136, 177–79, 185, 188, 192, 197, 200–213, 216–17, 223–28, 233, 235–36, 238–46
Metairie Cemetery, LA, ix, xvi, 221, 227
Mexico, 31, 34, 37, 89
Mitchell, H. C., 229
Mobile, Alabama, 132, 201, 205
Montgomery *Appeal*, 166
Montgomery, AL, 41, 44, 216
Moody, G. F., 229
Morris, John A., 232–33
Mount Sterling, KY, 4, 5, 6, 27, 36
Murfreesboro, TN, 128–29, 171
Murray, John H., 230

Napoleon club, 19
Napoleon guns, 61
Napoleonic tactics, 90
Nashville, TN, xvi, xvii, xviii, 85, 140, 144, 148, 151–54, 167, 169, 171–73, 175–77, 192, 202–3, 208, 213, 224, 239, 241; battle of, 156, 160–61; black troops, 161; casualties, 161; movement of Confederate forces towards, 158–59; Overton Hill, 161; reaction to battle, 161–63, 165; Shy's Hill, 161; winter weather, 160
Natchez, MS, 172, 176
Native Americans, xvi, xxii, 45; in California, 29–31; in Kentucky, 2–3; in Texas, 31, 34–39
Neal, Arthur, 174
New Hope Church, 115, 204
New Orleans, LA, 97, 125, 196, 198, 205; Cotton Exchange, 187; death of John Bell Hood, ix, 243; death of Robert E. Lee, 194–95; *Democrat*, 219; Hood's residence, x, xvii, 176–77, 224; and construction of war memory, 179–87, 190–93, 199, 200–201, 216, 227–28, 230–33, 235; and Union occupation, 142, 178; wartime history, 178; and yellow fever outbreak, x, xvii, 209, 215, 217, 223
Nichol, Alice McPhail, 157
Nicholls, Gen. F. T., 230
Nineteenth Alabama, 131
Nineteenth Tennessee, 154, 162

Ogden, Gen. Fred, 230
Ogden, H. N., 184
Orleans Dramatic Association, 230–31
Ours, 215, 231
Overton Hill, 161
Owingsville, Kentucky, 3, 5

Palestine, TX, 177
Palmer, Benjamin M., 194
Palmer, James, 124, 127
Palmer, Rev. Dr. B. F., 193, 198
Patrick, Robert, 118, 124, 134, 150, 167
Payton, Col. Isaac W., 230
Peachtree Creek, 117, 126–27
Petersburg, VA, xviii, 117, 119, 121, 123, 135, 137, 140, 144–45
Phelan, James, 165–66
Pickett, George, 19, 22, 23, 70, 72
Pierce, Franklin, 31, 32
Pierson, David, 164
Pirtle, William George, 167
Plumb Run, 72
Polk, Gen. Lucius, 91
Polk, Leonidas, 23, 116, 184, 188, 205, 207, 238; baptism of Hood, 112–13
Pollard, Edward, 99
Polley, J. B., 245
Pope, John, 57
Porter, Gov. James D., 210
Portland, OR, 215, 231, 235
posttraumatic stress disorder, xxii, 174
Preston, Jack, 102, 173
Preston, Mary, 87, 100

314   *Index*

Preston, Sally "Buck": and relationship with Hood, 1, 73, 101–6, 108, 173, 188
Preston, Willie, 173

Quintard, Chaplain Charles, 151, 159, 162

Ratchford, James W., 121, 197
rations, 37, 61, 69, 131, 150–51, 159
Reagan, John H., 177, 225–26
Reed, John, 72
Reed, Laura, 191
Religion, 9, 49, 91, 112, 143, 197
Resaca, GA, 111, 113, 149–50
Richards, Sam, 132
Richardson, Harry, 4
Richardson, T. G., 75
Richmond, VA, xvii, xix, 44–46, 49, 50–53, 56–58, 69, 72–74, 75, 77–78, 87, 90, 94, 97, 98, 100–105, 107–8, 111–12, 114, 117–18, 121, 129, 130, 139, 168–69, 181, 188, 193, 199, 209, 238
Richmond Bazaar, 184
Richmond *Enquirer*, 100
Richmond *Whig*, 139
Rise and Fall of the Confederate Government, 237
Ritter, Capt. William L., 241
Robb, Phil, 103
Robertson, Gen. John, 63, 100, 196
Robinson, Bob, 232
Robinson, James, 126
Rosecrans, William, 70, 74–75
Roy, Col. T. B., 210–11
Russell, David M., 233
Rutherford Creek, 152

San Antonio, Texas, 176
Sanders, Lt. M. M., 140
Saucier, John, 145
Schofield, John, 151–54, 156, 208, 213, 237; during Atlanta Campaign, 125; at West Point, 18, 20, 23

Scott, Winfield, 31, 38
Searcy, Captain Mark W., 244
Second Battle of Manassas, xvi, 58–61, 65, 198, 239
Second Cavalry (Dragoons), 30–35, 39, 40, 55, 140
Second Mission Church, 221
Seddon, James, 70, 77, 121
Seven Days Campaign, xix, 53–60
Seven Pines, 52, 108
Seventy-first Pennsylvania, 52
Shakespeare Club, New Orleans, 231
Sharpsburg, Battle of (Antietam), xvi, 61–63, 65–66, 70, 120, 128–29, 135, 198
Sheridan, Philip, 22, 24, 33, 134, 140
Sherman, William T., 145–46, 148–49, 151, 160–61, 164–66, 169, 170, 204, 208, 212, 213; and Atlanta campaign, 96, 110–18, 120–21, 124–28, 130–34, 137, 139, 140; correspondence with Hood, 140–44, 155; and Hood, 33; and memoir writing/dispute, 205–6, 211
Shiloh, 95, 119, 128–29, 186, 191
Short, Charles Wilson, 2
Shoup, Brig. Gen. Francis A., 130, 145–46
Shys Hill, 161
Sixteenth Kentucky
Sixth Mississippi, 116
Sixth North Carolina, 75
Smith, Edmund Kirby, xv, xvi, 23, 32–33
Smith, Gustavus W., 23, 51, 52, 78, 100, 127, 135–36
Smith, William L., 126
Snodgrass Hill, 84
Snow, John, 125
Southern Field and Fireside, 94
Southern Historical Society: and Hood's death, 225; memory of war, 192–93, 198, 200, 209–10, 212–14, 225, 236, 239–40, 243; move from Louisiana to Virginia, 199
Southern Hospital Association for Disabled Soldiers, 189–90, 192

Spanish Fort and Lake Railroad Company, 231
Spence, Captain Alex Erskine, 125, 139, 145
Spring Hill, xvii, 152–53, 155–56, 167, 177, 207–10, 213
St. Paul's Episcopal Church, 102
State National Bank, 227
Stephens, Col. M. D. L., 155–56
Stephenson, Philip Dangerfield, 242
Steven, Jonathan K.: and memory of Hood;
Stevens, C. H., 122
Stevenson, Sgt. James, 162
Stewart, Gen. Alexander P., 122, 127, 130, 152, 202, 242
Stewart, Maj. Joseph, 235
Stillwell, William, 145
Stockman, Maj. S. D., 230
Stone, Colonel, 156
Stone, Henry, 161
Stone, Kate, 169
Stoneman, George, 32, 39, 160
Sudduth, Massa, 2
Sudduth, William, 2–3

Taliaferro, General, 239
Taylor, Grant. 163
Taylor, Richard, 130, 148, 168, 186
Taylor, Zachary, 168
Temple College, 229
Texan Club of New Orleans, 195
Texas Brigade, 44, 46–49, 56, 57, 112 123, 195–97, 203, 222, 245–46; at Chickamauga, 74–76; and death of Hood, 230, 232, 234, 236; and death of Hood's family, 219, 220; and Eltham's Landing, 50–51; and Eighteenth Georgia, 47–48, 59, 62, 66, 196; at Fredericksburg, 65–67; First Texas, 48, 62; Fourth Texas, xv, 44–49, 62, 54–57, 59, 62, 71; Fifth Texas, 46–48, 57, 59, 69, 198, 242; Fifty Fourth North Carolina, 66; Fifty-Seventh North Carolina, 66; at Gaines Mill, 53–56; at Gettysburg, 71–73; and presentation of horse to Hood, 48; at Second Manassas, 58–60; at Sharpsburg, 61–63; winter encampment 1863, 67–69
Texas Rangers, 34, 39
Thayer, Sylvanus, 15, 19
The Confederate Dead, 179, 180
Thirty-First Mississippi, 155
Thomas, Ella, 145
Thomas, George, 75, 127, 149, 177, 208; correspondence with Grant, 159–60, 165; at Nashville, 153, 159–61, 241; on Texas frontier, 32, 34
Thomas, Henry, 196
Thompson, Col. C. R., 161
Thompson, John, 4
Todd, J. S., 229
Truman, W. L., 155
Tunnel Hill, 150
Tupelo, MS, 168
Turkey Hill, 53, 57
Twenty-First Alabama, 221
Twiggs, D. E., 38, 206

United States Military Academy. *See* West Point

Vann, Samuel King, 131
veterans, 88, 94, 174, 178, 181, 183–85, 190, 192, 194, 196–97, 217, 220, 224–25, 228, 230, 232, 235–37, 246
Viars, Gideon, 161

Waco, Texas, 197–98
Wadley, Sarah Louis, 143, 144, 164
Watkins, Sam, 91, 239–41
Wayne, Gen. Anthony, 3
Weaver, Capt. Henry Clay, 158
Weaver, Clark, 149
Weaver, Samuel, 181–82
Webb, Norma, 229
West Point, xix, xxi, xxii, 1, 13, 24–25, 27–28, 21–22, 36, 38, 40–41, 47, 51, 57, 61, 67, 118, 125, 129, 143, 206,

234; appointments to, 13, 14; brief history of, 14; changes to, 16, 17; Class of 1853, 23, 24; curriculum changes, 15, 16; daily activities, 17–19; and demerits, 20–22; and entrance exams, 14; final exams, 16; and hazing, 18, 19; meals, 18; rules and regulations, 16–17; summer encampments, 16
West, John C., xv, xvi, 71, 73
Western and Atlantic Railroad, 111, 113
Wharton, Richard, 128
Wheat, Major, 181
Whiskey, 4, 10, 91, 153, 156
White Sulphur Springs, VA, 199
Whites, LeeAnn, 94
Wigfall, Halsey, 109, 121
Wigfall, Lewis, 65
Wigfall, Louis T., 46–47, 102, 108, 173, 193, 239
Wigfall, Louly, 73, 101, 176
Wilcox, Gen. C. M., 212
Williamsburg, Battle of, 49, 50, 52
Wills, Francis, 3
Wills, Frederick William, 3
Wilmington, NC, 78, 100
Wilson's Creek, 129
Winchester, Kentucky, 6
Winchester, Virginia, 65–66, 182
Winkler, Mrs. C. M., 245
Witherspoon, Rev. A. J., 221–22
women, 13, 36, 38, 70, 106, 141–42, 155, 160; and definitions of manhood, xxii, 7, 8, 11, 88, 95–96; memory construction, xv, 175, 178–80, 182–85, 189, 190, 191, 195, 216, 230; reactions to amputees, 94–95, 97–98, 100, 102–3
Woods, Dr. J. S., 89
Woodworth, Steven, xviii, xix, 147
Wragg, William T., 218

yellow fever, x, xvii, 209, 214–20, 222, 227, 233
Yorktown, Virginia, 44, 49
Young, Mrs. M. J., 196–97
Youngblood, William, 71

John Bell Hood was designed and typeset on a Macintosh computer system using InDesign CS3 software. The body text is set in 10/13.5 Plantin Std Light and display type is set in Plantin Std Light Italic. This book was designed and typeset by Barbara Karwhite.

www.ingramcontent.com/pod-product-compliance
Lightning Source LLC
Chambersburg PA
CBHW030303080526
44584CB00012B/416